To my older daughter, Helen

TIMEL
WITN

TIMELESS WITNESS

CLASSIC CHRISTIAN LITERATURE
THROUGH THE AGES

— Written and Compiled by —

TONY LANE

HENDRICKSON PUBLISHERS

Timeless Witness: Classic Christian Literature through the Ages

Text copyright © 2004 A. N. S. Lane

Original edition published in English under the title *Lion Christian Classics Collection* by Lion Hudson plc, Oxford, England.

Copyright © Lion Hudson plc 2004

All copyright extracts appear by permission of the copyright holders (see pp. 405–413 for acknowledgements).

Published by
Hendrickson Publishers, Inc.
P. O. Box 3473
Peabody, Massachusetts 01961-3473

ISBN 1-56563-601-5

Printed in the United States of America

First Printing — October 2005

Library of Congress Cataloging-in-Publication Data

Timeless witness : classic Christian literature through the ages / written and
  compiled by Tony Lane.
      p. cm.
    Includes bibliographical references.
    ISBN 1-56563-601-5 (alk. paper)
    1. Christian literature. 2. Theology. I. Lane, A. N. S.
    BR53.T56 2005
    270—dc22
                                        2005011143

Contents

8

Preface

This book has been in the planning since 1984. Over the intervening years I have consulted many people for advice about which works to include – so many people that I shall not name any because inevitably many others will be forgotten. I profited much from the advice received, but none of them is to blame for the final selection, which is mine alone. It remained fluid until the very end in that a number of intended works were excluded as unsuitable once I started to read them. The final choice of items was not made until a week or so before the completion of the project.

My thanks go to a number of folk who have read all or part of the text and made helpful comments – especially to James Allcock and Chris Jack who read the whole and gave much useful feedback; also to Meic Pearse and my wife Maggie for reading part. Thanks are also due to Christian Meyer who suggested the extracts to be selected for two of the classics.

Finally, this volume is dedicated to my older daughter Helen, a fellow pilgrim on the way and a source of much joy and pride.

5 May 2003

Introduction

Mark Twain once commented that a classic is 'a book which people praise and don't read'. It is the aim of this book to begin to correct that. For each of the hundred classics selected, extracts are given to whet the appetite of the reader. Also, details are given of modern editions of the works as well as websites where the complete text (usually in older translations) may be found. My hope is that this book will stimulate readers to turn to the classics and read them for themselves.

How were these classics selected? Some wanted fewer works from the early and medieval periods, but I feel no need to apologise for the fact that in a selection of classics nearly half are chosen from the first three quarters of the church's life. I have also set a closing date of 1900 in that it seems inappropriate to call more recent works 'classics', though many will become such in due course. I have excluded short creeds (such as the Apostles' Creed) but have included some longer creeds and confessions. I have generally restricted myself to one work by each author, with two each from a select few (Athanasius, Bernard, Luther and Calvin) and three from Augustine in recognition of his towering stature. (Melanchthon, Cranmer and Edwards also have a second entry if one counts works in which they were involved.)

In this collection I have only included works that I consider useful and profitable to read, rather than selecting works based on their importance. But that does not mean that I have narrowly restricted myself to those with whom I am in full agreement. The selection is 'catholic' in that it includes Roman Catholic, Eastern Orthodox, Lutheran, Reformed, Anabaptist and other authors. The inclusion of a work does not imply an endorsement of its entire contents but only the judgment that it is an important Christian classic that can be read with profit, even though it may need to be read with discernment. So, unlike two recent books, this is not intended as a book on *literary* classics. Also, while many of the works selected include some exposition of Scripture, they are not chosen for that reason and this is not a book on *exegetical* classics. The majority of the works selected would fall into the category of *spiritual* classics. A smaller number would be *theological* or *apologetic* classics and a few others would be *historical* classics, such as Eusebius's pioneering *The History of the Church*. A very few books are included as much for their past as their present importance. Peter Lombard's *Sentences* is little read today, but served as a standard textbook for a quarter of the church's history and for much of that time held a position of unrivalled dominance. William Tyndale's *The New Testament* is included because of its immense influence upon most subsequent English translations. Both can still be read with profit today.

Why should one bother to read famous books from the past? Reading books from another age, like travelling to another country or conversing in another language, makes demands. There is much that is unfamiliar. In the introduction to each of the classics, I give a brief account of the author and the circumstances of the book. Occasionally it is very apparent that the author comes from an alien culture. Reading older English books requires a certain amount of translation where words have changed their meanings. All of this is more demanding than reading the latest popular Christian book – but it also offers greater rewards. If we read only today's books we are trapped in our own culture, with all of its blind spots and weaknesses. When we read books from the past we quickly spot the glaring weaknesses of past ages – but we can also be challenged by their strengths in areas where we are weak. There is no suggestion that the classics selected are without their blemishes and errors and in some instances these may be glaring. It is also doubtless true that there are recent works available which overall are superior to at least some of the classics selected. But the value of reading good books from the past is that they bring a different perspective from our own and that while they may be weak where we are strong, they may also have significant things to say that are being ignored today.

One example of this is the topic of martyrdom. The last hundred years have seen the martyrdom of literally millions of Christians, a point of contact with the Early Church. But, in the West at least, there is a profound difference in attitude. A recent book, with the title *Their Blood Cries Out*, bears the subtitle *The Worldwide Tragedy of Modern Christians Who are Dying for Their Faith*. The early Christians protested against their persecution, but 'tragedy' would not have been the first word that they would have chosen to describe it. They saw the martyrs as examples, as glorious witnesses to the faith, as a privileged elite who would inherit especial honour. The first of our classics, Ignatius's *Letters*, may strike the modern reader as distinctly odd. Yet Ignatius's willingness, not to say eagerness, to be martyred comes as a sharp challenge to modern western Christians, most of whom are willing to give up very little for their faith. In today's context it is perhaps also worth noting that the Christian concept of a martyr is one who dies bearing witness to their faith, not in the process of killing others.

For each classic I have selected extracts in order to give a flavour of the work. In making the selections I have generally sought to present material which has something to say to today's church. In 1973 at the Bangkok conference of the Commission on World Mission and Evangelism of the World Council of Churches, on the theme *Salvation Today*, there was a rebuke from a Roman Catholic observer: 'I haven't heard anyone speak on justification by faith. I've heard no one speak of everlasting life. What about God's righteous wrath against sin?' These are themes which are widely ignored today, and not just within the World Council of Churches. One aim of this volume is to serve as a reminder of neglected themes.

It is not anticipated that every reader will be enthused by all of the classics selected. Different readers will have different interests and the same reader will find different works relevant at different stages of life. But even if one were enthused by only half of the items and if one went on to read further in half of these, that would mean being exposed to twenty-five of the greatest works of our Christian heritage, a most worthwhile exercise.

At the end of the book I have cited the version that I have used for each extract. Where (for copyright reasons) these are older translations I have usually changed them, sometimes very considerably. Nineteenth-century translations of Greek and Latin often translated the words only, leaving the tortuous original sentence structure. I have sought to remedy this. I have also very occasionally taken slight liberties with the text in order to improve readability, such as removing a phrase like 'as I previously argued' or moving slightly in the direction of paraphrase. Also, in old English texts I have usually modernized spelling and changed 'hath' to 'has', and so on.

No attempt has been made to use 'inclusive language' in the extracts, for a variety of reasons. Where modern editions are used there is no question of changing the translation. Using inclusive language can also give the false impression that the writers concerned were 'politically correct' by today's standards in a way that they were not. Finally, 'traditional' English still remains the language of the great majority of discourse in Britain.

Ignatius of Antioch, *Letters* (c. 115)

Ignatius was bishop of Antioch in Syria at the beginning of the second century and was taken to Rome to be martyred, around the year AD 115. On the way he wrote seven letters, addressed to five churches in Asia Minor (at Ephesus, Magnesia, Tralles, Philadelphia and Smyrna), to the Roman church and to Polycarp, bishop of Smyrna. Polycarp went on to collect the letters and wrote one of his own as a covering letter for the collection. Ignatius's personality shines clearly through the letters and they are a most important source for our knowledge of the Christian church at this early and formative stage.

Ignatius is one of those who acquired a considerable posthumous literary heritage. Over the years further letters were added to the seven and these in turn were interpolated. Towards the end of the nineteenth century J.B. Lightfoot and other scholars managed to reconstruct the original texts and the authentic historical Ignatius again became visible. There do, however, remain minor uncertainties in detailed points of the text.

There are a number of themes that recur regularly in the letters:

● Ignatius saw two great threats facing the fledgling church, disunity and heresy, and warns repeatedly against them. In particular, he warns against Docetism, the belief that Jesus was human in outward appearance only.

● Ignatius is the first writer clearly to present the threefold pattern of ministry: one bishop in a church with his presbyters and deacons. He argues vigorously in defence of this pattern, an indication that it was not yet fully established. His letter to Rome is conspicuously silent about a single (monarchical) bishop there, showing that the threefold pattern had not yet reached the West. Ignatius's main concern is with the unity of the church. The bishop is seen as the focus of unity against both schism and heresy.

● He also sees the Eucharist as a focus of unity. He sees it as spiritual nourishment – 'breaking one bread, which is the medicine of immortality and the antidote to death, that we should live for ever in Jesus Christ' (Ignatius's *Letter to the Ephesians* 20).

● Finally, his own impending martyrdom preyed heavily on his mind and he welcomed it as the seal upon his discipleship. Through it he would become a true disciple, an imitator of Christ, and reach God. In places Ignatius's preoccupation with and longing for martyrdom can appear to be evidence of a mental instability, but it is unreasonable to expect someone facing up to being eaten by wild beasts to display a calm objectivity. In his letter to the Romans, most of which is found below, he repeatedly begs them not to work for his release whether by prayer or through political influence. At a time when many Christians are unwilling to make any significant sacrifices for their faith Ignatius's willingness to surrender his life comes as a stirring challenge.

The Letter to the Romans

1. Through prayer to God I have obtained the privilege of seeing your most worthy faces, and have been granted even more than I asked, for it is as a prisoner in Christ Jesus that I hope to greet you – if indeed it be God's will that I be counted worthy of reaching the end. For the beginning has been well ordered, if I may obtain grace to cling to my lot without hindrance unto the end. But what worries me is that your love may do me an injury, for it is easy for you to do what you please but difficult for me to reach God, unless you spare me.

2. My desire is not to please men, but God, even as you please him. I shall never again have such an opportunity as this of reaching God and nor will you ever be entitled to the honour of a better work, just by keeping quiet. For if you keep quiet and leave me alone, I shall become God's; but if you show your love to my flesh, I shall have to run my race again. Pray, then, do not seek to confer any greater favour upon me than that I be sacrificed to God while an altar is still prepared. Then, being gathered together in love, you may sing praise to the Father through Christ Jesus, for deeming me, the bishop of Syria, worthy to be summoned from the east to the west. It is good to set [in the west] from the world unto God, that I may rise again to him [in the east].

3. You have never envied any one; you have taught others. All I want now is for you to put into practice what you have taught. Just pray that I may have both inner and outer strength, that I may [genuinely] desire what I speak of and that I may not merely be called a Christian, but truly be found to be one. For if I be truly found [a Christian], I may also be called one and be deemed faithful at the point when I am no more visible to the world. Nothing visible is eternal. 'For the things which are seen are temporal, but the things which are not seen are eternal' [2 Corinthians 4:18]. For our God, Jesus Christ, is the more plainly visible now that he is with the Father. Christianity is not a matter of silence only, but also of [manifest] greatness.

4. I am writing to all the churches and assuring them that I shall die for God of my own free will – so long as you do not hinder me. I beg you not to show me an unseasonable kindness. Let me become food for the wild beasts, for it is through them that I can reach God. I am God's wheat so let me be ground by the teeth of the wild beasts, that I may become the pure bread of Christ. Rather entice the wild beasts that they may become my tomb and may leave no part of my body behind, so that I may be no bother to any one after my death. It is when my body

shall be no longer visible to the world that I shall truly be a disciple of Christ. Entreat Christ for me, that through these beasts I may become a sacrifice to God. I am not commanding you, as Peter and Paul did. They were apostles, but I am a mere convict. They were free, but I am a slave to this very hour. But when I suffer, I shall be the freed-man of Jesus, and shall rise again free in him. Now that I am a prisoner I am learning not to desire anything worldly or vain.

5. From Syria as far as Rome I am fighting with wild beasts, by land and sea, by night and day, being bound to ten leopards – I mean a band of soldiers, who only grow worse when they are kindly treated. Their injuries are training me to be a disciple of Christ, 'yet am I not justified by that' [1 Corinthians 4:4]. May I enjoy the wild beasts that are prepared for me and I pray that I will find them eager to rush upon me. Indeed I will entice them to devour me speedily rather than not touch me out of fear, as they have done to some. If they are unwilling to attack me, I will force them to do so. Bear with me. I know what is expedient for me. It is now that I am beginning to be a disciple. Let no power, visible or invisible, envy me reaching Jesus Christ. Come fire and cross, come crowds of wild beasts, come tearing, breaking and dislocation of bones, come hacking off of limbs, come crushing of my whole body and come the cruel tortures of the devil. Only let me reach Jesus Christ!

6. All the pleasures of the world, and all the kingdoms of this earth, shall profit me nothing. It is better for me to die for Jesus Christ than to reign over all the ends of the earth. 'For what shall it profit a man, if he gain the whole world but lose his own soul?' [Matthew 16:26] Him I seek, who died for us. Him I desire, who rose again for our sake. The pangs of a new birth are upon me. Bear with me, brethren. Do not hinder me from living, do not desire my death. I desire to belong to God, so do not give me over to the world. Allow me to receive pure light. When I have gone there, I shall indeed be a man of God. Allow me to be an imitator of the passion of my God. If any one has God within himself, let him understand what I desire and let him have sympathy with me, knowing how I am straitened.

7. The prince of this world would happily carry me away and corrupt my disposition towards God. Let none of you [Romans] therefore help him; rather be on my side, that is on God's side. Do not speak of Jesus Christ and yet set your desires on the world. Give no room to envy. Even though I myself, when I am with you, should exhort you to do so, do not listen to me then but rather give heed to what I am now writing to you. For though I am alive while I write to you, yet I am eager to die. My lust has been crucified and there is no fire of material desire in me, but only a living water that speaks to me within saying, 'Come to

the Father'. I have no delight in corruptible food, nor in the pleasures of this life. I desire the bread of God, the heavenly bread, the bread of life, which is the flesh of Jesus Christ, the Son of God, who became afterwards of the seed of David and Abraham. And I desire the drink of God, namely his blood, which is incorruptible love and eternal life.

8. I no longer wish to live after the manner of men, and this my desire shall be fulfilled if you consent. Consent, then, that your desires may also be fulfilled. I entreat you in this brief letter; believe me. Jesus Christ will reveal these things to you, [so that you shall know] that I am speaking the truth. He is the mouth altogether free from falsehood, by which the Father has truly spoken. Pray for me, that I may reach [the object of my desire]. I have not written to you according to the flesh, but according to the will of God. If I shall suffer, it will be because you wished me [well]; but if I am rejected, it will be because you hated me.

Justin Martyr, *First Apology* (150s)

Justin was born of pagan Greek parents in Palestine, early in the second century. He became a Christian after searching for the truth in Greek philosophy, a search which he describes in his *Dialogue with Trypho*. This is the record of a long and courteous debate which he had with a Jew called Trypho, which took place between AD 132 and 135 at Ephesus, the probable site of Justin's conversion.

Justin first attached himself to a Stoic philosopher. But after some time he was disappointed that he had not progressed in the knowledge of God, and that the philosopher did not seem even to consider this necessary. Then he followed an Aristotelian who was 'as he fancied, shrewd'. After a few days he pressed Justin for his fee, so Justin left him 'believing him to be no philosopher at all'. He next tried a follower of Pythagoras, but he expected Justin to study music, astronomy and geometry before coming to him for philosophy. Justin was impatient, and instead went to a well-known Platonist. He now 'made the greatest improvements daily', but proudly overestimated his progress, expecting 'forthwith to look upon God'. At this point he met an old man by the sea, who pointed him to the Old Testament Scriptures and to Christ. (Justin also refers to the impression that had been made upon him by the fearless way in which Christians faced martyrdom.) Justin then became a Christian, seeing 'this philosophy alone to be safe and profitable'. He concludes his account of his conversion with the statement that 'thus and for this reason I am a philosopher'. From then on Justin wore the philosopher's cloak. He was not just a Christian seeking to relate Christianity to Greek philosophy. He was a Greek who had come to see Christianity as the fulfilment of all that was best in philosophy, especially in Platonism.

Justin also wrote a two-part apology. His *First Apology* was a defence of the Christian faith, addressed to the emperor Antoninus Pius. To this he added his *Second Apology*, a shorter supplement to the first, addressed to the Roman senate. Justin's *Apology* is far more profound than the writings of the Apostolic Fathers. Justin spent his last years at Rome, where he taught. In the 160s he was arrested, with others, and put on trial for being a Christian. He refused to renounce his faith by offering sacrifice to the gods and went to his death confident of his salvation in Christ. As he pointed out in his *Apology*, death is a debt that all must pay eventually, so 'you can kill us, but not hurt us' (11, 2).

Justin's *Apology* is a masterly presentation of the Christian faith. He protests against the fact that Christians are condemned not for any crimes but for the 'mere name', i.e. merely for the fact of being Christians. He also refutes various false accusations against Christians. They were charged with being atheists because they would not worship the pagan gods. 'We confess that we are atheists as far as gods of that sort are concerned, but not with respect to the true God, the Father' (6). Christians were also accused of promiscuity because of the command to love one another, against which he makes it clear that for Christians sex is to be enjoyed within a faithful marriage relationship alone. 'If we marry, it is only that we may bring up children; if we decline marriage, we live chastely' (29). He also goes on to the attack by pointing out that Christians, unlike pagans, do not dispose of unwanted children. Justin argues at length that the coming of Christ was the fulfilment of Old Testament prophecy. He also sees analogies of Christian teaching and practice in pagan mythology, which he uses to argue that the persecution of Christians is unreasonable and which he sees as deliberate attempts by demons to mimic Christianity and thus deceive people.

Justin was resolutely opposed to paganism and had no time for syncretism. He gave his life rather than offer sacrifice to the gods. He was also very critical of Greek philosophy in places. But, at the same time, in his *Apologies*, he portrayed Christ not as a complete outsider but as the fulfilment of the best in Greek thought. He did this by exploiting the Greek concept of the *Logos* or Word in which all people participate.

> *We have been taught that Christ is the firstborn of God, and we have declared above that he is the Word [or reason] of whom all mankind partakes. Those who lived reasonably [with the Word] are Christians, even though they have been called atheists. For example: among the Greeks, Socrates, Heraclitus and men like them; among the barbarians [non-Greeks], Abraham. . . and many others whose actions and names we now decline to recount, because we know it would be tedious. (46)*

He also held that Plato and other philosophers had borrowed some of their ideas from the Old Testament.

Justin's *Apology* also gives us a reasonably full account of how Christian worship was conducted in Rome in the middle of the second century, describing (in the extract below) a baptism followed by communion for the newly baptized, and the regular weekly Eucharist.

---

61. I will also tell how we dedicate ourselves to God after we have been made new through Christ. As many as are persuaded and believe that what we teach and say is true, and undertake to be able to live accordingly, are taught to pray and to entreat God with fasting for the remission of their past sins, and we also pray and fast with them. Then we bring them to a place with water and they are born again in the same way that we were. For they are washed with water in the name of God, the Father and Lord of the universe, and of our Saviour Jesus Christ and of the Holy Spirit. For Christ also said, 'Unless you be

born again, you shall not enter the kingdom of heaven' [John 3:5]. . . .

We have learned from the apostles this reason for baptism. We were born by our parents coming together, without our own knowledge or choice, and were brought up in bad habits and wicked training. The name of God, the Father and Lord of the universe, is pronounced over those who choose to be born again and have repented of their sins, in order that we may not remain children of necessity and ignorance but may become children of choice and knowledge and obtain in the water the remission of sins previously committed. . . . We call this washing illumination, because those who learn these things are illuminated in their understanding. Those who are illuminated are washed in the name of Jesus Christ, who was crucified under Pontius Pilate, and in the name of the Holy Spirit who through the prophets foretold all things about Jesus.

65. Having thus washed those who have been convinced and have assented to our teaching, we bring them to the assembled brethren, to offer hearty communal prayers for ourselves, for those baptized and for all others everywhere. We pray that, now that we have learned the truth, we may be counted worthy and also that we may be found good citizens and keepers of the commandments by our works, so that we may obtain an everlasting salvation. After the prayers we salute one another with a kiss. Bread and a cup of wine mixed with water are then brought to the president of the brethren. He takes them, giving praise and glory to the Father of the universe, through the name of the Son and of the Holy Ghost, and offers thanks at considerable length for our being counted worthy to receive these things at his hands. When he has finished praying and giving thanks, all those present express their assent by saying Amen, the Hebrew word for 'So be it'. When the president has given thanks and all the people have assented, those whom we call deacons share with everyone present the bread and the wine mixed with water (over which the thanksgiving was pronounced) and take some away to those who are absent.

66. We call this food Eucharist and only allow those to partake who believe the things which we teach, who have received the washing [of baptism] for the remission of sins and for regeneration, and who are living as Christ taught. For we do not receive the [elements] as common bread and common drink. Just as Jesus Christ our Saviour, having been made flesh by the Word of God, had both flesh and blood for our salvation, so likewise we have been taught that the food which is blessed by the prayer of his word, and from which our blood and flesh are nourished by transformation, is the flesh and blood of that Jesus who was made flesh. For the apostles, in the memoirs composed by them which are called Gospels, have thus passed on to us what was enjoined upon them: that Jesus took bread, and when He had given thanks said, 'Do this in remembrance of me, this

is my body'; and that, in the same way, having taken the cup and given thanks, he said, 'This is my blood' and gave it to them alone.

67. Afterwards we continually remind each other of these things. The wealthy among us help the needy; we always stick together; and we bless the Maker of all for all that we receive, through his Son Jesus Christ and through the Holy Spirit. And on the day called Sunday, all who live in cities or in the country gather together in one place, and the memoirs of the apostles or the writings of the prophets are read for as long as time permits. When the reader has ceased, the president teaches and exhorts us to imitate these good things. Then we all rise together and pray and, as I said before, when our prayer is ended, bread and wine and water are brought, and the president similarly offers prayers and thanksgivings according to his ability and the people assent, saying Amen. Then that over which thanks have been given is distributed to all and partaken of, and a portion is sent by the deacons to those who are absent. Those who are well to do and willing give as they think fit and what is collected is deposited with the president, who assists the orphans and widows, those who are in need through sickness or any other cause, those who are in prison and strangers living among us. In a word, he takes care of all who are needy. Sunday is the day on which we all hold our common assembly because it is the first day [of the week] on which God made the world, having wrought a change in the darkness and matter, and also the day on which our Saviour Jesus Christ rose from the dead. For it was on the day before Saturn's [Saturday] that he was crucified and on the day after Saturn's, the Sun's day, that he appeared to his apostles and disciples and taught them these things, which we have submitted to you also for your consideration.

The Martyrdom of Polycarp (155–77)

Polycarp is one of the apostolic fathers and spans the period between the apostles and the late second-century church. As a youth he had sat at the feet of the apostles and in later life he met Irenaeus. His role as a living link was of vital importance given that the second-century church did not yet have a fixed creed or an agreed list of New Testament books. At a time when many wild and exotic theories were being spread abroad as Christian, Polycarp was able to point to the real nature of apostolic Christianity. Irenaeus himself bore witness to this in his *Against Heresies* 3:3:4, a passage quoted below (see pages 30–34).

Polycarp was bishop of Smyrna, in modern-day Turkey, and as such received a letter from Ignatius on the way to his martyrdom at Rome. He also himself wrote a letter to the church at Philippi. He is most famous for his martyrdom, an event which was recorded in a letter written by one Marcion on behalf of the church at Smyrna – the oldest surviving detailed account of Christian martyrdom. Polycarp, as bishop, was sought out after a number of his congregation had been cruelly martyred. He was martyred on Saturday 23rd February, but the year is not certain, being sometime between AD 155 and 177.

The narrative sets Polycarp's martyrdom in the context of a general persecution of the Smyrnan church at that time. After a number of Christians had been brutally put to death the crowd called out 'Away with the atheists; let search be made for Polycarp.' (The early Christians were called atheists because they refused to worship the pagan gods.) It then describes Polycarp's reluctant flight and eventual capture. He was taken to the stadium to face the proconsul and his 'trial' and martyrdom are described in the extract below. Polycarp is portrayed throughout as imitating Christ and there are a number of parallels with the Passion narratives in the Gospels. Another strong theme is the great hostility between Christians and the world, which is not surprising at a time when Christians were being cruelly put to death.

This work is of value as the oldest Christian martyrdom narrative outside the New Testament and also because of the importance of Polycarp for second-century Christianity. But aside from these factors it stands on its own merit as a superbly written account that, according to one edition, 'has moved and thrilled readers of all ages'.

---

5. The most admirable Polycarp, when he first heard [that he was sought for], far from being dismayed resolved to remain in the city. But he was persuaded by the majority to leave, so he departed to a farm not far from the city. There he stayed

with a few [friends], engaged in nothing else night and day than praying for all people and for the churches throughout the world, according to his usual custom. And while he was praying, three days before he was captured, he saw a vision in which his pillow seemed to be on fire. And he turned to those with him and said prophetically, 'I must be burnt alive.'

[Polycarp is captured.]

9. Now, as Polycarp entered the stadium, a voice came to him from heaven, 'Be strong, Polycarp, and play the man!' No one saw who spoke to him, but those brethren who were present heard the voice. And as he was brought forward, the commotion became great when they heard that Polycarp was taken. And when he came near, the proconsul asked him whether he was Polycarp. On his confessing that he was, [the proconsul] sought to persuade him to deny [Christ], saying, 'Have respect to your old age,' and other similar things according to their custom, [such as] 'Swear by the fortune of Caesar; repent and say, "Away with the Atheists".' Polycarp gazed with a stern countenance on all the wicked heathen in the stadium, waved his hand towards them, groaning and looking up to heaven, and said, 'Away with the Atheists.' Then the proconsul urged him, saying, 'Swear, and I will set you free. Revile Christ.' Polycarp declared, 'Eighty-six years have I served him and he never did me any injury. How then can I blaspheme my King and my Saviour?'

10. When the proconsul yet again pressed him and said, 'Swear by the fortune of Caesar,' he answered, 'Since you vainly urge me to swear by the fortune of Caesar, and pretend not to know who and what I am, hear me boldly declare, I am a Christian. If you wish to learn the doctrines of Christianity, fix a day and you shall hear them.' The proconsul replied, 'Persuade the people.' But Polycarp said, 'To you I have thought it right to offer an account [of my faith], for we are taught to give all due honour to the powers and authorities which are ordained by God. But as for these, I do not deem them worthy of receiving any account from me.'

11. The proconsul then said to him, 'I have wild beasts here and will throw you to them, unless you repent.' But he answered, 'Call them then, for we are not accustomed to repent of what is good in order to adopt that which is evil. It is a good thing for me to be changed from what is evil to what is righteous.' Again the proconsul said to him, 'If you will not repent I will have you burnt alive, seeing you despise the wild beasts.' But Polycarp said, 'You threaten me with fire which burns for an hour and is quenched after a little while, but you are ignorant of the fire of the coming judgment and of eternal punishment, reserved for the ungodly. But why do you delay? Do what you will.'

12. While he was speaking like this, he was filled with courage and joy and his countenance was full of grace, so that not merely did it not drop in dismay at the things said to him but on the contrary the proconsul was astounded. He sent his herald to proclaim three times in the midst of the stadium, 'Polycarp has confessed himself to be a Christian.' The whole multitude of pagans and Jews cried out at this proclamation with uncontrollable fury and in a loud voice, 'This is the teacher of Asia, the father of the Christians and the overthrower of our gods, who has been teaching many not to sacrifice or to worship the gods.' In such words they cried out and besought Philip the Asiarch to let a lion loose upon Polycarp. But Philip answered that this was illegal since the wild beast shows were already finished. Then they thought fit to cry out with one accord that Polycarp should be burnt alive. For the vision had to be fulfilled which was revealed to him concerning his pillow, when seeing it on fire as he was praying he prophesied, 'I must be burnt alive.'

13. This was carried into effect with greater speed than it takes to tell. The crowds immediately collected wood and faggots out of the shops and baths. . . . Immediately they surrounded him with the material that had been prepared for the funeral pile. When they were about also to fix him to the stake with nails he said, 'Leave me be, for he that gives me strength to endure the fire will also enable me to remain in the pile without moving, without your securing me by nails.'

14. So they did not nail him, but simply bound him. He placed his hands behind him and was bound like a noble ram [taken] out of a great flock for sacrifice, a burnt offering made ready and acceptable to God. He looked up to heaven and said:

> *O Lord God Almighty, the Father of your beloved and blessed Son Jesus Christ, through whom we have received the knowledge of you, the God of angels and powers and of all creation, and of the whole race of the righteous who live before you, I give you thanks that you have counted me worthy of this day and this hour, to have a part in the number of your martyrs, in the cup of your Christ unto the resurrection of eternal life, both of soul and body, through the incorruption [imparted] by the Holy Spirit. May I be accepted among them in your sight today as a rich and acceptable sacrifice as you, the ever-truthful God, fore-ordained and revealed to me and now have fulfilled. For this and all things I praise you, I bless you, I glorify you along with the everlasting and heavenly Jesus Christ, your beloved Son, with whom to you and the Holy Spirit be glory both now and for the ages to come. Amen.*

15. When he had concluded his prayer with 'Amen' the firemen lit the fire. And as the flame blazed forth in great fury, we to whom it was given to witness it beheld a great miracle and have been spared that we might report to others what happened. The fire, shaping itself into the form of an arch, like the sail of a ship filled with wind, made a wall round the body of the martyr. And he appeared within not like flesh which is burnt but like bread that is baked or gold and silver glowing in a furnace. We perceived such a sweet odour [coming from the pile] as if frankincense or some such precious spice had been smoking there.

16. At length the wicked men, perceiving that his body could not be consumed by the fire, ordered an executioner to go near and stab him with a dagger. When he had done this there came forth a dove and a great quantity of blood which extinguished the fire. All the people marvelled that there should be so great a difference between the unbelievers and the elect, including this glorious martyr Polycarp. In our own times he was an apostolic and prophetic teacher and bishop of the Catholic Church in Smyrna. For every word he spoke either has been or shall yet be fulfilled.

The Epistle to Diognetus
(2nd half of the 2nd century)

The so-called *Epistle to Diognetus* is in fact an anonymous apology, written probably in the latter half of the second century, addressed to one Diognetus, a high-ranking pagan. It was rediscovered in recent times and is known from only one late-medieval manuscript, in which parts of the seventh chapter are missing. Unfortunately this manuscript was destroyed in the Franco-Prussian war of 1870. It is known especially for its account of the lives of Christians in the world (5–6) and is one of the best and most beautifully written works from the early Christian centuries.

After a brief introduction (1) the author launches into a conventional attack on idolatry (2), echoing themes from the Old Testament. Having attacked pagan worship he then criticizes the Jews for their superstitious reliance upon the Old Testament ritual laws, such as sacrifices, circumcision, food laws, the sabbath and other special days (3–4). It is not stated in so many words but he appears to subscribe to the idea, found among some other Christian writers at the time, that the Jews were never intended to take these laws literally. After this negative polemical opening there is a beautiful and moving account of the relation between Christians and the world (5–6). The picture of Christian life at the time is doubtless idealized, but must have borne some relation to reality if it was to be credible. This is followed by an account of the role of Christ – the fact that God sent his own Son (7), the sorry state of the human race before his coming and the atonement that he made for us (8–9). Finally the author points to the blessing following acceptance of the Christian faith (10), its reasonableness (11) and the importance of a right response (12).

---

5. Christians are not distinguished from others by nationality or language or customs. For they neither inhabit cities of their own, nor employ a peculiar form of speech, nor lead an eccentric lifestyle. Their creed was not devised by any speculation or deliberation of inquisitive men nor do they, like some, proclaim themselves the advocates of any merely human doctrines. While they live in Greek as well as barbarian cities according as their lot has determined, and follow local customs in dress, food and the rest of their ordinary conduct, they display to us their wonderful and confessedly striking method of life.

They dwell in their own countries, but as transients. They share in all things with others as citizens, yet endure all hardships as foreigners. Every foreign land is to them as their fatherland, and their fatherland as foreign. They marry like others and beget children, but do not expose their offspring. They share their meals, but not their wives. They are in the flesh, but do not live after the flesh. They pass their days on earth, but are citizens of heaven. They obey the established laws, but surpass them in their private lives. They love all people, but are persecuted by all. They are ignored, and yet condemned. They are put to death, and yet restored to life. They are poor, yet make many rich. They lack everything, yet abound in everything. They are dishonoured, yet are glorified in their very dishonour. They are slandered, yet vindicated. They are reviled, yet bless. They are insulted, yet repay the insult with honour. They do good, yet are punished as evil-doers. When punished, they rejoice as if quickened into life. They are assailed by Jews as foreigners and are persecuted by Greeks, yet those who hate them are unable to give any reason for their hatred.

6. In a word, what the soul is in the body, Christians are in the world. The soul is spread through all the members of the body, and Christians are scattered through all the cities of the world. The soul dwells in the body, yet is not of the body; so Christians dwell in the world, yet are not of the world. The invisible soul is guarded by the visible body, and Christians are known indeed to be in the world, but their godliness remains invisible. The flesh hates the soul and wars against it, though itself suffering no wrong, because it is prevented from indulging its passions; the world also hates Christians, though in no way wronged by them, because they reject its pleasures. The soul loves the flesh that hates it and [loves also] the members of the body; Christians likewise love those that hate them. The soul is enclosed in the body, yet preserves that very body; Christians are confined in the world as in a prison, yet themselves hold the world together. The immortal soul dwells in a mortal tabernacle; Christians dwell as transients in a corruptible [world], looking for a heavenly incorruptibility. The soul improves when ill-provided with food and drink; in like manner Christians grow rapidly in number though subjected to daily punishment. God has assigned them this illustrious position, which it would be unlawful for them to desert.

7. As I said, it was no mere earthly invention which was entrusted to them, nor is it a mere human system of opinion which they take care to guard so carefully, nor is it a dispensation of mere human mysteries that has been committed to them. But truly God himself, the Almighty and invisible Creator of all things, sent from heaven [him who is] the truth, the holy and incomprehensible Word, and placed him among men and firmly established him in their hearts. He did not, as might have been imagined, send to men any servant, or angel, or ruler, or any one of those who bear sway over earthly things, or one of those to whom the government of things in the heavens has been entrusted, but the very Creator and Fashioner of all things. . . . This one he sent to them. Did he do this, as one might

imagine, in order to exercise tyranny or inspire fear and terror? By no means, but for motives of clemency and meekness. As a king sends his son who is also a king, so he sent him; as God he sent him, as [a man] to men he sent him; as a Saviour he sent him and as seeking to persuade, not to coerce us, for coercion has no place in the character of God. He sent him to call us, not to persecute us; he sent him to love us, not to judge us – though later he will indeed send him to judge us and who shall then endure his appearing? . . . Do you not see Christians thrown to wild beasts that they may be persuaded to deny the Lord, and yet not overcome? Do you not see that the more of them are punished, the more they grow in number? This does not look like the work of man; this is the power of God and these are the proofs of his presence.

9. . . . God acted when our wickedness had reached its height and it had been clearly shown that its reward (punishment and death) was about to come on us and when the time had come which God had ordained for manifesting his own kindness and power. Oh the great kindness and love of God! He did not hate us, nor reject us, nor bear any malice against us, but was long-suffering and patient. He took on himself the burden of our sins and gave his own Son as a ransom for us, the holy One for transgressors, the blameless One for the wicked, the righteous One for the unrighteous, the incorruptible One for the corruptible, the immortal One for the mortal. For what else was capable of covering our sins other than his righteousness? By whom else was it possible that we, the wicked and ungodly, could be justified than by the only Son of God? Oh sweet exchange, oh unsearchable creation, oh unexpected benefits, that the wickedness of many should be hidden in a single righteous One, and that the righteousness of One should justify many transgressors! Having therefore in former times convinced us that our nature was unable to attain to life, and having now revealed a Saviour who is able to save even those creatures which it was [formerly] impossible to save, he desired by both these facts to lead us to trust in his kindness and to esteem him our Nourisher, Father, Teacher, Counsellor, Healer, our Wisdom, Light, Honour, Glory, Strength, and Life, so that we should not be anxious about food and clothing.

Irenaeus, *Against Heresies* (180s)

Irenaeus was a Greek, born in Asia Minor in the middle of the second century into a Christian family. As a boy he listened to Polycarp, bishop of Smyrna, who had known the apostle John, as he describes in his *Letter to Florinus*, quoted in Eusebius's *History of the Church* (see pages 51–54). As a young man he moved to Lyons in Gaul (France) where he first became a presbyter before, in AD 177, succeeding to the martyred bishop. He is traditionally thought to have died at the beginning of the third century.

Irenaeus was influenced by Justin Martyr. He is a bridge between early Greek theology and western Latin theology, which began with his younger contemporary, Tertullian. While Justin was primarily an apologist, Irenaeus's main contribution lay in the refutation of heresy and the exposition of apostolic Christianity. His major work was his *Refutation and Overthrow of Knowledge Falsely So-called*, generally known by the shorter title of *Against Heresies*. This was written in the 180s primarily in opposition to Gnosticism. Irenaeus's defence against Gnosticism was largely successful and it was thanks to him and to those who followed in his footsteps that orthodox Christianity triumphed over Gnosticism.

Gnosticism is a modern term which covers a variety of second-century sects with certain common elements. The Gnostics believed in a supreme God who is totally remote from this world and had no part in its creation – that was the bungling work of a lesser deity, often identified with the God of the Old Testament. Between this evil world and the supreme God there is a hierarchy of divine beings. While our bodies, being physical, are part of this world, our souls are a divine spark, trapped in the body. Salvation is the escape of the soul from the body to the heavenly realms above. In order to reach the supreme God the soul needs to pass through the realms above this world, which are controlled by the stars and planets, potentially hostile divine beings. Salvation is by knowledge (Greek *gnosis*). This could be understood either in a crudely magical way as the knowledge of the passwords needed to pass by the divine beings on the way to the supreme God, or else in a more philosophical way as existential self-knowledge. Gnosticism was a radically different religion from orthodox Christianity. The different Gnostic groups had their own scriptures. They also appealed to secret traditions, which they claimed to have received from one or another apostle.

Irenaeus employed a number of arguments against Gnosticism, of which three can be mentioned:

● He described the different Gnostic systems in detail. For a long time he was a major source for knowledge of Gnosticism and more recent discoveries of Gnostic writings have confirmed the essential accuracy of his account. He sought to expose the ludicrous nature of many of their beliefs and to expose their inconsistencies. As he himself put it, 'merely to describe such doctrines is to refute them' (1:31:3). Indeed, having expounded one of their beliefs he anticipates that the reader 'will laugh heartily at their conceited foolishness' (1:16:3).

● He challenged the Gnostic claims to secret apostolic traditions. He argues that if the apostles had had special teaching to pass on, they would have entrusted it to the churches which they had founded. He points to the different churches founded by the apostles and shows how there has been a continuous succession of open public teaching in these churches since that time. In support of this, he lists the leaders of these churches, beginning with those appointed by the apostles themselves. Furthermore, these churches, scattered throughout the empire, all teach the same doctrine. This argument was powerful, given that Irenaeus himself knew Polycarp who had known the apostle John. Is one more likely to find apostolic Christianity in the apostolic churches whose teaching has been open and continuous since their foundation and who agree with one another – or among the Gnostics, whose claims to apostolic tradition are unverifiable and mutually contradictory and who disagree with one another?

I once discovered the power of Irenaeus's argument for myself when debating with two self-confessed 'Gnostics' who had given me a lift. I first tried to answer them from the New Testament but this did not work. They, like their second-century forebears, did not accept what they called 'your Scriptures'. As Irenaeus himself put it, 'when they are refuted from the Scriptures, they turn round and accuse these same Scriptures, as if they were not correct or authoritative' (3:2:1). Orthodox Christianity and Gnosticism are two religions, with two different sets of Scriptures. The question is: which religion and which set of Scriptures goes back to Christ and the apostles? It is this question which is answered by Irenaeus's argument – and it is hard to see how it could be answered otherwise.

● Irenaeus was one of the first to talk of New Testament Scripture alongside the Old Testament. Initially 'Scripture' for Christians meant the Old Testament. The apostolic writings were accorded authority, but it was only gradually that they were all gathered together into a New Testament. By the time of Irenaeus the New Testament was close to ours: four Gospels, Acts, Paul's letters and other writings. In a quaint passage, not to be taken too seriously, he argues that there could not be fewer or more than four Gospels. 'As there are four zones of our world and four main winds, while the church is scattered throughout the world and the pillar and foundation of the church is the gospel and the spirit of life, it is fitting that she should have four pillars breathing out immortality on every side and freshly vivifying people' (3:11:8).

Irenaeus appealed to apostolic Scripture (New Testament) and to the apostolic teaching handed down (tradition) in the apostolic churches. The latter was not intended to add to the message of the New Testament. It was because the Gnostics did not accept the New Testament that Irenaeus had to appeal to tradition. Tradition supplied a basic summary of apostolic Christianity (as found later in the Apostles' Creed, for example) in opposition to the radically different Gnostic beliefs.

Against Heresies is divided into five books. In the first book he begins by expounding the teaching of the Valentinians, a very influential Gnostic group, and goes on to describe other Gnostic systems in turn, with occasional critical comments. In the second book he argues more thoroughly against them, primarily on rational grounds. The third book refutes them on the basis of Scripture and the apostolic tradition. The fourth book relies more particularly on sayings of Christ from the Gospels. Finally, the fifth book treats the End Times, focussing on the resurrection of the flesh and also teaching about the millennium. *Against Heresies* is not well organized and at times rambles but it is the most important Christian work from the second century and lays solid foundations for the development of orthodox Christian theology.

1:10:1. The church, though scattered throughout the whole world to the ends of the earth, has received from the apostles and their disciples this faith: in one God, the Father almighty, maker of heaven and earth and the sea and all things in them; and in one Christ Jesus, the Son of God, who was made flesh for our salvation; and in the Holy Spirit, who through the prophets proclaimed God's saving dealings with man and the coming, virgin birth, passion, resurrection from the dead and bodily ascension into heaven of our beloved Lord Jesus Christ and his second coming from heaven in the glory of the Father to sum up all things and to raise up all human flesh so that. . . he should execute just judgment upon all people.

1:10:2. The church has received this preaching and this faith and, although scattered throughout the whole world, carefully preserves it as if living in but one house. . . . For although the languages of the world vary, yet the meaning of the tradition is one and the same. The churches planted in Germany do not believe or hand down anything different and nor do those in Spain, Gaul, the East, Egypt, Libya or the central regions. . . . The faith is always one and the same. Those who expound it at length do not add to it nor do those who say little diminish it.

3:3:1. All who wish to see the truth can clearly contemplate, in every church, the tradition of the apostles manifested throughout the whole world. We can list those who were by the apostles appointed bishops in the churches and their successors down to our own time. They neither taught nor knew anything like what these heretics rave about. Suppose the apostles had known hidden mysteries which they were in the habit of imparting to 'the perfect' privately and in secret. Surely they would have handed them down especially to those to whom they were also entrusting the churches themselves. For they wanted their successors to be perfect and blameless in everything.

3:3:4. Polycarp was instructed by apostles and conversed with many who had seen Christ. He was also appointed bishop of Smyrna in Asia, by apostles. I also saw him in my youth, for he lived a very long time. As a very old man he suffered a glorious and most noble martyrdom. He always taught the things that he had learned from the apostles, which the church has handed down and which alone are true. . . . There are people who heard him describe how John, the Lord's disciple, went to bathe at Ephesus, but seeing Cerinthus in the bath-house rushed out without bathing. 'Let us fly,' he exclaimed, 'in case the bath-house falls down because Cerinthus, the enemy of the truth, is inside.' Polycarp once met Marcion who asked him 'Do you recognize me?' 'Indeed I do recognize you – the firstborn of Satan,' Polycarp replied. Such was the horror which the apostles and their disciples had against even talking with any who perverted the truth.

3:4:1. As we have such proofs there is no need to look elsewhere for the truth that is easily obtained from the church. . . . Suppose there is a dispute about an important issue, should we not resort to the oldest churches, with whom the apostles were in constant contact, and learn from them an accurate and clear answer?

5:33:3. The predicted blessing [Genesis 27:27–29] unquestionably belongs to the time of the kingdom, when the righteous shall rise from the dead and rule; when also the creation, having been renewed and set free, shall be abundantly fruitful with all kinds of food, from the dew of heaven and the fertility of the earth. The elders who saw John, the Lord's disciple, related what they had heard from him – how the Lord used to teach about these times, saying:

> *The days are coming when vines shall grow, each with ten thousand branches, each branch with ten thousand twigs, each true twig with ten thousand shoots, each shoot with ten thousand clusters and each cluster with ten thousand grapes. Each grape will yield twenty-five measures of wine. When any of the saints takes hold of one cluster, another will cry out, 'I am a better cluster, take me; bless the Lord through me.*

[The Lord declared] likewise that a grain of wheat would produce ten thousand ears, that each ear should have ten thousand grains and that each grain would yield ten pounds of clear, pure, fine flour; also that all other fruit-bearing trees, seeds and grass would yield in similar proportions; also that all animals would feed on vegetation and would live in peace and harmony with each other, in perfect subjection to man.

5:33:4. If lions are going to eat straw [Isaiah 11:7], just think what the wheat will be like if its straw can feed lions!

Tertullian, *Apology* (197)

Quintus Septimius Florens Tertullianus was born into a pagan Roman family around the year AD 160 at Carthage (modern Tunis). He was educated in rhetoric and law. It is possible that he lived for a time at Rome and practised there as a lawyer. Sometime before the year 197, he became a Christian. For the remainder of his life he wrote extensively as an advocate for the Christian faith. He died an old man sometime after 220.

Tertullian was the first important Christian to write in Latin. He is the father of western Latin theology. Together with Origen, he is one of the two greatest Christian writers of the second and third centuries. Indeed, he was one of the greatest Latin writers ever and it is said that pagans used to read his works simply to enjoy the style. As a fifth-century writer put it, 'almost every word he uttered was an epigram and every sentence was a victory'. Or as a modern author said, Tertullian 'possessed an ability rare among theologians: he is incapable of being dull'!

Tertullian wrote always as an advocate – defending his own position and attacking all rivals. This he did with the full range of rhetorical skills at his disposal. He has been described as 'an apologist who never apologized'! His aim was the total annihilation of his opponents. They had to be shown to be totally wrong – and morally suspect to boot. Tertullian was not being vindictive or dishonest. He was completely convinced about the rightness of his cause and sincerely sought to argue it as best he could.

He wrote more than thirty works, which fall into three main groups: apologetic, practical and dogmatic. His most famous apologetic work, written in 197, is simply called *Apology*. Tertullian continued the work of the second-century apologists such as Justin, but with far greater brilliance. His *Apology* has been called 'by common consent the masterpiece and crown of all his writings'.

Tertullian argued with all his legal skills against the injustice of condemning believers to death simply for being Christians. He claimed that it was only evil emperors, such as Nero and Domitian, that persecuted Christians. He also refuted the charges brought against Christians – that they practised promiscuous and incestuous sex ('loving one another'), that they were cannibals (eating Christ's flesh and drinking his blood) and that they were atheists (not worshipping the pagan gods). While the Christians did not worship the gods, who were no gods, they did worship the one true God and pray for the well-being of the state. He complains that Christians are denied religious liberty, being the one group not allowed to worship freely.

1. Those who previously hated Christianity because they knew nothing about it, cease to hate it as soon as they come to know it. From being its haters they become its disciples. By simply finding out about it, they begin to hate what they used to be and to profess what they used to hate. Their numbers are as great as is claimed. The outcry is that the state is filled with Christians – that they are in the fields, in the cities, in the islands. They make lament, as if it were a calamity, that both sexes, every age and condition, even high rank are becoming Christians. For all that, their minds are not open to the idea that they may have overlooked some good in it. . . . They have no desire to look more closely. Here alone human curiosity slumbers. They prefer to be ignorant, even though the knowledge has been bliss to others.

37. If we are commanded to love our enemies whom have we to hate? If injured, we are forbidden to retaliate, lest we become as bad ourselves. Who can suffer injury at our hands? Think of your own experience – how often you inflict gross cruelties on Christians, partly of your own inclination and partly in obedience to the laws. How often too the hostile mob pays no regard to you but takes the law into its own hand, attacking us with stones and fire. . . . Yet, banded together as we are, ever so ready to sacrifice our lives, what single case of revenge for injury are you able to point to – though, if we were permitted to repay evil by evil, we could achieve an ample vengeance in a single night with a torch or two? . . .We are but of yesterday and we have filled all your places – cities, islands, forts, towns, market places, the very camp, tribes, companies, palace, senate, forum. We have left nowhere to you except the temples of your gods. Were it not counted better in our religion to be slain than to slay, would we not be fit and eager for war, even with unequal forces, we who so willingly yield ourselves to the sword?

39. We have a treasure-chest, but it is not made up of purchase-money, as of a religion that has its price. Once a month everyone who wants puts in a small donation, but only if he wants and is able. It is entirely voluntary with no compulsion. These gifts form a deposit fund of kindness. It is not spent on feasts, drinking-bouts or restaurants, but to support and bury poor people and to supply the wants of destitute orphan children and of housebound elderly folk; also of any who have been shipwrecked; also of any who are in the mines or banished to the islands or in the prison for nothing but their fidelity to the cause of God's church. These all become the nurslings of their confession. It is mainly because of such noble loving deeds that many label us. 'See,' they say, 'how they love one another' – while they themselves hate one another; 'how they are ready even to die for one another' – while they themselves will sooner put others to death. . . . One in mind and soul, we do not hesitate to share our earthly goods with each another. We have all things in common but our wives. We give up our community in the one

place that it is practised by others, who not only take their friends' wives, but most tolerantly also accommodate their friends with their own. Here they follow the example, I believe, of those wise men of ancient times, the Greek Socrates and the Roman Cato, who shared with their friends the wives whom they had married.

40. The name of faction is rightly given to those who conspire to bring odium on good and virtuous men and cry out against innocent blood. They offer as justification of their enmity the baseless plea that they think the Christians the cause of every public disaster, of every affliction with which the people are visited. If the Tiber rises as high as the city walls or if the Nile does not send its waters up over the fields, if the heavens give no rain, if there is an earthquake, if there is famine or pestilence, straightway the cry is, 'Away with the Christians to the lion!' What! Shall you give so many to a single beast? Tell me, how many calamities were there before the reign of Tiberius, that is before the coming of Christ?

42. But we are accused of doing harm on another ground, that of being useless in secular affairs. How in all the world can that be the case with people who live among you, eat the same food, wear the same clothes, have the same habits, under the same necessities of existence? We are not like Brahmins or Indian ascetics, who dwell in woods and exile themselves from ordinary human life. We do not forget our debt of gratitude to God, our Lord and Creator. We reject nothing that he has created, though we certainly restrain ourselves from an immoderate or sinful use of any of his gifts. So we live in the world with you and do not renounce forum, markets, baths, booths, workshops, inns, markets or any other place of commerce. We sail with you, fight with you, till the soil with you and trade with you. Even in the various arts we make public property of our works for your benefit. How we seem to be useless in your ordinary business when we live with you and by you, I can not comprehend. I may not join in your religious ceremonies, but on the sacred day I am still a man.

50. But go on zealously, good presidents, you will stand higher with the people if you sacrifice the Christians at their wish, kill us, torture us, condemn us, grind us to dust. Your injustice is the proof that we are innocent. That is why God allows us to suffer thus. Very recently, by condemning a Christian woman to the pimp rather than to the lion you admitted that we consider a taint on our purity more terrible than any punishment and any death. Your cruelty [against us] does not profit you, however exquisite. Instead, it tempts people to our sect. As often as you mow us down, the more we grow in number. The blood of the Christians is the seed [of the church]. . . . The very obstinacy you criticize teaches for us. For who on seeing it is not moved to find out what lies behind it? Who, having found

out, does not embrace our faith – and having done so, does not desire to suffer in
order to partake of the fulness of God's grace and obtain from God complete
forgiveness, in exchange for his blood? For martyrdom secures the remission of
all sins. That is why when you sentence us [to death] we give thanks on the very
spot. As the divine and human are always opposed, when you condemn us God
acquits us.

The Passion of Perpetua and Felicitas
(203)

Perpetua and Felicitas were a young Roman matron and her slave girl who were martyred at Carthage in AD 203, together with three male catechumens. The full account of their martyrdom is based upon the prison diaries of Perpetua and another of the martyrs, Saturus, and was put together by an unknown editor, whom some have claimed to be Tertullian.

In the narrative there are accounts of four visions that were given to Perpetua and another that was given to Saturus, taking up over a quarter of the text, which are described as their 'more eminent visions' (14). The emphasis upon visions shows the influence of Montanism, a late second-century prophetic movement that spread in Roman North Africa. The first of the visions showed Perpetua that 'it was to be a passion,' after which they 'ceased henceforth to have any hope in this world' (4). The visions play an important role in the morale of the martyrs and were obviously of considerable significance for them. As with *The Martyrdom of Polycarp* (see pages 23–26), there is a strong sense of hostility towards a sinful world. Their martyrdom is described as their victory and as a 'second baptism' (18).

This account has stood out among the many martyr narratives from the Early Church because the central figures are two young mothers. It has been described as 'one of the most beautiful pieces of ancient Christian literature'. It is unique in that the bulk of the text is actually written by the martyrs themselves. Most of the narrative concerns their time in prison, only a fifth being devoted to their actual martyrdom.

---

2. The young catechumens, Revocatus and his fellow-slave Felicitas, Saturninus and Secundulus were apprehended. Also among them was Vivia Perpetua, respectably born, liberally educated, a married matron, having a father and mother and two brothers, one of whom was, like herself, a catechumen, and a son an infant at the breast. She herself was about twenty-two years of age. From this point onward she shall herself narrate the whole course of her martyrdom, as she left it described by her own hand and with her own mind.

3. 'While' says she, 'we were still with the persecutors my father, because of his affection for me, persisted in seeking to turn me away from the faith. "Father," said I, "do you see, let us say, this vessel lying here to be a little pitcher or

something else?" And he said, "I see it to be so." And I replied to him, "Can it be called by any other name than what it is?" And he said, "No." "Neither can I call myself anything else than what I am, a Christian." Then my father, provoked at this saying, threw himself upon me as if he would tear my eyes out. But he only distressed me, and went away overcome by the devil's arguments. Then, in a few days after I had been without my father, I gave thanks to the Lord and his absence became a source of consolation to me. In that same interval of a few days we were baptized and to me the Spirit prescribed that in the water of baptism nothing else was to be sought for bodily endurance. . . . I suckled my child, which was now faint with hunger. In my anxiety for it, I addressed my mother and comforted my brother and commended my son to their care. I was languishing because I had seen them languishing on my account. Such cares I suffered for many days, and I obtained permission for my infant to remain in the dungeon with me. Immediately I grew strong and was relieved from distress and anxiety about my infant; and the dungeon became to me as it were a palace so that I preferred being there to being elsewhere.'

15. Felicitas was eight months with child (for she had been pregnant when she was apprehended) and as the day of their martyrdom drew near she was in great grief lest on account of her pregnancy she should be delayed (because pregnant women are not allowed to be publicly punished) and lest she should shed her sacred and guiltless blood among some who had been wicked subsequently. Her fellow martyrs were also painfully saddened lest they should leave so excellent a friend, and as it were companion, alone in the path of the same hope. Therefore they joined together in united prayer to the Lord three days before their martyrdom. Immediately after their prayer her pains came upon her, and when, with the difficulty natural to an eight months' delivery, in the labour of bringing forth she was sorrowing, one of the servants of the jailers said to her, 'You who are in such suffering now, what will you do when you are thrown to the beasts, which you despised when you refused to sacrifice?' And she replied, 'Now it is I that suffer what I suffer; but then there will be another in me, who will suffer for me, because I also am about to suffer for him.' Thus she brought forth a little girl, which one of the sisters brought up as her own daughter.

18. The day of their victory shone forth, and they proceeded from the prison into the amphitheatre, as if to an assembly, joyous and of brilliant countenances. If they shrank it was with joy, and not with fear. Perpetua followed with placid look and with step and gait as a spouse of Christ, beloved of God, casting down the lustre of her eyes from the gaze of all. Felicitas was rejoicing that she had safely brought forth, so that she might fight with the wild beasts, moving from the midwife to the gladiator, to wash after childbirth with a second baptism. . . .

Perpetua sang psalms; Revocatus, Saturninus and Saturus uttered threats against the people who were gazing on their martyrdom. When they came within sight of Hilarian the procurator, they said to him, 'You judge us, but God will judge you.' At this the people were exasperated and demanded that they should be scourged. And they rejoiced that they should have incurred one of their Lord's passions.

20. Moreover, for the young women the devil prepared a very fierce cow, provided especially for that purpose contrary to custom, rivalling their sex also in that of the beasts. And so, stripped and clothed with nets, they were led forth. The populace shuddered as they saw one young woman of delicate frame and another with breasts still dropping from her recent childbirth. So, being recalled, they were unbound. Perpetua was first led in to the cow. She was tossed and fell on her loins. When she saw her tunic torn from her side, she drew it over her as a veil for her middle, more mindful of her modesty than her suffering. Then she was called for again, and bound up her dishevelled hair, for it was not becoming for a martyr to suffer with dishevelled hair, lest she should appear to be mourning in her glory. So she rose up and when she saw Felicitas crushed, she approached and gave her her hand, and lifted her up. And both of them stood together. When the brutality of the populace was appeased they were recalled to the Sanavivarian gate. Then Perpetua was received by one Rusticus, who was still a catechumen, who kept close to her. So deeply had she been in the Spirit and in an ecstasy that she began to look round her, as if aroused from sleep, and to say to the amazement of all, 'I cannot tell when we are to be led out to that cow.' And when she heard what had already happened, she did not believe it until she noticed the signs of mauling on her body and on her dress and recognized the catechumen. Afterwards she asked the catechumen and the brother to approach and addressed them, saying, 'Stand fast in the faith, and love one another, all of you, and do not be offended at my sufferings.'

21. The populace called for them into the midst, so that they might make their eyes partners in the murder as the sword penetrated into the martyrs' bodies. They rose up of their own accord and moved themselves to where the people wished, having first kissed one another so that they might consummate their martyrdom with the kiss of peace. The others received the sword-thrust motionless and in silence. But Perpetua, that she might taste some pain, cried out loudly when she was pierced between the ribs and herself placed the wavering right hand of the youthful gladiator to her throat. Possibly such a woman could not have been slain unless she herself had willed it, because she was feared by the impure spirit.

O most brave and blessed martyrs! O truly called and chosen unto the glory of our Lord Jesus Christ! Whoever magnifies, honours and adores him assuredly ought to read these examples for the edification of the church, not less than the ancient ones, so that new virtues also may testify that one and the same Holy Spirit is always operating even until now, as is God the Father Almighty and his Son Jesus Christ our Lord, whose is the glory and infinite power for ever and ever. Amen.

Cyprian, *Letter to Donatus* (246)

Thascius Caecilius Cyprianus was born early in the third century into an upper-class pagan family. He taught rhetoric at Carthage and was probably destined for high public office, such as a provincial governorship. But in AD 245 or 246 he turned his back on his career prospects by becoming a Christian. Soon after, Cyprian was appointed a presbyter or elder and in 248 or 249, while still a relatively recent convert, became bishop of Carthage, the most important church office in the Roman province of Africa. He served as bishop for some ten years until his martyrdom in 258.

These happened to be years of immense turmoil for the church and Cyprian found his qualities of leadership tested more than if he had become a Roman provincial governor. He thought and wrote in response to the problems that he faced, being first and foremost a man of action rather than an intellectual. Almost as soon as he was appointed bishop the church faced the Decian persecution of 249–51, the first coordinated empire-wide persecution of the church. The emperor Decius planned a two-pronged attack on the church. First, the leading bishops were to be liquidated. Cyprian was warned in advance and fled into hiding in the country near Carthage, from where he directed the church during the persecution. The second phase of the persecution was an attempt to force all Christians to sacrifice to the gods. All were required, on pain of death, to obtain a certificate stating that they had done this. The church, which had known some years of relative peace and calm, was not prepared for this onslaught. Large numbers of Christians offered sacrifice to the gods and many others evaded the order by bribing the officials to give them the necessary certificate, without actually offering sacrifice.

Traditionally, those who had renounced their faith were not readmitted into the church. But what was to be done with the large numbers now seeking readmission? Should the lapsed be readmitted at once or only after public confession followed by a period of austere penitence or never? Who was to decide this question? Those who were imprisoned for their faith and ready to die for it (the 'confessors') were taking it upon themselves to reconcile the lapsed to the church. Did this authority lie with them or the bishops? Cyprian addressed this question in an important work, *The Lapsed*, insisting that the right lay with the bishops, although they were to heed the recommendations of the confessors. Cyprian fought hard for the authority of the bishop, for the 'church of the bishops' against the 'church of the martyrs', and it was fitting that he should seal his labours by dying as a martyr bishop. After the persecution Cyprian led a council at Carthage in 251 which decided that reconciliation was possible for the lapsed, after a period of penance.

These difficult decisions did not meet with universal approval. Some at Carthage thought Cyprian was being too strict and separated from him, forming a rival congregation with laxer discipline. In Rome, on the other hand, there was a split or schism in the other direction and Novatian, a gifted presbyter, set himself up as a rival bishop. Cyprian regarded the question of schism or division with the utmost seriousness and devoted to it his most important treatise, *The Unity of the Church*. The only true church is the Catholic Church and there is no room for a variety of denominations in one place. It is not possible to divide the church, only to leave it as Novatian had done. To leave the Catholic Church is to commit spiritual suicide. (By the third century the mainstream church called itself 'Catholic', the Greek for 'universal' or worldwide, to distinguish itself from heretical groups like the Gnostics and also from breakaway groups.) This doctrine remained normative for more than a thousand years and it is only recently that it has been relaxed in the Roman Catholic Church.

Cyprian wrote thirteen treatises, all brief apart from a lengthy work listing scriptural testimonies against the Jews. He also wrote a considerable number of letters, roughly equalling his treatises in bulk. His *Letter to Donatus*, which is reckoned as his first treatise, was written shortly after his baptism explaining his own conversion and exhorting his friend to follow suit. Stylistically it falls short of his later writings, but it is a charming work because he writes with the directness and immediacy of the new convert. As with other writings from the second and third centuries, it shows the early Christian commitment to sexual purity, to a correct use of possessions and to a readiness to suffer for their faith. In all of these matters it presents a sharp challenge to the modern western Christian.

Cyprian begins with an account of his own conversion, found below. He then invites Donatus to compare the Christian lifestyle with the corruption of the contemporary pagan world. He points to the prevalence of murder 'which in the case of an individual is seen as a crime but is called a virtue when committed wholesale [in war]' (6). He points to the cruelty of the gladiatorial games (7) and the corrupting influence of the theatre. 'Things which in the past were acts of vice now become examples to follow. . . . Adultery is learnt while it is seen. . . . The married woman who goes to the show chaste returns home lewd. [All sorts of immorality are portrayed.] Can those who view such things be healthy-minded or chaste?' (8). He points to the hypocrisy of those who condemn others in public for vices that they practise in private (9) and to the corruption of the legal and political systems (10–11). He points to the way in which the rich rob from the poor and yet are themselves enslaved to their possessions. The wealthy man 'is in bondage to his gold and is the slave of his luxury and wealth rather than their master'. The rich do not help the poor and are concerned only to hoard their wealth. But, 'their possession of it amounts to this only, that they can keep others from possessing it and – what a splendid perversion of language – they call those things "goods" which they put only to bad use' (12).

3. While I was still lying in darkness and gloomy night. . .completely ignorant of my real life and far removed from truth and light, I found some things hard to believe – especially hard given my character at that time: that a person can be born again (which the divine mercy had announced for my salvation); that a person animated to a new life in the saving water [of baptism] can put off what he had previously been; that he can be changed in heart and soul, while remaining physically the same. 'How,' I said, 'is such a conversion possible, that we can suddenly and speedily strip off all those things that are innate in us and have become hardened in the corruption of our material nature and all those things that we have acquired and which have become deep-rooted by lengthy habit? These things are deeply and radically ingrained within us. When does he who has been used to liberal banquets and sumptuous feasts learn thrift? And when does he who has been glittering in gold and purple and has been celebrated for his costly attire, reduce himself to ordinary and simple clothing? . . .It is inevitable, as it has always been, that the love of wine should entice, pride inflate, anger inflame, covetousness disturb, cruelty stimulate, ambition delight, lust hasten to ruin, with fascinations that will not let go their grip.'

4. These were my frequent thoughts. For as I was myself so entangled and constrained by the very many errors of my former life that I could not believe it possible for me to escape from them, for I was much enslaved to the vices that held me. Because I despaired of better things, I used to indulge my sins as if they were actually part of me and native to me. But the water of new birth [baptism] washed away the stain of my former life; a light from above was poured into my reconciled and purified heart; the Spirit breathed from heaven restored me so as to make me a new man by a second birth. Then in a wonderful way, my doubts at once began to be resolved, hidden things to be revealed, dark things to be enlightened, what had before seemed difficult was now easy, what had before seemed impossible was now possible. I could now acknowledge that which was born of the flesh and lived in the practice of sins belonged to the earth, but that it was now enlivened by the Spirit of holiness and had begun to be of God. You yourself assuredly know and recollect as well as I do what was taken away from us, and what was given to us by that death of evil and that life of virtue. You know this without my needing to tell you. Praising oneself is odious boasting, but to declare something a gift of God and not ascribe it to human virtue is gratitude rather than boasting. That we used to sin was the result of human error; that we have now ceased to sin is the beginning of the work of faith. All our strength comes from God. From him we have life and strength; it is by power derived and conceived from him that we act and, while yet in this world, recognize the signs of things to come. Let fear preserve our innocence, so that the Lord who has mercifully flowed into our hearts in his heavenly grace may remain a guest in our

grateful minds by a righteous submissiveness, lest the assurance we have gained give birth to carelessness and the old enemy creep up on us again.

14. There is only one peaceful and reliable serenity, only one solid, firm and constant security and that is to withdraw from the whirlpools of a distracting world, lay one's anchor in the harbour of salvation and lift up one's eyes from earth to heaven. . . . And this does not cost anything by way of bribes or hard work. Our elevation or dignity or power are not born of our elaborate efforts but are a free gift from God available to all. . . .

15. When you have enlisted in the spiritual camp of heavenly warfare, maintain a discipline that is uncorrupted and restrained by religious virtue. Be constant in prayer and [Bible] reading – speak with God and let him speak with you, instruct you in his commands and show you the way. Those whom he has made rich no one shall impoverish because he who has once been supplied with heavenly food cannot be poor. Gilded ceilings and houses adorned with costly marble mosaics will appear tawdry once you realize that it is you yourself who are to be perfected and decorated.

Origen, *Against Celsus* (246–48)

Origen was born around 185 of Christian parents in Alexandria. In 202 his father, Leonides, was martyred. Origen wrote to him urging him to remain firm and it is said that Origen was himself restrained from seeking martyrdom only by his mother hiding his clothes! He devoted himself totally to a life of austerity and scholarship. According to tradition, his dedication was so thorough that he took Matthew 19:12 literally and made himself a eunuch – although he later disapproved of such a course of action. He was loyal to the mainstream Catholic Church throughout his life and was appointed by Demetrius, bishop of Alexandria, as head of the catechetical school (where those seeking baptism were instructed). But in due course he fell out with Demetrius, who was seeking to extend his authority as bishop. Origen moved to Caesarea in Palestine, where he continued his work and was highly respected. In the Decian persecution (249–51) he was imprisoned and severely tortured, in the hope that he would renounce his faith, but he remained faithful and was eventually released. He died a few years later as a result of his injuries.

Origen was thoroughly acquainted with Greek philosophy, having studied under leading pagan philosophers. Some think that he studied under Ammonius Saccas, founder of Neoplatonism, but this is doubtful. Origen's theology was totally permeated by Platonism. The Platonist element is not like the icing on a cake or the currants in it, which can be removed, but like the brandy flavouring which is inseparable from the cake itself. His orthodoxy has been debated from his day to ours. In the fourth century there was a powerful anti-Origenist movement. In the sixth century he was formally condemned as a heretic and yet he remains the single most influential father of Greek theology.

Origen was a prolific writer, but much of his work has been lost. Much of it survives only in translation, sometimes 'doctored' to improve its orthodoxy. His major writings can be divided into four groups:

● Biblical. Origen produced a massive edition of the Old Testament with, in parallel columns, the Hebrew text, the Hebrew text in Greek characters and four or more Greek translations. He also wrote many commentaries (scholarly expositions), homilies (practical and edificatory) and 'scholia' (notes on particular passages).

● Practical works. Among other such works, he wrote *Prayer* and *Exhortation to Martyrdom*.

● *First Principles* was the first attempt in the Early Church to produce a systematic theology. It is divided into four books: on God, the world, freedom and the Scriptures.

● *Against Celsus* is Origen's reply to Celsus's *True Word*, a vehemently anti-Christian work written in the late 170s. This was ignored for some time but eventually Origen's wealthy patron Ambrose asked him to respond to it. This Origen did towards the end of his life, between 246 and 248. Celsus's work has been lost but it has been estimated that Origen quotes at least three quarters of it in his reply (italicized in the extract below) and it has been largely reconstructed. With Celsus and Origen, pagan-Christian polemics reached a new level. Celsus had studied Christianity carefully, reading the Bible and other Christian writings. He does not repeat the popular accusations of cannibalism and incest, although these were still widely believed when he wrote.

Origen's response in turn is the greatest and most substantial apology from the church of the second and third centuries. Earlier apologists like Justin and Tertullian were no intellectual lightweights, but Origen was the equal of any of his pagan contemporaries. In the Early Church, his *Against Celsus* was surpassed only by Augustine's massive *City of God* (see pages 99–101).

3:49. This statement [of Celsus] is also untrue, that it is *only foolish and low individuals, persons devoid of perception, slaves, women and children that the teachers of the divine word wish to convert.* Such people the Gospel does indeed invite, in order to make them better; but it also invites those who are very different, since Christ is 'the Saviour of all men, and especially of those that believe' [1 Timothy 4:10], whether they be intelligent or simple. 'He is the propitiation with the Father for our sins; and not for ours only, but also for the sins of the whole world' [1 John 2:2]. In the light of this there is no need for us to respond to questions of Celsus like the following: *Why is it an evil to have been educated, and to have studied the best teachings, and to have both the reality and appearance of wisdom? What hindrance does this offer to the knowledge of God? Why should it not rather be a help and a means by which one might be better able to arrive at the truth?* It is no evil to have been truly educated, for education is the way to virtue – but even the wise men among the Greeks would not rank amongst the number of the educated those who hold to erroneous teaching. On the other hand, who would not admit that it is a blessing to have studied the best teachings? But which teachings shall we call the best, except those which are true and which incite men to virtue? Moreover, it is an excellent thing to be wise, but not merely to appear wise, as Celsus says. And it is a help, not a hindrance, to the knowledge of God to have been educated, to have studied the best teachings and to be wise. And it becomes us rather than Celsus to say this, especially if it be shown that he is an Epicurean.

3:50. But let us examine those statements of his which follow next: *Moreover, we see that even those individuals, who in the marketplaces perform the most disgraceful tricks and who gather crowds around them, would never approach an assembly of wise men, nor*

dare to exhibit their arts among them; but wherever they see youths, and a mob of slaves, and
a gathering of unintelligent persons, thither they thrust themselves in and show themselves
off. Observe, now, how he slanders us in comparing us to those who in the
marketplaces perform the most disreputable tricks, and gather crowds around
them! What disreputable tricks, pray, do we perform? Or what is there in our
conduct that resembles theirs, seeing that it is by reading [biblical] texts and
explaining them that we lead men to the worship of the God of the universe and
to the cognate virtues, that we turn them away from despising the Deity and from
everything contrary to right reason? Even philosophers would wish to gather
together hearers like this for their discourses exhorting men to virtue – a practice
which certain of the Cynics especially have followed, conversing publicly with
whomever they happen to meet. Will they maintain, then, that these philosophers
who do not gather together persons who are considered to have been educated,
but who invite and assemble hearers from the public street, resemble those who
in the marketplaces perform the most disreputable tricks, and gather crowds
around them? Neither Celsus, however, nor any one who holds the same opinions,
will fault those who, motivated by philanthropy, address their arguments to the
ignorant populace.

3:51. And if they are not to be blamed for doing this, let us see whether Christians
do not exhort multitudes to the practice of virtue in a greater and better degree
than they. For philosophers who converse in public do not pick and choose their
hearers, but anyone who wishes stands and listens. The Christians, however, so
far as possible, test previously the souls of those who wish to become their
hearers. Having previously instructed them in private, they introduce them into
the community when they appear to have sufficiently demonstrated their desire
for a virtuous life – then, and not before. They privately form one class for
beginners who are receiving admission but have not yet obtained the mark of
complete purification; and another class for those who have manifested to the
best of their ability their intention to desire nothing that is not approved by
Christians. With the latter, certain persons are appointed to make inquiries about
the lives and behaviour of those who join them, in order to prevent those who
commit acts of infamy from coming into their public assembly; while those of a
different character they receive wholeheartedly, in order to make them better day
by day. This is how they deal with those who are sinners, and especially with
those who lead dissolute lives, whom they exclude from their community –
although, according to Celsus, they resemble those who in the marketplaces
perform the most shameful tricks! Now the venerable school of the Pythagoreans
used to erect cenotaphs to those who had apostatized from their system of
philosophy, treating them as dead; but the Christians lament as dead those who
have been vanquished by licentiousness or any other sin, because they are lost

and dead to God. And if they give evidence of an appropriate change they are afterwards received back as though risen from the dead – at some future time and after a greater interval than in the case of those first seeking admission. But those who lapsed and fell after professing the Gospel are not placed in any office or post of rank in the church of God.

Eusebius of Caesarea,
The History of the Church (324)

Eusebius was born in the early 260s in Palestine. He studied and worked with Pamphilus, who was in charge of Origen's library at Caesarea and who was martyred in 309 or 310. In gratitude to Pamphilus, Eusebius took his name becoming Eusebius Pamphili, as if he had been his son or slave. Like Pamphilus, Eusebius was an ardent admirer of Origen and they jointly wrote a defence of him. Eusebius was first and foremost a scholar but in 313 or 314 he became bishop of Caesarea. He died there in 339 or 340.

Eusebius is remembered above all as a historian, indeed as the father of church history. He wrote a *Chronicle* of the history of the world and also a history of *The Martyrs of Palestine* in the Great Persecution (303–13), events of which he was an eyewitness. But his greatest work is his *History of the Church*, which traces the progress of the church from the earliest times to 324, when Constantine became sole emperor of East as well as West. Eusebius also wrote a *Life of Constantine* as well as two lesser works on him, being an ardent admirer of the emperor. He believed strongly in monarchy and had a particularly exalted view of Constantine as a Christian emperor, seeing him as God's representative on earth. Eusebius has been accused of 'baptizing' the eastern concept of the absolute 'divine' monarch. The eastern Byzantine Christian emperors were happy to accept this understanding of their status. Eusebius also wrote a number of apologetic, biblical and dogmatic works. Most significant of these are two substantial apologetic works: *The Preparation for the Gospel* and *The Proof of the Gospel*.

Eusebius did not shine in terms of eloquence, originality or clarity of thought. He tended in his works to rely heavily on quotation. Ironically, this is one of the great strengths of his *History of the Church* because it preserves so many documents which are otherwise unknown. Writing the history of the Early Church without Eusebius has been compared to attempting to write the history of the Apostolic Church without the Acts of the Apostles. Eusebius saw the hand of providence in the life of the church – in the deaths of those who persecuted Christians and in the triumph of Christianity. His *History of the Church* may not have been particularly well written, but it laid a foundation for the history of the Early Church on which others built. In the following century Socrates, Sozomen and Theodoret wrote sequels to Eusebius's *History*.

The History of the Church is in ten books, organized according to the reigns of different emperors. The last three books cover the period from 303 to 324, for which Eusebius was himself an eyewitness. Eusebius was concerned throughout to record succession lists of bishops, accounts of orthodox Christian teachers and their heretical opponents, accounts of persecution and martyrdom and, supremely, the final victory of the Christian faith over paganism. For Eusebius, the conversion of Constantine and the establishment of a Christian empire was the natural and desirable outworking of the Christian faith. He had no qualms about the linking of Christianity with the empire. Eusebius wrote during the honeymoon years of the Christian state, when its negative features were only beginning to become apparent. A century later Augustine was to present a very different and less triumphalistic perspective in his monumental *The City of God* (see pages 99–101).

2:25. When Nero's government was firmly established, he began to plunge into unholy practices and even took up arms against the God of the universe. It is beyond the scope of the present work to describe the greatness of his depravity. Many have recorded his history in most accurate narratives, from which anyone may learn at their pleasure the coarseness of the man's extraordinary madness. After he had accomplished the senseless destruction of so many myriads, it led him into such blood-guiltiness that he did not spare even his nearest relatives and dearest friends, but destroyed his mother, his brothers, his wife and countless others of his own family as he would private and public enemies, with various kinds of deaths. But on top of all this he added one more crime, being the first emperor to show himself an enemy of the divine religion. Tertullian also bears witness to this:

> *Examine your records and you will find that Nero was the first to persecute this teaching when, having subdued all the east, he exercised his cruelty against all at Rome. We are proud to have such a man as the leader in our punishment. For anyone who knows him understands that he condemned nothing unless it was supremely excellent. [Tertullian, Apology 5 (see pages 35–38)]*

Having publicly announced himself as the first among God's chief enemies, he was led on to slaughter the apostles. It is recorded that in his reign Paul was beheaded in Rome itself, and that Peter likewise was crucified. This account of Peter and Paul is confirmed by the fact that their names are to this day preserved in cemeteries there. It is also confirmed by Gaius, a church member who arose when Zephyrinus was bishop of Rome. In his published disputation with Proclus, the leader of the Phrygian heresy [Montanism], he speaks as follows about the places where the sacred corpses of the aforesaid apostles are laid:

I can show you the monuments of the apostles. If you go to the Vatican or to the Ostian way
you will find the monuments of those who laid the foundations of this church.

That they were both martyred at the same time is stated by Dionysius, bishop of
Corinth, in his *Letter to the Romans*:

> *You have thus by such an admonition bound together the planting of Peter and*
> *Paul at both Rome and Corinth. For they both of them planted and likewise*
> *taught us in our Corinth as they also did in Italy, being martyred at the same*
> *time.*

I have quoted these things in order further to confirm the truth of the history.

5:20. Irenaeus wrote several letters against those who were disturbing the sound
ordinance of the church at Rome. One of these, to Blastus, was entitled *Schism*;
another, to Florinus, was entitled *Monarchy*, or *That God is not the Author of Evil*, a
view which Florinus seemed to be defending. Because Florinus was being led
astray by the error of Valentinus, Irenaeus wrote his work *The Ogdoad*, in which he
shows that he himself had known the first successors of the apostles. At the close
of this treatise I found a most beautiful note which I am constrained to insert in
this work:

> *Whoever copies this book, I adjure you by our Lord Jesus Christ and by his*
> *glorious advent when he comes to judge the living and the dead to compare what*
> *you write with this manuscript and carefully correct it. You are also to write this*
> *adjuration and include it in the copy.*

These things may be profitably read in his work and I have recorded them, that
we may have those ancient and truly holy men as the best example of painstaking
carefulness.

In the *Letter to Florinus*, to which I referred, Irenaeus again mentions his
intimacy with Polycarp:

> *Such doctrines, to put it mildly Florinus, are not of sound judgment. They disagree*
> *with the church and drive those who accept them into the greatest impiety. Not*
> *even the heretics outside of the church have ever dared to publish such doctrines.*
> *The presbyters who came before us and were companions of the apostles did not*
> *deliver such doctrines to you. When I was a boy I saw you in lower Asia with*
> *Polycarp, moving in splendour in the royal court and trying to gain his approval. I*
> *remember the events of that time more clearly than those of recent years, for what*
> *boys learn grows with their mind and becomes part of it. So I can describe the very*

place where the blessed Polycarp sat as he spoke, his goings out and his comings in, the manner of his life, his physical appearance, his discourses to the people and the accounts that he gave of his conversation with John and the others who had seen the Lord. He remembered their words and what he heard from them about the Lord, his miracles and his teaching, having received them from eyewitnesses of the Word of life. These things Polycarp told in harmony with the Scriptures. I listened attentively to these things which were told me by the mercy of God, noting them down not on paper but in my heart. By God's grace I constantly and faithfully recall them. I can bear witness before God that if that blessed and apostolic presbyter had heard any such thing, he would have cried out, stopped his ears and would have exclaimed, as was his way, 'Dear God, for what times have you spared me that I should endure these things?' And he would have fled from the place where he was sitting or standing when he heard such words. This is clear from the letters which he sent, either to confirm neighbouring churches or to admonish and exhort individual believers.

11

Athanasius,
The Incarnation of the Word (335–37)

Athanasius was born at the end of the third century. He entered the household of Alexander, bishop of Alexandria, in due course becoming a deacon and accompanying the bishop to the Council of Nicea in 325. When Alexander died in 328, Athanasius succeeded him as bishop of Alexandria, holding the post for forty-five years until his death in 373. He had nothing to do with The Athanasian Creed (see pages 115–17).

The chief preoccupation of Athanasius's life was the struggle against Arianism. Arius, who denied the deity of Christ, had been condemned at the Council of Nicea, but the Creed produced by the council was not acceptable to the majority of eastern bishops. The emperor sought unity above all else, so favoured a more tolerant approach to orthodoxy which could embrace a suitably chastened Arius. Athanasius would have none of this. He saw the deity of Jesus Christ as the foundation of the Christian faith and fought Arianism with every weapon at his disposal, including that of ecclesiastical politics. His uncompromising stand made him unpopular with bishops and rulers alike. Seventeen of his forty-five years as bishop were spent in five different exiles. Most important of his years in exile were those spent in Rome from 340 to 346. This was a time of considerable mutual influence between Athanasius and his hosts. After this exile he spent the 'Golden Decade' of 346–56 at Alexandria, his longest uninterrupted time as bishop. Most of Athanasius's works were dedicated to the struggle against Arianism and he made good use of the leisure given him by his exiles. Best known is his longest work, the *Orations against the Arians*.

Athanasius also wrote an apology in two parts: *Against the Greeks* and *The Incarnation of the Word*. Traditionally these were thought to have been written in about 318, before the Arian controversy, but the evidence seems to favour a date during his first exile, 335–37. We have here a different sort of apology from those so far considered. There is no more need to refute accusations made against Christians by a persecuting pagan society. Instead we have the exposition of a specific doctrinal theme seeking to give a rational response to objections made against it.

Jews and pagans claimed that the incarnation and crucifixion of God's Son were unfitting and degrading. In response to such charges Athanasius argues that the incarnation and cross are indeed suitable, fitting and eminently reasonable. This is because only the one through whom the world was created was able to restore it and this restoration could not take place in any way other than by the cross. God made the human race like the animals (nature) but added the extra gift of being made in his image (grace).

Adam and Eve had free will and their obedience was tested in the garden but they failed, turning from God to physical and sensual gratification. God had said that if they sinned they would die (Genesis 2:17) and he could not go back on his word. But the eternal Word, the same one through whom God had made the world in the first place, came to restore the human race. By his death in our place he paid the debt that we owed. He taught us about God and restored the lost image. He brought incorruption and immortality.

Athanasius's two-part apology has received much criticism, not all justified. He is accused of teaching that salvation comes by the incarnation rather than the cross and that it is automatic for the human race. Neither of these charges is fair to the argument of the books as a whole. They have also been accused of giving excessive weight to Greek thought, especially in the representation of the fall. Adam before the fall is portrayed as a Greek philosopher – contemplating the Word, the image of the Father. His mind had nothing to do with his body. It transcended all bodily desires and senses and contemplated 'intellectual reality'. But Adam turned from intellectual reality and began to consider his body and its senses, thus falling into fleshly desires (*Against the Greeks* 2–4). But it needs to be remembered that the primary purpose of these books is to answer the objections of unbelievers. As such it is a brilliant achievement and the argument of the work has been very influential. Anselm's *Cur Deus Homo* (see pages 146–49) uses basically the same line of argument, developing it very differently in a very different context.

---

6. For these reasons death having gained upon men, and corruption abiding upon them, the human race was perishing, rational man made in God's image was disappearing and God's handiwork was in the process of dissolution. Death had a legal hold over us from that time forth and it was impossible to evade the law, since it had been laid down by God because of the transgression. The result was truly both absurd and incongruous. For it was absurd that God, having spoken, should prove false. God had ordained that man should die if he disobeyed the command and it would be absurd if he were not to die after having transgressed and God's word should be broken. For God would not be true if man did not die, after he had said we should die. Again, it is incongruous that creatures who were created rational and had partaken of the Word, should be ruined and return to non-existence through corruption. For it is not worthy of God's goodness that the things he had made should waste away because the devil deceived men. It is especially incongruous that God's handicraft among men should be done away, either because of their own negligence or because of the deceitfulness of evil spirits.

8. The incorporeal, incorruptible and immaterial Word of God came to our realm. . . in condescension to show us love and to visit us. He saw that the race of rational creatures was perishing and that death reigned over them through corruption. He also saw that it was God's threat against transgression that gave a firm hold to the corruption that was upon us, and that it was absurd that the law should lapse without being fulfilled. He also saw the incongruity of the situation, that creatures made by him were fading away. He also saw the exceeding wickedness of men and how they were gradually increasing it to an intolerable pitch against themselves and, lastly, how all men were under penalty of death. He took pity on our race, had mercy on our infirmity, condescended to our corruption and could not bear for death to have the mastery. Lest the creature should perish and his Father's handiwork in men be wasted, he took to himself a body and that of no different sort from ours. For his aim was not simply to have a body or merely to appear. If he had wanted merely to appear he could have done so some better way, but he took a body like ours and that from a pure and spotless virgin who had not known a man, a body clean and truly pure of sexual intercourse. Though he was the mighty creator of everything, he prepared the body in the Virgin as a temple for himself and made it his very own as an instrument in which to be manifested and to dwell. So, because all were under the penalty of mortal corruption, he took from our bodies one of like nature and gave it over to death in the place of all, offering it to the Father. This he did because of his love so that the law involving man's ruin might be undone because all are held to have died in him in that the law's power was fully spent in the Lord's body and had no further claim on men like him. He also did it so that, whereas men had turned to corruption, he might turn them back to incorruption, and quicken them from death by the appropriation of his body and by the grace of the resurrection, eliminating death like straw in a fire.

9. The Word perceived that human corruption could not be undone except by fulfilling the necessary condition of death, but he was unable to suffer death, being immortal and the Son of the Father. So he took to himself a body which was capable of death so that it might be worthy to die in the place of everyone, through partaking of the Word who is above all, and remain incorruptible because of the Word dwelling in it. Thus corruption might be stayed from all by the grace of the resurrection. He offered the body he had taken unto death, as a spotless offering and sacrifice and thus put away death from all his fellows by the offering of an equivalent.

20. No one else but the Saviour himself, who in the beginning made everything out of nothing, could bring the corrupted to incorruption; no one else but the Image of the Father could recreate men in God's image; no one else but our Lord

Jesus Christ, who is Life itself, could make the mortal immortal; no one else but the Word, who orders everything and is alone the true and only-begotten Son of the Father, could teach men about the Father and destroy idolatry. Since the debt owed by all men had to be paid (for all men had to die), he came among us. After he had demonstrated his deity by his works, he offered his sacrifice on behalf of all and surrendered his temple [body] to death in the place of all. He did this to free men from the guilt of the first sin and to prove himself more powerful than death, displaying his own body incorruptible, as a first-fruit of the resurrection of all. . . . Two miracles happened at once: the death of all men was accomplished in the Lord's body, and death and corruption were destroyed because of the Word who was united with it. For there was need of death, and death must needs be suffered on behalf of all, that the debt owed by all might be paid. The Word was unable to die, being immortal, so he took to himself a mortal body in order to offer it as his own on behalf of all and in order, by suffering on behalf of all through his union with it, to 'destroy him who holds the power of death, that is the devil, and free those who all their lives were enslaved by their fear of death' [Hebrews 2:14–15].

54. By death immortality has reached all and by the Word becoming man the universal providence and its creator and leader, the very Word of God, has been made known. For he became human that we might become divine; he revealed himself in a body that we might understand the unseen Father; he endured human insults that we might inherit immortality.

Athanasius, *The Life of Antony* (c. 357)

Most of Athanasius's writings concern the person of Christ, whether works against Arianism or his two-part apology. But he also wrote the most important work on early monasticism, *The Life of Antony*, whom Athanasius portrays as the first monk. This was not a total distraction from his main concern. Athanasius defeated Arianism not just at the intellectual level and in the arena of church politics but also at the popular level. The support of simple Coptic Christians and monks like Antony provided him with the power base from which to conduct his offensive.

Antony was an illiterate Copt born in about 250. At the age of about twenty he heard Matthew 19:21 read in church: 'If you wish to be perfect, go and sell all you have and give to the poor.' Moved by this Antony began to lead an ascetic life, as had many before him. (In the second and third centuries there were those who lived an especially ascetic life – remaining single, embracing poverty and devoting themselves to prayer and fasting. Such people remained within the normal congregations and are called 'domestic ascetics' because they practised their asceticism at home, within society.) Gradually Antony withdrew from society until in about 286 he broke new ground by going out into the desert – in order to fight with the demons on their own ground. He spent about twenty years on his own in a disued fort at Pispir, his friends bringing him food twice a year.

Eventually they broke into the fort by force to see how he was. At this stage others began to join Antony, like him living a solitary life. Thus began the monastic movement in Egypt. A few years later Antony began to divide his time between Pispir (the 'Outer Mountain') and an 'Inner Mountain', a three-day journey away, where he could live on his own. He went twice to Alexandria, during the Great Persecution in the hope of attaining martyrdom and in about 338 to support Athanasius against Arianism. He died in 356 at the Inner Mountain, leaving his cloak to Athanasius. Not the least of Athanasius's achievements was to keep the monastic movement within the bounds of the mainstream Catholic Church and to keep it from schism.

Antony and early Egyptian monasticism were inspired and motivated by the words and example of Jesus. But there was another influence at work. Greek philosophy did not see the physical world as the creation of the supreme God. This encouraged the idea of salvation as the escape of the soul from the prison of the body and the world. The early Christian ascetic movement was influenced by this. Thus Antony preferred to eat in private because he was ashamed that he had to eat.

Traditionally Antony has been reckoned the first monk. This may not strictly be true but, as politicians know, it is the perception that counts. Athanasius's *Life of Antony*, written shortly after his death, provided him with worldwide publicity and became one of the most influential documents from the Early Church. It helped to spread monasticism throughout the whole Roman empire. It also played a significant role in the conversion of Augustine, described in his *Confessions* (see pages 91–94).

———————————

2. When his father and mother died Antony, who was about eighteen or twenty years old, was left alone with one little sister to take care of. Less than six months later he was going as usual to church. On the way he meditated and reflected how the apostles left all to follow the Saviour, how in Acts some sold their possessions and brought them to the apostles to be distributed to the needy and what a great hope was laid up for them in heaven. Pondering these things he entered the church when the Gospel was being read, and he heard the Lord's words to the rich man, 'If you wish to be perfect, go and sell all you have and give to the poor and you will have treasure in heaven' [Matthew 19:21]. It was as if God had reminded him of the saints and the passage had been read for his sake. Antony immediately left the church and gave his ancestral lands (three hundred productive and beautiful acres) to the villagers so that they should no longer bother him and his sister. He also sold his movable goods and gave the proceeds to the poor, keeping a little however for his sister.

8. Tightening his hold upon himself, Antony departed to the tombs which were some way from the village. Having asked a friend to bring him bread regularly, he entered one of the tombs and remained within alone, the friend having shut him in. When the enemy could no longer endure this but was afraid that in a short time Antony would fill the desert with the [monastic] discipline, he came one night with a multitude of demons and whipped him so severely that he lay on the ground speechless from pain. He claimed that the torture was so severe that no human blows could ever have hurt so much. In the providence of God (who never overlooks those that hope in him) his friend came the next day with the loaves. Having opened the door and seeing Antony lying on the ground as though dead, he lifted him up and carried him to the village church and laid him on the ground. Many of his relatives and the villagers sat around Antony as round a corpse, but about midnight he came to himself and arose. When he saw them all asleep and only his friend keeping watch, he summoned him and asked him to carry him back to the tombs without waking anybody.

14. Antony continued training himself in solitude for nearly twenty years, never leaving [the fort] and rarely being seen by anyone. By then many others were eager to imitate his discipline so his friends came and forcibly tore down and removed the door. Antony came out, as if from a shrine, initiated in the mysteries

and filled with the Spirit of God. This was the first time those who came to see him saw him outside the fort and when they saw him they were amazed at the sight. For his bodily condition was the same as before – he was neither fat from lack of exercise, nor lean from fasting and fighting with the demons, but just the same as they had known him before his withdrawal. His soul was free and unblemished, being neither contracted by grief, nor relaxed by pleasure, nor affected by laughter or dejection, for he was not troubled when he saw the crowd nor overjoyed at being greeted by so many. He was altogether even as being guided by reason, and abiding in a natural state. Through him the Lord healed many who were ill and cast out evil spirits from others. He gave Antony grace in speaking to comfort the sorrowful, reconcile those in dispute and exhort all to prefer the love of Christ above everything in the world. While exhorting and advising them to remember the good things to come and the loving-kindness towards us of God, 'who did not spare his own Son, but gave him up for us all' [Romans 8:32], he persuaded many to embrace the solitary life. Thus cells arose even in the mountains and the desert was colonized by monks who left their own people and enrolled themselves in a heavenly citizenship.

16. One day when he had gone out all the monks gathered together and asked him to speak to them. He addressed them in Coptic as follows: 'The Scriptures are enough for instruction, but it is good to encourage one another in the faith. . . . Let this especially be your common aim neither to surrender having once begun, nor to faint in difficulty, nor to say: "It is a long time that we have been living under the discipline" – but let us rather increase our zeal as though each day were a fresh start. Compared with the ages to come our whole life is very short and compared with eternal life all our time is nothing.'

17. 'Do not let desire for possessions take hold of anyone, for what gain is there in acquiring things which we cannot take with us? Why not rather gain those things which we can take with us, like prudence, justice, temperance, courage, understanding, love, kindness to the poor, faith in Christ, freedom from wrath and hospitality? If we possess these, we shall find them preparing a welcome for us in the land of the meek.'

23. 'If the demons see any Christians, especially monks, working cheerfully and advancing they first attack by tempting us and placing obstacles in our way, i.e. evil thoughts. But we need not fear their suggestions, for by prayer, fasting and faith in the Lord their attack immediately fails. Even then they do not stop, but attack again with wicked subtlety. For when they cannot deceive the heart openly with foul pleasures they approach in a different disguise and try to strike fear by changing their shape, taking the form of women, wild beasts, creeping things,

gigantic bodies and troops of soldiers. Even then you need not fear their deceitful displays for they are nothing and quickly disappear, especially if you fortify yourself with faith and the sign of the cross. Yet they are bold and very shameless for when thus worsted they attack in a different way, pretending to prophesy and foretell the future, appearing to be as high as the roof and very wide.'

30. 'So we should fear God alone and despise the demons, not being afraid of them. The more they do these things the more let us intensify our discipline against them, for a good life and faith in God is a great weapon. They fear the ascetics' fasting, sleeplessness, prayers, meekness, quietness, contempt of money and vainglory, humility, love of the poor, almsgiving, freedom from anger and, chief of all, their piety towards Christ.'

35. 'When the demons come to you at night and want to tell the future or say, "we are the angels," take no notice because they are lying. Even if they praise your discipline and call you blessed, do not listen to them and have nothing to do with them but rather sign yourselves and your houses [with the cross] and pray and you will see them vanish. For they are cowards and greatly fear the sign of the Lord's cross, because in it the Saviour stripped them and made an example of them. But if they shamelessly stand their ground, prancing and changing their appearance, do not fear them, nor shrink, nor heed them as though they were good spirits. For with God's help it is easy to distinguish between the presence of good and evil.'

44. While Antony was thus speaking all rejoiced. In some the love of virtue increased, in others carelessness was thrown aside, in others self-conceit was stopped. All were persuaded to despise the assaults of the Evil One and marvelled at the grace given by the Lord to Antony for discerning spirits. So their mountain cells were like tents filled with holy bands of men who sang psalms, loved reading, fasted, prayed, rejoiced in the hope of things to come, laboured in almsgiving and preserved mutual love and harmony. One could behold, as it were, a land set apart and filled with piety and justice. Instead of evil-doers, victims and complaining tax-collectors there was a multitude of ascetics whose one goal was to aim at virtue. Any one beholding the cells and seeing such good order among the monks, would lift up his voice and say, 'How beautiful are your dwelling-places, O Jacob, your tents, O Israel! Like shady glens and gardens by a river, like tents pitched by the Lord, like cedars beside waters' [Numbers 24:5–6].

Sayings of the Desert Fathers [and Mothers] (4th century)

After the pioneering work of Antony, Egypt became one of the chief centres of early monasticism. Very different from Antony was Pachomius, an educated Coptic soldier who was baptized on leaving the army. Around 323 he founded a community at Tabennesi on the Nile. His form of monasticism was based on community rather than solitary life, on a simple lifestyle (comparable to that of a Coptic peasant) rather than extremes of asceticism, on a hard working and disciplined life with the monasteries being efficient economic units modelled on the army. Pachomius's monks met four times daily for corporate worship and were expected to learn to read the Bible. By the time Pachomius died in 346 his movement embraced about three thousand monks in nine monasteries. Pachomius is seen as the founder of communal monasticism, the first to write a monastic 'rule'.

Very different was the emphasis in the desert region between Cairo and Alexandria, where there were three major settlements. Nitria was founded in about 330 by Ammun, a wealthy man who spent his wedding night converting his wife to a life of celibacy. Nitria was composed of a number of independent settlements with the monks meeting daily for worship and eating and worshipping together on Saturdays and Sundays. There was no common rule but there were three palm trees with whips on them – one for monks, one for robbers and one for guests! In 390 there were about five thousand monks at Nitria. Some found this life too lax and Macarius the Alexandrian moved twelve miles further into the desert to found Cellia, where about six hundred monks lived out of earshot of each other, meeting only at weekends. Further south, Macarius the Egyptian in about 330 founded Scetis (confusingly, in the Wadi Natrun) which was stricter than Nitria in that the monks did not drink wine. They all met together at weekends. There are Coptic monasteries to this day in the Wadi Natrun. In all three places the practice was semi-eremitic. That is, the monks lived a hermit life most of the time but met together at weekends. The ideal was to move from a communal to a solitary life as one progressed.

The sayings of and about these monks were collected towards the end of the fifth century into the *Apophthegmata Patrum* or *Sayings of the Fathers*. (A minority of the 'fathers' are in fact 'mothers'.) This collection is an invaluable source of information for early Egyptian desert monasticism and is largely free of the 'spin' that characterizes Athanasius's *The Life of Anthony* (see pages 59–62). Many of the sayings are highly 'occasional', being addressed to specific situations. The asceticism of the collection tends to the extreme. Monks sought to eat, drink and sleep as little as possible. Silence and the solitary life were prized. Despite the extreme rigour, many monks did not find peace easy to achieve. The struggle against demons, passions and temptation was fierce. Given the extreme ideals it would have been easy to lapse into legalism, but one of the attractive features of the *Sayings* is the repeated warnings against judging one another.

Most Christians, and even most monks, have not approved the extremes of asceticism. Most would not applaud Amma [Mother] Sarah for living sixty years beside a river without ever looking at it. But some of the sayings and stories have a timeless value. Rufinus elsewhere tells the story of how Macarius was given a bunch of grapes. He saw another monk who was sick and gave them to him. He in turn passed the grapes on and eventually they came round back to Macarius again! Another story not in this collection tells how Satan came to a monk, disguised as the angel Gabriel. The monk sent the angel away to check his facts, for he was not worthy to have an angel sent to him.

Abba [Father] Pambo asked Abba Anthony, 'What ought I to do?' and the old man said to him, 'Do not trust in your own righteousness, do not worry about the past, but control your tongue and your stomach.'

Blessed Archbishop Theophilus, accompanied by a magistrate, came one day to find Abba Arsenius. He questioned the old man, to hear a word from him. After a short silence the old man answered him, 'Will you put into practice what I say to you?' They promised him this. 'If you hear Arsenius is anywhere, do not go there.'

A brother who had sinned was turned out of the church by the priest; Abba Bessarion got up and went with him, saying, 'I, too, am a sinner.'

Abba Gerontius of Petra said that many, tempted by the pleasures of the body, commit fornication, not in their body but in their spirit, and while preserving their bodily virginity, commit prostitution in their soul.

[Epiphanius] also said, 'Ignorance of the Scriptures is a precipice and a deep abyss.'

Abba Theodore also said, 'If you are temperate, do not judge the fornicator, for you would then transgress the law just as much. And he who said, "Do not commit fornication," also said, "Do not judge."'

[Isisdore of Pelusia] also said, 'The desire for possessions is dangerous and terrible, knowing no satiety; it drives the soul which it controls to the heights of evil. Therefore let us drive it away vigorously from the beginning. For once it has become master it cannot be overcome.'

[Abba Matoes] also said, 'The nearer a man draws to God, the more he sees himself a sinner. It was when Isaiah the prophet saw God, that he declared himself "a man of unclean lips"' [Isaiah 6:5].

Abba Xanthius said, 'The thief was on the cross and he was justified by a single word; and Judas who was counted in the number of the apostles lost all his labour in one single night and descended from heaven to hell. Therefore, let no one boast of his good works, for all those who trust in themselves fall.'

[Abba Poemen] also said, 'Just as the king's bodyguard stands always on guard at his side, so the soul should always be on guard against the demon of fornication.'

Abba Poemen said, 'If a man has sinned and denies it, saying: "I have not sinned," do not reprimand him; for that will discourage him. But say to him, "Do not lose heart, brother, but be on guard in future," and you will stir his soul to repentance.'

[Abba Poemen] also said, 'A man who teaches without doing what he teaches is like a spring which cleanses and gives drink to everyone, but is not able to purify itself.'

[Abba Poemen] also said, 'Men speak to perfection but they do precious little about it.'

A brother asked Abba Poemen, 'What is a hypocrite?' The old man said to him, 'A hypocrite is he who teaches his neighbour something he makes no effort to do himself.'

A brother questioned Abba Poemen saying, 'What does it mean to repent of a fault?' The old man said, 'Not to commit it again in future. This is the reason the righteous were called blameless, for they gave up their faults and become righteous.'

Abba Poemen said that blessed Abba Anthony used to say, 'The greatest thing a man can do is to throw his faults before the Lord and to expect temptation to his last breath.'

Abba Poemen said, 'Teach your mouth to say what is in your heart.'

[Abba Poemen] also said, 'If a man understands something and does not practise it, how can he teach it to his neighbour?'

[Abba Pambo] also said, 'The monk should wear a garment of such a kind that he could throw it out of his cell and no one would steal it from him for three days.'

Abba Paul said, 'Keep close to Jesus.'

[Abba Silvanus] also said, 'Unhappy is the man whose reputation is greater than his work.'

Abba Sarmatas said, 'I prefer a sinful man who knows that he has sinned and repents, to a man who has not sinned and considers himself to be righteous.'

Amma Sarah said, 'If I prayed God that all men should approve of my conduct, I should find myself a penitent at the door of each one, but I shall rather pray that my heart may be pure towards all.'

[Amma Syncletica] also said, 'As long as we are in the monastery, obedience is preferable to asceticism. The one teaches pride, the other humility.'

[Amma Syncletica] also said, 'Just as one cannot build a ship unless one has some nails, so it is impossible to be saved without humility.'

Cyril of Jerusalem,
Catechetical Lectures (post-350)

Not much is known about the life of Cyril. He became bishop of Jerusalem in 348, probably in his early thirties and opposed Arianism, for which he was removed from his see three times, totalling fourteen years. He died in 386.

Cyril is famous for one particular work, a series of twenty-four *Catechetical Lectures*. These were given, probably in 350 at the Church of the Holy Sepulchre in Jerusalem, to those preparing for baptism. As the full title to the first lecture puts it, it is 'An introductory lecture to those who have come forward for baptism, delivered extempore at Jerusalem to those about to be enlightened [baptized].' The lectures were copied out by one of the hearers. They fall into two groups. The first nineteen were given during Lent, as the candidates prepared for their baptism on Easter day. After an initial *Procatechesis* or prologue there are five preliminary lectures on repentance, faith and baptism together with a summary account of Christian doctrine. These are followed by thirteen lectures expounding the local creed of the Jerusalem church, which was similar to the later Nicene Creed. The second group of five lectures, known as the *Mystagogic Lectures*, were delivered to the newly baptized and cover baptism, confirmation and communion. For a while it was held that these last lectures were given not by Cyril but by his successor, John, but there is now more support for the idea that Cyril himself gave them but at a later date than the other lectures.

These lectures are of great value. They give a unique insight into the instruction given to those preparing for baptism in the middle of the fourth century, what they were required to believe and how they were expected to live. They also describe in detail the practice of and belief about the sacraments at that time.

Lecture 20 (Mystagogic Lecture 2): Baptism

[The lecture begins by quoting Romans 6:3–14.]

1. These daily introductions into the mysteries and instructions into new truths are profitable to us and especially to you who have been renewed from an old state to a new. Following yesterday's lecture [on the outer chamber], today I will teach you what was symbolized by the things you did in the inner chamber.

2. As soon as you entered you took off your clothes, symbolizing taking off the old man with his deeds. Having stripped you were naked, thus imitating Christ who was stripped naked on the cross and by his nakedness disarmed the principalities and powers, triumphing over them on the tree. For since the enemy forces made their lair in your members, you may no longer wear that old garment; I am not referring to this visible garment, but to the old man, which was corrupted by its deceitful lusts. May the soul which has once taken him off, never again put him on, but say with the Bride of Christ in the Song of Solomon [5:3], 'I have taken off my robe, how shall I put it on?' How marvellous! You were naked in the sight of all and were not ashamed, like the first Adam who was naked in the garden and not ashamed.

3. Having stripped you were anointed with exorcized oil, from the very hairs of your head to your feet, and became part of the good olive tree, Jesus Christ. For you were cut off from the wild olive, and grafted into the good one, and were made to share the abundance of the true olive. The exorcized oil therefore symbolized participation in the richness of Christ, a charm to drive away every trace of hostile influence. For just as the breath of the saints and the invocation of God's name scorch and drive out evil spirits, like the fiercest flame, so also this exorcized oil receives power by the invocation of God and by prayer so as not only to burn and purge away the traces of sins, but also to chase away all the invisible forces of the Evil One.

4. You were next led to the holy pool of divine baptism, just as Christ was carried from the cross to the sepulchre which is before our eyes [here in Jerusalem]. And you were each asked whether you believed in the name of the Father, of the Son and of the Holy Spirit. Having made that saving confession, three times you descended into the water and ascended again, here again mystically signifying Christ's three-day burial. For as our Saviour spent three days and three nights in the heart of the earth, so you also when you first ascended out of the water represented the first day of Christ in the earth, and by your descent the night. Just as no one sees at night but in daytime we remain in the light, so in your descent you saw nothing as at night but when you ascended again it was like day. At the same moment you were both dying and being born and that water of salvation was both your grave and your mother. What Solomon said of others applies also to you: 'There is a time to be born and a time to die' [Ecclesiastes 3:2]. But for you the order was reversed – there was a time to die and a time to be born. Both of these took place at the same time and your birth coincided with your death.

5. How strange and inconceivable! We did not really die, we were not really buried, we were not really crucified and raised again. Our imitation was figurative

but our salvation is real. Christ was actually crucified, actually buried and really rose again; and all these things he has freely bestowed upon us, so that sharing his sufferings by imitation we might gain salvation in reality. What excellent love! Christ received nails in his undefiled hands and feet and suffered anguish; while on me without pain or toil by the fellowship of his suffering he freely bestows salvation.

6. Let no one then suppose that baptism merely bestows remission of sins together perhaps with adoption, like John's baptism which conferred only remission of sins. We know full well that as it purges our sins and ministers to us the gift of the Holy Ghost, so also it is the antitype of Christ's sufferings. This is why Paul said, 'Don't you know that all we who were baptized into Christ Jesus, were baptized into his death? We were buried therefore with him by baptism into his death' [Romans 6:3]. These words he spoke to some who were disposed to think that baptism ministers to us the remission of sins and adoption, but not also the fellowship of Christ's true sufferings, by representation.

7. So that we might learn that whatever Christ endured for us and for our salvation, he suffered in reality and not in appearance, and that we are also made partakers of his sufferings, Paul cried with all exactness of truth: 'For if we have been planted together with the likeness of his death, we shall be also with the likeness of his resurrection' [Romans 6:5]. He did well to say 'planted together', for since the true Vine was planted in this place we also by partaking in the baptism of death have been planted together with him. Pay close attention to the words of the apostle. He did not say, 'For if we have been planted together with his death,' but, 'with the likeness of his death'. For in Christ's case there was real death (his soul was really separated from his body) and real burial (his holy body was wrapped in pure linen) and it all really happened to him; but in your case there was only a likeness of death and suffering, while of salvation there was no mere likeness but the reality.

8. Now that you have been taught these things, I beg you to remember them so that, unworthy as I am, I may say of you, 'Now I love you, because you always remember me and hold fast the traditions which I delivered unto you' [1 Corinthians 11:2]. And God, who has brought you from death to life, is able to grant you to walk in newness of life because his is the glory and the power, now and for ever. Amen.

Basil of Caesarea, *The Long Rules*
(c. 358)

The Cappadocian Fathers were Basil of Caesarea, his friend Gregory of Nazianzus and his younger brother Gregory of Nyssa. They came from the Roman province of Cappadocia, in modern Turkey. They shared a common ambition to integrate Christianity with all that was good in classical culture.

Basil, sometimes known as Basil the Great, was born into a wealthy Christian family, in about 330. His grandparents had been martyred. He studied the classics and philosophy in various places ending at Athens, the leading university, where he studied from 351 and met Gregory of Nazianzus. On his return home he taught rhetoric for a while, but then was baptized and pursued the monastic life, under the influence of his older sister Macrina. He toured the leading monastic sites in the East and then set up a small community of his own on the family estates. His sister and mother were in a parallel community across the river. But his leisure was short-lived. In 364 he was appointed presbyter at Caesarea and in 370 he succeeded the bishop. He devoted himself to social schemes for the poor and to the struggle against Arianism, dying in 379.

Basil's writings cover a range of themes:

● He wrote two major works on the doctrine of the Trinity in opposition to the Arians, his *Against Eunomius* and his *The Holy Spirit*. He also wrote a number of highly important letters on this theme.

● While he wrote no commentaries on Scripture he did leave behind a number of series of homilies, especially on the six days of creation (the Hexaemeron), on the Psalms and on Isaiah.

● The *Liturgy of St Basil* attributed to him is still used on occasions in Eastern Orthodox churches of the Byzantine rite.

● Basil also wrote a number of ascetic treatises. The oldest of these, *The Morals*, is a set of eighty rules or moral instructions, composed mainly of extracts from the New Testament. At a later stage (around 358) he composed two 'rules' which respond to questions asked by his monks, the *Long Rules* which respond to 55 questions and the *Short Rules* which respond to 313 questions. Eventually a collection of thirteen ascetic writings, not all genuinely by Basil, were brought together under the title of *Ascetica*.

Basil had visited the monks in the Egyptian desert and observed the solitary life. He opted for a different approach, arguing at length (as in the extract below) for the superiority of a communal life. Whose feet will the solitary wash? Basil also valued work for its own sake and not merely as a way of earning one's keep and avoiding idleness. Like Pachomius in Egypt he urged moderation in asceticism. To some extent his various Rules lay out the way in which all Christians ought to live and Basil thought of the monk as the one who lives a fully consistent Christian life. He emphasized humility and obedience, the monk subjecting his will to the abbot. Basil's Rules are valuable for the wisdom that they contain and are also important because they influenced *The Rule of Benedict* (see pages 124–27).

───────────

Question 7. Since your words [answer to question 6] have convinced us that it is dangerous to live in company with those who hold the commandments of God in light regard, we consider it logical to inquire whether one who retires from society should live in solitude or with brethren who are of the same mind and who have set before themselves the same goal, that is, the devout life.

Reply: I consider that life passed in company with a number of persons in the same habitation is more advantageous in many respects. My reasons are, first, that no one of us is self-sufficient as regards corporeal necessities, but we require one another's aid in supplying our needs. . . . Again, apart from this consideration, the doctrine of the charity of Christ does not permit the individual to be concerned solely with his own private interests. 'Charity,' says the Apostle, 'seeketh not her own' [1 Corinthians 13:5]. But a life passed in solitude is concerned only with the private service of individual needs. This is openly opposed to the law of love which the Apostle fulfilled, who sought not what was profitable to himself but to many that they might be saved. Furthermore, a person living in solitary retirement will not readily discern his own defects, since he has no one to admonish and correct him with mildness and compassion. . . . The greatest commandment and the one especially conducive to salvation is not observed, since the hungry are not fed nor the naked clothed. Who, then, would choose this ineffectual and unprofitable life in preference to that which is both fruitful and in accordance with the Lord's command?

Besides, if all we who are united in the one hope of our calling are one body with Christ as our Head, we are also members, one of another. If we are not joined together by union in the Holy Spirit in the harmony of one body, but each of us should choose to live in solitude, we would not serve the common good in the ministry according to God's good pleasure, but would be satisfying our own passion for self-gratification. . . . He who lives alone, consequently, and has, perhaps, one gift renders it ineffectual by leaving it in disuse, since it lies buried within him. How much danger there is in this all of you know who have read the Gospel. On the other hand, in the case of several persons living together, each enjoys his own gift and enhances it by giving others a share, besides reaping benefit from the gifts of others as if they were his own.

Community life offers more blessings than can be fully and easily enumerated. It is more advantageous than the solitary life both for preserving the goods bestowed on us by God and for warding off the external attacks of the Enemy. If any should happen to grow heavy with that sleep which is unto death and which we have been instructed by David to avert with prayer: 'Enlighten my eyes that I never sleep in death' [Psalm 13:3], the awakening induced by those who are already on watch is the more assured. For the sinner, moreover, the withdrawal from his sin is far easier if he fears the shame of incurring censure from many acting together. . . and for the righteous man, there is a great and full satisfaction in the esteem of the group and in their approval of his conduct. . . . Besides these disadvantages, the solitary life is fraught with other perils. The first and greatest is that of self-satisfaction. Since the solitary has no one to appraise his conduct, he will think he has achieved the perfection of the precept. Secondly, because he never tests his state of soul by exercise, he will not recognize his own deficiencies nor will he discover the advance he may have made in his manner of acting, since he will have removed all practical occasion for the observance of the commandments.

Wherein will [the solitary] show his humility, if there is no one with whom he may compare and so confirm his own greater humility? Wherein will he give evidence of his compassion, if he has cut himself off from association with other persons? And how will he exercise himself in long-suffering, if no one contradicts his wishes? . . . Consider, further, that the Lord by reason of his excessive love for man was not content with merely teaching the word, but, so as to transmit to us clearly and exactly the example of humility in the perfection of charity, girded himself and washed the feet of the disciples. Whom, therefore, will you wash? To whom will you minister? In compassion with whom will you be the lowest, if you live alone?

Gregory of Nazianzus,
Theological Orations (380)

Gregory of Nazianzus, also known as Gregory Nazianzen, came from the Cappadocian nobility and was born in about 330. His father was bishop of Nazianzus. At the age of about twenty Gregory went to study at Athens where he met Basil. For a time after his studies he taught rhetoric, before devoting himself to Christian service. This fluctuated between monastic retreat, with Basil on his family estate, and church ministry with his father at Nazianzus. Gregory's ecclesiastical career was a succession of frustrations. His father appointed him presbyter at Nazianzus, but that was not a success. Then Basil pushed him into becoming bishop of a small town, in the interests of ecclesiastical politics and the struggle against Arianism. Gregory never took up his duties there. Finally, he became bishop of the Nicene party at Constantinople, the eastern capital. This was a crucial position and Gregory devoted himself wholeheartedly to it. In 381 he played a leading role at the Council of Constantinople but he fell foul of ecclesiastical rivalries and resigned his bishopric at the council. But while Gregory's ecclesiastical career was not a success, his theological heritage was greatly appreciated and he came to be known as 'Gregory the Theologian'. He died in 389 or 390.

The Cappadocians are remembered especially for their opposition to Arianism and their trinitarian teaching. They fused together the belief affirmed at the Council of Nicea (325) that Father and Son are of one substance and the older eastern belief (derived from Origen) that Father, Son and Holy Spirit are three hypostases or beings. The one substance of the Godhead exists simultaneously in three different hypostases or modes of being. But what does it actually mean to say that God is one substance in three hypostases? Each of the Cappadocian fathers (Basil, Gregory of Nazianzus and Gregory of Nyssa) developed this in their writings on the subject.

Gregory's greatest work was a series of forty-five Orations on a variety of themes. Most important of these was a series of five *Theological Orations* (*Orations* 27–31) preached in 380 at Constantinople on the doctrine of the Trinity. In the first he asks who may theorise about God and in what way this should be done, urging an approach of reverent caution. In the second he argues that God cannot be known fully, against heretics of the time who claimed to know God as fully as he knew himself! In stressing the limitation of our knowledge of God Gregory points to what is later known as the 'negative way' or the apophatic approach, which describes God by saying what he is not. In much of Eastern Orthodox theology this approach has been emphasized strongly and occasionally even regarded as the only way, something against which Gregory warns.

Gregory also warns of the opposite danger, by no means unknown today, of imagining that our language about God describes him fully. Gregory's oration is a timely message for today. The third and fourth orations are devoted to the Son, defending his deity and answering the objections of the Arians, both theological and exegetical. The last oration is on the Holy Spirit, again arguing for his full deity.

Theological Oration 2

4. To conceive God is difficult but to define him in words is impossible, as one of the Greek teachers of divinity [Plato] taught. His aim was to be thought to have apprehended God in that he says it is a hard thing to do and yet to escape the charge of ignorance because of the impossibility of expressing his apprehension. But in my view it is impossible to express God and yet more impossible to conceive him. For that which may be conceived may perhaps be made clear by language, if not fairly well at any rate imperfectly, to any one who is not quite deprived of hearing or slothful of understanding. But to comprehend the whole of so great a subject as this is quite impossible and impracticable, not merely to the utterly careless and ignorant, but even to those who are highly exalted and love God, and similarly to every created nature seeing that the darkness of this world and the thick covering of the flesh is an obstacle to the full understanding of the truth. I do not know whether it is the same with the higher natures and purer intelligences which, because of their nearness to God and because they are illumined with all his light, may possibly see if not the whole at any rate more perfectly and distinctly than we do – some perhaps more, some less than others in proportion to their rank.

6. Now our very eyes and the law of nature teach us that God exists and that he is the efficient and maintaining cause of all things: our eyes because they fall on visible objects and see them in beautiful stability and progress, immovably moving and revolving if I may so say; natural law because it reasons back from these visible things and their order to their author. For how could this universe have come into being or been put together unless God had called it into existence, and held it together? Every one who sees a beautifully made lute and considers the skill with which it has been fitted together and arranged or who hears its melody would think of none but the lute maker, or the lute player, and would turn their thoughts to him though they might not know him by sight. Thus to us also is manifested that which made and moves and preserves all created things even though he be not comprehended by the mind.

9. Thus we see that God is not a body. For no inspired teacher has yet asserted or admitted such a notion, nor does the church's teaching allow it. Nothing then remains but to conceive of him as incorporeal. But if we grant this term 'incorporeal' it does not set before us or contain within itself God's essence, any more than unbegotten, unoriginate, unchanging, incorruptible or any other predicate used of God or in reference to him. For what effect is produced upon his being or substance by his having no beginning and being incapable of change or limitation? No, the whole question of his being is still left for further consideration and exposition by him who truly has the mind of God and is advanced in contemplation. To say 'It is a body,' or 'It was begotten,' is not sufficient to present clearly to the mind the various objects of which these predicates are used, but you must also express the subject of which you use them if you would present the object of your thought clearly and adequately – for every one of these predicates (corporeal, begotten, mortal) may be used of a man, a cow or a horse. In the same way he who is eagerly pursuing the nature of the self-existent will not stop at saying what he is not, but must go on beyond what he is not and say what he is. For it is easier to take in some single point than to go on disowning point after point in endless detail, in order both by the elimination of negatives and the assertion of positives to arrive at a comprehension of this subject.

One who states what God is not without going on to say what he is acts much in the same way as someone who being asked how many twice five make answers, 'Not two, nor three, nor four, nor five, nor twenty, nor thirty, nor in short any number below ten, nor any multiple of ten,' but does not answer 'ten,' nor settle the mind of his questioner upon the firm ground of the answer. For it is much easier, and more concise to show what a thing is not from what it is, than to demonstrate what it is by stripping it of what it is not.

11. Why have I gone into all this, perhaps too minutely for most people to listen to, and in accordance with the present manner of discourse which despises noble simplicity and has introduced a crooked and intricate style? . . . My purpose in doing so was, not to get credit for myself for astonishing utterances, or excessive wisdom, through tying knots and solving difficulties, but to make clear the point at which my argument has aimed from the first. And what was this? That the divine nature cannot be apprehended by human reason and that we cannot even represent to ourselves all its greatness.

12. . . . . Therefore this darkness of the body has been placed between us and God, like the cloud of old between the Egyptians and the Hebrews. . . . . As it is impossible for a man to step over his own shadow, however fast he may move (for the shadow will always move on as fast as it is being overtaken), as it is

impossible for the eye to draw near to visible objects apart from the intervening air and light or for a fish to glide about outside of the waters, so it is quite impracticable for those who are in the body to be conversant with objects of pure thought altogether apart from bodily objects. For something in our own environment is always creeping in, even when the mind has most fully detached itself from the visible and collected itself, and is attempting to apply itself to those invisible things which are akin to itself.

17. What God is in nature and essence, no man ever yet has discovered or can discover. Whether it will ever be discovered is a question which he who will may examine and decide. In my opinion it will be discovered when that within us which is godlike and divine, I mean our mind and reason, shall have mingled with its like and the image shall have ascended to the archetype of which it has now the desire. And this I think is the solution of that vexed problem as to 'We shall know even as we are known' [1 Corinthians 13:12]. But in our present life all that comes to us is but a little effluence and as it were a small effulgence from a great light. So that if anyone has known God, or has had the testimony of Scripture to his knowledge of God, we are to understand such a one to have possessed a degree of knowledge which gave him the appearance of being more fully enlightened than another who did not enjoy the same degree of illumination and this relative superiority is spoken of as if it were absolute knowledge, not because it is really such but by comparison with the power of that other.

Pseudo-Macarius,
Fifty Spiritual Homilies (380s)

The Macarian homilies have been popular spiritual reading for many years. John Wesley came across them while a missionary in the North American colonies and famously wrote in his *Journal* (see pages 375–78) that he 'read Macarius and sang' (30 July 1736). He later went to make a new translation of twenty-two of them for his *Christian Library* series. They have a strong emphasis upon the Holy Spirit and Christian experience which has ensured their continued popularity.

But who is the author of these homilies? They claim simply to be by 'Macarius' and for many centuries this was taken to be Macarius the Egyptian, one of the desert fathers, who founded the monastic settlement at Scetis. This was questioned in the nineteenth century and it is now widely agreed that the author was a Syrian monk writing around the 380s. The issue is complicated by the fact the homilies show some affinity to Messalianism, a movement of the time which was criticized for playing down the sacraments and placing too much stress on dreams, visions and continual prayer.

The homilies partly take the form of questions and answers, like Basil of Caesarea's *Rules* (see pages 70–72). They are also in many ways 'occasional' writings addressed to specific situations, like the *Sayings of the Desert Fathers [and Mothers]* (see pages 63–66), thus retaining an element of immediacy. The author sees four stages of human existence. First comes the state of innocence before Adam's fall. His sin spoiled the image of God and left us in a state of bondage to sin. Through the Holy Spirit the grace of God is at work in our hearts and we are in a state of spiritual conflict between sin and grace. Finally there comes the point where sin is cast out by the Holy Spirit in cooperation with our wills and we are divinized. But this is not perfectly realized in this life and the struggle with temptation continues.

The Macarian homilies have exercised a considerable influence. In the eastern tradition writers like Symeon the New Theologian and Gregory Palamas were indebted to them. The western monk John Cassian was also significantly influenced by them and he in turn heavily influenced *The Rule of Benedict* (see pages 124–27).

Homily 16

1. All intellectual creatures, namely, angels, humans, and demons, have been created by the Creator, innocent and completely simple. That some fell away from these traits and turned to evil was a result of their free will. By their own will they turned away from right reason. If we assert that such fallen ones were created as such by the Creator, we are saying that God is an unjust judge who would cast Satan into fire. . . . Those who affirm that evil exists in itself are really most ignorant. For in God no evil can exist by itself since he himself is not subject to passions and he possesses his divinity. In us, however, it works with full power, especially in our senses, suggesting all sorts of obscene desires. In us it is not like, say, wine mixed with water. It is more like wheat in the same field by itself and the tares by themselves. It is like a robber in one part of the house and the owner in another.

3. There are some who, even though they have begun to develop a taste for divine things, nevertheless are disturbed and hassled by the adversary, so that they are surprised (still lacking experience) that after the divine visitation, they should still harbour doubts about the mysteries of the Christian religion. Those who have grown old in them are not surprised at all. As skilled farmers from long experience, if they have had a year of bountiful harvest, they do not live without some planning, but they foresee the time of dearth and tight times. On the contrary, if famine and penury hit them, they do not become despondent, as they think positively about the future. It is the same way with things in the spiritual world. When the soul falls into various temptations, it is not surprised nor does it lose all hope, because it knows that by God's permission it is being exposed to trials and is being disciplined by evil. Nor does it forget other circumstances when things go well and there is consolation, but it expects the time of trial.

4. When, therefore, a man is deep and rich in grace, there still remains inside of him a remnant of evil. But he has close at hand one who can help him. Wherefore, if one is overwhelmed by temptations, caught in the raging waves of passions, he ought not to lose hope. For if he acts in this way, sin builds up and takes over from within. If, however, one constantly puts his hope in God, evil to a certain degree diminishes and dries up. Certain people are afflicted with paralysis: some with mutilated members, others with fever, while others have sickness. All of this comes from sin. For sin is the root of all evils. The passions caused by the concupiscible powers of the soul and by evil thoughts also flow from sin.

10. There are those who claim that there is no sin in man. They are like people immersed in deep waters who still are afraid to recognize the fact, but say: 'We

have heard the sound of waters.' So plunged into the depth of the waves of evil, they deny that there is sin in their minds or thoughts. Some people talk a great deal, but they are not seasoned with a heavenly salt. They speak a great deal about the royal table, but they have never eaten there or enjoyed it. But different is the one who has seen the king, one to whom the treasures have been opened. He enters in and inherits them. He eats and drinks of these costly foods.

12. Such a one regards himself as the greatest of all sinners. He carries this thought ever with him as a part of his very makeup. And the more he progresses in knowledge of God, the more simple and unlearned he considers himself. And the more he studies and learns, the less he feels he knows. This grace acts as a guiding force, almost second nature to him. Just as an infant is carried about by a young man who carries him and does with him whatever he wishes, so also the grace that operates in the depths of the soul's powers. It feeds the mind and lifts it up to Heaven, to the perfect world, to everlasting rest. But in such a grace there are many degrees and perfections.

John Chrysostom, *The Priesthood*
(c. 386)

John Chrysostom was born at Antioch in the middle of the fourth century. He was baptized as a young man and after a while devoted himself to the monastic life. He lived for several years in a cave outside Antioch and damaged his health by his austerities, which forced him to return to Antioch. There he became first deacon and then presbyter (or priest, as it was now called) and studied under Diodore of Tarsus, who introduced him to the world of biblical scholarship. The school of Antioch was noted for its opposition to allegory and insistence that the Bible should be interpreted according to its natural meaning, the 'literal' sense as it was called. There was scope for typology (drawing parallels between God's dealings with humanity at different times), but not for fanciful interpretations which evaded the plain historical meaning of the text. Chrysostom adopted this Antiochene approach.

The name Chrysostom or 'golden-mouthed' was first given to him in the sixth century as a tribute to his excellence as a preacher. He preached regularly, normally working his way through an entire book of the Bible. These sermons were then published as commentaries. Apart from Genesis, Psalms and Isaiah, he devoted himself mainly to the New Testament, covering Matthew, John, Acts, Paul and Hebrews. He also preached sermons on specific subjects and wrote a number of treatises. Best-known of these is his *The Priesthood*, a classic work on pastoral care. Chrysostom was not especially gifted in theological matters – his sermons are above all practical and devotional.

As a presbyter at Antioch and a preacher Chrysostom was in his natural element and excelled. He was an extremely able orator and his sermons were very popular, but he was not allowed to remain there. In 397 there was fierce competition to fill the vacant bishopric at Constantinople, the capital. Imperial officials sought to resolve the matter by appointing an outsider and Chrysostom was chosen and forced to accept the post. The bishops of Alexandria were especially jealous of Constantinople because it had, at the Council of Constantinople in 381, replaced Alexandria as the second see or bishopric of Christendom. Theophilus, bishop of Alexandria, who had hoped to have his own man elected bishop of Constantinople, was forced to consecrate Chrysostom bishop with his own hands.

Chrysostom had been landed in a position which was fraught with danger for even the most skilful politician. He, by contrast, was quite without guile, preaching fearlessly and setting about correcting abuses. His relations with the court deteriorated, thanks to Theophilus's intrigues and slanders, and eventually he was exiled on trumped-up charges – in 403 and, after a brief return, in 404. In 407 he was forcibly marched to another distant site of exile and died as a result. At first there was controversy between East and West over his case, but eventually all came to recognize his sanctity and greatness. As a modern writer put it, 'he whose life was embittered and destroyed by his enemies now has no enemies at all'.

    The Priesthood is Chrysostom's best known and most translated work and was written in about 386. It is set out in six books and presented in the form of a dialogue between Chrysostom and an otherwise unknown friend, Basil. It is regarded as one of the really great works on pastoral care. Chrysostom discusses an issue that exercised many minds at the time, the relative merits of a contemplative life in withdrawal from the world and an active life involved in Christian ministry. In the fourth century many monks were ordained, sometimes forcibly against their will. It was not for nothing that the early desert fathers proclaimed, 'Flee women and bishops'! Chrysostom's verdict is that the active life may be less pleasant but it is a higher calling, as well as harder and more dangerous, because it puts into practice the command to love.

2:3. As regards human infirmities, in the first place it is not easy for the pastor to discern them, for no man 'knows a man's thoughts, except the man's spirit within him' [1 Corinthians 2:11]. How can any one apply the remedy for a disease whose nature he does not know, often indeed being unable to understand it even when suffering from it himself? It causes him yet more trouble when it does becomes clear, for it is not possible to doctor all people with the same authority with which the shepherd treats his sheep. As with sheep, it is necessary to bind wounds, restrain from food and to cauterize or cut, but with human beings this requires the cooperation of the patient not just the will of the doctor. That wonderful man [Paul] perceived this when he said to the Corinthians: 'Not that we lord it over your faith, but help you for your joy' [2 Corinthians 1:24]. For Christians above all are not permitted forcibly to correct the failings of those who sin. Secular judges indeed show their authority to be great when they capture criminals and prevent them, even against their will, from following their own devices, but we have to improve wrong-doers by persuasion not by force. For neither have we been given legal authority to restrain sinners by force nor, if it had been given, would we have any scope to exercise it inasmuch as God rewards those who abstain from evil voluntarily, not of necessity. Consequently we need much skill both to induce our patients to submit willingly to the prescribed treatment and even to be grateful for the cure. For if any one struggles when he is bound (which is in his power) he makes his condition worse and if he should pay no heed to words of warning which cut like steel he inflicts another wound on himself by this contempt. Thus the attempt to heal only becomes the occasion of a worse disorder, for it is not possible to cure a man forcibly against his own will.

2:4. What then is one to do? If you deal too gently with those needing a drastic application of the knife and do not cut deep into those requiring such treatment, you remove one part of the ulcer but leave the other. If, on the other hand, you mercilessly make the needed incision the patient, driven to despair by pain, will often cast everything away at once, both the remedy and the bandage, and throw himself down headlong – 'breaking the yoke and bursting the band' [Jeremiah 5:5]. I could tell of many who have run into extreme evils because the strict penalty of their sins was exacted. When applying punishment we should not merely proportion it to the scale of the offence but rather keep in view the disposition of the sinner. Otherwise while wishing to mend what is torn you make the rent worse and in your zealous endeavours to restore what is fallen you make the ruin greater. Weak and careless characters, addicted for the most part to the pleasures of the world and with reason to be proud because of their birth and rank, may yet, if gently and gradually brought to repent of their errors, be delivered (partially at least if not perfectly) from the evils by which they are possessed. But to inflict this discipline all at once would deprive them of this slight improvement. For when once the soul has been forced to abandon shame it becomes callous. It neither yields to kindly words, nor bends to threats, nor is susceptible of gratitude, but becomes far worse than that city which the prophet reproached, saying, 'you had the face of a harlot, refusing to be ashamed before all men' [Jeremiah 3:3]. So the pastor needs considerable discretion and a myriad eyes to observe on every side the condition of the soul. For while many are uplifted to pride and then sink into despair of their salvation, through their inability to endure severe remedies, others fall into carelessness through paying no penalty appropriate to their sins and become far worse, being impelled to greater sins. The priest therefore must leave none of these things unexamined, but after a thorough inquiry into all of them must apply such remedies as he has that are appropriate to each case, lest his zeal prove to be in vain.

One can see that the priest has much to do, not only in this matter but also in the work of knitting together the severed members of the church. For sheep follow the shepherd wherever he leads them; and if any stray out of the straight path and desert the good pasture to feed in unproductive or rugged places, a loud shout suffices to collect them and bring back to the fold those who have strayed from it. But if a human being wanders away from the right faith, great exertion, perseverance and patience are required; for he cannot be dragged back forcibly, nor constrained by fear, but must be led back by persuasion to the truth from which he originally swerved. The pastor therefore needs a noble spirit, so as not to lose heart or despair of the salvation of those wandering from the fold, but continually to reason with himself and say, 'Perhaps God will give them repentance leading them to acknowledge the truth and they may escape from the snare of the devil' [2 Timothy 2:25–26]. Therefore the Lord, when addressing his disciples, said, 'Who then is the faithful and wise servant?' [Matthew 24:45]. For he indeed who disciplines himself achieves only his own advantage, but the benefit of the pastoral office extends to the whole people. Those who dispense money to the needy or otherwise succour the oppressed benefit their neighbours to some extent, but as much less than the priest as the body is inferior to the soul. Rightly therefore did the Lord say that zeal for the flock was a proof of love for himself.

Ambrose, *The Duties of Ministers*
(387–97)

Ambrose was born at Trier in 339. His father was prefect of Gaul (France) and both his parents were Christians. Ambrose followed in his father's footsteps and became a provincial governor in Italy. In 374 there was strife over the appointment of a new bishop of Milan and Ambrose was chosen as an outsider, despite the fact that he was not yet baptized but only a catechumen. It was normal in the fourth-century church for those in public office, and therefore liable to have to put people to death, to delay baptism. Since baptism was seen as a one-off washing away of all sins, this was best deferred until the moral dangers of public office were past.

Ambrose devoted himself wholeheartedly to his new task and became the greatest Western Church leader of the fourth century. He fought hard and successfully for acceptance of the full deity of Christ. In the previous twenty years the emperors had favoured a less dogmatic Christianity, more open to Arian ideas. Ambrose led the struggle for a church based firmly on the truth of the deity of Jesus Christ. He was a gifted and popular preacher. He introduced from the East the method of allegory. This approach to the Bible, which turned the Old Testament into a 'spiritual' book pleasing to Platonists, paved the way for the conversion of Augustine at Milan, as described in his *Confessions* (see pages 91–94).

Ambrose's most important contribution lay in his dealings with the imperial court. He established important principles of the independence of the church and the duties of the Christian ruler, which were to be developed in the Middle Ages. He opposed the emperor Valentinian when he was inclined to show greater tolerance to paganism. He refused to hand over a church building for the use of Christians who did not accept the (anti-Arian) Council of Nicea. It was at this time that he introduced to the West the practice of congregational hymn-singing – to keep up the spirits of the congregation occupying the church. Finally, in 390, he disciplined the emperor Theodosius, who had ordered a particularly brutal massacre of thousands of citizens at Thessalonica, following a riot there. Ambrose died in 397.

Ambrose was a prolific author. He left behind numerous exegetical writings, especially on the Old Testament which he allegorized in the manner of Origen. He wrote a number of dogmatic treatises, the most important of which were two works in defence of the doctrine of the Trinity, his *The Faith* and *The Holy Spirit*. He also wrote a number of moral and ascetical writings, of which the best known is his *The Duties of Ministers*, composed in the last decade of his life. This was addressed especially to his clergy in Milan, though most of the content applies to all Christians. The structure of the work loosely follows that of a work by the Stoic philosopher Cicero called *Duties* and one can see both the influence of Stoic ethics upon Ambrose and his correction of them from a Christian perspective. He makes heavy use of Scripture, drawing especially on examples from the Old Testament.

Ambrose distinguishes between what is fitting or right and what is expedient or useful. Regarding the latter, 'we state nothing to be useful unless it help us to the blessing of eternal life – certainly nothing that helps us merely to enjoy this life' (1:9:28). He follows the Stoics in referring to four virtues: prudence, justice, fortitude and temperance – later known as the four 'cardinal' or 'natural' virtues. The work begins with a sustained warning against the dangers of speech. While some of Ambrose's teaching may be dated there is a considerable amount of valuable and timeless wisdom in his writing.

1:2:5. Before all else we should learn to be silent, in order that we may be able to speak – lest my own voice should condemn me before that of another acquits me, for it is written: 'By your words you will be condemned' [Matthew 12:37]. What need is there to rush into the danger of condemnation by speaking, when you can be safer by keeping silent? I have seen many fall into sin by speaking, but scarcely one by keeping silent, and so it is harder to know how to keep silent than how to speak. I know that most people speak because they do not know how to keep silent. It is seldom that any one is silent even when speaking is of no value. He is wise, then, who knows how to keep silent.

1:2:6. The saints of the Lord loved to keep silence, because they knew that a man's voice is often the utterance of sin and a man's speech is the beginning of human error. The Lord's saint said: 'I will watch my ways, lest I offend with my tongue' [Psalm 39:1]. . . . As he saw no one can keep their mouth free from evil speaking, he laid upon himself the law of innocence by a rule of silence, aiming to avoid by silence that fault which he could with difficulty escape while speaking.

1:2:7. The law says: 'Hear, O Israel, the Lord thy God' [Deuteronomy 6:4] – not 'speak' but 'hear'. Eve fell because she said to the man what she had not heard from the Lord her God. God's word to you says: Hear! If you hear, take heed to your ways; and if you have fallen, quickly amend your way. For: 'How can a young man amend his way, except by taking heed to the word of the Lord?' [Psalm 119:9]. So be silent first of all, and pay attention, lest you fail in your tongue.

1:2:8. It is a great evil to be condemned by your own mouth. If we shall each give account for a careless word [Matthew 12:36], how much more for impure and shameful words? For words uttered hastily are far worse than careless words. If, therefore, an account is demanded for a careless word, how much more will punishment be exacted for irreverent language?

1:3:9. What then? Ought we to be dumb? Certainly not. For: 'there is a time to keep silence and a time to speak' [Ecclesiastes 3:7]. If we are to give account for each careless word, let us take care that we do not have to give it also for a careless silence.

1:3:10. Let us then guard our hearts and our mouths, both of which are written about in Scripture. In this place we are told to take heed to our mouth; in another place you are told: 'Keep your heart with all diligence' [Proverbs 4:23]. If David took heed, will you not take heed? If Isaiah had unclean lips, saying: 'Woe is me, for I am ruined, for I am a man of unclean lips' [Isaiah 6:5], if a prophet of the Lord had unclean lips, how shall ours be clean?

1:3:13. Let there be a door to your mouth to be shut when need arises, and let it be carefully barred that no one may rouse your voice to anger causing you to pay back abuse with abuse. You have heard it read today: 'Be angry and sin not' [Ephesians 4:26]. So while we may be angry (arising from the motions of our nature, not of our will) let us not utter one evil word with our mouth, lest we fall into sin; but let there be a yoke and a balance to your words (humility and moderation) so that your tongue may be subject to your mind. Let it be held in check with a tight rein; let it have its own means of restraint whereby it can be recalled to moderation; let it utter words tested by the scales of justice, that there may be seriousness in our meaning, weight in our speech and due measure in our words.

1:4:14. Any one who takes heed to this will be mild, gentle and modest. For to guard one's mouth, restrain one's tongue and not to speak before examining, pondering and weighing one's words (whether this should be said, that should be answered or whether it be a suitable time for this remark) is certainly to practise modesty, gentleness and patience. So he will not burst out into speech through displeasure or anger, nor give sign of any passion in his words, nor proclaim by his language that the flames of lust are burning or that what he says is motivated by anger. Let him act thus for fear that his words, which ought to grace his inner life, should in the end plainly show and prove that his morals are corrupt.

1:4:15. It is especially when he sees passions hatched in us that the enemy lays his plans – he supplies tinder and he lays snares. . . . Too often we say something that our foe takes hold of, thus wounding us as though by our own sword. It is far better to perish by someone else's sword than by our own!

1:5:17. We must also guard against visible enemies who provoke us, spur us on, exasperate us and supply material to excite us to licentiousness or lust. If any one reviles us, irritates us, stirs us up to violence or tries to make us quarrel, let us keep silence and not be ashamed to become dumb. For those who irritate us and do us an injury are committing sin and wish us to become like themselves.

Gregory of Nyssa, *The Life of Moses*
(390–94)

Gregory of Nyssa, who was born in about 335, was the younger brother and disciple of Basil of Caesarea. He was the most intellectual of the three Cappadocian fathers and for a time became, like his father, a teacher of rhetoric. He also married but after a while embraced the monastic life, joining Basil's monastery. In 371 or 372 Basil bullied him into becoming bishop of Nyssa, a small town in Cappadocia under Basil's control. He remained bishop there for the rest of his life, apart from a few years when he was deposed and replaced by an Arian bishop. All three Cappadocian fathers were Origenists, but Gregory of Nyssa was the most ardent disciple of Origen. He was more interested than the others in philosophy and theological speculation, though he also distinguished himself as a defender of orthodoxy. He died in 394 or soon after.

The Life of Moses is one of Gregory's latest works, from the last few years of his life when he devoted more time to spiritual writings. The work falls into two main parts. There is a brief first Book which gives the 'history' and simply paraphrases the biblical account of Moses' life. This is followed by a considerably longer second Book which offers 'contemplation' or a spiritual and allegorical interpretation of the narrative. In adopting this two-stage approach to the life of Moses, Gregory was following the pattern of the first-century Jewish spiritual writer Philo, who also wrote a Life of Moses.

The emphasis of the book lies on spirituality and Christian discipleship. The Christian life is one of progress. Perfection is unattainable in this life, except perhaps in the sense of growing in goodness (1:8–10; 2:305–307). Gregory makes a selective use of pre-Christian Greek philosophy, justifying this in the traditional way, seeing it as the deeper meaning of Moses' apparently unjust command to the people of Israel to 'spoil' the Egyptians (Exodus 12:35–36) (2:112–16). In particular, he adopts Aristotle's precept that virtue lies in the mean or middle way between extremes (2:287f.). The great enemy of spiritual life is the passions or sinful desires, among which Gregory discusses envy, pride and pleasure at some length. The Christian is called to control these passions and to cultivate a life of virtue. In an age where the road to happiness is seen as the fulfilment of all of our desires, with little care to distinguish between legitimate desires and excessive lusts, Gregory's work has not lost its relevance.

2:122. Who does not know that the Egyptian army [that was lost in the Red Sea] – those horses, chariots and their drivers, archers, slingers, heavily armed soldiers, and the rest of the crowd in the enemies' line of battle – are the various passions of the soul by which man is enslaved? For the undisciplined intellectual drives and the sensual impulses to pleasure, sorrow and covetousness are indistinguishable from the aforementioned army. Reviling is a stone straight from the sling and the spirited impulse is the quivering spear point. The passion for pleasures is to be seen in the horses who themselves with irresistible drive pull the chariot.

2:125. Moreover, the history teaches us by this what kind of people they should be who come through the water, bringing nothing of the opposing army along as they emerge from the water. For if the enemy came up out of the water with them, they would continue in slavery even after the water, since they would have brought up with themselves the tyrant still alive, whom they did not drown in the deep. If anyone wishes to clarify the figure, this lays it bare: Those who pass through the mystical water in baptism must put to death in the water the whole phalanx of evil – such as covetousness, unbridled desire, rapacious thinking, the passion of conceit and arrogance, wild impulse, wrath, anger, malice, envy, and all such things. Since the passions naturally pursue our nature, we must put to death in the water both the base movements of the mind and the acts which issue from them.

2:127. Many of those who receive the mystical baptism, in ignorance of the commandments of the Law, mix the bad leaven of the old life with the new life. Even after crossing the water they bring along the Egyptian army, which still lives with them in their doings.

2:128. Take for instance the one who became rich by robbery or injustice, or who acquired property through perjury, or lived with a woman in adultery, or undertook any of the other things against life which have been forbidden before the gift of baptism. Does he think that even after his washing he may continue to enjoy those evil things which have become attached to him and yet be freed from the bondage of sin, as though he cannot see that he is under the yoke of harsh masters?

2:129. For uncontrolled passion is a fierce and raging master to the servile reasoning, tormenting it with pleasures as though they were scourges. Covetousness is another such master who provides no relief to the bondsman, but even if the one in bondage should slave in subservience to the commands of the master and acquire for him what he desires, the servant is always driven on to more. And all the other things which are performed by evil are so many tyrants and masters. If someone should still serve them, even if he should happen to have passed through the water, according to my thinking he has not at all touched the mystical water whose function is to destroy evil tyrants.

2:256. No longer does any offence which comes about through evil withstand the one who in this manner follows God. After these things the envy of his brothers arose against [Moses]. Envy is the passion which accuses evil, the father of death, the first entrance of sin, the root of wickedness, the birth of sorrow, the mother of misfortune, the basis of disobedience, the beginning of shame. Envy banished us from Paradise, having become a serpent to oppose Eve. Envy walled us off from the tree of life, divested us of holy garments, and in shame led us away clothed with fig leaves.

2:257. Envy armed Cain contrary to nature and instituted the death which is vindicated seven times. Envy made Joseph a slave. Envy is the death-dealing sting, the hidden weapon, the sickness of nature, the bitter poison, the self-willed emaciation, the bitter dart, the nail of the soul, the fire in the heart, the flame burning on the inside.

2:258. For envy, it is not its own misfortune but another's good fortune that is unfortunate. Again, inversely, success is not one's own good fortune but the neighbour's misfortune. Envy is grieved at the good deeds of men and takes advantage of their misfortunes. It is said that the vultures which devour corpses are destroyed by perfume. Their nature is akin to the foul and corrupt. Anyone who is in the power of this sickness is destroyed by the happiness of his neighbours as by the application of some perfume; but if he should see any unfortunate experience he flies to it, sets his crooked beak to it, and draws forth the hidden misfortunes.

Augustine, *Confessions* (397–401)

Augustine is the greatest Christian theologian since the apostle Paul and *the* Father of the Western Church. His thought dominated the Middle Ages – the good and the bad alike. In the sixteenth century the Reformation and the Catholic Counter-Reformation were both rediscoveries of Augustine.

Aurelius Augustine was born in 354 at Thagaste, in modern Algeria, of a pagan father and a Catholic Christian mother, Monica. In his student days at Carthage he resolved to devote himself to a life of philosophy. As a Catholic catechumen (candidate for baptism) he naturally turned to the Old Testament. But a rude shock awaited him there. To the mind attuned to Greek philosophy, the Old Testament appears crude and unspiritual. Augustine reacted against it and allied himself with the Manichees. Manicheism was a Persian religion with two ultimate principles or gods: Light and Darkness. These are in constant conflict. The physical universe originates from the Darkness, while the human soul is the product of the Light, thus explaining the origin of evil. It also served to deny our responsibility for our evil deeds (which originate with the dark element) – which suited Augustine for whom Carthage brought not just a search for truth but a surrender to sexual desire. After about ten years he came to see that Manicheism raises as many problems as it solves and began to search for the truth elsewhere.

While still searching, in 384, Augustine was appointed professor of rhetoric at Milan, an important post which could lead naturally to high government office. He began to read some Neoplatonist works and found there a more satisfactory answer to the problem of evil. Evil is not a positive principle, independent of God. It is not something which exists in its own right, but is rather the absence or lack of the good. In more modern terms, we might say that evil is parasitic on goodness or that it is something good which has been spoiled. Lust, for instance, is misdirected love. Augustine also began to attend the sermons of the bishop, Ambrose. He was impressed by the way in which Ambrose reconciled the Old Testament with Platonist spirituality, allegorically interpreting its very earthy stories to refer to invisible spiritual realities. This prepared the way for his return to the Christian faith.

Augustine was challenged by the accounts of the conversions of the prominent Neoplatonist philosopher Victorinus and the simple monk Antony, as set out in Athanasius's *The Life of Antony* (see pages 59–62). He was intellectually convinced about the truth of Christianity but balked at the prospect of celibacy. (He assumed, as was normal at this time, that a wholly dedicated Christian life involved celibacy.) Torn two ways, he one day rushed out into the garden. There he heard a child's voice crying, 'Take it and read.' Augustine opened his copy of Paul's letters at Romans 13:13–14. He got no further than 'Arm yourselves with the Lord Jesus Christ; spend no more thought on nature and nature's appetites.' His doubts and uncertainties vanished and his heart was resolved. This was in August 386 and Augustine was baptized by Ambrose the following Easter.

After his conversion Augustine, with a number of like-minded companions, devoted himself to an ascetic life of study. In the next few years he wrote a number of philosophical works. He also, between 387 and 400, wrote thirteen works against the Manichees. He felt a particular responsibility to do this because of his own first-hand experience of Manicheism and also because he had himself led people into the heresy. In these works he argued for human free will (denied by the Manichees). Sin is not created by God, nor coeternal with him, but arises from the misuse of free will. The will is free, not coerced, and we are therefore responsible for our deeds.

In 388 Augustine returned to Africa. There he took care to avoid towns without a bishop, since he was aware of the danger of being forced into the office. But in 391, while visiting Hippo, he was spotted and 'forcibly' ordained as presbyter or priest. When the bishop died, in 396, Augustine succeeded him. He remained bishop of Hippo until his death in 430.

Through his pastoral work, his deeper experience of human nature and his deeper study of the apostle Paul, Augustine came by the year 397 to a fuller realization of human dependence upon the grace of God. He then wrote his *Confessions*, in which he recounts the story of his life until the death of his mother, shortly after his conversion, interpreting it in the light of his new beliefs about God's grace. These found expression in a famous prayer: 'Give me the grace to do as you command, and command me to do what you will!' (10:29:40). This expression of dependence upon God offended Pelagius, whose views Augustine opposed in the last twenty years of his life, as in his *The Spirit and the Letter* (see pages 95–98).

The *Confessions* is one of Augustine's greatest works and justifiably the most widely read. It was the first work ever written to explore at length the inner workings of the human soul and set the pattern for later introspective works. But although it is inward looking it is also written in the form of a prayer addressed to God. The title is chosen for its deliberate ambiguity. Augustine is both confessing his sins in penitence and confessing God's greatness and mercy in praise. There are thirteen books, the first nine of which cover his life until his baptism and the death of his mother in 387. Book 10 then covers his present state as a Christian in the struggle against sin. Finally, books 11–13 expound the first chapter of Genesis. The work as a whole is more unified than this would suggest as there are unifying themes which run throughout.

———————

1:1:1. Can any praise be worthy of the Lord's majesty? How magnificent his strength! How inscrutable his wisdom! Man is one of your creatures, Lord, and his instinct is to praise you. He bears about him the mark of death, the sign of his own sin, to remind him that you thwart the proud. But still, since he is a part of your creation, he wishes to praise you. The thought of you stirs him so deeply that he cannot be content unless he praises you, because you made us for yourself and our hearts find no peace until they rest in you.

2:1:1. I must now carry my thoughts back to the abominable things I did in those days, the sins of the flesh which defiled my soul. I do this, my God, not because I love these sins, but so that I may love you. For love of your love I shall retrace my wicked ways. The memory is bitter, but it will help me to savour your sweetness, the sweetness that does not deceive but brings real joy and never fails.

3:1:1. I went to Carthage, where I found myself in the midst of a hissing cauldron of lust. I had not yet fallen in love, but I was in love with the idea of it, and this feeling that something was missing made me despise myself for not being more anxious to satisfy the need. I began to look around for some object for my love, since I badly wanted to love something. I had no liking for the safe path without pitfalls, for although my real need was for you, my God, who are the food of the soul, I was not aware of this hunger. I felt no need for the food that does not perish, not because I had had my fill of it, but because the more I was starved of it the less palatable it seemed. . . . So I muddied the stream of friendship with the filth of lewdness and clouded its clear waters with hell's black river of lust.

8:5:10. When your servant Simplicianus told me the story of Victorinus, I began to glow with fervour to imitate him. This, of course, was why Simplicianus had told it to me. . . . I longed to do the same, but I was held fast, not in fetters clamped upon me by another, but by my own will, which had the strength of iron chains. The enemy held my will in his power and from it he had made a chain and shackled me. For my will was perverse and lust had grown from it, and when I gave in to lust habit was born, and when I did not resist the habit it became a necessity.

8:5:12. I was quite sure that it was better for me to give myself up to your love than to surrender to my own lust. But while I wanted to follow the first course and was convinced that it was right, I was still a slave to the pleasures of the second. I had no answer to make when you said 'Awake, you who sleep, and arise from the dead, and Christ shall give you light' [Ephesians 5:14]. You used all means to prove the truth of your words, and now that I was convinced that they were true, the only answers that I could give were the drowsy words of an idler – 'Soon', 'Presently', 'Let me wait a little longer'. But 'soon' was not soon and 'a little longer' grew much longer. . . . For the rule of sin is the force of habit, by which the mind is swept along and held fast even against its will, yet deservedly, because it fell into the habit of its own accord.

8:12:29. I was asking myself these questions, weeping all the while with the most bitter sorrow in my heart, when all at once I heard the sing-song voice of a child in a nearby house. Whether it was the voice of a boy or a girl I cannot say, but again and again it repeated the refrain 'Take it and read, take it and read'. At this I looked up, thinking hard whether there was any kind of game in which children used to chant words like these, but I could not remember ever hearing them before. I stemmed my flood of tears and stood up, telling myself that this could only be a divine command to open my book of Scripture and read the first passage on which my eyes should fall. For I had heard the story of Antony, and I remembered how he had happened to go into a church while the Gospel was being read and had taken it as a counsel addressed to himself when he heard the words 'Go home and sell all that belongs to you. Give it to the poor, and so the treasure you have shall be in heaven; then come back and follow me' [Matthew 19:21]. By this divine pronouncement he had at once been converted to you.

So I hurried back to the place where Alypius was sitting, for when I stood up to move away I had put down the book containing Paul's Epistles. I seized it and opened it, and in silence I read the first passage on which my eyes fell: 'Not in revelling and drunkenness, not in lust and wantonness, not in quarrels and rivalries. Rather, arm yourselves with the Lord Jesus Christ; spend no more thought on nature and nature's appetites' [Romans 13:13–14]. I had no wish to read more and no need to do so. For in an instant, as I came to the end of the sentence, it was as though the light of confidence flooded into my heart and all the darkness of doubt was dispelled.

Augustine, *The Spirit and the Letter*
(412)

In his earliest days as a Christian, Augustine believed that we need God's grace, the inner help of the Holy Spirit, to live the Christian life. But he also believed that unbelievers can, of their own unaided free will, make the first move and turn to God. In other words, God gives his grace (or the Holy Spirit) to those who respond to the gospel in faith. But after a few years, Augustine came to a deeper understanding of grace. He came to see that even faith is a gift of God, the work of his grace. 'What do you have that you did not receive?' (1 Corinthians 4:7). Salvation is all of God's grace – the beginning as well as the continuance. This grace is not given to all (not all believe) but to those whom God has chosen, his elect. 'It does not . . . depend on human desire or effort, but on God's mercy' (Romans 9:16). Augustine reached these views by 397. They arose from his deeper experience of human nature and his deeper study of the apostle Paul. He then wrote his *Confessions* (see pages 91–94), in which he recounts the story of his life until the death of his mother, shortly after his conversion, interpreting it in the light of his new beliefs about God's grace.

While Augustine's mature views were essentially complete by 397, it was the controversy with Pelagius that led to their detailed outworking. Pelagius was a Scots or Irish monk – Jerome suggested that his wrong ideas came because his mind was befuddled by too much porridge! He held a high view of human nature. God has graciously shown us what to do and given us the free will to do it, so all that is needed is for us to get on with it. Should we sin from time to time, God will also graciously forgive us. But Pelagius did not believe that we need the inner help of the Holy Spirit in order to obey God. With this optimistic view of human nature he was offended when he heard Augustine's prayer from the Confessions: 'Give me the grace to do as you command, and command me to do what you will!' (10:29:40). He felt that this detracted from human responsibility and encouraged laziness.

Augustine became aware of Pelagius's views in 411 and spent the rest of his life campaigning furiously against them – by ecclesiastical and secular politics and above all by writing. He wrote eleven major works against Pelagius and his followers and another four related works in his closing years. Perhaps the greatest of these works was one of his earliest, *The Spirit and the Letter*, written in 412. The title is taken from 2 Corinthians 3:6 ('the letter kills, but the Spirit gives life') while the argument of the book is drawn mainly from Romans, especially chapter 7.

● 'The letter kills.' Augustine interprets the letter as the outward law, whether the Ten Commandments or the two great commandments to love God and our neighbour.

If we are left to our free will alone these commands are unable to produce obedience. 'Through the law comes the knowledge of sin' (Romans 3:20) or, as Augustine puts it, 'the law causes sin to be known rather than shunned' (5:8). The best that the law can produce is an external obedience arising from fear of the consequences, while the righteousness that God seeks is an obedience from the heart motivated by love of righteousness. This is something that unaided human free will cannot produce.

● So we are reliant on the fact that 'the Spirit gives life'. Augustine interprets the Spirit as the work of the Holy Spirit within, giving us love. 'The love of God is shed abroad in our hearts by the Holy Spirit' (Romans 5:5). When the Holy Spirit thus works in our heart we are motivated by love and so are able to obey God truly from the heart. This work of the Holy Spirit Augustine also calls 'grace'.

● Throughout *The Spirit and the Letter* the contrast is drawn between the external law written on tablets of stone (the letter) and the internal law written on our hearts by the Holy Spirit (the Spirit). This is drawn especially from Jeremiah 31:31–34, echoed by Paul in 2 Corinthians 3. The outward law demands and threatens but the inward law gives us the ability to fulfil it.

● Augustine describes the process by which God works in our hearts. The written law is the tutor to lead us to God's grace (Galatians 3:24) and through that grace we are then able to fulfil the law. 'Law is given that grace be sought; grace is given that the law be fulfilled' (19:34). This process Augustine sets out as follows: 'Through the law comes the knowledge of our sin; by faith we acquire grace to overcome sin; by grace the soul is healed from the disease of sin; through the healing of the soul the will becomes free; the freed will now loves righteousness; through the love of righteousness we are now able to fulfil the law' (30:52).

● Are we able of our own free will to turn to God or do we need God to make the first move? In other words, do we need 'prevenient grace', the grace which comes before any move on our part and moves us to turn to God? In the first decade after his conversion Augustine had thought that we could make the first move on our own but ten years later, as described above, he had changed his mind. Augustine is careful in *The Spirit and the Letter* not to make that the issue. Whatever their views about who makes the first move, Christians ought to be able to unite round the fact that we do need grace, the inner help of the Holy Spirit, in order to obey God from the heart. That is the thrust of *The Spirit and the Letter*.

Towards the end of the work, however, he notes that in the process he has described, quoted above (30:52), it appears that we take the first move by believing. He goes on to put forward his own view that it is only through God's work within by his Spirit that we are able to come to faith. As the controversy progressed Augustine became less tentative about this, arguing vigorously for the need for prevenient grace. Not all were convinced and John Cassian, in the thirteenth of his *Conferences* (see pages 102–105), presented a contrary view. The debate continued for another hundred years until the Second Council of Orange (529) issued *Canons* (see pages 121–23) which condemned the view that we can make the first step on our own, later known as 'Semi-Pelagianism'.

The Spirit and the Letter is one of Augustine's greatest works, setting out very clearly the contrast between the demands of the law and the gift of the gospel. After the Bible it was the single most influential book in the Protestant Reformation.

⸻

3:5. Man's free will avails for nothing except sin, if he does not know the way of truth; and even after he begins to know his duty and proper aim, unless he also take delight in it and feel a love for it, he neither does his duty, nor sets about it, nor lives rightly. It is in order that such a course may engage our affections that God's 'love is shed abroad in our hearts', not through the free will which arises from ourselves, but 'through the Holy Spirit, who is given to us' [Romans 5:5].

5:8. Attend carefully to the apostle's explanation in his Epistle to the Romans where he shows clearly enough that what he wrote to the Corinthians ('The letter kills, but the spirit gives life') must be understood in the sense which we have already indicated – that the letter of the law, which teaches us not to commit sin, kills if the life-giving Spirit be absent. The law causes sin to be known rather than shunned and so (because transgression of the law is now added to evil lust) to be increased rather than diminished.

12:22. What the law of works enjoins by threat, the law of faith secures by faith. . . . By the law of works, God says to us, 'Do what I command'; by the law of faith we say to God, 'Give me what you command.' This is why the law commands – to advise us what faith ought to do, so that he to whom the command is given, if he is as yet unable to perform it, may know what to ask for. If he immediately has the ability and complies with the command, he should be aware from whose gift this ability comes.

17:29. [In the Old Testament] the finger of God worked on tablets of stone; [in the New Testament] it was on the hearts of men. There the law was given outwardly to terrify the unrighteous; here it was given inwardly, so that they might be justified. For 'the commandments, do not commit adultery, do not kill, do not covet, and any other commandments that there may be,' (written, of course, on those tablets) 'are summed up in this one saying: love your neighbour as yourself. Love does no harm to its neighbour: therefore love is the fulfilment of the law' [Romans 13:9–10]. This law was not written on the tablets of stone, but 'is shed abroad in our hearts by the Holy Spirit, who is given to us' [Romans 5:5]. God's law, therefore, is love. 'The carnal mind is not subject to it, nor indeed can it be' [Romans 8:7]. When the works of love are written on tablets to alarm the carnal mind, there arises the law of works and 'the letter which kills' the transgressor; but when love itself is shed abroad in the hearts of believers, then we have the law of faith and the Spirit who gives life to him that loves.

31:56. This is the faith which works not by fear but by love, not by dreading punishment but by loving righteousness. From where does this love come, by which faith works, if not from the same source from which faith obtained it? For there would be no love within us, however little, if it were not shed abroad in our hearts by the Holy Spirit who is given to us. Now 'the love of God' that is said to be shed abroad in our hearts is not his love for us, but that by which he makes us love himself – just as 'the righteousness of God' is that by which we are made righteous by his gift and 'the salvation of the Lord' is that by which we are saved by him; and 'the faith of Jesus Christ' is that by which he makes us believers in him. This is that righteousness of God, which he not only teaches us by the commandment of the law, but also bestows upon us by the gift of his Spirit.

23

Augustine, *The City of God* (413–27)

In his final years Augustine wrote some of his most important works. Between 399 and 419 he wrote his greatest dogmatic work, *The Trinity*. In this he draws together the achievements of the early Fathers before his time and presents a systematic account of the doctrine of the Trinity. Not contenting himself with stating the doctrine, he seeks by reason to understand what faith believes. Augustine attempts to do this by using analogies, drawn from the human soul made in the image of God. He examines a range of possible analogies, mostly based on the trio of being, knowing and willing. His final and best analogy is the mind remembering, understanding and loving God. By examining the relationship between the mind's memory, understanding and love of God, Augustine sought insights into the relationships of the persons of the Trinity. But at the end of the day he recognizes that even the best analogy is imperfect, for now we see only 'in a glass darkly' (1 Corinthians 13:12).

Between 413 and 427 Augustine wrote his longest work, *The City of God*. In 410 Rome had fallen to barbarian invaders. This unprecedented disaster was blamed on Christianity – the gods were angry because they were no longer being worshipped. Augustine responded to this crisis with the greatest apologetic work of the Early Church. The first part (Books 1–10) is a refutation of paganism. He argues that the pagan gods had not in fact provided either earthly (Books 1–5) or heavenly (Books 6–10) fortune. For Augustine, Christianity does not offer temporal worldly success, contrary to the high hopes of Eusebius of Caesarea and others, following Constantine's conversion. The gospel offers inner peace and an eternal destiny. The second part (Books 11–22) presents the Christian alternative. Augustine contrasts two different cities or societies: the city of God and the city of Satan; the heavenly and the earthly city; Jerusalem and Babylon. These are not two rival nations, nor two organizations (such as the church and the state) but two groups of people. They are marked by two different loves: the love of God versus the love of self; the love of the eternal versus the love of temporal things. Books 11–14 trace the origins of the two cities, the one from God and the other from the world. Books 15–18 trace their growth and progress from creation to eternity. Finally, Books 19–22 explain the different destinies of each city.

Augustine spelt out more clearly than those before him the doctrine of the 'invisible church'. Not all within the church are genuine Christians – many are Christians in name alone. We cannot distinguish the true from the false. It is God alone who can read the hearts of men and who knows who are his. Thus the boundaries of the true church are invisible, known to God alone. Augustine distinguishes between the visible church (the outward organization) and the invisible church (the body of true Christians), seen only by

God. For Augustine, the invisible church lies entirely within the Catholic Church and there are no true Christians outside it.

Augustine died in 430, as an invading barbarian army was about to take the city of Hippo. Western Roman civilization was crumbling. But in his *City of God* he had taken classical culture and transposed it into a new Christian culture. This, one of the greatest works of the Early Church, was in many ways a blueprint for the Middle Ages.

———————————————

1:8. There is a very great difference in the purpose served both by those events which we call evil and those called blessings. The good man is neither uplifted with the good things of this world, nor broken by its ills; but the wicked man, because he is corrupted by this world's happiness, feels himself punished by its misfortune. Yet God often shows his own working plainly, even in the present distribution of temporal things. For if every sin were now manifestly punished, it would appear that nothing was reserved for the final judgment; on the other hand, if no sin now received a plainly divine punishment, it would be concluded that there is no divine providence at all. Similarly with the good things of this life: if God did not by a very visible liberality confer these on some who ask for them, we would say that these good things were not at his disposal; and if he gave them to all who sought them, we should suppose that such were the only rewards of his service – and such service would make us not godly but greedy and covetous.

So, though good and bad suffer alike, the identity of the suffering does not imply the identity of the sufferers. The suffering may be the same, but there remains a difference in the sufferers; virtue and vice are not the same thing even though exposed to the same anguish. Just as the same fire causes gold to glow brightly and chaff to smoke; just as under the same flail the straw is beaten small, while the grain is cleansed; and just as the lees are not mixed with the oil, though squeezed out of the vat by the same pressure – so the same violence of affliction proves, purges and clarifies the good, but damns, ruins and exterminates the wicked. Thus under the same affliction the wicked detest God and blaspheme, while the good pray and praise. So what matters is not what ills are suffered, but what kind of man suffers them. For stirred up with the same movement, mud exhales a horrible stench and ointment emits a fragrant odour.

4:4. Without justice, what are kingdoms but great bands of robbers? For what are robber bands themselves, but little kingdoms? The band itself is made up of men; it is ruled by the authority of a prince, it is knit together by a pact of the association; the booty is divided by an agreed law. If, by recruiting abandoned men, this evil increases to such a degree that it occupies territory, fixes abodes, takes possession of cities, and subdues peoples, it assumes the more openly the name of a kingdom, because the reality is now manifestly conferred on it, not by the removal of covetousness but by the addition of impunity. Indeed, Alexander the Great received an apt and true reply from a pirate whom he had captured. When the king had asked the man what he meant by keeping hostile possession of the sea, he answered with bold pride: 'the same as you mean by seizing the whole earth. Because I do it with a little ship I am called a pirate; because you do it with a great fleet you are called emperor.'

14:28. Two cities have been formed by two loves: the earthly city by the love of self, leading to contempt of God and the heavenly city by the love of God, leading to contempt of self. The former glories in itself, the latter in the Lord. The one seeks glory from men, but for the other the greatest glory is God, the witness of conscience. . . . In the one city, the rulers and the nations that it subdues are ruled by the lust for domination; in the other city, rulers and subjects serve one another in love – the subjects by obeying, the rulers by caring for all. The one city delights in its own strength, represented in the person of its own rulers; the other says to God, 'I will love you, O Lord my strength' [Psalm 18:1]. Therefore the wise men of the former city, living by human standards, sought bodily or mental profit or both. Any who knew God 'neither glorified him as God, nor gave thanks to him. . . .' [Romans 1:21–25]. In the other city, however, there is no human wisdom but only godliness which offers due worship to the true God and looks for its reward in the company of saints (holy angels as well as holy people), 'that God may be all in all' [1 Corinthians 15:28].

15:1. We have divided the human race into two parts: those who live by human standards and those that live according to God. We also mystically call these the two cities or two communities of men. The one is predestined to reign eternally with God, the other to suffer eternal punishment with the devil.

John Cassian, *Conferences* (421–30)

John Cassian was born in about 365, in modern-day Romania. He spent ten years in a monastery at Bethlehem and also travelled extensively in the East, touring Egyptian monasteries and gathering a collection of sayings of the desert fathers. At Constantinople he met John Chrysostom, who influenced him, and he also spent some time at Rome. At the age of about fifty he settled down in Marseilles, in the south of France, founding two monasteries, one for men and one for women. He died in the early 430s.

Cassian wrote two important monastic works. His *Institutes*, in twelve books, introduce the western reader to the customs and rules of Egyptian monasticism and then discuss eight major sins: gluttony, fornication, covetousness, anger, dejection, accidie (spiritual sloth or sluggishness), vanity and pride. These overlap to some extent with the later list of seven deadly sins. His twenty-four *Conferences*, probably written in the 420s, are his account of dialogues with fifteen different Egyptian 'abbas' (fathers), each conference being on a specific theme. Cassian's aim was to mediate the fruits of Egyptian monasticism to the monks of southern Gaul and in the process he set his own stamp on it. While he drew extensively on his Egyptian experiences, the topics selected and to some extent the slant given to the teaching are determined by western needs. Benedict in turn drew upon Cassian when writing his *Rule* (see pages 124–27), which was to become normative for western monasticism.

In the eleventh Conference Abba Chaeremon tackles an important theme which is often misunderstood today, the role of fear in our relationship to God. He steers a middle course between two opposite errors. On the one hand, fear on its own is an inadequate basis for our relationship to God. As Augustine graphically put it, the person who fears hell fears burning, not sin (*Letter* 145:4). But on the other hand, Chaeremon did not fall into the mistake, popular today, of claiming that fear has no role to play – an unlikely theory given that 'the fear of the Lord is the beginning of wisdom' (Proverbs 9:10). He shows how we should progress from fear to love, much as children are initially constrained at least in part by fear and grow up to follow the right path of their own accord. He also shows that there is a sense in which those who love perfectly do not cease to fear God. Fear and the desire for reward are valid motivations, but not sufficient on their own.

Conference 11: The First Conference of Abbot Chaeremon: On Perfection

6. There are three things which enable men to control their sins: fear of hell or of earthly laws; hope for and desire of the kingdom of heaven; a liking for goodness itself and the love of virtue. For we read that fear loathes the contamination of evil: 'The fear of the Lord hates evil' [Proverbs 8:13]. Hope also shuts out all the assaults of sin, for 'those who hope in him shall not fail' [Psalm 34:22]. Love also fears no destruction from sin, for 'love never fails' [1 Corinthians 13:8] and again: 'love covers a multitude of sins' [1 Peter 4:8]. Therefore the blessed apostle summarizes the whole of salvation in the attainment of those three virtues: 'these three remain: faith, hope and love' [1 Corinthians 13:13].

It is faith that makes us shun the contagion of sin from fear of future judgment and punishment; it is hope that anticipates heavenly rewards and withdraws our mind from present things to despise all bodily pleasures; it is love that fires us with zeal for the love of Christ and the fruit of spiritual goodness and makes us hate with a perfect hatred whatever is opposed to these. These three virtues all seem to aim at the same end of inciting us to abstain from everything unlawful – yet they differ greatly from each other in degree of excellence. [Faith and hope] belong to those who aim at goodness but have not yet acquired the love of virtue, while [love] belongs specially to God and to those who have appropriated his image and likeness. For God alone does good simply for its own sake, not motivated by fear, thanks or reward. . . .

7. Any one aiming at perfection should rise from that first stage of fear which we rightly called servile . . . and climb to the next stage, the higher path of hope. There he can be compared not to a slave but to an employee because he looks for the payment of a reward. No longer worried about forgiveness of sins or afraid of punishment, he is conscious of his own good works and anticipates the promised reward. But he has not yet reached the love of a son who trusts in his father's kindness and liberality and has no doubt that all that belongs to the father is his. . . . We ought to hasten on so that by means of the indissoluble grace of love we may rise to the third stage of sonship, believing that all that the Father has is ours and thus being counted worthy to receive the image and likeness of our heavenly Father. . . .

These are stages on the way. We start by avoiding sin from fear of punishment or hope of reward and are then enabled to progress to the stage of love, for 'there is no fear in love, but perfect love casts out fear: for fear has to do with torment, but he who fears is not perfect in love. We therefore love because God first loved us' [1 John 4:18–19]. We can only ascend to true perfection when we love him solely because he loved us, just as he first loved us for no other reason but our salvation. So we must zealously strive to ascend from fear to hope and from hope to love of God and of virtue. . . .

8. There is a great difference between those who extinguish the inner fire of sin by means of fear of hell or hope of future reward and those who have a horror of sin itself and of uncleanness, moved by love for God. These keep themselves pure simply because they love purity and long for it, not looking for a future promised reward but delighted with the knowledge of present good things, motivated not by fear of punishment but by delight in virtue. Such people do not take the opportunity to sin when no one is looking nor are they corrupted by the secret allurements of thoughts. They keep the love of virtue in their hearts and anything opposed to it they not only do not admit into their heart but actually hate with the utmost horror. It is one thing to hate the stains of sins and of the flesh out of delight for some present good, and another thing to restrain unlawful desires by contemplating future reward; it is one thing to fear present loss and another to dread future punishment; finally it is much better for the sake of goodness itself to be unwilling to forsake good than to withhold consent from evil for fear of evil. For in the former case the good is chosen voluntarily, but in the latter it is coerced and dragged out of a reluctant party either by fear of punishment or by greed for reward. He who abstains from the delights of sin because of fear will, as soon as the obstacle of fear is removed, return once more to what he loves and thus will not acquire any stability in good, nor will he ever be free of temptation.

13. Whoever then has been established in this perfect love must ascend to a higher and more sublime stage, to the fear which belongs to love. This arises not from dread of punishment or greed for reward, but from the greatest love – just as a son fears with earnest affection a most generous father, or a brother fears his brother, a friend his friend, or a wife her husband. There is no dread of blows or reproaches, but only of a slight injury to his love, while in every word as well as act care is ever taken by anxious affection lest there should be any cooling in the other's love for oneself. . . . To this fear then not sinners but saints are invited by the prophetic word where the Psalmist says: 'Fear the Lord, you his saints, for those who fear him lack nothing' [Psalm 34:9] – for nothing is lacking to the perfection of those who fear the Lord in this way.

When the apostle John said that 'He who fears is not made perfect in love, for fear has to do with punishment' [1 John 4:18] he was referring to that other penal fear. So there is a great difference between this fear, which lacks nothing and is the treasure of wisdom and knowledge, and that imperfect fear which is called 'the beginning of wisdom' [Proverbs 9:10]. The latter fears punishment and so is expelled from the hearts of those who are perfect by the incoming of the fullness of love. For 'there is no fear in love, but perfect love casts out fear' [1 John 4:18]. If the beginning of wisdom consists in fear, what will its perfection be except in the love of Christ which, as it contains in it the fear which belongs to perfect love, is called not the beginning but the treasure of wisdom and knowledge? So there are two stages of fear. The one for beginners, for those who are still subject to the yoke and to servile terror, of which we read: 'The servant shall fear his Lord' [Malachi 1:6]; the other in the gospel: 'I no longer call you servants, for the servant does not know what his Lord does' [John 15:15] and therefore 'the servant,' he tells us, 'does not remain in the house for ever, but a son remains for ever' [John 8:35]. For he is instructing us to pass on from that penal fear to the fullest freedom of love, and the confidence of the friends and sons of God.

Cyril of Alexandria,
Third Letter to Nestorius (430)

Cyril became bishop of Alexandria in 412, in succession to his uncle Theophilus. His main claim to fame lies in his controversy with Nestorius, bishop of Constantinople. Since Constantinople had been promoted in 381 to second see in the place of Alexandria, there had been bitter rivalry between the two sees. Cyril's uncle Theophilus had secured the exile of John Chrysostom and Cyril was to follow suit with Nestorius. But it would be wrong to see this purely as an ecclesiastical political struggle. Cyril opposed Nestorius because of fundamental differences concerning the person of Jesus Christ.

Nestorius was a popular preacher who in 428 became bishop of Constantinople. He belonged to the Antiochene school of thought on the person of Jesus Christ. That meant that he followed the 'Word-man' approach – he saw Christ as composed of Jesus the man who was indwelt by God the Word. There is the closest possible conjunction between Jesus the man and God the Word – they are united in purpose and will. But when all is said and done, despite Nestorius's attempts to unite them, they remain two individuals. Nestorius has been accused of teaching a 'pantomime horse' theory of the incarnation, in which there is an outward unity but underneath two individuals are at work. In 1910 a long-lost work of Nestorius, *The Bazaar of Heracleides*, was discovered. This confirms Nestorius's desire to be orthodox and to affirm the unity of Jesus Christ – but not his success in this aim.

Nestorius, in his preaching at Constantinople, denied that the virgin Mary was *theotokos* ('God-bearer' or 'Mother of God'). It was Jesus the man who was born of Mary, not God the Word. Cyril heard of this and reacted. First he wrote Nestorius a polite but firm letter, explaining his own position and urging Nestorius to accept *theotokos* and be at peace with him. Nestorius remained adamant and in the meantime Cyril obtained the support of Rome, where in August 430 a synod decided against Nestorius and required him to recant within ten days of being informed. Cyril was entrusted with the task of executing this. He then wrote Nestorius an uncompromising letter, his *Third Letter to Nestorius* (number 17 among his Letters), demanding submission and requiring him to sign twelve 'anathemas' – that is, to condemn twelve statements setting out what Cyril considered to be his heresies. Nestorius refused and the emperor called the Council of Ephesus, which met in 431 and deposed Nestorius. Cyril died in 444.

The essence of Cyril's position is very simple. Jesus Christ is not a man indwelt by or conjoined to God the Word – he *is* God the Word, made flesh. The doctrine for which Cyril fought against Nestorius was simply the doctrine of the incarnation. God the Word, who is eternally begotten or born of God the Father, was in time born of the virgin Mary as man. This is why Mary is *theotokos* – because the baby born of her was God. Christ is not a combination of Jesus the man and God the Word, but rather 'the Word became flesh' (John 1:14) – that is, God the Word united to himself complete human nature (including a soul) and became a man. This union makes of Jesus Christ one being.

The difference between Cyril and Nestorius can be summarized as follows: Nestorius spoke of Jesus *and* God the Word, while Cyril believed that Jesus was the Word. Again, who was the man Jesus? Nestorius believed him to be a man united with the Word in a unique and perfect way. Cyril insisted that Jesus himself was the Word, incarnate. Nestorius very revealingly stated: 'I could not call a baby two or three months old God' (Socrates, *Church History* 7:34). Cyril's opposition to Nestorius, like that of Athanasius to Arius, was motivated by a concern for the doctrine of salvation – which is not to suggest that it was a totally unpleasant duty for him to unseat the bishop of Constantinople. Cyril believed that in the communion service we receive life from Jesus' life-giving flesh (John 6:48–58). His flesh gives life because it is the flesh not of a mere man but of the incarnate Word.

Cyril's attack on Nestorius has often been criticized. In part this is because the anathemas at the end of this *Third Letter* were soon detached from the preceding letter. Read out of their context they can easily be misunderstood – and were. In part, however, it is because of the brutal clarity with which Cyril saw the fundamental issue at stake and exposed the inadequacies of Nestorius and those like him. It is to Cyril more than any other that we owe the faithful preservation of the doctrine of the incarnation, that Jesus is God the Word made flesh. There are other truths about Jesus that also need preserving and twenty years later Leo in his *Tome* (see pages 110–12) would stress the importance of the full humanity of Christ, a point not questioned by Cyril but one on which he lays less emphasis.

He did not indeed lay aside what he was, but even though he became a human being by assuming flesh and blood he still remained God in nature and in truth. And we say neither that the flesh was changed into the nature of Godhead, nor indeed that the inexpressible nature of God the Word was converted into that of flesh, for he is unchanging and unalterable, ever abiding the same, according to the Scriptures. But while visible as a babe in swaddling clothes, and at the breast of the Virgin who bore him, he was filling all creation as God, and was enthroned with his Father. . . .

We do not say that the Word from God dwelt in an ordinary man who was born of the holy Virgin, lest Christ should be thought of as a man carrying God (within him). It is true that 'the Word dwelt among us' [John 1:14], and that in Christ there dwelt 'all the fullness of the Godhead bodily' [Colossians 2:9]. But when the Word became flesh, God's indwelling in Christ is not to be defined in the same way as his indwelling in the saints. Rather, being naturally united with flesh without being turned into it, the Word effected such an indwelling as the soul of man may be said to have in its own body. . . .

We confess that he himself, the Son begotten of God the Father, the only-begotten God, remaining impassible in his own nature, suffered in the flesh for us according to the Scriptures, and was in his crucified body impassibly making his own the sufferings of his own flesh. For 'by the grace of God he tasted death for everyone' [Hebrews 2:9], yielding his own body to it, while yet by nature he was life and himself 'the resurrection' [John 11:25]. For he trampled upon death in his unspeakable power, in order to become in his own flesh 'the firstborn from the dead' [Colossians 1:18] and 'the first fruits of those that sleep' [1 Corinthians 15:20], and open a way for human nature to return to incorruption. . . .

And we must add this also. We proclaim the death in the flesh of the only-begotten Son of God, that is, of Jesus Christ, and confess his return to life from the dead and his ascension into heaven, when we celebrate the [Eucharist] in the churches. We thus approach the sacramental gifts and are sanctified, being partakers both of the holy flesh and of the precious blood of Christ the saviour of us all. We do not receive it as a common flesh – surely not! – nor as the flesh of a man sanctified and associated with the Word in a unity of dignity, or having some divine indwelling, but as truly life-giving as the Word's very own flesh. For being by nature life as God, when he became one with his own flesh he rendered it life-giving. So that although he says to us, 'I tell you the truth, unless you eat the flesh of the Son of Man and drink his blood' [John 6:53], we shall not reckon it to be the flesh of a man like one of ourselves – for how could the flesh of a mere man be life-giving in its own nature? – but as having become truly the own flesh of him who for our sakes both became and was called Son of Man. . . .

Since the holy Virgin brought forth after the flesh God substantially united to flesh, we say that she is *theotokos*. It is not as though the nature of the Word had its beginning of existence from flesh, for 'he was in the beginning', and 'the Word was God', and 'the Word was with God' [John 1:1]. He is himself the maker of the ages, coeternal with the Father, and the creator of the universe. But, as we have already said, we call her that because it was from her womb that he substantially united humanity to himself and underwent a fleshly birth.

It was not for his own nature that he needed the birth in time, in the last days of the world. It was rather that he might bless the very beginning of our existence by a woman's bearing him united to flesh. Also that the curse on all the race which sends our earthly bodies to death, might be made to cease; and that when he annulled the sentence 'in pain you will give birth to children' [Genesis 3:16], the prophet's words should be shown to be true: 'Death in its might swallowed [us] up, and on the other hand God wiped away all the tears from every face' [Isaiah 25:8]. This is why we say that he himself blessed marriage by his incarnation and went when invited to Cana of Galilee with his holy apostles.

These doctrines we have been taught to hold by the holy apostles and evangelists and all the God-breathed Scriptures, and from the true confession of the blessed fathers. Your reverence must agree to all this and maintain it without any guile. The points which your reverence must anathematize are appended to this our letter:

1. If anyone does not acknowledge that Emmanuel is truly God and therefore that the holy Virgin is *theotokos* (for she gave fleshly birth to the Word of God made flesh), let him be anathema.

2. If anyone does not acknowledge that the Word of God the Father has been substantially united with flesh; and that he is one Christ with one flesh so that the same one [Christ] is at once both God and human, let him be anathema.

5. If anyone has the nerve to state that Christ is a God-bearing man [i.e. indwelt by God] instead of saying that he is truly God, being [God's] one Son by nature, because 'the Word became flesh' and 'shared in flesh and blood like us' [Hebrews 2:14], let him be anathema.

11. If anyone does not acknowledge that the Lord's flesh is life-giving and that it belongs to the very Word of God the Father, but instead says that it belongs to someone different joined to him [the Word] by dignity or merely indwelt by God, rather than being (as we said) life-giving because it has become the flesh of the Word who is able to give life to all, let him be anathema.

12. If anyone does not acknowledge that the Word of God suffered in the flesh, was crucified in the flesh, tasted death in the flesh and became firstborn from the dead because as God he is life and life-giving, let him be anathema.

Leo, *Tome* (449)

Leo was bishop of Rome from 440 to 461 and was one of the greatest of the popes –
he is often called 'Leo the Great'. He was a formidable person. In 452 he personally
persuaded Attila the Hun to turn back from attacking Rome. Three years later, when the
Vandals did take Rome, he managed to slow the destruction and killing. Leo is famous
especially for his teaching on the person of Jesus Christ, found above all in his *Letter* 28
(generally known as his *Tome*) written in refutation of the heretic Eutyches.

Eutyches was accused of blurring the two natures of Jesus Christ (deity and
humanity) into one and creating a mixture. If yellow paint is mixed with blue (to use a
modern analogy), the outcome is green paint, which is neither yellow nor blue; if a horse
is crossed with a donkey, the outcome is a mule, which is neither a horse nor a donkey.
Likewise, Eutyches was accused of making of Jesus Christ a mixture of deity and humanity,
a *tertium quid* or 'third something', which is neither God nor man but a sort of mongrel.

Eutyches was an elderly and highly respected monk at Constantinople. In 448
he was accused of heresy and the bishop, Flavian, was forced to put him on trial. The
outcome was that Eutyches was condemned for confusing the two natures of Jesus Christ –
though it has been argued that it was Eutyches himself who was confused or muddled,
rather than wilfully heretical. This played into the hands of Dioscorus, bishop of Alexandria
since 444. He was eager to enter the fray on Eutyches' side, and thus to follow in the
footsteps of his predecessor Cyril. Eutyches appealed to Dioscorus, who persuaded the
emperor to call a council, which met at Ephesus in 449. It was meant to be a replay of the
431 Council of Ephesus, with Flavian playing Nestorius to Dioscorus's Cyril. But there was
one vital difference – this time the West, in the person of Leo, supported Constantinople
instead of Alexandria. Leo wrote a letter to Flavian, his *Tome*, opposing Eutyches. But the
council was effectively controlled by Dioscorus, through the imperial officials. Leo's *Tome*
was not allowed to be read, Eutyches was restored and his opponents were deposed.
Flavian died a few days later of the rough treatment that he had received.

Leo's *Tome* draws together the western teaching on Christology up to his time. His
understanding of the person of Jesus Christ is based on his understanding of salvation. In
order to save us, Jesus Christ needed to be both God and man. His humanity needed to
be 'complete in what belonged to us', though without sin. It follows therefore that he has
two natures: deity and humanity. Against Eutyches, Leo stressed that 'each nature retains
without loss its own properties'. Jesus hungered and yet fed the five thousand – the former
was human, the latter divine. As man he wept for his friend Lazarus, as God he raised him
from the dead. He is one person, but this must not be misunderstood in such a way as to
blur the distinction between the natures – there must be no *tertium quid*. Leo placed less

stress than Cyril on the unity of Jesus Christ, but it was not absent from his teaching. It was the Son of God, the second person of the Trinity, who was born of Mary. 'The impassible God did not disdain to be a passible human being.'

At the Council of Chalcedon in 451, Leo's *Tome* was read and the bishops shouted, 'Peter has spoken through Leo. Thus Cyril taught. Leo and Cyril teach the same.' That statement has been contested ever since. One thing is for sure: Leo and Cyril did not teach the same in the sense that there is no difference between them. Whether or not they taught the same in the sense that it is possible to accept both without contradicting oneself remains a matter for debate.

━━━━━━━━━━━━━━

3. So the properties of both natures and substances [of Jesus Christ] were preserved and both met in one person. Humility was embraced by majesty, weakness by strength, mortality by eternity. And in order to pay the debt of our condition the invulnerable nature was united to a passible nature. The appropriate remedy for our ills was 'one and the same Mediator between God and humanity, the man Jesus Christ' [1 Timothy 2:5], who was capable of death in one nature and incapable of it in the other. True God was born in the complete and perfect nature of true humanity – complete in what belonged to him and complete in what belonged to us.

By 'what belonged to us' we mean that [nature] which the Creator put in us from the beginning and which he took upon himself to restore. For there was no trace in the Saviour of that [sin] which the Deceiver brought upon us and which deceived humanity accepted. It does not follow that because he shared in human weakness he therefore shared in our sins. What he assumed was 'the form of a servant' without the stain of sin, enriching what was human, not diminishing what was divine.

The 'self-emptying', by which he who is invisible rendered himself visible and the Creator and 'Lord of all' chose to be mortal, was a condescension of pity not a loss of power. So he who made the human race while remaining in 'the form of God' was the same one who was made human in the 'form of a servant'. For each nature retains its own properties without loss. Just as the 'form of God' does not take away the 'form of a servant', so the 'form of a servant' does not detract from the 'form of God'.

4. One and the same one is truly the Son of God and truly the Son of Man. Son of God, inasmuch as 'In the beginning was the Word, and the Word was with God, and the Word was God' [John 1:1]. Son of Man, inasmuch as 'the Word became flesh and dwelt among us' [John 1:14]. Son of God, inasmuch as 'through him all things were made, and without him nothing was made that has been made'

[John 1:3]. Son of Man, inasmuch as 'he was born of a woman, born under law' [Galatians 4:4]. The birth of the flesh is a manifestation of his human nature; birth from a virgin is proof of his divine power. His lowly cradle shows the infancy of the little child; the angels' voices declare the greatness of the Most High. He whom Herod impiously tries to slay is like a human infant, but he whom the Magi rejoice to adore on their knees is Lord of all.

When he came to be baptized by his forerunner John, lest he should escape notice because the deity was veiled in flesh, the Father's voice thundered from heaven: 'This is my Son, whom I love; with him I am well pleased' [Matthew 3:17]. So to the same one whom the devil craftily tempts as a man, the angels minister as God. To feel hunger and thirst, to be weary and to sleep is evidently human. To satisfy five thousand people with five loaves, to give to the Samaritan woman living water (a drink of which would cause her to thirst no more), to walk on the surface of the sea with feet that do not sink, to rebuke the storm and bring down the uplifted waves – all this is without doubt divine.

So, to pass over many other examples, it does not belong to the same nature to weep with pity for a dead friend and to raise that same friend from the dead with a word of power, after the removal of the stone over the tomb where he had been buried for four days. Nor to hang on the cross and to make the elements tremble by changing light into darkness. Nor to be pierced with nails and to open the gates of Paradise to the faith of the robber. Likewise it does not belong to the same nature to say 'I and the Father are one' [John 10:30] and 'the Father is greater than I' [John 14:28]. For although in the Lord Jesus Christ there is one person who is God and man, yet the source of the common injury is one thing; the source of the common glory is another. For it is from us that he has a humanity inferior to the Father and it is from the Father that he has a deity which is equal to the Father.

5. It is because of this unity of person, which must be understood to exist in both natures, that we read, on the one hand, that the Son of Man descended from heaven inasmuch as the Son of God took flesh from the Virgin from whom he was born. And again, on the other hand, that the Son of God is said to have been crucified and buried, inasmuch as he suffered these things not in his deity itself (in virtue of which the Only-begotten is both coeternal and consubstantial with the Father) but in the weakness of his human nature. This is why we all also confess in the creed that the only-begotten Son of God was crucified and buried, in accordance with the apostolic saying: 'For had they known, they would not have crucified the Lord of glory' [1 Corinthians 2:8].

The Definition of Chalcedon (451)

The year after the Council of Ephesus (449) at which Eutyches was condemned, the emperor died. His successor, Marcian, was not happy with the outcome of the council and so agreed to Leo's request for another. This council met at Chalcedon (across the Bosphorus from Constantinople) in October 451. It came to be seen as the fourth of the general or ecumenical councils.

The council reinstated those bishops condemned at the 'Robber Synod' of Ephesus in 449. Eutyches and Dioscorus of Alexandria were deposed. The creeds of the Councils of Nicea and Constantinople, two of Cyril's letters and Leo's *Tome* (see pages 110–12) were all read and approved. The bishops wished to stop there, but the emperor was determined to have a confession of faith to unite the empire. And so the *Definition of Chalcedon* was born.

A case can be made for seeing the Definition as primarily positive, as an exposition of the Creeds of Nicea and Constantinople. But the purpose of this exposition was the exclusion of heresy and it is more helpful to think of it primarily in these negative terms – as the safeguard against the four ancient heresies. Chalcedon does not lay down one normative Christology – it sets out the limits within which an orthodox Christology must remain. It is to be seen as a boundary fence rather than a straitjacket.

The Definition makes four points in opposition to the four ancient Christological heresies: In Jesus Christ, true deity (against Arius) and full humanity (against Apollinaris) are indivisibly united in the one person (against Nestorius), without being confused (against Eutyches). Its teaching can be summarized in the phrase 'one person in two natures'. But what does this actually *mean*? What is the difference between 'person' and 'nature'? The two terms can best be thought of as the answers to two different questions: *Who* was Jesus Christ? The one person of God the Word, made flesh. *What* was he? Truly divine and truly human – two natures. To put it differently, there was in Jesus Christ only one 'I', only one 'subject' of all that he experienced. This one subject or person is God the Word – there is not someone else (another 'person') who was the human Jesus. The Word remained God, with no lessening of his deity or divine nature, and yet he also took everything that belongs to humanity or human nature.

The Definition draws together material from the different traditions in the Early Church – from Alexandria (Cyril), Antioch, Constantinople (Flavian) and the West (Tertullian and Leo). But the dominant hand was western. It was at Roman insistence that the final text read 'in two natures' rather than 'out of two natures' as the majority of eastern bishops preferred. In the West the Definition was accepted at once but in the East the story was totally different. The emperor intended this document to cement unity with the Eastern Church. Its effect was more like dynamite than cement. Egypt and other areas have never accepted Chalcedon to this day.

Many have mistakenly spoken of Chalcedon as the culmination of the Early Church debates about the person of Christ. Almost the reverse is true. Chalcedon kindled a fierce debate that continued in the East for two hundred and thirty years leading to the next two general councils, at Constantinople in 553 and again from 680 to 681. But while it is wrong to suppose that Chalcedon concluded the debate, it is without question the most important definition of the person of Christ that has ever been produced. It by no means says everything that one would want to say on the issue, but the four errors that it condemns remain errors and it continues to function usefully as a boundary fence for modern theories.

─────────────────────

[The Creeds of Nicea and Constantinople are quoted. These ought to have sufficed for the establishment of orthodoxy, but unfortunately the teaching of Nestorius and Eutyches meant that more was required. Two of Cyril's letters were received as a refutation of Nestorianism, and Leo's *Tome* was received as an antidote for Eutychianism.]

[The Synod] opposes those who would rend the mystery of the incarnation into a duality of Sons [of which Nestorius was accused]; it expels from the priesthood those who dare to say that the Godhead of the Only-begotten is capable of suffering [Arius]; it resists those who imagine a mixture or confusion of the two natures of Christ [Eutyches]; it drives away those who fancy that the 'form of a servant' [i.e. humanity] which he took from us was of a heavenly or some other [non-human] substance [of which Apollinaris was falsely accused]; and it anathematizes those who imagine that the Lord had two natures before their union, but only one afterwards [Eutyches].

Following the holy fathers, we confess with one voice that the one and only Son, our Lord Jesus Christ, is perfect in deity and perfect in humanity, truly God and truly man, that he has a rational soul and a body. He is of one substance with the Father as God, he is also of one substance with us as human. He is like us in all things except sin. He was begotten of his Father before the ages as God, but in these last days and for our salvation he was born of Mary the virgin, the God-bearer, as a man. This one and the same Christ, Son, Lord, Only-begotten is made known in two natures [which exist] without confusion, without change, without division, without separation. The distinction of the natures is in no way taken away by their union, but rather the distinctive properties of each nature are preserved. [Both natures] unite into one person and one hypostasis. They are not separated or divided into two persons but [they form] one and the same Son, Only-begotten, God, Word, Lord Jesus Christ, just as the prophets of old [have spoken] concerning him and as the Lord Jesus Christ himself has taught us and as the creed of the fathers has delivered to us.

The Athanasian Creed (c. 500)

It is said of the Athanasian Creed that it is neither by Athanasius nor a creed. It was certainly not written by Athanasius, but was attributed to him from the seventh century, probably because he was seen as the father of the orthodox doctrine of the Trinity. This tradition was questioned in the sixteenth century and demolished in the seventeenth. There is no general consensus concerning its origin, but the evidence seems to indicate that it was written around the year 500 in the south of Gaul (France). It is often known as the *Quicunque Vult*, the opening words in the original Latin.

Strictly speaking, the Athanasian Creed is a definition rather than a creed, but this is perhaps an over-pedantic distinction. In the earliest times it was used as a test of orthodoxy for the clergy and as a simple compendium of Catholic doctrine for instructing the laity. By the thirteenth century it had come to be seen in the West as one of the 'three creeds', together with the Nicene and Apostles' Creeds. It was widely accepted by Protestant churches (e.g. in the Anglican *Thirty-nine Articles* [see pages 264–68], the Lutheran *Formula of Concord* [see pages 269–73] and at the Reformed *Synod of Dort*). The eastern churches were torn between respecting its Athanasian authorship and rejecting its *filioque* teaching (that the Holy Spirit proceeds from the Father *and the Son*). They either denied that Athanasius wrote it or claimed that the *filioque* was a later addition. The Creed was used frequently in Anglican and Roman Catholic worship, but in the last century it fell largely out of use. There has been considerable opposition to the Creed, not so much because of the theology it proclaims as because it consigns to eternal damnation those who do not accept it.

The Creed consists of two sections: one on the Trinity and one on the person of Jesus Christ. Each section is preceded and followed by a 'damnatory clause', stating the necessity to believe it if one is to be saved. While the Creed tells us how to think or speak about God, the emphasis is also on rightly worshipping him. The Creed is more than an exercise in speculative theology.

The trinitarian section is a masterly summary of the western doctrine of the Trinity, drawing heavily upon Augustine. Indeed, it has been called 'codified and condensed Augustinianism'. It presents the paradox of the unity and the trinity, the oneness and the threeness of God. These are set against the two errors of Monarchianism ('confusing the persons') and Arianism ('dividing the substance'). The Monarchians resolved the paradox of the Trinity by teaching that the Father is the Son is the Holy Spirit and there was a contemporary Spanish movement, Priscillianism, which tended in the same direction. The 'Arianism' opposed by the Creed is in fact the Origenism of the barbarian Gothic rulers in the West, who had been converted to Christianity at a time when the official eastern doctrine fell short of affirming the full deity of Jesus Christ. The Creed opposes two errors that the Goths were deemed to hold: it upholds the full deity of Christ against their belief that the Father is greater than the Son; it upholds the unity of the Godhead against their tendency towards three Gods. Thus the Athanasian Creed affirms the three main elements of the doctrine of the Trinity: that there is one God; that Father, Son and Holy Spirit are God; that the Father is not the Son is not the Holy Spirit.

The Christological section presents a doctrine similar to that of the Council of Chalcedon, but expressed in western terms. The four heresies condemned at Chalcedon are all clearly excluded. The first paragraph maintains the full deity and full humanity of Christ, excluding Arianism and Apollinarianism. The second paragraph affirms that he is one person, but without any confusion of his substances (natures), thus excluding Nestorianism and Eutychianism.

The 'damnatory clauses' stipulate that without correct belief salvation is not possible. This was long held to be so, but today there is a greater readiness on all sides to allow for sincerely-held error. Making a small mistake on the finer details of the doctrine of the Trinity need not result in eternal damnation. If the Athanasian Creed were taken at its face value, all easterners who reject the western *filioque* would be lost. It is sad that these damnatory clauses have diverted attention from the rest of the Creed. The trinitarian section, in particular, is a masterly concise summary of a difficult doctrine in simple terms.

———————————

Whoever wants to be saved must first of all hold the Catholic faith. Unless one keeps this faith whole and inviolate, he will without doubt perish eternally.

Now this is the Catholic faith: that we worship one God in trinity and trinity in unity – neither confusing persons, nor dividing the substance. For the Father's person is one, the Son's another and the Holy Spirit's another. But the deity of Father, Son and Holy Spirit is one. Their glory is equal and their majesty coeternal.

Whatever the Father is, such is the Son and such also the Holy Spirit. The Father is uncreated, the Son uncreated and the Holy Spirit uncreated. The Father is infinite, the Son infinite and the Holy Spirit infinite. The Father is eternal, the Son eternal and the Holy Spirit eternal. Yet there are not three eternals but only one eternal – just as there are not three uncreateds nor three infinites but only one uncreated and only one infinite. Likewise, the Father is almighty, the Son almighty and the Holy Spirit almighty – yet there are not three almighties but only one almighty.

Thus the Father is God, the Son is God and the Holy Spirit is God – yet there are not three Gods but only one God. Thus the Father is Lord, the Son Lord and the Holy Spirit Lord – yet there are not three Lords but only one Lord. For just as

Christian truth compels us to acknowledge each person by himself to be God and Lord, so the Catholic religion forbids us to speak of three Gods or Lords.

The Father is neither made nor created nor begotten from anything. The Son is from the Father alone – not made nor created but begotten. The Holy Spirit is from the Father and the Son – not made nor created nor begotten but proceeding. So there is one Father, not three Fathers; one Son, not three Sons; one Holy Spirit, not three Holy Spirits. And in this trinity no one is before or after another; no one is greater or less than another, but all three persons are coeternal and coequal with each other. Thus in all things, as has been said, both trinity in unity and unity in trinity are to be worshipped. This is how to think of the Trinity if you want to be saved.

But for eternal salvation it is also necessary to believe faithfully in the incarnation of our Lord Jesus Christ. For correct faith is believing and confessing that our Lord Jesus Christ, the Son of God, is equally God and man. God he is, begotten from the Father's substance before time; man he is, born from his mother's substance in time. He is both perfect God and perfect man, composed of a rational soul and human flesh. He is equal to the Father, as God; less than the Father, as man.

Although he is both God and man, yet he is not two but one Christ. He is one however, not by the conversion of his deity into flesh, but by the taking up of his humanity into God. He is one indeed, not by confusion of substance, but by unity of person. For just as rational soul and flesh make one man, so also God and man make one Christ.

He suffered for our salvation, descended into hell, rose from the dead, ascended into the heavens and sat at the right hand of the Father. He will come from there to judge the living and the dead. When he comes, all men will rise again with their bodies and will render account for their own deeds. Those who have done good will go to eternal life, those who have done evil to eternal fire.

This is the Catholic faith. Unless one believes it faithfully and firmly, one cannot be saved.

Boethius, *The Consolation of Philosophy* (c. 525)

Anicius Manlius Severinus Boethius was born in about 480 into an aristocratic Roman family and was related to two former emperors. His father died when he was young and he was brought up by Symmachus, who later became head of the Senate. Symmachus brought Boethius up as his own son and in due course became his father-in-law and his close friend. Boethius had a first-rate education and acquired a perfect command of Greek, then a rarity in the West.

Boethius dedicated himself to a life of philosophy, seeing himself as 'schoolmaster of the West'. His great aim was to make the philosophies of Plato and Aristotle accessible to Latin westerners. He planned to translate all of Aristotle's writings, with his own explanatory commentary, and then to do the same for all of Plato's dialogues. Unfortunately, however, he managed to translate only part of Aristotle (his works on logic), and none of Plato.

Boethius might have completed his translation project had he not entered public life. In 476 the last western emperor was deposed and Rome was ruled by Gothic barbarian kings. In 510 Boethius was appointed sole consul for the year, a high honour since normally two were appointed. In 522 his two young sons were chosen as the two consuls, also a great honour for their father and the pinnacle of his worldly success. He accepted high office under the king, Theodoric, as chief of the civil service, but became the victim of a combination of political intrigue and his own indiscretion. He was convicted of treason and exiled to Pavia to await execution, which came in about 525.

Boethius's last and most famous work, written during his final imprisonment, is his *Consolation of Philosophy*. It is a short work in five books, taking the form of a dialogue between Boethius and the lady Philosophy.

● In Book 1, Boethius tells Philosophy of his misfortunes. She points him to the true nature of his problem – it is not so much that he has been banished from his home, but that he has wandered away from himself and forgotten his true nature. What concerns her is not where he is, nor even what will happen to him, but his present state of mind.

● In Book 2, Philosophy shows him the true character of Fortune and outward prosperity. The essence of Fortune is change and it is this that Boethius has learned through his sudden reversal. She seeks to show him that in Fortune he neither had nor lost anything of lasting value nor anything that truly belonged to him. 'If the things whose loss you are bemoaning were really yours, you could never have lost them' (2:2). There is nothing more precious to a person than their own self and that is something that Fortune can neither give nor take away – all else is merely transitory. That is why bad fortune is of more value than good fortune.

● In Book 3, they discuss the nature of true happiness and examine the different places that people seek it – in wealth, status, power, fame and bodily pleasures. The problem is that 'nature is satisfied with little, whereas nothing satisfies greed' (3:3). Boethius comes to recognize that true happiness is found only in God.

● In Book 4, Philosophy meets an objection raised by Boethius: how can evil exist and remain unpunished in a world ruled by a good God who is omniscient and omnipotent? Philosophy does not deny God's omnipotence. Providence, which is divine reason, is set at the head of all things and controls them and this happens according to justice, despite the apparent injustices of this life. Good people are rewarded by good fortune or disciplined by bad fortune, as Providence deems necessary. Evil people are corrected by bad fortune, while good fortune does not bring them real happiness. Thus, 'All fortune whether pleasant or adverse is meant either to reward or discipline the good or to punish or correct the bad. We agree, therefore, on the justice or usefulness of fortune, and so all fortune is good' (4:7).

● In Book 5, Philosophy reconciles God's foreknowledge with human free will. God's knowledge is to be considered 'not as a kind of foreknowledge of the future, but as the knowledge of a never ending presence' and so 'God sees all things in his eternal present' (5:6). Thus God's eternal knowledge of all my actions does not contradict my freedom of will.

Boethius's work is rightly regarded as a classic, written as it is in the immediacy of his looming execution. The prospect of losing all of the benefits of this life brings home to Boethius the value of eternity in comparison with time. There is a problem, though. Boethius's book is a work of devotional piety towards God, but there is nothing distinctively Christian in it. There is no mention of Christianity, Jesus Christ, revelation, grace, faith, forgiveness of sins or the church. The comfort that Boethius finds comes from a Neoplatonist contemplation on eternity. Why is this? Boethius was writing at a time when Christianity had been blended with Neoplatonism and the categories of Neoplatonism were widely used in theology. In expressing himself in the way that he did Boethius would not have thought of himself as writing other than as a Christian. His work can be viewed as a valuable philosophical contribution, while recognizing that the Christian faith has much more to say on the topics concerned.

1:5. And so it is not the sight of this place which gives me concern but your own appearance. It is not the walls of your library with their glass and ivory decoration that I am looking for, but the seat of your mind. That is the place where I once stored away – not my books, but – the thing that makes them have any value, the philosophy they contain. . . . In your present state of mind, while this great tumult of emotion has fallen upon you and you are torn this way and that by alternating fits of grief, wrath and anguish, it is hardly time for the more powerful remedies. I will use gentler medicines. It is as if you had become swollen and calloused under the influence of these disturbing passions, and by their more gentle action they will temper you ready to receive the strength of a sharper medicament.

2:8. Bad fortune, I think, is more use to a man than good fortune. Good fortune always seems to bring happiness, but deceives you with her smiles, whereas bad fortune is always truthful because by changing she shows her true fickleness. Good fortune deceives, but bad fortune enlightens. With her display of specious riches good fortune enslaves the minds of those who enjoy her, while bad fortune gives men release through the recognition of how fragile a thing happiness is. And so you can see Fortune in one way capricious, wayward and ever inconstant, and in another way sober, prepared and made wise by the experience of her own adversity. And lastly, by her flattery good fortune lures men away from the path of true good, but adverse fortune frequently draws men back to their true good like a shepherdess with her crook. Do you think it is of small account that this harsh and terrible misfortune has revealed those friends whose hearts are loyal to you? She has shown you the friends whose smiles were true smiles, and those whose smiles were false; in deserting you Fortune has taken her friends with her and left you those who are really yours. Had you remained untouched and, as you thought, blessed by Fortune, you would have been unable to get such knowledge at any price. So you are weeping over lost riches when you have really found the most precious of all riches – friends who are true friends.

Council of Orange, *Canons* (529)

Augustine's teaching on grace and predestination met with opposition in the south of Gaul (France), where some monks felt that too much stress on God's grace and man's inability could encourage laziness. They thought that it was important to stress what we can do and the need to get on with it. They agreed that God's help is necessary in order to live the Christian life, but also believed that we are able to make the first move on our own. When it comes to righteousness the sinner is sick, not dead, and those who are sick can take the initiative in asking the doctor for help. If we ask, it will be given to us; if we seek, we will find; if we knock, it will be opened to us. In short, their teaching can be summarized by the slogan, 'God helps those who help themselves.' This position is called Semi-Pelagianism (a term coined around 1600). The Semi-Pelagians included some of the leading figures of the day, such as John Cassian at Marseilles, who defended such views in the thirteenth of his *Conferences* (see pages 102–105).

Augustine wrote two works against the Semi-Pelagians at the end of his life: *The Predestination of the Saints* and *The Gift of Perseveranc*e. He treated them with respect as erring brethren, not as heretics. Semi-Pelagian views were common in the church before the time of Augustine and he himself had held them in his early years as a Christian. After Augustine's death, his cause was defended in Gaul by Prosper of Aquitaine. The controversy dragged on for a whole century, with different councils taking different sides. It was brought to a conclusion by the Council of Orange in 529, which was led by Caesarius of Arles with the support of the pope, Felix IV. By the tenth century, however, the canons of Orange had been forgotten and there was a revival of Semi-Pelagian views in the later Middle Ages. They were rediscovered and printed in 1538.

The council produced twenty-five canons or short doctrinal statements, followed by a conclusion. Above all else, Semi-Pelagianism is rejected, thirteen of the twenty-five canons denying that we can take the initiative in turning to God. We need 'prevenient grace' – i.e. the inner work of the Holy Spirit must precede or come before any move to God on our part. This is necessary because Adam's fall has changed the whole of human nature (body and soul) for the worse. Prevenient grace is necessary if we are to start on the Christian way and cooperating grace is necessary if we are to keep going.

The canons affirm our need for grace, but this grace is tied to the sacraments. Free will is healed by the grace of baptism. With the grace of baptism and the aid and cooperation of Jesus Christ, we have the power to do all that is necessary for salvation, if we so desire. By this time infant baptism was universal, so the teaching on grace is pushed back to a forgotten infancy. The practical emphasis lies in the baptized Christian's present ability to do all that is necessary for salvation. Finally, the council condemns, not Augustine's doctrine of predestination to salvation, but the idea of predestination to evil.

———————

Canon 1. If anyone denies that it is the whole man, that is, both body and soul, that was 'changed for the worse' through the offence of Adam's sin, but believes that the freedom of the soul remains unimpaired and that only the body is subject to corruption, he is deceived by the error of Pelagius and contradicts the Scripture which says, 'The soul that sinneth, the same shall die' [Ezekiel 18:20]; and 'Know you not, that to whom you yield yourselves servants to obey, his servants you are whom you obey?' [Romans 6:16]; and, 'For by whom a man is overcome, of the same also he is the slave' [2 Peter 2:19].

Canon 4. If anyone maintains that God awaits our will to be cleansed from sin, but does not confess that even our will to be cleansed comes to us through the infusion and working of the Holy Spirit, he resists the Holy Spirit himself who says through Solomon, 'The will is prepared by the Lord' [Proverbs 8:35, in the Septuagint translation] and the salutary word of the Apostle, 'It is God who worketh in you both to will and to accomplish' [Philippians 2:13].

Canon 10. The succour of God is ever to be sought by the regenerate and converted also [i.e. as well as the unconverted], so that they may be able to come to a successful end or persevere in good works.

Canon 12. God loves us for what we shall be by his gift, and not by our own deserving.

Canon 13. The freedom of will that was destroyed in the first man can be restored only by the grace of baptism, for what is lost can be returned only by the one who was able to give it. Hence the Truth itself declares: 'If the Son makes you free, you will be free indeed' [John 8:36].

Canon 18. Recompense is due to good works, if they are performed; but grace, to which we have no claim, precedes them, to enable them to be done.

Canon 20. God does much that is good in a man that the man does not do; but a man does nothing good for which God is not responsible, so as to let him do it.

Conclusion. And thus according to the passages of Holy Scripture quoted above or the interpretations of the ancient Fathers we must, under the blessing of God, preach and believe as follows. The sin of the first man has so impaired and weakened free will that no one thereafter can either love God as he ought or believe in God or do good for God's sake, unless the grace of divine mercy has preceded him. . . . There are innumerable passages of Holy Scripture which can be quoted to prove the case for grace, but they have been omitted for the sake of brevity, because further examples will not really be of use where few are deemed insufficient.

According to the Catholic faith we also believe that after grace has been received through baptism, all baptized persons have the ability and responsibility, if they desire to labour faithfully, to perform with the aid and cooperation of Christ what is of essential importance in regard to the salvation of their soul. We not only do not believe that any are foreordained to evil by the power of God, but even state with utter abhorrence that if there are those who want to believe so evil a thing, they are anathema. We also believe and confess to our benefit that in every good work it is not we who take the initiative and are then assisted through the mercy of God, but God himself first inspires in us both faith in him and love for him without any previous good works of our own that deserve reward, so that we may both faithfully seek the sacrament of baptism, and after baptism be able by his help to do what is pleasing to him. We must therefore most evidently believe that the praiseworthy faith of the thief whom the Lord called to his home in paradise, and of Cornelius the centurion, to whom the angel of the Lord was sent, and of Zacchaeus, who was worthy to receive the Lord himself, was not a natural endowment but a gift of God's kindness.

The Rule of Benedict (post-530)

The only original account of the life of Benedict is found in the *Dialogues* of Pope Gregory I. Benedict was born in about 480 at Nursia in central Italy. As a student he went to Rome, but was disgusted by its low moral standards. He therefore withdrew from the world in about 500, becoming a hermit in a cave at Subiaco. In due course others came to join him and he founded a number of small monasteries in the area. In about 529 local tensions forced him to leave and he moved with some of his disciples to Monte Cassino, where he founded a monastery. He remained there until his death in the middle of the century.

Benedict is remembered primarily for his *Rule* for the monastic life. For this he drew heavily on the work of his predecessors (such as Basil the Great and John Cassian) and, especially, on an earlier *Rule of the Master*, from which he copied extensively. But this is not to deny Benedict's originality. He set his own mark on his sources and created a distinctive work of great genius – one of the most influential documents in European history. Initially it was not widely used, but in the eighth century Benedict of Aniane helped to increase its influence. In 817 a synod at Aachen, the capital of Charlemagne's empire, made *The Rule of Benedict* the official rule for all monks. But while it came to be accepted everywhere, it was not the sole rule. Monasticism at this time drew on other sources of inspiration. Cassiodore, who was a disciple of Boethius and founder of a monastery at Vivarium, was also influential, viewing the monastery as a centre of learning.

Benedict's *Rule* combines brevity with completeness in that it covers a wide range of eventualities in a short space. It is a mixture of clarity and explicitness with a lack of rigidity – it is a very flexible document when it comes to application. Benedict adopted a policy of mildness. This is a rule which can be kept by beginners, not a goal for veterans to aim at. The monastery is seen as a family, with the abbot as father. Asceticism is to be moderate. The monk's life was comparable to that of the contemporary peasant. Provision is made for human weakness and frailty. Benedict was realistic when it came to the standards to be anticipated – a whole chapter is devoted to telling the monks not to strike one another.

Central to the *Rule* is obedience. The monk was not seen as especially poor – in fact provision is made for giving the monks' cast-off clothes to the poor. But the monk is someone who has submitted himself to obedience – to Christ, to the *Rule* and to the abbot, whose commands are to be obeyed as if from God himself. This obedience is the first step to humility. It is to be an obedience from the heart – without delay, coldness, grumbling or reluctance. The *Rule* is famous especially for the chapter on the twelve steps of humility. Bernard of Clairvaux picked up on this, taking it as the basis for his *The Steps of Humility and Pride* (see pages 150–53).

There were three main occupations for the monk: manual work (which was often dropped in medieval monasticism); 'divine reading' (reading and meditation on the Bible and other spiritual works, such as Basil's *Rules* [see pages 70–72] and Cassian's *Conferences* [see pages 102–105], which he names); and the 'work of God' (liturgical worship). The monks were to worship seven times daily, in accordance with Psalm 119:164.

A striking tribute to the *Rule* came from the modern evangelical leader David Watson, who noted that many of the problems faced by communities in the church today 'could have been avoided if the remarkably wise sixth-century *Rule of Benedict* had been known or followed more closely'.

Prologue. Listen, my son, to the precepts of your master and take them to heart. Willingly receive and faithfully fulfil the admonition of your loving father. By the work of obedience you will return to [God] from whom you departed through the laziness of disobedience. . . . If we want to escape the pains of hell and arrive at eternal life we must hasten to do now what will profit us in eternity, while there is yet time, while we are still in the flesh and are able to fulfil all these things by the light given us. Our aim therefore is to establish a school of the Lord's service. In setting it up we hope to order nothing harsh or rigorous. But if, following sound reason, anything has been laid down rather strictly in order to amend vices or preserve love, do not therefore be frightened away from the path of salvation, which has to be narrow and difficult at the beginning.

Chapter 7. Holy Scripture cries out to us, brethren, 'Everyone who exalts himself shall be humbled and he who humbles himself shall be exalted' [Luke 14:11]. It thus teaches us that all exaltation is a kind of pride against which the prophet showed himself to be on guard when he said, 'Lord, my heart is not exalted nor my eyes lifted up; nor have I aspired to great things, nor things too wonderful for me.' Why? 'If I did not think humbly but exalted my soul, you would have driven my soul away like a weaned child from its mother' [Psalm 131:1–2]. So, brethren, if we wish to arrive at the peak of humility and speedily reach that heavenly exaltation, to which we rise through the humility of this present life, we must ascend by our works and erect a ladder like that which Jacob saw in his dream, on which he saw angels descending and ascending. This descent and ascent signify that we descend by exalting ourselves and ascend by our humility. The ladder which we thus erect is our life in this world, which the Lord lifts up to heaven if our heart be humbled. The sides of the ladder are our body and soul, in which our divine calling has placed various steps of humility or discipline for us to ascend.

The first step of humility is for a man always to keep the fear of God before his eyes, avoiding all forgetfulness. He should always remember what God has commanded and that those who despise God will burn in hell for their sins while eternal life is prepared for those who fear him. He should uproot carnal lusts, keeping himself always from sin and vice, whether of thought, speech, vision, deed or will. . . .

The second step of humility is for a man to love not his own will nor delight in fulfilling his own desires, but carry out in his deeds that saying of the Lord, 'I came not to do my own will but the will of him who sent me' [John 6:38]. . . .

The third step of humility is for a man, for the love of God, to submit himself to his superior in all obedience, imitating the Lord of whom the apostle said, 'He was made obedient even unto death' [Philippians 2:8].

The fourth step of humility is for him, if in the course of this obedience he meets with hardship, contradiction or even injury, to embrace them patiently, with a quiet conscience and not grow weary or give in, as the Scripture says, 'He who perseveres to the end shall be saved' [Matthew 24:13]. . . .

The fifth step of humility is not to hide from the abbot any of the evil thoughts that beset one's heart nor those sins committed in secret, but humbly to confess them. Concerning this, Scripture thus exhorts us, 'Make your ways known to the Lord and hope in him' [Psalm 37:5] and again, 'Confess to the Lord, for he is good and his mercy endures for ever' [Psalm 106:1]. . . .

The sixth step of humility is for a monk to be contented with the meanest and worst of everything and in all that is commanded him to reckon himself a bad and worthless labourer, saying with the prophet, 'I was senseless and didn't know it; I was a beast before you. Yet I am always with you' [Psalm 73:22–23].

The seventh step of humility is for him not only with his tongue to call himself lower and viler than all but also to believe it in his heart, humbling himself and saying with the prophet, 'I am a worm and no man, scorned by men and despised by the people' [Psalm 22:6], 'I have been exalted and cast down and confounded' [Psalm 88:15, in the Septuagint translation]. And again, 'It is good for me that you humbled me, so that I may learn your commands' [Psalm 119:71].

The eighth step of humility is for a monk to do nothing not authorized by the common rule of the monastery or the example of his seniors.

The ninth step of humility is for a monk to refrain his tongue from speaking, keeping silent until asked a question, as the Scripture shows, 'Where words are many, sin is not absent' [Proverbs 10:19] and 'The talkative shall not be directed upon the earth' [Psalm 140:11].

The tenth step of humility is for him not to laugh easily or quickly, because it is written, 'The fool lifts up his voice in laughter' [Ecclesiasticus 21:20].

The eleventh step of humility is for a monk when he speaks to do so gently, without laughter, humbly, gravely. His words should be few and reasonable and he should not raise his voice, as it is written, 'The wise man is known by the fewness of his words' [*Sentences of Sixtus*].

The twelfth step of humility is for the monk always to show his humility to all that see him, not just in his heart but in his outward behaviour, i.e. in the work of God, in the oratory, in the monastery, in the garden, on the road, in the field or wherever he may be. Sitting walking or standing, he should always keep his head bowed down and his eyes fixed on the earth and should always think of the guilt of his sins and imagine himself already present before the terrible judgment seat of God. He should always say in his heart what the publican in the Gospel said with his eyes cast down, 'Lord, I a sinner am not worthy to raise my eyes to heaven' [Luke 18:13]. And again with the prophet, 'I am bowed down and humbled on every side' [Psalm 119:107, in the Septuagint translation].

Chapter 73. We have written this rule so that, by keeping it in the monasteries, we may show ourselves to have some virtue and a beginning of holiness. Those who wish to press on to a perfect life should read the teaching of the holy fathers. . . . Whoever you are, then, that hastens to the heavenly country, keep, with the help of Christ, this little rule for beginners. Eventually, with God's protection, you will arrive at the lofty heights of doctrine and virtue which we have described above.

Gregory the Great, *Pastoral Rule*
(590–604)

Gregory was born in 540 at Rome. He came from a godly and aristocratic family, his great-great-grandfather being Pope Felix III. In 572 or 573 he was appointed Prefect of the City of Rome, a high post for one so young. Soon afterwards, his father died. Gregory then founded six monasteries on the family estates in Sicily and one at Rome, overlooking the Colosseum. The last he entered himself, as an ordinary monk. But before long he was appointed one of the seven Roman deacons by the pope, who then sent him for five years (about 578–83) as his representative to Constantinople. This time in the East convinced Gregory that the papacy needed to pursue a policy more independent of the eastern emperors, from whom he saw little prospect of practical help for the West. On his return to Rome he resumed his monastic life. In 590 the pope died and Gregory was elected to succeed him, the first monk to occupy that post. He accepted only with genuine reluctance but then threw himself with fervour into the task. He is known as Gregory the Great and is one of the few popes to be both a great leader and a genuinely saintly figure. He died in 604. He is seen as the last of the four Doctors of the Latin Church, together with Ambrose, Jerome and Augustine.

Gregory was an able administrator and extended the power of the papacy in the West. He assumed some of the tasks previously exercised by the eastern emperor, a move which in the long term led to the papacy ruling the papal states in central Italy. He is remembered for his concern for the English ('not Angles but angels') and it was Gregory who, in 596, sent Augustine to England to become the first archbishop of Canterbury. This was described by Bede in his *A History of the English Church and People* (see pages 137–39). He also gave his name to the 'Gregorian chant' but his role in it was minimal.

Gregory wrote extensively, though some of his works have been lost. Four writings are worthy of special mention.

● *Letters*. Some 850 of Gregory's letters survive. These tell us a lot about both Gregory himself and his times.

● *Dialogues*. These contain the life and miracles of Benedict and other Latin saints. Gregory is often accused of not being able to distinguish between fact and legend. He mentions Benedict's *Rule* (see pages 124–27) but there is no evidence that it was adopted by his own monastery.

● *Book of Morals* or *Exposition of Job*. This is the longest of Gregory's works, in which he expounds Job in three different ways, giving the historical meaning, the allegorical meaning (interpreting it in terms of Jesus Christ and his church) and the moral or ethical meaning. Gregory also wrote homilies on Ezekiel and the Gospels.

● *Pastoral Rule*. This was Gregory's greatest work and became the textbook for the medieval bishop. Like Chrysostom's *The Priesthood* (see pages 80–83), this sets out to guide the pastor, 'since the rule of souls is the art of arts' (1:1). The work is divided into four books of very uneven length. The first, brief, book explains how one becomes a pastor, lest some decline the responsibility through excessive humility. The second book explains how the pastor should live, lest his life undermine his ministry. The third book, which occupies almost two thirds of the whole, gives thirty-six admonitions to the pastor and preacher. These concern especially the need to handle each individual differently according to their station in life, their gender, their spiritual and moral condition, etc. The final, extremely brief, book reminds pastors of the need to maintain their own spiritual life, lest they lapse into the sin of presumption. While some things in this work are specific to Gregory's context, most of what he teaches is sound practical wisdom that is of value to the pastor in any generation.

1:9. Those who did not cease to be proud while occupying a low position will not be able to learn humility in a high one; those who learned to pant for praise when it was lacking will not know how to fly from it when it abounds; those whose own means do not suffice for themselves will not be able to overcome greed when entrusted with funds for many. . . . It is generally true that the practice of good deeds which was maintained in tranquillity is lost in the pressures of ruling – just as even an unskilful person can steer a ship along a straight course in a calm sea, but in a storm even the skilled sailor is defeated.

2:6. Supreme rule is well-ordered when he who presides lords it over vices rather than over his brethren. When superiors correct their delinquent subordinates, punishing faults with due discipline as appropriate to their authority, they must take care humbly to acknowledge that they are on the same level as the very brethren they are correcting – indeed in our silent thought it is proper even to prefer the brethren whom we correct to ourselves. For their vices are disciplined by us but our own sins are not even corrected by a word of rebuke. . . . So we should maintain humility in the heart and discipline in action. . . . Let rulers act outwardly for the benefit of others and inwardly remain fearful in their estimate of themselves. They should also let even their subjects perceive their inward humility, by appropriate outward signs, so that they will both see something to be afraid of in their authority and acknowledge something to imitate with respect to their humility. So those in command should always take care that to the extent that their power is seen to be great outwardly it should be kept down within themselves inwardly. It must not conquer their thought to the point that the heart is carried away to delight in it, for fear that the mind become unable to control that to which it submits itself in lust of domination.

3:Prologue. Now that we have shown what sort of man the pastor should be, let us explain how he should teach. For, as Gregory of Nazianzus taught long ago, the same exhortation does not suit everyone since all do not have the same character. What profits some people often hurts others – just as herbs which nourish some animals are fatal to others; the gentle hissing that quietens horses incites puppies; the medicine which cures one disease aggravates another; and food which strengthens the strong kills little children. Teachers should craft their sermons according to the condition of their hearers, so as to meet the different needs of each and every one, while never deviating from the art of edifying all. For the intent minds of the hearers can be compared to the various strings in a harp, which the skilful player strikes differently in order to produce a harmonious sound. The strings respond with a consonant modulation, being struck with the same quill but with different kinds of stroke. So also every teacher should touch the hearts of his hearers drawing on a single set of beliefs, but not using the same exhortation for each one in order that he may edify them all in the one virtue of charity.

3:1. Admonition 2. The young and the old are to be admonished differently; because the former are usually directed to improvement by severe rebuke, while kind remonstrance disposes the latter to better deeds. For it is written, 'Rebuke not an elder, but entreat him as a father' [1 Timothy 5:1].

3:3. Admonition 4. The joyful and the sad are to be admonished differently. The sad consequences of punishment are to be set before the joyful; but before the sad the promised glad things of the kingdom. Let the joyful learn by the bitterness of threat what to fear; let the sad hear what joys of reward they may look forward to.

3:7. Admonition 8. The impudent and the bashful are to be admonished differently. Nothing but hard rebuke restrains the former from the vice of impudence; while a modest exhortation usually disposes the latter to amendment.

3:8. Admonition 9. The forward and the faint-hearted are to be admonished differently. For the former presume on themselves too much and disdain all who reprove them; but the latter are too conscious of their own weakness and usually fall into despondency.

3:17. Admonition 18. The humble and the haughty are to be admonished differently. . . . Let the humble hear how eternal are the things that they long for, how transitory the things which they despise; let the haughty hear how transitory are the things they court, how eternal the things they lose. . . . Let the humble, then, be told that, when they abase themselves, they ascend to the likeness of God; let the haughty be told that, when they exalt themselves, they fall into imitation of the apostate angel [Satan]. . . . There is, however, another point to be carefully considered in these cases – some are often deceived by a false show of humility, while others are beguiled by ignorance of their own haughtiness. For commonly some who think themselves humble are led by fear of other people; while speaking freely commonly goes with being haughty. When any vices need to be rebuked, the former hold their peace out of fear, but imagine that they are being silent out of humility; the latter speak in the impatience of haughtiness, yet believe themselves to be speaking in the freedom of uprightness. The one group are held back by timidity, under a show of humility, from rebuking what is wrong; the other group are impelled by the unbridled impetuosity of pride, under the semblance of freedom, to rebuke things they ought not, or to rebuke them more than they ought. Therefore the haughty are to be warned not to be freer than is becoming, and the humble are to be warned not to be more submissive than is right – lest either the former turn the defence of righteousness into a display of pride, or the latter, while studying more than necessary to submit themselves to men, be driven even to pay respect to their vices.

3:40. Every preacher should give forth a sound more by deeds than by words, and rather by his good life make footprints for others to follow than by his words show them the way to walk. . . . Those who utter words of holy preaching should first be wide awake in the zeal of living well, lest they rouse others with their voice while themselves being apathetic in performance. . . . They should first punish their own faults by mourning them, before denouncing others for things worthy of punishment. Before exhorting others with words they should proclaim by their own deeds all that they are about to teach.

Maximus the Confessor,
Four Hundred Chapters on Love (pre-662)

Maximus was born in about 580 into a wealthy Christian family. He became chief secretary to the emperor at Constantinople, but in about 614 renounced his secular career to become a monk, soon rising to become abbot. In 626 he fled from a Persian invasion to North Africa, spending about twenty years in a Byzantine monastery at Carthage.

Maximus is best known for his teaching on the person of Jesus Christ. In the seventh century there was controversy over whether Jesus had a single will or two wills, human and divine. The former view was advocated by the Eastern Church and, for a time, by Rome. Maximus opposed it, being a firm believer in the two wills of Christ. He was captured and brought back to Constantinople where pressure was brought to bear upon him. He was twice exiled and it is said that his tongue and right hand were cut off. He died in 662, exiled in Georgia. He is called 'the Confessor' because he suffered for the truth. His beliefs triumphed at the Council of Constantinople in 680–81.

Maximus was the most significant Orthodox theologian of the seventh century. Indeed, he has been called 'the real father of Byzantine theology'. He wrote some ninety works on a wide range of topics, including influential commentaries on pseudo-Dionysius, an early sixth-century Syrian monk who claimed to be Paul's disciple Dionysius the Areopagite (Acts 17:34).

Maximus is also renowned as a mystical teacher. He drew together the earlier teaching of Evagrius (a fourth-century disciple of Origen) and pseudo-Dionysius. Their teaching was corrected in the light of Gregory of Nazianzus and Gregory of Nyssa, thus curbing some of the imbalance of each of them. The goal of the life of prayer is the vision of God. Here Maximus anticipates the distinction, later made by Gregory Palamas, between God's essence and his energies.

One of his best-known spiritual writings was his *Four Hundred Chapters on Love*. This was a collection of brief sayings arranged in four (the number of the Gospels) sets of one hundred (a sacred number) sayings. Maximus modestly claimed no originality, having gleaned them from the Fathers, but he summarized their teaching in his own words. Rather like the book of Proverbs, each saying is free-standing but sometimes related sayings are grouped together.

In common with most of early monasticism, Maximus is excessively negative about the body and about human feelings. Thus self-love is described as 'the passion for the body' (2:8). But at the same time he is careful to teach that it is not God's creation itself that is at fault, but our misuse of it (3:4, 4:66), a point which remains highly relevant. There is much in this work which is as applicable today as when it was first written.

1:26. The disposition of love is made manifest not only in the sharing of money but much more in sharing the word of God and physical service.

1:31. As the memory of fire does not warm the body, so faith without love does not bring about the illumination of knowledge in the soul.

1:63. We carry along with us the voluptuous images of the things we once experienced. Now the one who overcomes these voluptuous images completely disdains the realities of which they are images. In fact, the battle against memories is more difficult than the battle against deeds, as sinning in thought is easier than sinning in deed.

1:81. The fear of the Lord is twofold. The first type is produced in us from threats of punishment, and from it arise in proper order self-control, patience, hope in God, and detachment, from which comes love. The second is coupled with love itself and constantly produces reverence in the soul, lest through the familiarity of love it become presumptuous of God.

1:82. Perfect love casts out the first fear from the soul which by possessing it no longer fears punishment. The second fear it has always joined to it, as was said.

2:8. The one who throws off self-love, the mother of the passions, will very easily with God's help put aside the others, such as anger, grief, grudges, and so on. But whoever is under the control of the former is wounded, even though unwillingly, by the latter. Self-love is the passion for the body.

2:9. On account of these five reasons men love one another whether to their praise or blame: for God's sake, as when the virtuous person loves everyone and the one not yet virtuous loves the virtuous person; or for natural reasons, as parents love their children and vice versa; or out of vainglory, as the one who is honoured loves the one who honours him; or for greed, as the one who loves a rich man for what he can get; or for the love of pleasure, as the one who is a servant of his belly or genitals. The first of these is praiseworthy, the second is neutral, and the rest belong to the passions.

2:37. When you hear the Scripture saying, 'You will render to each one according to his works' [Psalm 62:12], know that God will reward good works but not those done apart from a right intention even if they appear good, but precisely those done with a right intention. For God's judgment looks not on what is done but to the intention behind it.

2:43. So long as you have evil habits, do not refuse to undergo hardships, so that you may be humbled by them and vomit out pride.

2:59. Keep yourself away from self-love, the mother of vices, which is the irrational love of the body. For from it surely arise the first three passionate and capital thoughts, gluttony, greed, and vainglory, which have their starting point in the seemingly necessary demands of the body and from which the whole catalogue of vices comes about. Therefore, as was said, one must necessarily keep away from and do battle with this self-love with full determination, for when this is overcome then are all its offspring likewise brought into line.

2:60. The passion of self-love suggests to the monk that he should be kind to the body and to indulge in food more than is appropriate. Thus under the pretence of proper guidance it means to drag him little by little to fall into the pit of voluptuousness. To the worldly person it proposes that he make provision for himself right away in the matter of lust.

2:72. As much as it is easier to sin in thought than in deed, so is a war with thoughts more exacting than one with things.

2:81. For these five reasons will the soul abstain from sin: the fear of men, the fear of judgment, the future reward, the love of God, or finally the prompting of conscience.

2:87. There are three general moral states among monks. The first is not to sin in deed, the second is not to dally over passionate thoughts in the soul, and the third is to look with a detached mind on the forms of women or of those who have offended us.

2:89. Some owners have possessions without attachment, and thus do not grieve when they are deprived of them, as those who accepted with joy the seizure of their goods [Hebrews 10:34]. But others possess with attachment and become filled with grief when about to be deprived, like the one in the Gospel who went away sad [Matthew 19:22]; and if they are deprived, they grieve until death. So it is that deprivation attests the condition of whether one is detached or attached.

3:4. It is not food which is evil but gluttony, not the begetting of children but fornication, not possessions but greed, not reputation but vainglory. And if this is so, there is nothing evil in creatures except misuse, which stems from the mind's negligence in its natural cultivation.

3:7. Excessive and sumptuous eating are causes of intemperance; greed and vainglory cause hatred of neighbour. But their mother, self-love, is the cause of both.

3:13. If you want to prevail over your thoughts, take care of your passions and you will easily drive them from your mind. Thus for fornication, fast, keep vigil, work hard, keep to yourself. For anger and hurt, disdain reputation and dishonour and material things. For grudges, pray for the one who has hurt you and you will be rid of them.

3:14. Do not compare yourself to weaker men, but rather reach out to the commandment of love. For by comparing yourself to these you fall into the pit of conceit; in reaching out for the latter you advance to the heights of humility.

3:48. In everything that we do God looks at the intention, as has frequently been said, whether we do it for him or for any other motive. Therefore when we wish to do something good, let us not have human applause in view but rather God, so that always looking to him we might do everything on his account; otherwise we shall undergo the labour and still lose the reward.

3:71. The blameworthy passion of love engrosses the mind in material things. The praiseworthy passion of love binds it even to divine things. For generally where the mind devotes its time it also expands, and where it expands it also turns its desire and love, whether this be in divine and intelligible things which are its own or in the things of the flesh and the passions.

3:74. There is not just one reason why sinners commit the same sin in deed, but several. For instance, it is one thing to sin from habit and another to sin by being carried away. In this case the sinner did not fully reflect either before or after the sin but rather was deeply grieved over the incident. The one who sins from habit is quite the reverse, for first he does not cease sinning in thought and after the act he maintains the same disposition.

4:7. God, along with divine realities, is in one sense knowable and in another sense unknowable: knowable in ideas about him, unknowable in himself.

4:40. Love of God is always fond of flying off to hold converse with him; love of neighbour prepares the mind to think always well of him.

4:59. Since 'knowledge makes boastful but love edifies' [1 Corinthians 8:1], link up love with knowledge and you will not be puffed up but rather a spiritual architect building up yourself and all those around you.

4:66. Scripture takes away none of the things given by God for our use but it restrains immoderation and corrects unreasonableness. For example, it does not forbid eating or begetting children or having money or managing it, but it does forbid gluttony, fornication, and so forth. Nor does it even forbid us to think of these things, for they were made to be thought of; what it forbids is thinking of them with passion.

4:94. Friends are abundant – that is, in times of prosperity. In time of trial you can barely find one.

4:99. 'A faithful friend is a strong defence' [Ecclesiasticus 6:14], for when his friend is prospering he is a good counsellor and and sympathetic collaborator, and when he is in distress he is his sincerest supporter and most sympathetic defender.

Bede, *A History of the English Church and People* (731)

Bede was born in around AD 673 at Wearmouth in the north-east of England. Soon after, the king gave lands to Benedict Biscop so that he could found the new monastery of St Peter. Bede's parents entrusted him to the care of Benedict when he was seven and soon after he was entrusted to the care of the first abbot of the newly founded daughter house of St Paul at Jarrow. There Bede remained as a monk until his death in 735. He was ordained deacon at the age of nineteen and priest at the age of thirty. He rarely travelled out of the immediate locality.

Bede wrote a number of books, mostly expositions of passages of Scripture, but his fame rests primarily on one work, his *History of the English Church and People*, which is divided into five books. This starts with the earliest known history of the island, including the Roman invasions of Julius Caesar and Claudius and the account of the martyrdom of St Alban. But the bulk of the narrative concerns the period from 596, when Pope Gregory the Great sent Augustine to evangelize England, to 731, the time of writing. Bede is rightly known as the 'Father of English History' and he gives an invaluable account of an otherwise little known, but foundational, period of English history. Much that is described explains why this period has been called the 'Dark Ages' but there are also moving accounts of the heroism of those who made great sacrifices to establish the gospel in England.

There had been a church in Roman Britain but after the withdrawal of the legions in the fifth century England was overrun by pagan tribes. Much of Bede's narrative is about the reconversion of England during the seventh century especially. Pride of place is given to Augustine, who was sent from Rome in 596 (1:23–33, 2:2–3). There is also a full account of the mission of Columba, who came to Scotland from Ireland and founded a monastery at Iona (3:4), and Aidan who took the gospel from there to northern England, founding the monastery at Lindisfarne off the coast of Northumbria.

In due time there was a clash between the older Celtic Christianity in the north and the newly reintroduced Roman Christianity in the south, which was to generate some heat. The issues concerned seem very trivial today. The major difference was the fact that the two churches calculated the date of Easter differently – which could cause some practical inconvenience when the two practices clashed in the same place. Another point of controversy was the different shape of the tonsure or shaved patch on the head worn by the clergy. Both of these were serious issues for Bede and he devotes his longest chapter (5:21) to explaining why the Roman way was right. Underlying both of these questions was the issue of authority and, in particular, the authority of Rome. The matter was finally resolved at the Synod of Whitby in 664 where the Celtic churches gave way (3:25). The clinching argument came from Wilfrid, who had spent some time on the Continent, as described in the extract below (3:25).

2:1. One day some merchants who had recently arrived in Rome displayed their many wares in the marketplace. Among the crowd who thronged to buy was Gregory, who saw among other merchandise some boys exposed for sale. These had fair complexions, fine-cut features, and beautiful hair. Looking at them with interest, he enquired from what country and what part of the world they came. 'They come from the island of Britain,' he was told, 'where all the people have this appearance.' He then asked whether the islanders were Christians, or whether they were still ignorant heathens. 'They are pagans,' he was informed. 'Alas!' said Gregory with a heartfelt sigh: 'how sad that such bright-faced folk are still in the grasp of the Author of darkness, and that such graceful features conceal minds void of God's grace! What is the name of this race?' 'They are called Angles,' he was told. 'That is appropriate,' he said, 'for they have angelic faces, and it is right that they should become joint-heirs with the angels in heaven.' . . .

Approaching the Pope of the apostolic Roman see – for he was not yet Pope himself – Gregory begged him to send preachers of the word to the English people in Britain to convert them to Christ, and declared his own eagerness to attempt the task should the Pope see fit to direct it. This permission was not forthcoming, for although the Pope himself was willing, the citizens of Rome would not allow Gregory to go so far away from the city. But directly Gregory succeeded to the Papacy himself, he put in hand this long cherished project. He sent other missionaries in his place; but it was his prayers and encouragement that made their mission fruitful.

2:13. [King Edwin of Northumbria is deciding whether or not to turn from paganism to Christianity.] He summoned a council of the wise men, and asked each in turn his opinion of this strange doctrine and this new way of worshipping the godhead that was being proclaimed to them.

Coifi, the Chief Priest, replied without hesitation: 'Your Majesty, let us give careful consideration to this new teaching; for I frankly admit that, in my experience, the religion that we have hitherto professed seems valueless and powerless. . . . If on examination you perceive that these new teachings are better and more effectual, let us not hesitate to accept them.'

Another of the king's chief men signified his agreement with this prudent argument, and went on to say: 'Your Majesty, when we compare the present life of man on earth with that time of which we have no knowledge, it seems to me like the swift flight of a single sparrow through the banqueting-hall where you are sitting at dinner on a winter's day with your thanes and counsellors. In the midst there is a comforting fire to warm the hall; outside the storms of winter rain or snow are raging. This sparrow flies swiftly in through one door of the hall, and out through another. While he is inside, he is safe from the winter storms; but after a few moments of comfort, he vanishes from sight into the wintry world from which he came. Even so, man appears on earth for a little while; but of what went before this life or of what follows, we know nothing. Therefore, if this new teaching has brought any more certain knowledge, it seems only right that we should follow it.' The other elders and counsellors of the king, under God's guidance, gave similar advice.

. . . And when [the king] asked the Chief Priest who should be the first to profane the altars and shrines of the idols, together with the enclosures that surrounded them, Coifi replied: 'I will do this myself; for now that the true God has granted me knowledge, who more suitably than I can set up a public example and destroy the idols that I worshipped in ignorance?'

3:25. [Wilfrid concedes that Columba and earlier Celtic saints were innocent, being sincere though misguided.] '. . . You and your colleagues are most certainly guilty of sin if you reject the decrees of the Apostolic See, indeed of the universal church, which are confirmed by Holy Writ. For, although your Fathers were holy men, do you imagine that they, a few men in a corner of a remote island, are to be preferred before the universal church of Christ throughout the world? And even if your Columba – or, may I say, ours also if he was the servant of Christ – was a Saint potent in miracles, can he take precedence before the most blessed Prince of the Apostles, to whom our Lord said: "Thou art Peter, and upon this rock I will build my church, and the gates of hell shall not prevail against it, and I will give unto thee the keys of the kingdom of heaven" [Matthew 16:18–19]?'

[The king of Northumbria then ascertained that this had indeed been said to Peter and that no similar authority had been given to Columba.] 'Then, I tell you, Peter is guardian of the gates of heaven, and I shall not contradict him. I shall obey his commands in everything to the best of my knowledge and ability; otherwise, when I come to the gates of heaven, there may be no one to open them, because he who holds the keys has turned away.'

John of Damascus,
The Orthodox Faith (pre-750)

John Mansour was born in the third quarter of the seventh century, at Damascus. Syria was by then under Muslim rule and John followed his father in working for the Muslim caliph. He later left this work and became a monk in the monastery of Mar Saba, where his cell remains to this day. He died in the middle of the eighth century. John is often called the last of the Greek Fathers. His main achievement was to gather together the earlier teaching of the Fathers into a systematic manual. This was how he himself saw his aim:

> *Like a bee I shall gather all that conforms to the truth, even deriving help from the writings of our enemies. . . . I am not offering you my own conclusions, but those which were laboriously arrived at by the most eminent theologians, while I have merely collected them and summarized them, as far as was possible, into one treatise. (Dialectic, Prologue)*

This comes at the beginning of his most famous work, his *Fount of Knowledge*, which is divided into three parts:

● *Dialectic* or *Philosophical Chapters*: a discussion of philosophical terms and concepts, especially those used in formulating the doctrines of the Trinity and the person of Jesus Christ.

● *Heresies in Epitome*: a brief summary of 103 heresies, drawing heavily on the earlier works of Epiphanius and Theodoret. Interestingly, Islam is listed as a heresy, not yet being seen as distinct religion.

● *Exact Exposition of the Orthodox Faith* (usually referred to simply as *The Orthodox Faith*): a systematic summary of the teaching of the Greek Fathers in a hundred chapters (later divided into four books). This concentrates especially on the doctrines of the Trinity and the person of Jesus Christ. On the Trinity, he expounds the teaching of the Cappadocian Fathers, supplemented by an important seventh-century work, *The Holy Trinity*, falsely attributed to Cyril of Alexandria. On the person of Jesus Christ he expounds the teaching of *The Definition of Chalcedon* (see pages 113–14), supplemented by Maximus the Confessor. He begins (as in the extract below) by raising the question of whether God can be known. Like Gregory of Nazianzus in his *Theological Orations* (see pages 73–76), he points to both the reality and the limitations of our knowledge of God.

John also took part in the Iconoclast Controversy, which plagued the Eastern Church for over a hundred years. Icons are pictures of Jesus Christ and the saints which had become widespread in the Orthodox Church and were venerated: that is, people would bow down before them, kiss them and pray to them. In the eighth century there was a reaction against icons by the iconoclasts (destroyers of icons). The first steps were taken in 719 or 720 by a Muslim ruler, Islam being completely opposed to such images. A few years later the cause was taken up by the Byzantine emperor Leo III who ordered the destruction of all icons. This provoked fierce opposition from the iconodules (worshippers of icons), including John who wrote three *Orations in Defence of Sacred Images*. In 754 a council was held at Hieria which upheld the iconoclast position and anathematized John. Some years later an iconodule Council of Nicea was held, in 787, which came to be seen as the seventh ecumenical council, at which John's views prevailed.

John also wrote the first known refutation of Islam in Greek. Parts of the *Fount of Knowledge* were translated into Latin in the twelfth and thirteenth centuries and Thomas Aquinas drew upon it for his *The Sum of Theology* (see pages 172–76).

———————

1:1. 'No one has seen God at any time but the only-begotten Son, who is in the bosom of the Father, has made him known' [John 1:18]. The deity, therefore, is ineffable and incomprehensible. 'For no one knows the Father except the Son, nor the Son except the Father' [Matthew 11:27]. The Holy Spirit also knows the things of God as the spirit of a man knows the things that are in him [1 Corinthians 2:11]. Moreover, after the first and blessed nature no one, whether human, angelic, Cherubim or Seraphim, has ever known God, except those to whom he has revealed himself.

God, however, did not leave us in complete ignorance. He has implanted the knowledge of his existence in all by nature. The creation also, its maintenance and government, proclaim the majesty of the divine nature. Moreover, God disclosed to us the knowledge of himself so far as was possible for us, in former times by the Law and the Prophets and afterwards by his only-begotten Son, our Lord, God and Saviour Jesus Christ. We therefore receive, know and honour all that has been delivered to us by Law and Prophets and by Apostles and Evangelists, and seek for nothing beyond these. For God, being good, is the cause of all good, subject neither to envy nor to any passion. Envy is far removed from the divine nature, which is both impassible and purely good. Knowing all things, therefore, and providing for each what is profitable for them, he revealed what it was profitable for us to know but kept secret what we were unable to bear. Let us be satisfied with these things and abide by them, neither removing everlasting boundaries nor transgressing the divine tradition.

1:2. Anyone who wishes to speak or hear of God needs to understand clearly that in the doctrines of God and of the incarnation alike, neither everything nor nothing can be expressed in words; neither everything nor nothing can be known. Things that can be known belong to one group and things that can be expressed in words to another – just as it is one thing to speak and another thing to know. Many of the things of God, therefore, that are dimly understood cannot be put into suitable words. But with things above us we can do no other than express ourselves according to our limited capacity. So, for example, we use terms like sleep, wrath, indifference, hands, feet, and such expressions when speaking of God.

We, therefore, both know and confess the following points: God is without beginning, without end, eternal and everlasting, uncreated, unchangeable, invariable, simple, uncompounded, incorporeal, invisible, impalpable, uncircumscribed, infinite, unknowable, indefinable, incomprehensible, good, just, maker of all things created, almighty, all-ruling, all-seeing, overseer of all, sovereign, judge. God is one, that is to say, one essence. He is known and has his being in three subsistences (Father, Son and Holy Spirit). Father, Son and Holy Spirit are one in all respects, except in that of being unbegotten, being begotten, and proceeding. The only-begotten Son and Word of God and God, out of his mercy, for our salvation, by the good pleasure of God and the cooperation of the Holy Spirit, was conceived without seed and born without corruption of Mary (the Holy Virgin and Mother of God) by the Holy Spirit, becoming perfect man. The same [Son] is at once perfect God and perfect man, of two natures (deity and humanity) and in two natures, possessing intelligence, will, energy and freedom – in a word, perfect according to the measure and proportion proper both to each [nature] (deity and humanity) and to one composite person. He suffered hunger, thirst and weariness; he was crucified and for three days submitted to the experience of death and burial; he ascended to heaven, from where he both came to us and will come again. The Holy Scriptures and the whole company of the saints bear witness to this.

But we neither know, nor can say, what the essence of God is, nor how it is in all things, nor how the only-begotten Son being God, emptied himself and became man from virgin blood, contrary to the laws of nature, nor how he walked with dry feet upon the waters. It is not within our capacity, therefore, to say anything about God or even to think of him, beyond the things which have been divinely revealed to us, whether by word or by manifestation, by the divine oracles of both Old and New Testaments.

Symeon the New Theologian,
Catechetical Discourses (980–98)

Symeon was born of noble parents in Asia Minor, in 949. At the age of fourteen he became a disciple of Symeon the Studite, a leading spiritual teacher. After a period in secular employment on Symeon's advice, he joined him in the Studion monastery at Constantinople. Soon after he left there to join the St Mamos monastery, remaining Symeon's disciple. He was abbot of St Mamos from 980 to his retirement in 1005. During this time he was involved in controversy – with his own monks, who found his regime too strict, and later with Bishop Stephen of Nicomedia, the official court theologian. The controversy with Stephen resulted in a period of exile, from 1009. Symeon died, restored to favour, in 1022. His *Life* was written by his disciple Nicetas Stethatos.

Symeon has been called 'the most outstanding of Byzantine medieval mystics' and has been given the title 'New Theologian'. Previously John the apostle and Gregory of Nazianzus (one of the Cappadocian Fathers) were called 'theologian' for their teaching on God. Symeon's teaching was considered worthy of comparison with theirs. He was the first systematic exponent of the technique of inward prayer. He was also unique among medieval Orthodox mystics in speaking freely of his own personal spiritual experiences, usually in the third person under the name of George.

His controversy with Stephen involved the conflict between two different approaches. Stephen's approach to theology was philosophical and abstract, similar to the later approach of western Scholastic theology. Symeon's approach was monastic and spiritual, with a great stress on the need to experience that about which one talks. The conflict between Symeon and Stephen has been compared to that between Bernard and Abelard in the West. Abelard was condemned through the intervention of Bernard, but the essence of his approach was found in Peter Lombard's *Sentences* (see pages 157–59) and was to predominate in the West. In the East, by contrast, it was the mystic, Symeon, who won the ultimate victory.

The controversy with Stephen was also a conflict between the 'institutional' and the 'charismatic' approaches. Symeon was not opposed to the institutional authorities of the church and did not deny the importance of the sacraments. But at the same time he maintained that sins could be confessed to unordained monks and taught that baptism is of no value unless we go on to bear fruit in the form of a holy life. Symeon was opposed to formalism, to a merely nominal Christianity which did not involve a changed life. He taught the need for a 'baptism in the Holy Spirit' to follow water baptism. This involves repentance and conversion to Jesus Christ and awareness of him as Lord and Saviour. It means a personal experience of God for oneself, understood in terms of deification, and a life of obedience.

In his mystical teaching Symeon follows the tradition of Dionysius the Areopagite and Maximus the Confessor. He portrayed the vision of God as the vision of the divine light, uncreated and invisible. This experience is not just for an elite, it is not even confined to monks who can devote all their time to it, but is for all Christians.

Symeon is the author of a number of works. Most important are his *Catechetical Discourses*, a series of thirty-four sermons preached to monks together with two other pieces in the form of thanksgiving to God. These were delivered during the years that he was abbot of St Mamos. They vary considerably in length with the longest being eight times as long as the shortest. They are Christ-centred and there is an emphasis throughout on the work of the Holy Spirit. Penitence is also a major theme, appearing in the titles of five of the discourses including the two longest. His second most important work was his fifty-eight *Hymns of Divine Love*, which convey the same teaching as the *Catechetical Discourses* but in poetic form. He also wrote a number of treatises, of which three theological and fifteen ethical treatises survive but others have been lost.

16:3. So I entered the place where I usually prayed and, mindful of the words of the holy man [Symeon the Studite] I began to say, 'Holy God'. At once I was so greatly moved to tears and loving desire for God that I would be unable to describe in words the joy and delight I then felt. I fell prostrate on the ground, and at once I saw, and behold, a great light was immaterially shining on me and seized hold of my whole mind and soul, so that I was struck with amazement at the unexpected marvel and I was, as it were, in ecstasy. . . . 'Whether I was in the body, or outside the body' [2 Corinthians 12:2–3], I conversed with this Light. The Light itself knows it; it scattered whatever mist there was in my soul and cast out every earthly care. It expelled from me all material denseness and bodily heaviness that made my members to be sluggish and numb. What an awesome marvel! It so invigorated and strengthened my limbs and muscles, which had been faint through great weariness, that it seemed to me as though I was stripping myself of the garment of corruption. Besides, there was poured into my soul in unutterable fashion a great spiritual joy and perception and a sweetness surpassing every taste of visible objects, together with a freedom and forgetfulness of all thoughts pertaining to this life. In a marvellous way there was granted to me and revealed to me the manner of the departure from this present life. Thus all the perceptions of my mind and my soul were wholly concentrated on the ineffable joy of that Light.

22:8. To this end we were brought into being, that having received some small benefits in this life we may, by giving thanks to God and loving him, enjoy in that life blessings far greater that endure forever. But alas! We have no concern whatever for the blessings that are to come and are even ungrateful for the blessings that are at hand, and so, to tell the truth, we become the equals of demons or even worse! Therefore we deserve an even worse punishment in proportion to the greater benefits we have received, for we know that God for our sakes became like us (apart from sin), in order that he might deliver us from error and set us free from sin. But why should I say this? We truly believe all these things, but in word only; we deny them by our deeds! Is not Christ's name spoken everywhere – in cities, in villages, in monasteries, on the mountains [where hermits dwell]? Search, if you will, and examine carefully whether men keep his commandments. Truly, among thousands and tens of thousands you will scarcely find one who is a Christian in word and deed.

32:2. It is heresy when someone turns aside in any way from the dogmas that have been defined concerning the right faith. But to deny that at this present time there are some who love God, and that they have been granted the Holy Spirit and to be baptized by him as sons of God, that they have become gods by knowledge and experience and contemplation, that wholly subverts the incarnation of our God and Saviour Jesus Christ! It clearly denies the renewal of the image that had been corrupted and put to death and its return to incorruption and immortality.

32:3. Just as it is impossible for one to be saved who has not been baptized by water and the Spirit, neither is it for him who has sinned after baptism, unless he be baptized from on high and be born again. This the Saviour confirmed when he said to Nicodemus, 'Unless one is born from on high, he cannot enter the kingdom of heaven' [John 3:3, 5].

Anselm, *Cur Deus Homo* (1090s)

Anselm was born in about 1033 at Aosta, in Italy. As a young man of twenty-six he entered the Benedictine monastery at Bec in Normandy. Before long, in 1063, he became prior of the monastery, in succession to Lanfranc, who became abbot elsewhere. Thereafter his life falls into three periods of about fifteen years each – as prior of Bec (1063–78), as abbot of Bec (1078–93) and as archbishop of Canterbury (1093–1109), again in succession to Lanfranc. Anselm clashed with successive kings over the question of the independence of the English Church from the king and the role of the pope in England. As a result, most of his time as archbishop was spent in exile on the Continent.

Anselm was the first truly great theologian of the medieval West and is seen by some as the founder of Scholasticism. He allowed philosophy to play a significant, though limited, role in theology. It is revelation, not philosophy, that gives us the content of the Christian faith, but the theologian who believes can then seek, by the use of reason, to understand more fully that which he believes. Reason can show the rationality and inner coherence of Christian doctrine. Anselm follows Augustine's method of 'faith seeking understanding'.

Anselm pursued this method in three major writings, the first two of which offer 'proofs' for the existence of God. The *Monologion* (1077), originally called *An Example of Meditation on the Grounds of Faith*, argues that because we can discern degrees of goodness, then there must be an absolute Good by which we can measure it. This being is God. Anselm's argument was not original, having been used previously by Augustine. The following year, Anselm broke new ground with the publication of his *Proslogion*, originally called *Faith Seeking Understanding*. In this work Anselm presents his famous 'ontological argument' for the existence of God. God is defined as 'that, than which nothing greater can be conceived' or, to put it more simply, 'the greatest conceivable being'. This being must exist. Were he not to exist, he would be inferior to an identical being that did exist and thus would not be 'the greatest conceivable being'. Anselm has, with some justice, been accused of attempting to define God into existence. His approach reflects the supreme confidence of the eleventh century in the power of reason to explain things.

Anselm's most ambitious work was his *Cur Deus Homo (Why God Became Man)* , written in the 1090s. Anselm, like Athanasius in his *The Incarnation of the Word* (see pages 55–58), faces the charge that it is unfitting and degrading for God to become man and die to save us. Anselm's defence is that it is fitting because there was no other way possible. The work takes the form of a dialogue between Anselm and one of his monks, Boso. As in his earlier works, Anselm follows the method of 'faith seeking understanding'. He writes as a believer seeking to show how reasonable faith is, to demonstrate the inner harmony of the Christian faith. Starting with certain presuppositions that would be shared by Jews and Muslims (such as the existence of God and his character, the nature of humanity and sin against God) he sought to show that the incarnation and cross were the only option open to God – and therefore were a fitting and reasonable course of action.

The basic structure of Anselm's argument is simple. By our sin we have failed to render to God the obedience that we owe and thus have dishonoured him. It would not be sufficient for us now to begin to obey God; we must also offer to him some satisfaction or compensation for his lost honour. But can God not simply forgive us? No. As God he needs to uphold the principles of justice and law and there can be no greater injustice than for God to lose his honour to a creature. Only two remedies are possible. Either some satisfaction must be offered for God's lost honour or it must be restored by the punishment of sinners. The latter option meets the problem of God's honour, but undermines God's purposes in the creation of humanity. The dilemma is both that we can offer no satisfaction since we already owe God perfect obedience and that the satisfaction required must be of greater value than the whole universe (for which Anselm has an intricate argument).

God's dilemma is that humanity owes a debt that it cannot pay, his justice prevents him from overlooking it and yet his purposes require him to save humanity. The size of the satisfaction required means that only God is able to provide it; yet as it was man that sinned, it must be a man that provides the satisfaction. The solution for God's dilemma, therefore, is for the Son to become human in order, as man, to offer this satisfaction by his voluntary death.

Anselm's argument is impressive, but not without its weaknesses. He went beyond the usual Christian claim that the cross was necessary (i.e. that God had to do something) to claim that it was absolutely necessary (i.e. that God could not have done anything else). There are also weaknesses in Anselm's understanding of the atonement itself – such as his emphasis on God's honour rather than his justice, and the stress on the cross to the exclusion of the life, resurrection and ascension of Jesus Christ. But Anselm's argument is very flexible and it can be modified to take account of these criticisms. His basic case, suitably modified, remains today a powerful argument that the incarnation and the cross are indeed fitting and reasonable.

1:1. I have often been asked most earnestly, both by word of mouth and in writing, by many people, to set down a written record of the reasoned explanations with which I am in the habit of answering people who put enquiries to me about a certain question of our faith. . . . They make this request, not with a view to arriving at faith through reason, but in order that they may take delight in the understanding and contemplation of the things which they believe, and may be, as far as they are able, 'ready always to give satisfaction to all who ask the reason for the hope that is in them' [1 Peter 3:15]. The question is one which unbelievers, deriding Christian simplicity as foolish, are in the habit of raising as an objection against us, and many believers too are in the habit of pondering in their hearts. The question is this. By what logic or necessity did God become man, and by his death, as we believe and profess, restore life to the world, when he could have done this through the agency of some other person, angelic or human, or simply by willing it?

Boso: On the one hand, right order demands that we should believe the profundities of the Christian faith before we presume to discuss it logically, but, on the other, it seems to me negligence if, after we have been confirmed in the faith, we do not make an effort to understand what we believe. Thanks to the grace of God which goes before us, I think I adhere to faith in our redemption in such a way that, even though I cannot understand what I believe in any rational way, yet there is nothing which can tear me away from its steadfastness. I ask you, therefore, to reveal to me something which, as you know, many people besides me ask about, namely this: by what necessity or logic did God, almighty as he is, take upon himself the humble standing and weakness of human nature with a view to that nature's restoration?

1:4. Surely there seems a sufficiently cogent reason why God had a need to do the things of which we are speaking: the human race, clearly his most precious piece of workmanship, had been completely ruined; it was not fitting that what God had planned for mankind should be utterly nullified, and the plan in question could not be brought into effect unless the human race were set free by its Creator in person.

1:11. [Obedience] is the debt which an angel, and likewise a man, owes to God. No one sins through paying it, and everyone who does not pay it, sins. This is righteousness or uprightness of the will. It makes individuals righteous or upright in their heart, that is, their will. This is the sole honour, the complete honour, which we owe to God and which God demands from us. For only such a will, when it can act, performs actions which are pleasing to God. . . . Someone who does not render to God this honour due to him is taking away from God what is his, and dishonouring God, and this is what it is to sin. As long as he does not repay what he has taken away, he remains in a state of guilt.

2:18. Boso: The substance of the question was: why God became man, so that he might save mankind through his death, when it appears that he could have done this in another way. You [Anselm] have responded to this question with many cogent lines of reasoning, and have thereby shown that it was not right that the restoration of human nature should be left undone, and that it could not have been brought about unless man repaid what he owed to God. This debt was so large that, although no one but man owed it, only God was capable of repaying it, assuming that there should be a man identical with God. Hence it was a necessity that God should take man into the unity of his person, so that one who ought, by virtue of his nature, to make the repayment and was not capable of doing so, should be one who, by virtue of his person, was capable of it.

Bernard of Clairvaux,
The Steps of Humility and Pride (c. 1125)

Bernard was born in 1090 at Fontaines (near Dijon), of noble parentage. In 1112 he entered the recently-founded abbey of Cîteaux, the first abbey of the new Cistercian order. Three years later, Bernard was appointed abbot of a new monastery at Clairvaux. Under his leadership this monastery grew rapidly and also became parent to some seventy new Cistercian monasteries during his lifetime.

Bernard went to Cîteaux to flee the world, but in time he became one of the most widely-travelled and active leaders of the twelfth-century church. During the 1130s he fought hard for Pope Innocent II, against the rival Pope Anacletus, helping to secure Innocent's eventual victory. After this, he was engaged in controversy with the theologian Peter Abelard, securing his condemnation at the Council of Sens in 1140 and thereafter by the pope. In 1145 his authority was further enhanced when a former monk of Clairvaux, Bernard Paganelli, became Pope Eugenius III. In the next two years, at Eugenius's request, Bernard preached round Europe, raising support for the Second Crusade. This was launched in 1148, but failed dismally, a severe blow for Bernard. But his reputation was great enough to survive such a setback. He died in 1153 and his popularity has never really waned.

Bernard has been called 'the last of the Fathers'. He was the last great representative of the early medieval tradition of monastic theology and a brilliant writer, earning himself the title 'mellifluous' or sweet as honey. He preached regularly and many of his sermons survive – some in an unpolished state, probably much as preached; others in a highly polished literary form designed for reading. More than five hundred of his letters survive, ranging from the personal and devotional to the official and political.

Bernard is known especially as a spiritual writer. Sometime around 1125 he wrote the first of his works, his *Steps of Humility and Pride*, based on the twelve steps of humility described by Benedict in his Rule (see pages 124–27). In this work he displayed his considerable literary gifts, channelling them into one of the great spiritual classics of the Middle Ages. Bernard was writing for and about monks, but his insights into human nature and motivation make it a simple task to apply what he says to ordinary life today. His work is very relevant to an age that values self-esteem above self-knowledge, assertiveness above humility.

Benedict had described twelve steps of humility. Bernard begins his work with the way of humility, which he defines as 'a virtue by which a man has a low opinion of himself because he knows himself well' (1:2). He sees three stages in the perception of truth: as we find it in ourselves (leading to humility), in others (leading to love) and in itself (leading to the contemplation of it). There is a logic in this order with one step leading to the next. 'You will never have real mercy for the failings of another until you know and realize that you have the same failings in your soul' (3:6).

The emphasis of the book is more on the reverse process, the twelve descending steps of pride, which Bernard describes with some very perceptive insights into human nature doubtless drawn from observation of his own monks. In the extracts below I have used as headings the description of each step of pride as found in a list at the beginning of Bernard's work.

―――――――――――――

The Descending Steps of Pride

I. Curiosity; when the eyes and the other senses attend to what is not one's concern

10:28. The first step of pride is curiosity. . . . He used to watch over his own conduct; now all his watchfulness is for others. . . . My man! If you gave yourself the attention you ought, I do not think you would have much time to look after others.

II. Levity of mind, known by words that bespeak unreasonable joy and sadness

11:39. The monk who observes others instead of attending to himself will begin before long to see some as his superiors and others as his inferiors; in some he will see things to envy, in others, things to despise. . . . One moment he is sulky and silent except for some bitter remarks; the next sees a full spate of silly chatter. Now he is laughing, now doleful; all without rhyme or reason. . . .

III. Silly mirth, with over-much laughing

12:40. The monk that has come down the two steps of curiosity and levity of mind will find much to upset him. He is saddened every time he sees the goodness of others, impatient with humiliation. He finds an escape in false consolations. His eyes are closed to anything that shows his own vileness or the excellence of others, wide open to what flatters himself. . . . He is careful not to remember anything he has done which could hurt his self-esteem; but all his good points will be remembered, and added up, and if need be, touched up by imagination. He is like a well-filled bladder that has been pricked and squeezed. The air, not finding a free vent, whistles out through the little hole with squeak after squeak. . . .

IV. Boasting and too much talking

13:41. When vanity has swelled the bladder to its limits a bigger vent must be made or the bladder will burst. . . . His hunger and thirst are for listeners, someone to listen to his boasting, on whom he can pour out all his thoughts, someone he can show what a big man he is. . . . He does not wait to be asked. His information comes before any question. He asks the questions; gives the answers; cuts off anyone who tries to speak. . . . [He talks] not to edify the listeners, but to show off his learning. He may have the capacity to help others but that is the least of his concerns. His aim is not to teach you nor to be taught by you, but to show how much he knows. . . .

V. Singularity, proud esteem of one's own ways

14:42. When a man has been bragging that he is better than others he would feel ashamed of himself if he did not live up to his boast and show how much better than others he is. The common rule of the monastery and the example of the seniors are no longer enough for him. He does not so much want to be better as to be seen to be better. He is not so much concerned about leading a better life as appearing to others to do so. . . . After sleeping through the night office while the others were singing psalms, he stays to pray alone in the oratory while they are resting in the cloister. . . .

VI. Self-assertion: believing one is holier than others

15:43. He swallows all the praise others give him. He is quite complacent about his conduct and never examines his motives now; the good opinion of others is all he needs. About everything else he thinks he knows more than anybody, but when they say something favourable about him he believes them against his own conscience. So now not only in words and affected conduct does he display his piety but he believes in his inmost heart that he is holier than others. . . .

VII. Presumption: meddling with everything

16:44. When a man thinks he is better than others will he not put himself before others? He must have the first place in gatherings, be the first to speak in council. He comes without being called. He interferes without being asked. He must rearrange everything, re-do whatever has been done. What he himself did not do or arrange is not rightly done or properly arranged. . . .

VIII: Defending one's sins

17:45. There are many ways of excusing sins. One will say: 'I didn't do it.' Another: 'I did it, but I was perfectly right in doing it.' If it was wrong he may say: 'It isn't all that bad.' If it was decidedly harmful, he can fall back on: 'I meant well.' . . .

IX. Hypocritical confession, which can be tested by harsh reproof

18:46. There is something even more dangerous than this stubborn and obstinate self-defence, and that is hypocritical confession springing from pride. There are some who, when they are caught out in wrong-doing and know that if they defend themselves they will not be believed, find a subtle way out of the difficulty in deceitful self-accusation. . . . They will not merely admit what has happened but will exaggerate their guilt. They accuse themselves of things so great, so incredible, that you begin to doubt the charges you were certain of before. . . . The candour of their confession is all in outward show. It does not come from the heart and cancels no sin.

X. Rebellion against superiors and brethren

19:48. The divine mercy may yet rescue such a man and inspire him to submit to the judgment of the community; but such a character finds this a very hard thing to do, and instead, he may take an attitude of brazen insolence and in desperation take the final plunge as far as the tenth step of pride. He has already shown his contempt for his brethren by insolence, and now his contempt for superiors flashes out in open revolt.

XI. Freedom in sinning

20:50. The man in revolt has reached the tenth step of pride and will leave or be expelled from the monastery. Without delay he goes down to the eleventh step. . . We may style this step freedom in sinning. The monk has no longer a superior to fear nor brethren to respect, so with fewer qualms he happily gives himself up to his sinful desires which in the monastery fear and shame held in check. . . .

XII. The habit of sin

21:51. The first steps in sin are taken apprehensively and no blow falls from the dreaded judgment of God. Pleasure in sin has been experienced. Sin is repeated and the pleasure grows. Old desires revive, conscience is dulled, habit tightens its grasp. The unfortunate man sinks into the evil depths, is tangled in his vices and is swept into the whirlpool of sinful longings while his reason and the fear of God are forgotten.

22:57. We have described the stages of the downward road and you will see them as you climb up and down them better from your own experience than from the description of our book.

Bernard of Clairvaux, *Loving God*
(1125–41)

In his last years Bernard wrote two of his greatest works. In 1145 a former monk of Clairvaux, Bernard Paganelli, became Pope Eugenius III and between 1148 and 1152 Bernard wrote for him a treatise on *Consideration* in which he urges the pope to find time for reflection or meditation in his busy life. He should consider himself (his person and his office), those placed under him, those around him at Rome and those above him (in the heavenly world). Bernard had a high view of the papacy. The pope is 'the unique vicar of Christ who presides not over a single people but over all', and he has fullness of power, but Bernard was equally emphatic in his opposition to papal tyranny.

Bernard's most famous work is his eighty-six *Sermons on the Song of Solomon*, which he began in 1135 and which were incomplete when he died in 1153. These are ostensibly sermons as preached but are now seen as a literary production intended to be read, rather than preached sermons. In them Bernard teaches his monks about the spiritual life and about the steps towards mystical union with God. He gives an account of his own experience:

> I want to tell you of my own experience, as I promised. . . . I admit that the Word has also come to me – I speak as a fool [2 Corinthians 11:21] – and has come many times. But although he has come to me, I have never been conscious of the moment of his coming. I perceived his presence, I remembered afterwards that he had been with me; sometimes I had a presentiment that he would come, but I was never conscious of his coming or his going. (74:5)

He also comments on the different motivations for study:

> There are some who long to know for the sole purpose of knowing, and that is shameful curiosity; others who long to know in order to become known, and that is shameful vanity. To such as these we may apply the words of the Satirist [Persius]: 'Your knowledge counts for nothing unless your friends know that you have it.' There are others still who long for knowledge in order to sell its fruits for money or honours, and this is shameful profiteering; others again who long to know in order to be of service, and this is charity. Finally, there are those who long to know in order to benefit themselves, and this is prudence. (36:3)

Bernard's dismissal of motivation by curiosity, the desire for recognition or the seeking of academic or professional qualifications would rightly be seen as extreme today. But the essential point, that these are all selfish motivations and that there needs to be a deeper motivation of love, the desire to serve others, is profound and of abiding validity.

In 1125, at the time that he was writing his *The Steps of Humility and Pride* (see pages 150–53), Bernard wrote a letter to the Carthusians about the different stages of love for God. He distinguishes between the love of a slave that is motivated by fear of the master, the love of an employee which is motivated by self-interest and the desire for gain, and the love of a son which is alone a true love. (This is similar to the teaching of Cassian in the eleventh of his *Conferences* [see pages 102–105], as quoted above.) He then goes on to describe four stages of love.

Sometime after this and before 1141 Bernard developed this theme in another of his greatest works, his *Loving God*, which is also rightly regarded as a spiritual classic. In this he describes more fully the four stages of love – how we are to move from loving ourselves for our own sakes, to loving God because of the benefits that we receive from him, to loving God because of his own goodness, to loving ourselves for God's sake only. At the conclusion of this work Bernard includes the text of his earlier letter to the Carthusians (12:34–15:40). Many of Bernard's writings are soaked in scriptural phraseology and there are many parts of this work where every sentence contains an allusion to a passage of Scripture.

1:1. You wish me to tell you why and how God should be loved. My answer is that God himself is the reason why he is to be loved. As for how he is to be loved, there is to be no limit to that love. . . . I insist that there are two reasons why God should be loved for his own sake: no one can be loved more righteously and no one can be loved with greater benefit.

8:23. The First Degree of Love: Man Loves Himself for His Own Sake
Since nature has become more fragile and weak, necessity obliges man to serve it first. This is carnal love by which a man loves himself above all for his own sake. He is only aware of himself.

8:25. Man who is animal and carnal, and knows how to love only himself, yet starts loving God for his own benefit, because he learns from frequent experience that he can do everything that is good for him in God and that without God he can do nothing good.

The Second Degree of Love: Man Loves God for His Own Benefit
9:26. Man, therefore, loves God, but for his own advantage and not yet for God's

sake. Nevertheless, it is a matter of prudence to know what you can do by yourself and what you can do with God's help to keep from offending him who keeps you free from sin. If man's tribulations, however, grow in frequency and as a result he frequently turns to God and is frequently freed by God, must he not end, even though he had a heart of stone in a breast of iron, by realizing that it is God's grace which frees him and come to love God not for his own advantage but for the sake of God?

The Third Degree of Love: Man Loves God for God's Sake

Man's frequent needs oblige him to invoke God more often and approach him more frequently. This intimacy moves man to taste and discover how sweet the Lord is. Tasting God's sweetness entices us more to pure love than does the urgency of our own needs. . . . This love is pleasing because it is free. It is chaste because it does not consist of spoken words but of deed and truth. It is just because it renders what is received. Whoever loves this way, loves the way he is loved, seeking in return not what is his but what belongs to Christ, the same way Christ sought not what was his, but what was ours, or rather, ourselves. . . .

The Fourth Degree of Love: Man Loves Himself for the Sake of God

10:27. Happy the man who has attained the fourth degree of love, he no longer even loves himself except for God. . . . I would say that man is blessed and holy to whom it is given to experience something of this sort, so rare in life, even if it be but once and for the space of a moment. To lose yourself, as if you no longer existed, to cease completely to experience yourself, to reduce yourself to nothing is not a human sentiment but a divine experience.

15:39. Man first loves himself for himself because he is carnal and sensitive to nothing but himself. Then when he sees he cannot subsist by himself, he begins to seek for God by faith and to love him as necessary to himself. So in the second degree of love, man loves God for man's sake and not for God's sake. When forced by his own needs he begins to honour God and care for him by thinking of him, reading about him, praying to him, and obeying him, God reveals himself gradually in this kind of familiarity and consequently becomes lovable. When man tastes how sweet God is, he passes to the third degree of love in which man loves God not now because of himself but because of God. No doubt man remains a long time in this degree, and I doubt if he ever attains the fourth degree during this life, that is, if he ever loves only for God's sake. Let those who have had the experience make a statement; to me, I confess, it seems impossible.

Peter Lombard, *Sentences* (1147–51)

In 1122 the theologian Peter Abelard wrote a major work called *Sic et Non (Yes and No)*, in which he juxtaposed apparently conflicting passages from the Bible, the early Fathers and other authorities. His aim was not, as used to be believed, to discredit these authorities. He saw reason as the arbiter to reconcile conflicting authorities and, if necessary, to decide between them. He did not invent this method himself. Lawyers had already begun to use philosophical methods to decide or arbitrate between conflicting authorities. Where one law appeared to conflict with another, logic was used to reconcile them and to determine the law. Abelard's novelty lay in the way that he applied this method to theology and to the documents of revelation and also in his unwillingness to show due reverence to authority.

Behind the *Sic et Non* lay Abelard's basic approach to theology. Anselm of Canterbury, still in this respect within the monastic tradition, followed Augustine's method of faith seeking understanding, in his *Cur Deus Homo* (see pages 146–49) and other writings. 'I believe in order that I may understand.' Abelard reversed this, introducing the method of doubt. The way to reach the truth is to doubt, to ask questions and thus to find the answer. In the preface to *Sic et Non* Abelard stated that 'by doubting we come to enquire and by enquiring we reach truth'. Doubt is seen not so much a sin (the traditional understanding of it) as the necessary beginning of all knowledge. Abelard sought to understand Christian doctrine in order to know what to believe – a reversal of the method of Augustine and Anselm. Theology had become a science instead of a meditation.

Peter Abelard was condemned, through the intervention of Bernard of Clairvaux. But his work was continued by another Peter – Peter Lombard. This Peter was born at around the end of the eleventh century in Lombardy (northern Italy). He studied at Bologna, Reims and Paris (probably under Abelard). From about 1140 he taught at Paris and in 1159 he became bishop of that city. He died the following year.

Before 1143 he wrote major commentaries on the Psalms and the Pauline Epistles, drawing mainly on the writings of the church fathers, but his chief contribution was his *Four Books of Sentences*, written between 1147 and 1151. This is a compilation of extracts ('sentences' meaning maxims, opinions) from the Bible, the Fathers and other authorities. Lombard's method is similar to Abelard's – he uses reason, dialectic and logic to arbitrate between the different authorities. But he combined Abelard's methods with a reverence for authority, with the result that he won the support even of Bernard. His aim was not to introduce new ideas of his own but simply to decide the truth on the basis of the established authorities – as with his reconciling of Psalm 19:9 and 1 John 4:18 below. The extract below also illustrates the extent of dependence upon quotation from the Fathers. If

Peter thought that he was improving on the work of his predecessors, it would only be in the way described by Bernard of Chartres (as quoted by John of Salisbury, *Metalogicon* 3:4):

> *We are like dwarves sitting on the shoulders of giants [the ancients]. We see more than them and things that are further away – not because our sight is better than theirs, nor because we are taller than they were, but because they raise us up and add to our stature by their enormous height.*

Peter Lombard's theology was questioned immediately after his death, but he was vindicated at the Fourth Lateran Council in 1215. Lombard's *Sentences* became a standard theological textbook until the time of the Reformation and beyond. Writing a commentary on it became a regular part of the preparation for a doctorate in theology and Lombard came to be known as the 'Master of the Sentences'. It is probably safe to say that no one today reads Lombard apart from historians and theologians. But a book that served as a standard textbook for a quarter of the church's history and for much of that time held a position of unrivalled dominance deserves the title of classic and perhaps has more to offer than is generally recognized today.

Book 3. The Incarnation of the Word and the Restoration of the Human Race

Prologue. Now in order to understand and discuss those matters which have to do with the mystery of the Incarnate Word, let us concentrate the full attention of our minds in order that we may be capable, by God's revelation, of saying at least something about ineffable matters. For the order of reason so lays it down that we who in Book 1 said something concerning the inexplicable mystery of the Supreme Trinity by the indisputable attestation of the saints, and then in Book 2 proceeded to the order of the creation of things and the fall of man under certain rules of authority, should proceed in Books 3 and 4 to examine its restoration provided through the grace of the Mediator between God and man [in Book 3], and, [in Book 4] the sacraments of human redemption, by which man's contritions are bound, and the wounds of sins are healed, how the Samaritan comes to the wounded man, the physician to the sick and grace to the wretched.

Book 3; Distinction 34; Chapter 5: Pure and Servile and Initial Fear
Augustine discusses these fears more fully: Someone begins to believe in the day of judgment; if he begins to believe, he also begins to fear. But he who fears to such a degree does not yet have trust in the day of judgment, nor yet is there in

him perfect love – 'if there were perfect love in him, he would not fear. For perfect love would make perfect righteousness and would have nothing to fear, but would rather have something to long that iniquity might pass away and the kingdom of God come. Therefore fear is not found in love. But in what sort of love? Not in incomplete love. In what love then? In perfect love. "Perfect love," it is said, "casts out fear" [1 John 4:18]. Therefore let fear begin, because "the fear of the Lord is the beginning of wisdom" [Proverbs 9:10]. Fear as it were prepares a place for love, but when loves begins to dwell there, the fear which prepared the place for it is expelled. For the more love increases, the more fear decreases; and the more love enters within, the more is fear forced out. The greater the love, the less the fear; the less the love, the greater the fear. But if there is no fear there is no way for love to enter – just as in sewing the thread is introduced through a needle and the needle enters first, but unless the needle leaves the thread cannot follow. Thus fear first occupies the mind, but does not remain there for it entered in order to introduce love' [Augustine, *Homilies on 1 John* 9:4].

'But there is another opinion which appears to contradict this if it is not understood correctly. For it says in the Psalm, "the pure fear of the Lord endures for ever and ever" [19:9]. This shows us a certain eternal but pure fear. But if the Psalm shows us an everlasting fear, is this not contradicted by the Epistle which says, "There is no fear in love, but perfect love casts out fear" [1 John 4:18]? The latter was said by John, the former by David, but do not think that there are two Spirits. . . . If filled by one spirit, that is by one breath, two trumpets sound in harmony, can two tongues filled by the Holy Spirit produce a dissonance? No, there is a certain harmony and concord here, but it requires a zealous not a lazy hearer. . . . There is a fear which is called pure and there is fear which is not pure. Let us distinguish the two fears and thus understand the harmony of the trumpets. . .' [Augustine, *Homilies on 1 John* 9:5].

Chapter 6: How Pure and Servile Fear Differ

'The one trumpet speaks of the fear by which the soul fears lest it be condemned; the other speaks of the fear by which the soul fears lest it be forsaken. The one is a fear that excludes love; the other is a fear which "endures for ever and ever"' [Augustine, *Homilies on 1 John* 9:8]. Here Augustine clearly shows what sort of fear is pure and what sort is servile and how they differ.

Richard of St Victor,
The Twelve Patriarchs (1153–62)

A major theological centre for the twelfth-century church was the abbey of St Victor in Paris, a community of Augustinian canons founded in about 1108. Its two most influential figures were Hugh of St Victor (who died in 1141) and Richard of St Victor. Richard was born in Scotland or possibly Ireland. He joined the abbey in the early 1150s and in 1162 was appointed prior. He remained in this post until his death in 1173. Richard never met Hugh, but was influenced by his writings. Richard was interested in the psychology of religious experience, which informs and gives a depth to his spiritual writings.

Between about 1153 and 1162 Richard wrote two important works of spiritual theology:

● *The Twelve Patriarchs* (sometimes known as *Benjamin Minor*), an allegorical description of the children of Jacob (based on the account of each in Genesis) and of the Transfiguration of Jesus. The theme of the book is the preparation of the soul for contemplation.

● *The Mystical Ark* (sometimes known as *Benjamin Major*), an allegorical account of the Ark of the Covenant and the Seraphim (Exodus 25:10–22). The theme of the book is the six ascending stages of the contemplation of God, a theme which is taken up by Bonaventure in his *The Soul's Journey into God* (see pages 168–71).

Richard also later wrote an influential work entitled *The Trinity* in six books. Here he argues that perfect love requires not just two persons but a third with whom to share that love. While mainstream western theology has always tended to emphasize the unity of the Trinity above the threeness, Richard lays greater stress on the latter with a 'social' doctrine of the Trinity. This has excited interest in recent years because of its potential to bring together eastern and western approaches to the Trinity and because of interest today in the social implications of the doctrine of the Trinity.

In *The Twelve Patriarchs* the soul's progression from sin is portrayed in terms of Jacob's thirteen children, who are considered in order of age. Their four mothers are also significant – thus the seven children of Leah are seven virtues. The order is as follows:

Four sons of Leah, who is seen as the earnest desire for righteousness:
● Reuben = fear of God
● Simeon = grief for sin

- Levi = hope of forgiveness
- Judah = love for God

Two sons of Rachel's handmaid Bala, who is seen as the imagination:
- Dan = reminder of future punishment, restraining vice
- Naphtali = reminder of future rewards, encouraging virtue

Two sons of Leah's handmaid Zelpha, who is seen as the sensations of the five senses:
- Gad = abstinence from worldly pleasures
- Asher = patience in worldly adversity

Leah's other three children:
- Issachar = inner joy
- Zebulun = hatred of vices
- Dinah = shame

Two sons of Rachel, who is seen as reason in pursuit of wisdom:
- Joseph = discretion or self-knowledge
- Benjamin = ecstatic contemplation of God

Such an allegorical interpretation of the Old Testament has since fallen out of favour, though in recent years there is a much greater willingness to recognize that a variety of different approaches to reading Scripture may all have some validity. One cannot simply disregard Richard's work because of the use of allegory. The heart of it is an account of the soul's progress from sin to the contemplation of God. The relating of this to the Genesis narrative is more than superficial and Richard genuinely believed that he was drawing out part of the deeper spiritual meaning of the text. But his teaching can stand in its own right as a spiritual classic, irrespective of the link with the Patriarchs. Read on these terms it contains much abiding wisdom about the spiritual life.

———————

7. The seven offspring of Leah are seven virtues since a virtue is nothing other than an ordered and moderated affection of the soul: ordered when it is directed to that toward which it ought to be; moderated when it is as great as it ought to be. Thus there are seven principal affections that rise by turns from the one affective disposition of the soul: Hope and fear; joy and grief; hatred, love and shame. All these can be ordered at one time and disordered at another. But only when they have been ordered are they then to be counted among the sons of Jacob. If there were no disordered fear the divine word would never have said: 'They trembled from fear in that place, where there was no fear' [Psalm 14:5, in

the Septuagint translation]. Again, if there were no ordered fear it would not have been written: 'Fear of the Lord is holy, enduring for all ages' [Psalm 19:9]. Again, if love were not ordered at one time and disordered at another sacred Scripture would neither teach the former nor prohibit the latter: 'You shall love your God with all your heart, and with all your mind, and with all your strength, and your neighbour just as yourself' [Deuteronomy 6:5; Matthew 22:37, 39]. And elsewhere, 'Love neither the world nor things that are in the world' [1 John 2:15]. We should understand similarly concerning the other affections: sometimes ordered and for that reason good; sometimes disordered and for that reason evil. . . .

8. It is written: 'The fear of the Lord is the beginning of wisdom' [Psalm 111:10]. Therefore this offspring is the first of the virtues. Without it you are not able to have the others. He who desires to have such a son should consider not only frequently but also carefully the evil that he has done: on one side, the magnitude of his crimes; on the other side, the power of the judge. From such consideration fear is born. . . .

9. After the first son has been born and gradually has grown up, the second is born because it is necessary that grief follow great fear. For the more vehemently a person fears the punishment he deserves, the more sharply he laments the fault he has committed. But it should be known that, at whatever hour a sinner shall have been converted and shall have mourned, he will be saved, according to this: 'A contrite and humbled heart, O God, you will not despise' [Psalm 51:17].

41. Some, as if from the constraint of humility, do not dare to rebuke delinquent persons. Others, in order not to seem to disturb brotherly love, fear to denounce sinners. And so others, in other ways, because they are unwilling to be zealous for the Lord, suppose this is virtuous, or they believe it is a virtue. But on the contrary, many persons, because without doubt they are acting in a spirit of fury, think that they act with zeal of uprightness, and the things they enforce in truth from hatred of men, they think or pretend that they practise because of hatred of vices. . . . Those who have known by means of experience those inner joys to which they invite them by so many griefs ought to trust pursuing delinquent persons with compassion, not cruelty.

46. Learn first to hate sin, and then you will begin truly to feel ashamed of it. If you truly hate, you feel quickly ashamed of it. That shame is known to be true when hatred of vices precedes and accompanies it. Otherwise, if you are caught in sin and confounded with shame when you are caught, I do not believe that you feel ashamed at the fault, but of the infamy. For such shamefacedness descends

not so much from sin itself as from the damage to our reputation. . . . Even perverse men have shame, but if only it were good, if only it were ordered! For if they had good shame, perhaps they would not be perverse. For indeed, if they felt perfectly ashamed, they would not commit sin so easily.

66. One ought to keep cautious watch over all the virtues so that they are not only ordered but also moderated. For excessive fear often falls into despair; excessive grief, into bitterness; immoderate hope, into presumption; overabundant love, into flattery; unnecessary joy, into dissolution; intemperate anger, into fury. And so in this way virtues are turned into vices if they are not moderated by discretion.

Thomas of Celano,
First Life of Francis of Assisi (1228)

Francis of Assisi is the best-loved of medieval saints. He was born in 1181 or 1182, the son of Peter Bernardone, a wealthy cloth merchant of Assisi. His life was uneventful until, in his early twenties, he had a number of encounters with God which led him to draw back from his worldly life and embrace a life of simplicity and poverty. While praying in a ruined church outside Assisi he heard a voice telling him to rebuild the church. This he began to do, but in an excess of zeal he sold some of his father's cloth to raise money. His father was not amused and took him to the bishop's court in an attempt to recover the money. Francis, in a dramatic gesture, stripped naked and returned all of his clothes to his father. From now on he would have only one father, his Father in heaven.

Francis began to live a wandering life of poverty. One day he heard Matthew 10:7–10 read in church and this came to him as a personal call – he was to go forth and minister in poverty, as had the apostles. Disciples began to gather round him and in 1209 or 1210 Francis wrote a *Primitive Rule*. This is now unfortunately lost, but it seems to have been composed mainly of passages from the Gospels. Francis went to Rome and presented it to the pope, Innocent III, who after initial misgivings gave his qualified verbal approval. This was a crucial decision since not long before a group called the Waldenses had begun much like the Franciscans, but unwise handling had provoked them into dissent and a separate Waldensian church survives to this day.

The novelty in Francis's ideal was the central position given to poverty, which he saw not as a mere means to an end but as an end in itself. He was married to Lady Poverty, the bride of Jesus Christ who had been a widow since he died. Francis's ideal was not merely a simple lifestyle, it was the total renunciation of all property. It included not just individual poverty (as with other religious orders) but the collective poverty of the order.

In 1212 Francis was joined by Clare, a young heiress from Assisi, who had come to accept his ideals. With Francis's help, she founded the 'Poor Clares', the female version of the Franciscans. After this Francis made various unsuccessful attempts to convert the Muslims, actually meeting the Sultan in Egypt. When he returned he found that others had taken control of his followers. On the advice of Cardinal Ugolino, a friend of the Franciscans, Francis resigned as leader in 1220. The following year he wrote the *First Rule*. This was further revised, with help from the cardinal, to make it acceptable to the church authorities and in 1223 the *Second Rule* was confirmed by Pope Honorius III.

In 1224, while praying on Mount Alverna, Francis had a vision of the cross and received the 'stigmata', the five wounds of Jesus Christ in the hands, feet and side. (He was the first, but by no means the last, to receive them.) Two years later, in 1226, he died, having written a final *Testament* to the order. His *Canticle of Brother Sun*, written in 1225, is also well known, but he was not the author of the nineteenth-century prayer which is popular today under the title *Prayer of St Francis*.

Francis lived a free and spontaneous life of total poverty. But was this possible for a medieval religious order? As one writer has put it, a 'vast and unwieldy phalanx was attempting to follow in the footsteps of the most spontaneous and unconventional genius of many ages – and with the natural result'. Already in Francis's lifetime adjustments were being made. The Franciscans were not to own property, but a 'spiritual friend' could own it for them and allow them to make use of it. Before long the Franciscans had churches as large and as lavish as any others. This led to conflict in the order between those who wanted a strict observance of the *Rule* and those who wished to be more practical. To some extent this conflict was resolved by Bonaventure, the 'Second Founder' of the order, but it lingered for centuries.

The earliest accounts of Francis's life are by one of his early followers, Thomas of Celano (c. 1185–c. 1260), who joined the order in about 1215. He wrote a *First Life* in 1228 at the request of the pope (Gregory IX, formerly Cardinal Ugolino) in order to justify Francis's canonization as a saint. Between 1246 and 1247 he wrote a longer *Second Life* at the request of the General of the Franciscans and a few years later (1250–53) added an account of *The Miracles of Blessed Francis*. Shorter works based on Thomas's *First Life* were produced by Thomas himself (about 1230), by Julian of Speier (1232–39) and by Henry d'Avranches (about 1232–34). In 1260 the General Chapter of the order commissioned Bonaventure to write a new biography of Francis, drawing upon this material. In 1263 Bonaventure's *Life of St Francis* became the official biography. In 1266 a decree ordered the destruction of all copies of earlier accounts – but mercifully failed to suppress them completely. The aim was to 'sanitize' the historical Francis and to exclude all that might conflict with the newly-established order. Bonaventure also later wrote a shorter *Life* for liturgical use. Two later accounts which are widely read today are *The Mirror of Perfection*, written in 1318, and *The Little Flowers of Saint Francis*, written about a hundred years after Francis's death.

Thomas's *First Life* has been chosen here not because it is better written than the others but because it takes us back nearest to the original, uncensored Francis. It is a relatively brief work of 151 paragraphs, further divided into parts and chapters. Apart from the Prologue and Epilogue there are three parts, devoted to his life until 1223 (thirty chapters), his final years (ten chapters) and his canonization and miracles (two chapters). The three scenes described below will be familiar to many readers from a variety of paintings depicting them.

14. His father saw that he would never be able to deter Francis from the course he meant to pursue, and now concentrated all his efforts on recovering the money he had lost. Francis had wanted to give it all away for the feeding of the poor and for rebuilding the church. . . . When the money was found where Francis had thrown it into the dust of the window ledge, his father's rage abated a little and his mercenary instincts were somewhat pacified. He then took Francis before the bishop of Assisi and demanded that he renounce all his possessions before the prelate and give up everything he had. This Francis agreed to do, and not only that, but he happily and readily offered to do what his father demanded.

15. When Francis was brought before the bishop he could not bear to wait a moment longer. At once, before a single word was spoken, he took off his clothes, threw them all to the ground and gave them back to his father. He removed even his undergarment. He stripped himself stark naked in front of everyone. And the bishop, seeing how passionately he felt, and deeply moved by his fervour and determination, rose at once from his seat, gathered Francis in his arms and covered him with the mantle he himself was wearing.

58. While, as has been said, many were flocking to join the Brothers, Francis was journeying through the valley of Spoleto and reached a place near Bevagna where an enormous number of different sorts of birds were gathered: there were doves, and crows, and those the people call 'daws'. When Francis saw them, being an impulsive man and one who felt great tenderness towards all dumb creatures, he left his companions on the road and ran off towards them in a great surge of affection.

 As he approached them, he realized that they were waiting for him, and he greeted them in his usual manner. To his great surprise they did not fly away as birds do, and this filled him with happiness, and he humbly begged them to hear the word of God. After speaking to them at length he added:

> *My brother birds, you really ought to praise your Creator Lord and love him for ever: he has given you feathers for clothing, wings for flight, and everything you need. God has made you noble among his creatures: he has given you a home in the pure air of heaven, and though you neither sow nor reap he still protects and guides you, so that you have not a care in the world.*

At this the little creatures showed their birdlike joy in a quite remarkable fashion, stretching their necks, spreading their wings and opening their beaks and gaping at him, and Francis went to and fro among them brushing their heads and bodies with his cloak. Finally he blessed them, and making the sign of the cross gave them leave to fly away elsewhere.

94. Two years before he gave his soul back to heaven. . . Francis had a vision in which he saw a man like a seraph: he had six wings and was standing above him with his hands outstretched and his feet joined together, and was fixed to a cross. . . . When Francis saw this he was utterly amazed: he could not fathom what this vision might mean. He was overcome with happiness and filled with intense joy at the kindly and gracious way the seraph was looking at him, and the seraph's beauty was indescribable, but the fact that he was nailed to a cross, and the sight of his cruel suffering terrified Francis. Consequently he was both sad and happy, if I can so describe him; joy and grief alternated in him. He wondered anxiously what the vision could possibly represent, and racked his brains trying to make sense of it. But still he could grasp no clear idea of its meaning, and as the strangeness of the vision continued to haunt him, the marks of nails began to appear on his hands and feet just like those he had seen on the crucified figure above him.

95. His hands and feet seemed to be pierced by nails, the heads of the nails appearing on the inside of his hands and the upper side of his feet, and their points protruding on the other side.

Bonaventure,
The Soul's Journey into God (post-1258)

John of Fidanza was born in Tuscany (central Italy) in 1217. In about 1234 he went to Paris to study and there joined the Franciscan friars in 1243, being given the name Bonaventure. He says that he was attracted to Francis because he was like the early apostles in his unlearned simplicity. But Bonaventure also believed that just as the church had gone on to produce learned doctors, so the Franciscans should rise to the highest academic levels. He taught at Paris from 1248 to 1255 and in 1250–52 lectured on Peter Lombard's *Sentences* (see pages 157–59), producing his own commentary. In 1255 the friars (Franciscans and Dominicans, founded by the Spaniard Dominic in 1216) had to leave the university because of opposition from their enemies. But in 1257 they returned, with Bonaventure as a professor.

The thirteenth century was an age of crisis for Christian theology. Previously in the medieval West, Aristotle had been known only through his works on logic. Now, in the thirteenth century, translations were made from the original Greek, and western thinkers were faced with the full impact of his philosophy. This challenged the Platonist world view, which had until then been unquestioned in the medieval West. Thomas Aquinas adopted Aristotle's philosophy and sought to reconcile it with Christian theology, supremely in his *The Sum of Theology* (see pages 172–76). Bonaventure, on the other hand, held firm to the traditional Neoplatonist philosophy. He read Aristotle and borrowed ideas from him, but these were fitted into an essentially Platonist framework. He used Aristotle, but he did not call him master.

A striking example of Bonaventure's Neoplatonism lies in his theory of illumination. With Augustine, he believed that unchanging concepts, such as justice or beauty, cannot be learned through the bodily senses – through observation or through reading or hearing about them. Instead, they are learned directly in the soul, through the eternal Ideas of justice or beauty. How can we judge one action to be more just than another unless we see the eternal unchanging Idea of justice? This truth is seen in 'the true light that gives light to every man' (John 1:9). 'In your light, we see light' (Psalm 36:9).

In 1257 Bonaventure was appointed to lead the Franciscan order as its Minister General. He inherited conflict within the order over the practicality of Francis's rule and the need to modify it. He also favoured the move from the simplicity of the first Franciscans to top rank intellectual study. Bonaventure helped to resolve these tensions and is known as the 'Second Founder' of the order. In 1260 he was commissioned to write a new biography of Francis and in 1263 his *Life of St Francis* became the official biography. Bonaventure was offered the archbishopric of York in 1265, but declined. In 1273 he succumbed to pressure and became the cardinal bishop of Albano. He died the following year, at the important Council of Lyons where East and West were negotiating reunion. In 1588 the pope declared him a doctor of the universal church with the title 'Seraphic Doctor'.

Bonaventure is remembered as much as a spiritual writer as a theologian. He wrote *The Tree of Life* which focusses on the human Jesus, his origins, his passion and his glorification. His best-known work is *The Soul's Journey into God*, which focusses rather on the mystical crucified Christ. The inspiration for the work came in 1259 while he was meditating at the spot where Francis had received the 'stigmata' (wounds of Jesus Christ). The framework for the book comes from the six-winged seraph that appeared to Francis on that occasion, the six wings corresponding to six steps or stages on the journey into God. One chapter of the book is devoted to each of these, with a seventh chapter on the final stage of mystical ecstasy.

The journey divides into three parts:

● Meditation on nature (chapters 1–2), a fitting topic for a Franciscan given Francis's interest in nature. As we express ourselves in language, so God expresses himself through creation, so his creatures are signs or symbols of him, his shadows or vestiges. We can behold God both *through* these vestiges (chapter 1) and *in* them (chapter 2).

● Meditation on the soul (chapters 3–4). Following Augustine, Bonaventure held that the image of the Trinity is to be found in the human soul, in our memory, understanding and will (chapter 3). Because of sin the soul needs to be restored for us to appreciate this (chapter 4). Bonaventure's theory of divine illumination comes into play here. The mind knows unchanging eternal truths through the divine light. God is so present that the soul actually grasps him. One cannot say that one thing is better than another without some knowledge of the highest good by which to judge.

● Meditation on God (chapters 5–6). Drawing on the early sixth-century writings of Pseudo-Dionysius especially, Bonaventure describes how we can meditate directly on God as Being (chapter 5) and as Good (chapter 6). The final chapter of the book goes on to describe the ecstasy of mystical communion with God.

Prologue: 4. I invite the reader to the groans of prayer through Christ crucified, through whose blood we are cleansed from the filth of vice – so that he not believe that reading is sufficient without unction, speculation without devotion, investigation without wonder, observation without joy, work without piety, knowledge without love, understanding without humility, endeavour without divine grace. . . . To those, therefore, predisposed by divine grace, the humble and the pious, the contrite and the devout . . . I propose the following considerations, suggesting that the mirror presented by the external world is of little or no value unless the mirror of our soul has been cleaned and polished. Therefore, man of God, first exercise yourself in remorse of conscience before you raise your eyes to the rays of Wisdom reflected in its mirrors, lest perhaps from gazing upon these rays you fall into a deeper pit of darkness.

Chapter 1: On the Stages of the Ascent into God and on Contemplating Him Through His Vestiges in the Universe

1:8. Whoever wishes to ascend to God must first avoid sin, which deforms our nature, then exercise his natural powers mentioned above: by praying, to receive restoring grace; by a good life, to receive purifying justice; by meditating, to receive illuminating knowledge; and by contemplating, to receive perfecting wisdom. Just as no one comes to wisdom except through grace, justice and knowledge, so no one comes to contemplation except by penetrating meditation, a holy life and devout prayer.

Chapter 2: On Contemplating God in His Vestiges in the Sense World

2:1. Concerning the mirror of things perceived through sensation, we can see God not only through them as through his vestiges, but also in them as he is in them by his essence, power and presence.

Chapter 3: On Contemplating God Through His Image Stamped Upon Our Natural Powers

3:1. The two previous stages, by leading us into God through his vestiges, through which he shines forth in all creatures, have led us to the point of re-entering into ourselves, that is, into our mind, where the divine image shines forth. Here it is that, now in the third stage, we enter into our very selves; and, as it were, leaving the outer court, we should strive to see God through a mirror in the sanctuary.

3:5. When, therefore, the soul considers itself, it rises through itself as through a mirror to behold the blessed Trinity of the Father, the Word and Love: three persons, coeternal, coequal and consubstantial.

Chapter 4: On Contemplating God in His Image Reformed by the Gifts of Grace

4:2. Our soul could not rise completely from these things of sense to see itself and the Eternal Truth in itself unless Truth, assuming human nature in Christ, had become a ladder, restoring the first ladder that had been broken in Adam.

4:6. By Scripture we are taught that we should be purged, illumined and perfected according to the threefold law handed down to it: the law of nature, of Scripture and of grace.

Chapter 5: On Contemplating the Divine Unity Through its Primary Name Which is Being

5:1. We can contemplate God not only outside us and within us but also above us: outside through his vestiges, within through his image and above through the light which shines upon our minds, which is the light of Eternal Truth.

Chapter 6: On Contemplating the Most Blessed Trinity in its Name Which is Good

6:1. After considering the essential attributes of God, the eye of our intelligence should be raised to look upon the most blessed Trinity.

Chapter 7: On Spiritual and Mystical Ecstasy in Which Rest is Given to Our Intellect When Through Ecstasy Our Affection Passes Over Entirely into God

7:5. Transcending yourself and all things, by the immeasurable and absolute ecstasy of a pure mind, leaving behind all things and freed from all things, you will ascend to the superessential ray of the divine darkness.

7:6. But if you wish to know how these things come about, ask grace not instruction, desire not understanding, the groaning of prayer not diligent reading, the Spouse [Jesus Christ] not the teacher, God not man, darkness not clarity, not light but the fire that totally inflames and carries us into God by ecstatic unctions and burning affections.

Thomas Aquinas,
The Sum of Theology (1264–74)

Thomas Aquinas was born in 1225 near Naples as the younger son of the count of Aquina. He went to the university of Naples and while there, in 1244, joined the relatively new Order of Preachers, the Dominican friars. In disgust, his family kidnapped him and held him captive for some months, but to no avail. Thomas continued his studies at Paris and at Cologne under the famous Dominican theologian Albert the Great, who greatly influenced him. In 1252 he returned to Paris to lecture. Thereafter he taught at Paris and in Italy until his death in 1274, on the way to the Council of Lyons.

Thomas faced the burning issue of the thirteenth century – how to react to the philosophy of Aristotle. He did not agree with those who wanted to suppress Aristotle and he did not follow his older contemporary Bonaventure, who kept to the traditional Neoplatonist world view. Thomas followed Aristotle's philosophy but parted company with those who followed Aristotle to the point of contradicting Catholic doctrine (e.g. by teaching that the universe was eternal and had no beginning). Thomas's aim was to construct a synthesis between reason and faith, philosophy and theology, Aristotle and Catholic doctrine. He followed Aristotle's philosophy, but not blindly. Occasionally he felt the need to correct him, as with his opinion concerning the age of the universe, but generally he followed him because he believed him to be right. He maintained that Aristotelian philosophy and Catholic theology could be held together, with no conflict between the two.

Thomas did not see philosophy and theology as merely compatible with one another – like music and geology, say. He believed that correct philosophy can greatly aid theology. The aim of God's grace is not to destroy human nature, nor to act separately from it, but to perfect it. Human reason, by the use of philosophy, can discover much that is true about the world, mankind and even God. The purpose of divine revelation is to perfect human philosophy by adding to it, building on it, completing it. Revelation does not basically oppose human philosophy (though it will oppose *false*, incorrect philosophy), but rather supplements it and brings it to completion and perfection. But for Thomas it is always revealed theology that is primary, a fact that his interpreters have not always recognized, although his interpretation of revealed theology was greatly influenced by Aristotle.

Thomas wrote extensively – commentaries on Scripture, philosophical and theological treatises, commentaries on Aristotle. But two of his works stand out especially:

● *The Manual against the Heathen* was written in the early 1260s, in four books. It was written for the benefit of unbelievers, like Jews and Muslims. It exemplifies Thomas's nature/grace approach. In Books 1 to 3 he argues on the basis of reason/philosophy alone. Scripture and tradition are invoked only to confirm conclusions already reached by reason. On this basis Thomas seeks to establish the existence of God, his attributes (such as love, wisdom, omnipotence), his creation of the world, his providence and predestination. In the final book, Thomas goes on to present those doctrines which cannot be reached without Christian revelation – the Trinity, the incarnation of Jesus Christ, the sacraments, the resurrection of the body. These doctrines are beyond the grasp of unaided reason, but they are not *contrary* to reason.

● *The Sum of Theology*, written in the last ten years of Thomas's life, was intended as a textbook to replace Peter Lombard's *Sentences* (see pages 157–59), though it did not succeed in this aim for some centuries. It is a massive work of more than two million words. Since it is addressed to Catholics rather than to unbelievers, the distinctive truths of revelation are not kept to the end. But Thomas still distinguishes between that which can be discerned by reason and that which can be known only by revelation. In this, his greatest work, Thomas takes the theology of Augustine which was presented in Neoplatonist terms, and restates it in Aristotelian terms. It is one of the greatest systematic presentations of the Christian faith ever produced. Thomas did not live to complete this work, but some of his disciples supplied a *Supplement* drawn from his other works to complete it. Near the end of his life Thomas had a vision while saying mass, which caused him to stop writing. He stated that in comparison with what had then been revealed to him, all that he had written seemed like straw.

The layout of the *Sum of Theology* is distinctive. It is divided into three parts, the second of which is subdivided into two further parts. The whole work is divided into 512 questions (613 counting the *Supplement*), each of which is normally divided into a number (from one to ten) of articles or points of inquiry. Under each point, Thomas begins by marshalling evidence which appears to contradict his position. This consists of philosophical arguments or quotations from authorities such as the Bible or the Fathers. But he then counters this with a reason or a quotation in favour of his own position. (In the extract below, this contrary view is, exceptionally, another incorrect view diametrically opposed to the first.) Then in a 'reply' he resolves the question to his satisfaction. Aristotle is the most frequently quoted (as 'the philosopher') and, after the Bible, Augustine heads the list of theological authorities. For the benefit of those without the leisure to read the whole of the *Sum*, Thomas also wrote a relatively brief *Compendium of Theology*. Thomas's *Sum* is hardly light reading and at times requires a grasp of Aristotle to be understood. But at the same time the two million words are broken down into 3125 articles, each of which is of modest length. Thomas was one of the greatest theologians of all time and his *Sum* is rightly taken seriously today as a classic theological text of abiding value.

Thomas was a large man who moved slowly and always remained calm. His fellow students used to call him the 'dumb ox'. But his teacher, Albert the Great, once prophesied that 'this dumb ox will fill the world with his bellowing'. Thomas's reputation was considerable in his own day, but his views did not go unopposed and some of them were condemned shortly after his death. It was not until after his canonization as a saint in 1323 that opposition died down. Even then, his influence in the fourteenth and fifteenth centuries was not very great. It is more recently that he has become pre-eminent. In 1879, Pope Leo XIII instructed all theological students to study Thomas's works. However, since the Second Vatican Council and the desire for modernization in the Roman Catholic Church, Thomas's influence has somewhat declined.

Thomas is famous for his teaching about analogy. What do we mean when we speak of God – e.g. 'God is good' or 'the Lord is my rock'? Is such language univocal – i.e. do the words 'good' and 'rock' mean exactly the same as when used of people or boulders in everyday language? If God is transcendent, they cannot. Is such language then equivocal – i.e. do the words mean something completely different from their everyday usage, as a dog's bark is totally different from a tree's bark? If that were so, we would have to say that we know *nothing* about God.

Thomas distinguishes two different types of statement about God. Some are metaphorical – such as 'the Lord is my rock'. This is a metaphor because the word rock applies primarily to physical rocks and only in a secondary way to God, to draw out certain points of comparison, such as God's reliability. Other words are used properly and strictly of God – as when we say that God is good. Such a statement lies between the univocal and the equivocal. God's goodness can be compared to ours, so there is a ground for using the same word. But the word good does not have exactly the same meaning when applied to God and to us. (Thomas uses the argument that our goodness is distinct from our being – we can cease to be good – while God's is not.)

If God and people are both called good, but in different senses, which sense is primary? As regards our language, the latter. It is human goodness that we know first. But Ephesians 3:14–15 implies that human fatherhood is named after God's fatherhood. While the word rock applies primarily to physical rocks, words like good apply primarily to God (and therefore are used of him properly and accurately, not metaphorically). That is, it is God who is the cause of all creaturely goodness. Furthermore, God's goodness is perfect. Therefore the word good is used most appropriately of God. 'No one is good – except God alone' (Mark 10:18). But our understanding of the term is derived from human goodness. Thus Thomas leaves us with a real, but imperfect, knowledge of God. 'God surpasses human understanding and speech. He knows God best who acknowledges that whatever he thinks and says falls short of what God really is.'

Part I, question 13, article 5.

Are words predicated univocally of both God and creatures?

Objection 1: It would appear that the things said of God and creatures are univocal. For every equivocal term is based upon the univocal, just as the many are based upon the one. The word 'dog' can only be used equivocally of barking dogs and dogfish because it is first used univocally – of all barking dogs. . . . Therefore it seems that the first cause to which all other causes are reduced is a univocal cause. Thus what is said of God and creatures, is predicated univocally.

Objection 2: Further, there is no likeness between equivocal things. Therefore as creatures have a certain likeness to God, according to the word of Genesis [1:26], 'Let us make man in our image and likeness,' it seems that something can be said of God and creatures univocally. . . .

On the contrary, when the same word is used of various things with different meanings it is predicated equivocally. But no word is used of God in the same sense as of creatures. For instance, wisdom is a quality in creatures, but not in God. . . . Therefore whatever is said of God and of creatures is predicated equivocally. Furthermore, God is more distant from creatures than any creatures are from each other. But some creatures are so different from each other that nothing can be predicated of them univocally, as with things belonging to different categories. Therefore it is much less possible for anything to be predicated univocally of God and creatures – and so only equivocal predication can be applied to them.

My reply is that univocal predication is impossible between God and creatures. . . . All perfections which exist in creatures in a separate and various way, pre-exist in God unitedly. Thus when any term expressing perfection is applied to a creature, it signifies that perfection distinct from others. When we apply the term 'wise' to a man, we signify some perfection distinct from his essence, power, existence, etc. But when we apply the term to God, we do not mean to signify anything distinct from his essence, power or existence. . . . Hence it is evident that the term 'wise' is not applied to God in the same way as to man. The same applies to other terms. Hence no word is predicated univocally of both God and creatures.

Neither, on the other hand, are words applied to God and creatures in a purely equivocal sense, as some have said. Because if that were so, it would follow that nothing could be known or demonstrated about God at all from creatures – for such reasoning would always be guilty of the error of equivocation. Such a view is contrary to the philosophers, who proved many things about God, and also against the teaching of the Apostle, who says: 'The invisible things of God are clearly seen, being understood from what has been made' [Romans 1:20]. Therefore it must be said that these terms are applied to God and creatures in an analogical or proportional sense. . . .

In this way some things are said of God and creatures analogically, not in a purely equivocal or univocal sense. For we can speak of God only in language derived from creatures. So whatever is said of God and creatures is said according to the relation between the latter and God, who is their principle and cause in which all their perfections pre-exist excellently. Now this way of speaking lies somewhere between the purely equivocal and the simply univocal. For in analogies the idea is not (as with univocals) one and the same, yet it is not totally different (as with equivocals), but a word which is thus used in a multiple sense signifies various proportions to some one thing. . . .

Reply to Objection 2: The likeness of the creature to God is imperfect, for it does not represent one and the same generic thing. . . .

The arguments adduced in the contrary sense prove indeed that these words are not predicated univocally of God and creatures; yet they do not prove that they are predicated equivocally.

Johann Tauler, *Sermons* (pre-1361)

The fourteenth and fifteenth centuries saw a flowering of mysticism. Many of the greatest mystical writers of all time lived then – such as Catherine of Siena, Walter Hilton, Julian of Norwich, Richard Rolle and Henry Suso. There were two strands in the mystical tradition – the intellectual and speculative approach, influenced by Neoplatonism, and a more practical approach which stressed the imitation of Jesus Christ. The first approach was found in Meister Eckhart (died 1327 or 1328). He was a popular and respected teacher, but incautious in some of his statements – for example, in referring to a 'divine spark' within the human soul. Neoplatonism stressed the unity of all things, so Neoplatonist mysticism was always in danger of lapsing into pantheism and in 1326 Eckhart was accused of heresy. While there is no doubt about his desire to be orthodox, in 1329 twenty-eight of his statements were condemned by the pope – eleven as 'dangerous', seventeen as heretical. Eckhart's influence continued through his disciples, especially Tauler and his friend Suso.

Johann Tauler was born at Strassburg (later to become the French city Strasbourg) in about 1300 and in about 1314 joined the Dominican friars there. He was influenced by Eckhart's ideas, spending some time at Cologne while he was there. The rest of his life was spent mostly at Strassburg, apart from a few years at Basel from 1339. Tauler himself became a leading spiritual teacher and helped to spread some of Eckhart's ideas, but he learned from Eckhart's condemnation, being more cautious and pastorally sensitive in his teaching. He laid his stress on the practical side of mysticism and aimed his teaching not at a spiritual elite but at all Christians. During the Black Death (1348–49) he devoted himself to caring for the sick, which enhanced his reputation. He died in 1361. He was a preacher rather than a writer. The only genuine works which survive are some sermons, which were preached before nuns and recorded at a later date. It was Tauler's brand of mysticism which became popular in the fourteenth and fifteenth centuries. It was influential in the 'Rhineland school' of mysticism (which produced a work called *The German Theology* [see pages 180–82], admired by Luther), in the English mystical tradition and in the Modern Devotion, of which Thomas à Kempis's *The Imitation of Christ* is the best-known representative.

Tauler, like many spiritual writers, had a clear understanding of the obstacles that stand in the way of progress. In the sermon from which the extracts below are taken he warns clearly against a self-centred form of religion which is more concerned about ourselves than about God. This is a message that needs to be heeded at a time when so much religion is about meeting our needs and making us feel better rather than repentance and submission to God and to his agenda.

Sermon 19 (Ascension II) on Ephesians 4:8: 'Ascending on high, he led captivity captive'

Our Lord Jesus Christ ascended into Heaven and with him he led captivity captive. We find five types of captivity in this world to which people are subjected and robbed of their freedom, but when Christ takes us up in his Ascension, he frees us from all our bonds.

The first type of captivity consists in man's dependence on creatures, animate or inanimate, when he loves them without reference to God. This is particularly true of the love of human beings, for who is closer to man than man? The damage that is caused by such inordinate affection cannot be sufficiently stressed. . . .

The second type of captivity is the lot of those who, after being released from the first – the love of creatures and the world – fall into the captivity of self-love. This love fills them with such complacency that it makes one wonder. No one rebukes them, least of all do they rebuke themselves. Their self-love is so beautifully cloaked, so splendidly projected, that no one could possibly object. Eventually it makes them seek their own in everything. Personal advantage is what they pursue in their pleasures, their consolations, their comfort and their honour. So totally are they absorbed in themselves that they even make use of God. Alas, what will come to light when the depths of such souls are searched! What appears as sanctity will be found fraudulent throughout. Oh how hard it will be to help such people with their soft natures and worldly dispositions! How hard it will be to free them from their captivity! . . . They seem to require so many things, their needs are so extensive and various, and they consider themselves so fragile and sensitive. But when it happens, as it often does, that their possessions are taken from them or threatened, whether it is some convenience or a friend, or another precious thing that lends them comfort, then they immediately reject God with angry words and spiteful actions, speaking untruths openly or by insinuation. . . .

The third type of captivity is that of natural reason. This is the downfall of many, because they spoil everything which should be born in the spirit – be it doctrine or truth of whatever kind – by lowering it to the level of their reasoning powers. They give themselves great airs, because whatever it is, they interpret it rationally and hold forth on it, which greatly increases their self-esteem. . . .

And now we come to the fourth captivity, which is that of spiritual sweetness. Many a man has been led astray by it, because he pursued it in an undisciplined way, sunk down in it, and came to a standstill there; it seemed to him a good thing to possess and to abandon himself to with pleasure. But nature will claim its share, and when we think we have grasped God, it is only our enjoyment we have grasped. Still, there is a way of telling whether God or nature is the source of our joy. If we feel restless and distressed and are troubled as soon as the sweetness begins to fade and diminish, if we are unable to serve God as willingly and as faithfully as before, then we may be sure that it was not really God we served. . . .

The fifth captivity is self-will. By this we mean the will to have one's own way, even in the things of God, even in God himself. Suppose God were to give himself to our very will and desires, so much that we might be rid of all our shortcomings and gain every virtue and perfection; it would indeed be folly to reject such an offer. And yet I can think of something better. Even if I could have my way, with God's consent, I would still say: 'No, Lord, not my graces or gifts are what I desire; not my will, Lord, but yours I shall accept; and should you will that I have nothing, I will surrender for the sake of your will.'

To think in such a way, and to renounce self-will with such a disposition, is to possess and receive more than could ever have been gained by having one's own way. Whatever a man may desire to have according to his will, be it God or creatures, it would be infinitely more beneficial to forgo it willingly and humbly and to hold whatever he has, in a spirit of true abandonment, surrendering the will completely to God. For that reason I would prefer a man who has utterly surrendered, with fewer works and accomplishments, to one of dazzling works of virtue whose surrender was imperfect.

The German Theology (mid-14th century)

The *German Theology* is an anonymous work from the middle of the fourteenth century. Its fame is due in part to Martin Luther's enthusiastic advocacy of it. In 1516 he found a shorter version of it and had it published at Wittenberg. Two years later he found a fuller manuscript and published this. In his Preface to the latter edition he spoke in glowing terms of the work: 'Next to the Bible and Saint Augustine no other book has come to my attention from which I have learned – and desired to learn – more concerning God, Christ, man, and what all things are.'

There are two slightly different versions of the text. In 1851 a manuscript was discovered dating from 1497, known as the Würzburg version. Since then there has been ongoing debate about which is the more authentic version. For some time the Würzburg version was favoured, but more recent scholarship has begun to favour Luther's version.

Protestant attitudes to this work have varied. While Luther was very enthusiastic about it, later Lutheran scholastic theology came to view it with considerable suspicion. Calvin observed that while it contained no notable errors it obscures the simplicity of the gospel. Yet later Pietist authors admired it greatly and Spener commended it in his *Holy Desires* (see pages 332–35). Despite this controversy it has remained a popular work and has been published about two hundred times over the centuries in a variety of languages.

The anonymous author belonged to a fourteenth-century mystical movement known as 'The Friends of God', which was influenced by the *Sermons* of Johann Tauler (see pages 177–79). This group taught the need for denying oneself and for a personal relationship with God. The stress on an individual relationship with God could lead to a rejection of the organized church with its hierarchy and sacraments. The Friends did not go that way but there were others, known as 'Brothers and Sisters of the Free Spirit', who did, also rejecting conventional morality. The Friends were in danger of being confused with the Free Spirits and being persecuted, which may explain the anonymity of the *German Theology* – which repeatedly condemns the Free Spirits.

The *German Theology* teaches humility. We must ascribe no good to ourselves and recognize our total dependence upon God's grace – themes that would have appealed to the young Luther. But at the same time (as with Luther's *Freedom of a Christian* [see pages 194–97]) it is important not to neglect external good works. The key to spirituality lies in the elimination of all self-will, in the obedient subjugation of our own will to God's. The book has a lot to say about the path of discipleship (which explains its popularity with the Pietists) but all but nothing to say about our being accepted by God through faith (which explains the reserve of other Protestants). There are warnings about the dangers of a purely academic knowledge, including a description of the danger facing all who study theology, that 'knowledge and learning are indeed more loved than that which is the object of knowledge' (40).

The *German Theology* does indeed have its weaknesses and blind spots, as some have pointed out, but at the same time there is much of value in what it does say and it has rightly remained an ever-popular spiritual classic.

─────────────────────

11. When a person comes to know and see himself he discovers that he is wicked and unworthy of the goodness and comfort that he has received from God or from fellow beings. He then feels that he is damned and lost and unworthy even of that. Yes, he thinks that he is unworthy of the sufferings that he may undergo in his earthly life. . . . He also deems it right that he should be eternally damned and be a footstool for all the devils in hell and, again, that he is unworthy even of that. . . .

12. So we should note and observe the kind of peace Christ left for his disciples in his parting days. He spoke to them and said: 'My peace I give to you; not as the world gives do I give to you.' For the world's gifts are treacherous. What kind of peace does Christ mean? He means the inner peace that comes in the midst of hardship, distress, much anguish and misfortune, strain, misery, disgrace, and whatever setbacks there are. Through this peace we become cheerful and patient amid tribulations, just as Christ's dear disciples were – and not they alone but all chosen friends of God and true Christ-followers.

32. All self-will must be done away with, as we said. God would gladly help man toward this. When man seeks his own good, he never actually finds it. For man's highest good would be and truly is that he should not seek and love himself or his own.

36. The life in Christ is not chosen because one derives use from it or can obtain something thereby but on account of love for its nobility and because it is dear to God and highly rated by him. Whoever says that he has had enough of it or that he wants to put it aside has never tasted it or come to know it from within. For the person who has in truth felt it or tasted it can never give it up. Therefore, the person who leads a life in Christ with the intention of obtaining some use or earning some glory from it embraces this life as a hireling who is out for recompense and not from love; he possesses none of Christ's life. He who is not devoted to it out of love has no part of it. He might fancy he has it but he is mistaken.

39. The truly righteous would rather die than cause unrighteousness and this for no reason than for love of righteousness. Righteousness becomes the reward of the truly righteous; she gives herself as reward. This is how a righteous person lives. He would rather die a hundredfold than live unrighteously.

47. One says that self-will is the most widespread commodity in hell. That is certainly true. Hell is and consists of self-will. If there would be no self-will there would be no hell and no devil. When we read that the devil, Lucifer, fell from heaven and turned away from God, and so forth, it means only that he was anxious to maintain his own self-will and that he did not wish to tune his will to the eternal Will. This was also the case with Adam in paradise. When we say self-will we mean willing to be other than the one eternal Will wills. . . . In all that exists around us nothing is forbidden, nothing is basically contrary to God, save one thing. That one thing is self-will, or to will and intend otherwise than the eternal Will wills.

51. In hell everyone wants to have a self-will. Therefore all is misery there, and wretchedness. The case is, correspondingly, the same in our temporal existence. Supposing a denizen of hell surrendered his self-will and were released from his desire to call something his own. He would then come out of hell into the kingdom of heaven. In this earthly life man finds himself between heaven and hell. He can turn his will to whichever he chooses. The greater the desire to possess and own, the more hell and wretchedness he will have; the less self-will, the less hell and the closer to the kingdom of heaven.

56. May we abandon our selfish ways and die away from our own will and live only to God and his will. May we be helped to this by him who surrendered his will to his heavenly Father, and who lives and rules with God, the Father, in union with the Holy Spirit, in perfect Trinity.

Catherine of Siena, *The Dialogue*
(1377–78)

Caterina di Giacomo di Benincasa was born in 1347 to a Sienese wool dyer. She was the twenty-fourth of twenty-five children. When she was seven years old she had a vision of Jesus with Peter, Paul and John, as a result of which she resolved to lead a life of celibacy. It took her family some time to come to terms with this and when she was fifteen Catherine had to cut off her hair in order to avoid marriage.

Her first confessor was her sister's brother-in-law Tommaso della Fonte, who was a Dominican. It was as a result of his influence that she became a Dominican lay sister, which meant that she would live a 'religious' life in the world. For a time she lived a life of solitude at home, during which she learned to read. This period culminated in 1368 with her experience of 'mystical betrothal' to Christ.

From 1368 to 1374 Catherine was active in Siena. She devoted herself to the care of the poor. She also embarked upon a wider pastoral ministry through letter writing. Nearly four hundred of her letters have come down to us. In 1370 she also underwent an experience of 'mystical death', a four-hour period of union with God during which her body appeared to be totally lifeless.

From 1375 Catherine's ministry widened beyond Siena. She found herself playing a role in wider church politics, including negotiations between the pope and the city of Florence. In 1375 she claimed to have received the 'stigmata', the five wounds of Christ, as had Francis of Assisi, but in such a way that they were visible only to herself. In 1377 she had further experiences of God which moved her to write her *Dialogue,* her major work.

Since 1305 the pope had been in Avignon under French control. Catherine repeatedly urged Gregory XI to return to Rome, which he finally did in 1377. But he died the following year and his successor Urban VI behaved in such a totalitarian fashion that he soon prompted the election of a rival pope, Clement VII. Thus began the forty-year Great Schism. Catherine sided with Urban and threw herself into the task of supporting him. She went to Rome, at Urban's request, but her health deteriorated and she died there in 1380, a mere thirty-three years old. In 1970 Catherine was granted the title Doctor of the [Roman Catholic] Church.

Catherine made no original contribution to theology, but her gift was to absorb the spiritual teaching of her time and to re-express it vividly in the local (Italian) dialect. The *Dialogue* was before long divided into [167] chapters and in the sixteenth century further (and very misleadingly) divided into four 'treatises', arising from a misunderstanding of some chapter headings. Catherine gives an account of various of her own experiences but most of the work takes the form of God speaking to her. There is a heavy use of imagery.

The longest and most important section, comprising over a quarter of the whole, is an extended development of the theme of Christ as the bridge between earth and heaven, through his incarnation. This is the only way to heaven, opened up by Christ's death for us on the cross. Those who instead try to pass through the river of temptation, sin and death will be lost. The allegory is extended with three stairs to heaven, a gate, walls on the sides of the bridge, etc. The entire work is focussed practically on how to progress from a state of sin to the goal of loving union with God.

───────────

59. [God to Catherine:] I told you no one can cross over the bridge and so escape the river without climbing the three stairs. Such is the truth, and some climb imperfectly, some perfectly, and others with great perfection.

Those who are motivated by slavish fear climb and gather their powers together only imperfectly. When they see the penalty that must follow upon their sin, they climb up and gather together their powers: memory to recall their vices, understanding to see the punishment they expect for their sin, and finally the will to hate it.

Since this is the first step upward and the first gathering together, they must act on it. Their mind's eye, through the pupil, which is most holy faith, should consider not only the punishment but the reward of virtue and the love I bear them. Then they will climb in love, with the feet of their affection stripped of slavish fear. In this way they will become faithful rather than faithless servants, serving me out of love rather than fear. And if they set their hatred to the task of digging up the root of their selfish love of themselves, and if they are prudent, constant, and persevering, they will succeed.

But there are many who begin their climb so sluggishly and pay what they owe me in such bits and pieces, so indifferently and ignorantly, that they quickly fall by the way. The smallest wind makes them hoist their sails and turn back. They had climbed only imperfectly to the first stair of Christ crucified, and so they never reach the second, which is that of his heart.

60. There are others who become faithful servants. They serve me with love rather than that slavish fear which serves only for fear of punishment. But their love is imperfect, for they serve me for their own profit or for the delight and pleasure they find in me. Do you know how they show that their love is imperfect? By the way they act when they are deprived of the comfort they find in me. And they love their neighbours with the same imperfect love. This is why their love is not strong enough to last. No, it becomes lax and often fails. It becomes lax toward me when sometimes, to exercise them in virtue and to lift them up out of their imperfection, I take back my spiritual comfort and let them experience struggles

and vexations. I do this to bring them to perfect knowledge of themselves. . . . And though I may take away their comfort, I do not take away grace.

But it makes such as these grow lax, and they turn back with impatient spirit. . . . Because they are imperfect they serve me only for their own profit and let their love for their neighbours grow lax.

The first souls I spoke of fail because of their fear of suffering. These second grow lax, desisting from the service they were giving their neighbours and pulling back from their charity if it seems they have lost their own profit or some comfort they had formerly found in them. And this comes about because their love was not genuine. They love their neighbours with the same love with which they love me – for their own profit. . . .

To have eternal life it is essential to love without regard for one's own interest. Fleeing sin for fear of punishment is not enough to give eternal life, nor is it enough to embrace virtue for one's own profit. No, one must rise from sin because sin displeases me, and love virtue for love of me. . . .

Souls who climb this first stair with only slavish fear and mercenary love fall into all sorts of troubles. What they need is to get up and be my children and serve me without regard for their own interest. . . . If these souls do not give up the exercise of holy prayer and other good works, but go on strengthening their virtue perseveringly, they will come to filial love. And I will love them as my children, because with whatever love I am loved, with that love I respond. . . . As long as their love remains mercenary I do not show myself to them. But they can, with contempt for their imperfection and with love of virtue, use hatred to dig out the root of their spiritual selfishness. They can sit in judgment on themselves so that motives of slavish fear and mercenary love do not cross their hearts without being corrected in the light of most holy faith. If they act in this way, it will please me so much that for this they will come to the love of friendship. And then I will show myself to them.

Thomas à Kempis,
The Imitation of Christ (pre-1427)

Thomas Hemerken was born in 1379 or 1380 at Kempen (near Cologne), from which he has acquired the name Thomas à Kempis. His parents sent him to a school at Deventer (in Holland) run by the Brethren of the Common Life – a movement pioneered by Geert de Groote (1340–84), a wealthy canon of Utrecht who was converted from his worldly life. He started informal lay communities and his followers became involved in the task of education. In 1387 some of his disciples founded a house of Augustinian canons at Windesheim, near Zwolle in Holland, which became the mother house of an expanding 'order', with about a hundred daughter houses by 1500. This movement was known as the Modern Devotion. Despite the name, it was essentially traditional rather than novel, with an emphasis on conversion, on the importance of practical Christian living and holiness, on meditation (especially on the life and death of Jesus) and on frequent communion. It was based especially on the teaching of Augustine, Bernard and Bonaventure, but the idea of lay communities involved in secular work in towns without living under a rule was new.

In 1399 Thomas entered the house of Augustinian canons at Mount St Agnes, near Zwolle, a recent offshoot from Windesheim. He remained there until his death in 1471, writing, preaching, copying manuscripts and acting as a spiritual adviser. He wrote many works, of which the best known is *The Imitation of Christ*, which is composed of four books. Originally these were four separate treatises, all of which were in circulation by 1427. It was customary to include a number of shorter treatises on one manuscript and as these four were especially popular they were often found together. The first printed version, from 1473, contains these four books as we now have them and this rapidly became the standard form. The treatises were originally anonymous, which led to speculation as to their authorship, but it is generally accepted today that Thomas was the author.

The Imitation of Christ is one of the most popular classics of all times and a recent edition claimed that 'after the Bible, this is perhaps the most widely read book in the world'. It reached its ninety-ninth printed edition by the end of the fifteenth century and has by now reached well over two thousand printings. In some ways its greatness lies in its very lack of originality. It is the best representative of the spirituality of the Modern Devotion and the ideas that it proclaims are not peculiar to any one school but belong to the mainstream of Christian spirituality.

The title *The Imitation of Christ* is misleading. In fact it is the title of only the first chapter of the first book and is not an accurate indication of the contents of the work as a whole. (In the extracts below, chapter titles are given, dropping the initial 'On'.)

The keynotes of the work are self-examination and humility, self-denial and discipline, acceptance of one's lot and trust in and love for God. Book I is especially devoted to the beginnings of the spiritual life (in a monastery) while the last book is devoted to the subject of receiving holy communion. The middle books are on the inner life and on spiritual comfort.

As with most monastic writings the asceticism is in danger of denying that the good things of this life are gifts of God for us to enjoy, but for most modern Christians the danger lies in the opposite direction – living for this life alone. John Calvin, in the section of his *Institutes of the Christian Religion* (see pages 218–21) on the Christian life, embraces Thomas's teaching but warns against the danger of asceticism. Thomas also illustrates another weakness which recurs throughout the Christian tradition – anti-intellectualism. Thomas is surely right, in his reaction against the barren scholastic theology of his time, to proclaim that it is better to 'feel contrition than be able to define it' (1:1). But it is better still both to experience it and to be able to define it. While scholars who have no experience of what they study and teach are sadly deficient, those who are able to explain that which they have experienced are well equipped to help others. But no book is perfect and these blemishes are minor compared with the immense wisdom of this work.

―――――――――――――

1:1. The Imitation of Christ

Of what use is it to discourse learnedly on the Trinity, if you lack humility and therefore displease the Trinity? Lofty words do not make a man just or holy; but a good life makes him dear to God. I would far rather feel contrition than be able to define it. If you knew the whole Bible by heart, and all the teachings of the philosophers, how would this help you without the grace and love of God? . . .

1:2. Personal Humility

Restrain an inordinate desire for knowledge, in which is found much anxiety and deception. Learned men always wish to appear so, and desire recognition of their wisdom. But there are many matters, knowledge of which brings little or no advantage to the soul. Indeed, a man is unwise if he occupies himself with any things save those that further his salvation. A spate of words does nothing to satisfy the soul, but a good life refreshes the mind, and a clean conscience brings great confidence in God.

1:15. Deeds Inspired by Love

Without love, the outward work is of no value; but whatever is done out of love, be it never so little, is wholly fruitful. For God regards the greatness of the love that prompts a man, rather than the greatness of his achievement. Whoever loves much, does much. Whoever does a thing well, does much. And he does well, who serves the community before his own interests. Often an apparently loving action really springs from worldly motives; for natural inclination, self-will, hope of reward, and our own self-interest will seldom be entirely absent. . . .

1:16. Bearing with the Faults of Others

Strive to be patient; bear with the faults and frailties of others, for you, too, have many faults which others have to bear. If you cannot mould yourself as you would wish, how can you expect other people to be entirely to your liking? For we require other people to be perfect, but do not correct our own faults. We wish to see others severely reprimanded; yet we are unwilling to be corrected ourselves. We wish to restrict the liberty of others, but are not willing to be denied anything ourselves. We wish others to be bound by rules, yet we will not let ourselves be bound. It is amply evident, therefore, that we seldom consider our neighbour in the same light as ourselves. Yet, if all men were perfect, what should we have to bear with in others for Christ's sake?

1:23. A Meditation on Death

Very soon the end of your life will be at hand: consider, therefore, the state of your soul. Today a man is here; tomorrow he is gone. And when he is out of sight, he is soon out of mind. Oh, how dull and hard is the heart of man, which thinks only of the present, and does not provide against the future! You should order your every deed and thought, as though today were the day of your death. Had you a good conscience, death would hold no terrors for you; even so, it were better to avoid sin than to escape death. If you are not ready to die today, will tomorrow find you better prepared? Tomorrow is uncertain; and how can you be sure of tomorrow?

2:11. The Few Lovers of the Cross of Jesus

Jesus has many who love his kingdom in heaven, but few who bear his cross. He has many who desire comfort, but few who desire suffering. He finds many to share his feast, but few his fasting. All desire to rejoice with him, but few are willing to suffer for his sake. Many follow Jesus to the breaking of bread, but few to the drinking of the cup of his passion. Many admire his miracles, but few follow him in the humiliation of his cross. Many love Jesus as long as no hardship touches them. Many praise and bless him, as long as they are receiving any comfort from him. But if Jesus withdraw himself, they fall to complaining and utter dejection. They who love Jesus for his own sake, and not for the sake of comfort for themselves, bless him in every trial and anguish of heart, no less than in the greatest joy. And were he never willing to bestow comfort on them, they would still always praise him and give him thanks.

Oh, how powerful is the pure love of Jesus, free from all self-interest and self-love! Are they not all mercenary, who are always seeking comfort? Do they not betray themselves as lovers of self rather than of Christ, when they are always thinking of their own advantage and gain? Where will you find one who is willing to serve God without reward?

3:16. How True Comfort is to Be Sought in God Alone

Whatever I can wish or imagine for my consolation, I do not expect now, but hereafter. For if I were to enjoy all the pleasures of the world, and were able to taste all its delights, they would surely pass away. Therefore my soul can never find full satisfaction or perfect refreshment save in God alone, who is the comfort of the poor and protector of the humble. Be patient, my soul; await the fulfilment of God's promise, and you shall enjoy the abundance of his goodness in heaven. But if you hanker inordinately after the good things of this life, you will lose those of heaven and eternity. Therefore make right use of this world's goods, but long only for those that are eternal. This world's good things can never satisfy you, for you are not created for the enjoyment of these alone.

3:28. Against Slander

My son, do not take it to heart if others think ill of you, and say unpleasant things about you. Consider yourself to be even worse than they imagine, and regard yourself as the weakest of men.

3:35. How There is No Security from Temptation

If you look for rest in this life, how can you gain eternal rest? Dispose yourself not to rest, but to patient endurance. Seek true peace not on earth but in heaven; not in man, nor in any other creature, but in God alone. For love of God cheerfully endure everything – labour, sorrow, temptation, provocation, anxiety, necessity, weakness, injury and insult; censure, humiliation, disgrace, contradiction and contempt. All these things foster your growth in virtue, for they test the unproved servant of Christ, and form the jewels of his heavenly crown. I will grant an eternal reward for your brief toil, and boundless glory for your passing trouble.

Desiderius Erasmus,
The Praise of Folly (1509)

Desiderius Erasmus was born in the late 1460s, the illegitimate son of a priest. He was educated for some years by the Brethren of the Common Life. The Modern Devotion, as found in Thomas à Kempis's *The Imitation of Christ* (see pages 186–89), influenced him, though he rejected some aspects of the Brethren. He reluctantly entered one of their monasteries, but before long obtained permission to leave. After a period of study at Paris, from 1495 he became a freelance scholar, travelling widely throughout Europe. For a time he was a professor at Cambridge. From 1521 he settled at Basel, but in 1529 the Reformation there progressed beyond his liking and he left for nearby Catholic Freiburg. He returned to Basel in 1535 and died there the following year.

Erasmus was the most famous scholar of his time. He was a convinced Christian Humanist, believing that the best way to reform the church was by good scholarship – by a study of the Bible in Hebrew and Greek and by a return to the Early Church Fathers. He was a master of satire and one modern writer has stated that 'only when humour illuminated that mind did it become truly profound'. His satire was directed against the abuses of the contemporary church – the scandalous lives of the pope and many of the clergy, the state of the monasteries and the obscurities of medieval scholastic theology. Erasmus's own desire was for peaceful reform of the church.

In this way Erasmus laid the foundations for the Protestant Reformation. As the adage goes, 'Erasmus laid the egg which Luther hatched.' In the early years of the Reformation, a papal agent in Germany wrote to Rome that the satires of Erasmus were harming the papacy more than the denunciations of Luther. By making people laugh at the Roman system Erasmus had more effect than the protests of Reformers. But Erasmus was not an unqualified supporter of Luther. He approved of Luther's desire for reform, but could not follow him in his breach with the papacy and his division of the church. In the early years of the Reformation Erasmus forbore from criticizing Luther and this greatly helped the latter at a critical and dangerous time. But in 1524 Erasmus bowed to pressure from the pope and others and wrote an attack on Luther's doctrine of the bondage of the human will. Luther promptly replied and relations between the two great men were permanently soured.

Erasmus fell out with Luther, whose education had been in scholastic theology with little humanist influence. But he remained on friendly terms with other Reformers, such as Melanchthon. His disciples were found among Roman, Lutheran and Reformed theologians. He himself was left high and dry by the progress of the tide of history. His preference was for a liberal Catholic reform, while Protestantism was met by an increasingly dogmatic and illiberal Roman Catholicism. Erasmus enjoyed the support of successive popes, but his teaching was condemned in Paris in 1527. As the Counter-Reformation progressed his ideas were seen as dangerous and all his works were placed on the Index of Forbidden Books in 1559.

Erasmus wrote prolifically and edited many works:

● The *Adages* is one of his most entertaining works, being a compilation of proverbial sayings from classical times with Erasmus's comments. The first edition appeared in 1500 with 818 adages and it grew in size until the final edition in 1536 with 4151 adages arranged into four 'chiliads' or thousands.

● *The Praise of Folly* was written in 1509 at the home of his friend Thomas More and dedicated to him. This is written in the first person by Folly herself who complains of human ingratitude since all make use of her but none have bothered to present her with a speech of thanks. Folly points out how her way is followed by different groups – doctors, lawyers, teachers, theologians, monks, rulers, etc. This is one of Erasmus's best satires and of all of his works it is the one most read today.

● In 1516 Erasmus published an edition of the New Testament in Greek, with his own Latin translation. This was the first ever printed edition of the New Testament in Greek. It was a hasty work based on too few manuscripts – partly because Erasmus knew of a team working in Spain on a similar project and wished to publish first. It was revised in several later editions. Erasmus's aim was that the Bible should be made available to all. 'I would to God that the ploughman would sing a text of the Scripture at his plough and that the weaver would hum them to the tune of his shuttle.' This Greek New Testament influenced many towards Protestantism.

● Erasmus supervised the publication of many editions of the Early Church Fathers. This was part of his programme for church reform – a return to the Scriptures and the early Fathers.

● In 1524 Erasmus wrote *The Freedom of the Will*, an attack on Luther's doctrine that the fallen human will is in bondage and unable to do any good. He objected to Luther's position – both because he thought it wrong and because he felt it improper to be dogmatic on what he saw as an obscure issue.

At this point too I think I should copy the rhetoricians [academics] of today who fancy themselves practically gods on earth if they can show themselves twin-tounged [i.e. bilingual], like horse-leeches, and think it a splendid feat if they can work a few silly little Greek words, like a piece of mosaic, into their Latin speeches, however out of place these are. Then, if they still need something out of the ordinary, they dig four or five obsolete words out of mouldy manuscripts with which to cloud the meaning for the reader. The idea is, I suppose, that those who can understand are better pleased with themselves, and those who can't are all the more lost in admiration the less they understand.

* * *

Then there are the theologians, a remarkably supercilious and touchy lot. I might perhaps do better to pass over them in silence. . . lest they marshal their forces for an attack with innumerable conclusions and force me to eat my words. If I refuse they'll denounce me as a heretic on the spot, for this is the bolt they always loose on anyone to whom they take a dislike. Now there are none so unwilling to recognize my good services to them, and yet they're under obligation to me on several important counts, notably for their happiness in their self-love, which enables them to dwell in a sort of third heaven, looking down from aloft, almost with pity, on all the rest of mankind as so many cattle crawling on the face of the earth. . . .

These subtle refinements of subtleties are made still more subtle by all the different lines of scholastic argument, so that you'd extricate yourself faster from a labyrinth than from the tortuous obscurities of realists, nominalists, Thomists, Albertists, Ockhamists and Scotists and I've not mentioned all the sects, only the main ones. Such is the erudition and complexity they all display that I fancy the apostles themselves would need the help of another Holy Spirit if they were obliged to join issue on these topics with our new breed of theologian. . . .

Peter received the keys, and received them from one who would not have entrusted them to an unworthy recipient, yet I doubt whether Peter understood (nowhere does he show signs of subtle reasoning power) how a man who has not knowledge can still hold the key to it. The apostles baptized wherever they went, yet nowhere did they teach the formal, material, efficient, and final cause of baptism, nor did they ever mention the delible and indelible marks of the sacraments. . . .

Nothing will make me believe that Paul, from whose learning we may judge all the other apostles, would so often have condemned questions, arguments, genealogies, and what he himself called 'battles of words', if he had been well up in these niceties, especially when all the controversies and disagreements of that time would have been clumsy and unsophisticated affairs in comparison with the more than Chrysippean subtleties of the schoolmen of today. . . .

They are happy too while they're depicting everything in hell down to the last detail, as if they'd spent several years there, or giving free rein to their fancy in fabricating new spheres and adding the most extensive and beautiful of all in case the blessed spirits lack space to take a walk in comfort or give a dinner-party or even play a game of ball. Their heads are so stuffed and swollen with these absurdities, and thousands more like them, that I don't believe even Jupiter's brain felt so burdened when he begged for Vulcan's axe to help him give birth to Athene. And so you mustn't be surprised if you see them at public disputations with their heads carefully bound up in all those fillets – it's to keep them from bursting apart. . . .

The happiness of these people is most nearly approached by those who are popularly called 'religious' or 'monks'. Both names are false, since most of them are a long way removed from religion, and wherever you go these so-called solitaries are the people you're likely to meet. I don't believe any life would be more wretched than theirs if I [Folly] didn't come to their aid in many ways. The whole tribe is so universally loathed that even a chance meeting is thought to be ill-omened – and yet they are gloriously self-satisfied. In the first place, they believe it's the highest form of piety to be so uneducated that they can't even read. . . . There are others again who shrink from the touch of money as if it were deadly poison, but are less restrained when it comes to wine or contact with women.

Martin Luther,
The Freedom of a Christian (1520)

Martin Luther was born in 1483 at Eisleben (in Germany). He was on his way to becoming a lawyer when a close brush with death frightened him into becoming a monk. He joined the Augustinian friars at Erfurt, where he went on to study theology. In due course he rose to become professor of theology at the new university of Wittenberg. But Luther had problems. His theological training had taught him that in order to please God and earn his grace he must 'do his very best' – which included loving God above all else. But this God was portrayed to Luther as a judge weighing up his merits. Luther was trapped – he could not love the God who was condemning him, but until he loved him he would not be accepted. One verse in particular caused Luther difficulty – Romans 1:17 – 'In [the gospel] the righteousness of God is revealed.' Luther hated God for righteously condemning us not only by the law but also by the gospel. Then one day his eyes were opened and he saw the meaning of 'the righteousness of God'. It is not the righteousness by which God *condemns* us but the righteousness by which he justifies us by faith. The gospel reveals not God's condemnation and wrath but his salvation and justification. Once Luther saw this he felt as if he had been born again and entered paradise.

Luther began to preach and teach his new insights. In 1517 he produced ninety-seven theses for debate in the university (a common procedure) in which he put forward a strongly Augustinian line and rejected the teaching of late-medieval Semi-Pelagianism that we can make the first move towards God. To Luther's disappointment, these theses aroused little interest. But later that year Luther produced some more theses which *did* arouse interest. 'Indulgences' were being sold near Wittenberg. The theory was that the purchase of an indulgence could free a departed soul from purgatory – though *not* from hell. But ordinary folk believed that their sins could be forgiven simply by the purchase of an indulgence. Luther was outraged and wrote ninety-five theses against the indulgences. A copy of these fell into the hands of an enterprising printer who saw their potential and published the theses in German. The theses rapidly became a best-seller and all Germany was aroused. Luther became a hero overnight. The theses were relatively conservative, proposing only minor reforms of the existing system. For example, Luther did not question the existence of purgatory, the authority of the pope or the limited validity of indulgences. But the theses were of the greatest importance as they touched the papacy where it hurt most – in the pocket. They encouraged German unrest over the excessive taxes paid to Rome. For this reason, steps were taken to silence Luther, but he had the support of his ruler, Frederick the Wise.

In 1519 Luther and some colleagues went to Leipzig to debate with John Eck, a leading theologian. The topics were those of the ninety-five theses. But Eck was a clever debater. He pushed Luther into admitting that a general council could err and into approving some of the teaching of Hus and Wyclif, who had been condemned as heretics. The controversy had moved from points of doctrine to the very nature of authority. The following year the pope issued a bull threatening Luther with excommunication unless he recanted within sixty days. Luther responded by burning the papal bull. This was open rebellion. The following year he was summoned to the Diet of Worms, where the young emperor, Charles V, ordered him to recant. While Luther probably did not say the famous words, 'Here I stand, I can do no other', they accurately summarize his reply.

The breach with Rome was now complete. In the space of four years, the loyal subject of the pope had been pushed into the position that the papacy was the Antichrist prophesied in the New Testament. Luther's chances of survival would have been slight, but Frederick supported him and the emperor was unable to act against him. The Turks were besieging Vienna and Charles needed a united Germany to provide troops for its defence. He could not afford to divide Germany over the religious issue until it was too late – by then Lutheranism was well established and could not be eradicated by force.

In 1520 Luther wrote three major works in which he set out his programme for reform:

● *Appeal to the German Ruling Class*: Luther calls upon rulers to reform the church. This is necessary because the church will not put its own house in order. Rulers are to fulfil their responsibility to govern by acting against oppression and extortion by the church. Furthermore, as baptized Christians, rulers share in the 'priesthood' common to all believers. Luther rejects the Roman Catholic view of the clergy as a separate priestly caste and the common practice of calling the clergy 'the church'. All Christians are 'religious' and have a common status. The 'religious' in the church (clergy and monks) do not have a different status or dignity but merely exercise a different function. If they fail to exercise that function, others can step in and take their place.

● *Babylonian Captivity of the Church*: Luther attacked the seven sacraments of the Roman Catholic Church. He reduced these to the two which were instituted by Jesus Christ himself – baptism and the eucharist. (About penance Luther was ambiguous – he calls it a sacrament yet he also limits the sacraments to baptism and the eucharist, seeing penance as 'simply a means of reaffirming our baptism'.) But Luther did not merely reduce the number of sacraments. He radically opposed the Roman Catholic doctrine of the eucharist, rejecting the withholding of the cup from the laity, transubstantiation and, especially, the idea that the mass is a sacrifice that we offer to God.

● *The Freedom of a Christian*: Luther distinguishes between the inner and the outer person. As regards the inner person, he stresses that we are justified by faith alone. It is only by faith that we become righteous, not by good works. Faith lays hold of God's promises, unites us to Jesus Christ and indeed even fulfils the law (in that it honours God, as the first of the ten commandments requires). Good works are not the *means* of becoming righteous but only the *fruit* of righteousness, the result in the outer person of righteousness in the inner person. Works are to righteousness as fruit is to a tree. Here Luther was closely following the teaching of Augustine's *The Spirit and the Letter* (see pages 95–98).

To make the way smoother for the unlearned – for only them do I serve – I shall set down the following two propositions concerning the freedom and the bondage of the spirit:

A Christian is a perfectly free lord of all, subject to none. A Christian is a perfectly dutiful servant of all, subject to all.

These two theses seem to contradict each other. If, however, they should be found to fit together they would serve our purpose beautifully. Both are Paul's own statements, who says in 1 Corinthians 9[:19], 'For though I am free from all men, I have made myself a slave to all,' and in Romans 13[:8], 'Owe no one anything, except to love one another.' Love by its very nature is ready to serve and be subject to him who is loved.

* * *

First of all, remember what has been said, namely, that faith alone, without works, justifies, frees, and saves; we shall make this clearer later on. Here we must point out that the entire Scripture of God is divided into two parts: commandments and promises. Although the commandments teach things that are good, the things taught are not done as soon as they are taught, for the commandments show us what we ought to do but do not give us the power to do it. They are intended to teach man to know himself, that through them he may recognize his inability to do good and may despair of his own ability. . . . Here the second part of Scripture comes to our aid, namely, the promises of God which declare the glory of God. . . . That which is impossible for you to accomplish by trying to fulfil all the works of the law – many and useless as they all are – you will accomplish quickly and easily through faith. . . . Thus the promises of God give what the commandments of God demand and fulfil what the law prescribes so that all things may be God's alone, both the commandments and the fulfilling of the commandments. He alone commands, he alone fulfils.

* * *

'Good works do not make a good man, but a good man does good works; evil works do not make a wicked man, but a wicked man does evil works.' Consequently it is always necessary that the substance or person himself be good before there can be any good works, and that good works follow and proceed from the good person, as Christ also says, 'A good tree cannot bear evil fruit, nor can a bad tree bear good fruit' [Matthew 7:18]. It is clear that the fruits do not bear the tree and that the tree does not grow on the fruits, also that on the contrary, the trees bear the fruits and the fruits grow on the trees. As it is necessary, therefore, that the trees exist before their fruits and the fruits do not make trees either good or bad, but rather as the trees are, so are the fruits they bear; so a man must first be good or wicked before he does a good or wicked work, and his works do not make him good or wicked, but he himself makes his works either good or wicked.

* * *

Who then can comprehend the riches and the glory of the Christian life? It can do all things and has all things and lacks nothing. It is lord over sin, death and hell, and yet at the same time it serves, ministers to and benefits all men. But alas in our day this life is unknown throughout the world; it is neither preached about nor sought after; we are altogether ignorant of our own name and do not know why we are Christians or bear the name of Christians. Surely we are named after Christ, not because he is absent from us, but because he dwells in us, that is, because we believe in him and are Christs one to another and do to our neighbours as Christ does to us. But in our day we are taught by the doctrine of men to seek nothing but merits, rewards and the things that are ours; of Christ we have made only a taskmaster far harsher than Moses.

* * *

Our faith in Christ does not free us from works but from false opinions concerning works, that is, from the foolish presumption that justification is acquired by works. Faith redeems, corrects and preserves our consciences so that we know that righteousness does not consist in works, although works neither can nor ought to be wanting; just as we cannot be without food and drink and all the works of this mortal body, yet our righteousness is not in them, but in faith; and yet those works of the body are not to be despised or neglected on that account.

William Tyndale,
The New Testament (1526)

William Tyndale was born in the 1490s on the Welsh border. He was educated at Magdalen Hall, Oxford and later at Cambridge. He then became tutor to the family of Sir John Walsh at Little Sodbury Manor, north of Bath. While living in this household, Tyndale experienced at first hand the ignorance of the local clergy. To one cleric he is reported to have declared that 'if God spare my life, ere many years pass, I will cause a boy that driveth the plough shall know more of the Scriptures than thou dost', echoing Erasmus's Preface to his Greek New Testament. This task became Tyndale's life-work.

The only English translation of the Bible at this time was the Wyclif Bible, which was distributed clandestinely by the Lollards, the followers of John Wyclif. This was available only in manuscript form and was inaccurate, having been translated from the Latin Vulgate. For fear of the Lollards, the church had banned the English Bible since 1408. Tyndale's aim was to make a new, accurate translation from the original Hebrew and Greek, for which he hoped to win the patronage of Cuthbert Tunstall, the scholarly bishop of London who was a friend of Erasmus. But the bishops were more concerned to prevent the spread of Luther's ideas to England than to promote the study of the Bible and Tunstall refused to support Tyndale. In due course Tyndale obtained financial support from a number of London merchants.

England was clearly no safe place to be translating the Bible so Tyndale left for Germany in 1524, never to return. By early 1525 the New Testament was ready for the press. It was being printed at Cologne when the authorities were alerted and raided the press. Tyndale managed to escape in time, taking with him some of the printed leaves. He went to Worms, where the first complete English New Testament was printed in 1526. There were a number of later revised editions.

Tyndale's New Testament was smuggled into England. At the end of 1526, Tunstall preached against it and had copies ceremonially burnt at St Paul's Cross. The following year Tunstall was at Antwerp and an English merchant called Packington offered to buy the remaining copies for him so that they could be burnt – thus financing a further printing! 'And so forward went the bargain, the bishop had the books, Packington had the thanks, and Tyndale had the money.'

At some stage after 1526 Tyndale moved to Antwerp, a major centre of printing where there was a sizeable community of English merchants, who paid him a regular stipend. It was there in 1530 that his translation of the Pentateuch, made with the help of Miles Coverdale, was printed. The following year saw the publication of his translation of

Jonah. Tyndale himself published no more of the Old Testament, but there is strong evidence that the translation of the historical books (Joshua to II Chronicles) in the 1537 Matthew's Bible was Tyndale's, the rest of the Old Testament being Coverdale's translation. Tyndale had planned to translate the entire Old Testament, but in 1535 he was betrayed by a fellow-Englishman at Antwerp and arrested. The following year he was strangled and then burnt at Brussels. According to Foxe's Book of Martyrs (see pages 259–63) his final words were: 'Lord, open the king of England's eyes.'

Tyndale's translation was banned in England and destroyed when it was found, but its influence was considerable. In 1535 Miles Coverdale produced the first ever complete printed edition of the Bible in English. For diplomatic reasons Tyndale was not named, but the translation was heavily dependent upon his. Henry VIII approved the publication of the Coverdale translation and by 1539 every parish church in England was required to make a copy of the English Bible available to all of its parishioners. All of the available translations were substantially based upon Tyndale's, so while Tyndale had not been personally rehabilitated his cause had triumphed, as had the substance of his translation. Tyndale can justly be called 'the father of the English Bible'. It would not be much of an exaggeration to say that almost every English New Testament until recently was merely a revision of Tyndale's. Some 90 per cent of his words passed into the King James Version and about 75 per cent into the Revised Standard Version.

Tyndale also wrote a number of other works:

● *The Parable of Wicked Mammon* (1528) is on the theme of justification by faith alone, though with an Augustinian emphasis on faith bringing about a moral renewal leading to good works.

● *The Obedience of a Christian Man* (1528) is Tyndale's most influential treatise, in which he argues the duty of obedience to civil authority, except where loyalty to God is concerned. Henry VIII read parts of this work and was delighted with its subordination of the church to royal authority.

● Henry was less delighted with Tyndale's strong rejection of divorce in his *The Practice of Prelates* (1530). Here he chronicles the relations between the crown and the papacy and presents an unfavourable portrait of the king. This book served to turn Henry against Tyndale.

● In 1530 Tyndale published an expanded version of the preface to his first, incomplete New Testament, entitled *A Pathway into the Holy Scripture*.

● Tyndale is also famous for his literary battle with Thomas More. In 1529 More attacked 'the captain of English heretics' in his *Dialogue Concerning Heresies*. Two years later Tyndale replied with an *Answer to Sir Thomas More's Dialogue*. More responded with a lengthy and tedious *Confutation* in two volumes (1532 and 1533).

A number of Tyndale's works could be called classics, but he is rightly known above all else for his translation of the Bible. In a recent television series on the history of the English language Tyndale's New Testament was described as 'probably the most influential book there's ever been in the history of any language, English or any other'. It is a work of such immense significance that it has been selected for this volume, despite being only a Bible translation. It remains worth reading today – for Tyndale's superb use of the English language, for the refreshing directness of his style and because of its historical significance. In the extracts below the original spelling and punctuation have been retained (except that i and j, and u and v have been distinguished). At that stage there was no standard spelling and the same word can be spelt a number of different ways – as below with 'shal' and 'shall', 'perfet' and 'parfet'.

Matthew 5:1–12

When he sawe the people, he went up into a mountayne, and when he was set, his disciples cam unto hym, and he openned his mought, and taught them, saynge: Blessed are the poure in sprete: for theirs is the kyngdome off heven. Blessed are they that morne: for they shal be comforted. Blessed are the meke: for they shall inheret the erth. Blessed are they which honger and thurst for rightewesnes: for they shal be filled. Blessed are the mercifull: for they shall obteyne mercy. Blessed are the pure in herte: for they shall se God. Blessed are the maynteyners of peace: for they shal be called the chyldren of God. Blessed are they which suffre persecucion for rightewesnes sake: for theirs ys the kyngdome off heven. Blessed are ye when men shall revyle you, and persecute you, and shall falsly say all manner of yvell saynges agaynst you ffor my sake. Rejoyce and be glad, for greate is youre rewarde in heven. For so persecuted they the prophets which were before youre dayes.

John 3:1–16

There was a man off the pharises named Nicodemus a ruler amonge the jewes. He cam to Jesus be nyght, and sayde unto him: Master, we knowe that thou arte, a teacher whyche arte come from god. For no man coulde do suche miracles as thou doest, except God were wyth hym. Jesus answered, and sayde unto hym: Verely verely I saye unto the: except that a man be boren anewe, he cannot se the kingdom of god. Nicodemus sayde unto hym: howe can a man be boren, when he is olde? can he enter into hys moders body and be boren agayne? Jesus answered: verely, verely I saye unto the, except that a man be boren of water, and of the sprete, he cannot enter into the kyngdom of god. That whych is boren of the flesshe, is flesshe. And that which is boren of the sprete, is sprete. Marvayle nott that I sayd to the, ye must be boren anewe. The wynde bloweth where he listeth, and thou hearest his sounde: butt thou canst nott tell whence he commeth and whether he goeth. So is every man that is boren of the sprete.

Nicodemus answered and sayde unto him: howe can these thynges be? Jesus answered and sayde unto hym: Arte thou a master in Israhell, and knowest nott these thynges? Verely verely, I saye unto the, we speake that we knowe, and testify that we have sene: And ye receave not oure witnes. Yff I have tolde you erthely thynges and ye have not beleved: howe shulde ye beleve if I shall tell you of hevenly thynges?

And noo man hath ascended uppe to heven, butt he that cam doune from heven, that ys to saye the sonne of man, which is in heven.

And as Moses lifte uppe the serpent in wyldernes, even soo must the sonne off man be lifte uppe, that noo man which beleveth in hym perisshe: but have eternall lyfe.

God soo loved the worlde, that he gave his only sonne for the entent, that none that beleve in hym shulde perisshe: Butt shulde have everlastynge lyfe.

1 Corinthians 13

Though I speake with the tonges of men and angels, and yet had no love, I were even as soundynge brasse: and as a tynklynge Cynball. and though I coulde prophesy, and understode all secretes, and all knowledge: yee, if I had all fayth so that I coulde move mountayns oute of there places, and yet had no love, I were nothynge. And though I bestowed all my gooddes to fede the poure, and though I gave my body even that I burned, and yet have no love, it profiteth me nothynge.

Love suffreth longe, and is corteous. love envieth nott. Love doth nott frawardly, swelleth not, dealeth not dishonestly, seketh nott her awne, is not provoked to anger, thynketh not evyll rejoyseth not in iniquite: but rejoyseth in the trueth, suffreth all thynge, beleveth all thynges hopeth all thynges, endureth in all thynges. Though that prophesyinge fayle, other tonges shall cease, or knowledge vanysshe awaye: yet love falleth never awaye.

For oure knowledge is unparfet, and oure prophesyinge is unperfet: but when thatt which is parfet is come: then that which is unparfet shall be done awaye. When I was a chylde, I spake as a chylde, I understode as a childe, I ymmagened as a chylde: but as sone as I was a man I put awaye all childesshnes. Nowe we se in a glasse even in a darke speakynge: but then shall we se face to face. Nowe I knowe unparfectly: but then shall I knowe even as I am knowen. Nowe abideth fayth, hope, and love, even these thre: but the chefe of these is love.

The Schleitheim Confession (1527)

The magisterial Reformers reformed the church's doctrine, but there was much that they left unchanged. In particular, they shared with medieval Catholicism the ideal of a Christian state in which all citizens are baptized members of a single church with a uniform creed – which inevitably implies the coercion of dissenters. This ideal was challenged by some, known as Anabaptists, for whom the Protestant Reformation was not radical enough. The two ideals came into open conflict in Zurich. In the early years of the reform, Zwingli worked hand in hand with a group of radicals: Conrad Grebel, Felix Manz and others. They maintained a common front until 1523, but the issues of the state church and infant baptism divided them. It seems that Zwingli himself questioned infant baptism for a time, but drew back when he realized that it is essential if a state church is to be maintained. The radicals' opposition to infant baptism hardened and in 1525, after a public disputation with Zwingli, they began to (re)baptize believers. The town council responded by ordering the exile of all those rebaptized, and in the following year the death penalty was introduced for rebaptizing. In January 1527 Felix Manz was executed by drowning.

Infant baptism was the obvious point of disagreement but the issues were more fundamental. The Anabaptists rejected the state church, to which all were forced to belong. For them, Christian faith was free and voluntary, not to be coerced. The church is a voluntary association of committed disciples. The Reformers recognized that not all citizens were true Christians, but they saw the elect as an unknown number within the state church – we cannot know for sure who they are. The Anabaptists disagreed. They thought that the church should consist only of true believers, of committed disciples. The true church is not the unknown number of the elect within the all-embracing state church, but a visible group of disciples who have separated themselves from the world (which includes the state church). The church's purity is to be maintained by excluding unrepentant sinners. All church members are committed Christians and are to be actively involved in spreading the faith. The Anabaptist ideal of the church was rejected in the sixteenth century. But the rise of a secular society and the decline of nominal Christianity has led to a sharper contrast in modern western society between committed Christians and non-Christians. Today all churches are forced by circumstances to accept at least part of the Anabaptist concept of the church.

The early Anabaptist leaders had little opportunity to write. Most of them survived only for a few years, on the run. The most important and authoritative statement of early Anabaptist faith is found in the *Schleitheim Confession*. A number of Anabaptist leaders met in February 1527 at Schleitheim (on the Swiss-German border not far from Schaffhausen) and produced seven articles of faith. The main author appears to have been Michael Sattler, a former prior who spent some time at both Zurich and Strassburg (where he debated with the Reformers Bucer and Capito). In May 1527 he was apprehended by the Roman Catholic authorities and burnt at Rottenburg, near Tübingen. His wife was drowned a few days later.

The seven articles are not a comprehensive statement of faith, but cover the main points of difference between the Anabaptists and the Reformers, as well as points where the Anabaptists had previously disagreed among themselves.

———————

Article I. Notice concerning baptism. Baptism shall be given to all those who have been taught repentance and the amendment of life and [who] believe truly that their sins are taken away through Christ, and to all those who desire to walk in the resurrection of Jesus Christ and be buried with him in death, so that they might rise with him; to all those who with such an understanding themselves desire and request it from us; hereby is excluded all infant baptism, the greatest and first abomination of the pope. For this you have the reasons and the testimony of the writings and the practice of the apostles. We wish simply yet resolutely and with assurance to hold to the same.

Article II. We have been united as follows concerning the ban. The ban shall be employed with all those who have given themselves over to the Lord, to walk after [him] in his commandments; those who have been baptized into the one body of Christ, and let themselves be called brothers or sisters, and still somehow slip and fall into error and sin, being inadvertently overtaken. The same [shall] be warned twice privately and the third time be publicly admonished before the entire congregation according to the command of Christ [Matthew 18:15–17]. But this shall be done according to the ordering of the Spirit of God before the breaking of bread so that we may all in one spirit and in one love break and eat from one bread and drink from one cup.

Article III. Concerning the breaking of bread, we have become one and agree thus: all those who desire to break the one bread in remembrance of the broken body of Christ and all those who wish to drink of one drink in remembrance of the shed blood of Christ, they must beforehand be united in the one body of Christ, that is the congregation of God, whose head is Christ, and that by baptism. For as Paul indicates [1 Corinthians 10:21], we cannot be partakers at the same time of the table of the Lord and the table of devils. Nor can we at the same time partake and drink of the cup of the Lord and the cup of devils. That is: all those who have fellowship with the dead works of darkness have no part in the light. Thus all who follow the devil and the world, have no part with those who have been called out of the world unto God. All those who lie in evil have no part in the good. . . .

Article IV. We have been united concerning the separation that shall take place from the evil and the wickedness which the devil has planted in the world, simply in this; that we have no fellowship with them, and do not run with them in the confusion of their abominations. So it is; since all who have not entered into the obedience of faith and have not united themselves with God so that they will to do his will, are a great abomination before God, therefore nothing else can or really will grow or spring forth from them than abominable things. Now there is nothing else in the world and all creation than good or evil, believing and unbelieving, darkness and light, the world and those who are [come] out of the world, God's temple and idols, Christ and Belial, and none will have part with the other. . . .

Article V. We have been united as follows concerning shepherds in the church of God. The shepherd in the church shall be a person according to the rule of Paul, fully and completely, who has a good report of those who are outside the faith. The office of such a person shall be to read and exhort and teach, warn, admonish, or ban in the congregation, and properly to preside among the sisters and brothers in prayer, and in the breaking of bread, and in all things to take care of the body of Christ, that it may be built up and developed, so that the name of God might be praised and honoured through us, and the mouth of the mocker be stopped. . . .

Article VI. We have been united as follows concerning the sword. The sword is an ordering of God outside the perfection of Christ. It punishes and kills the wicked and guards and protects the good. In the law the sword is established over the wicked for punishment and for death, and the secular rulers are established to wield the same. But within the perfection of Christ only the ban is used for the admonition and exclusion of the one who has sinned, without the death of the flesh, simply the warning and the command to sin no more. . . .

Article VII. We have been united as follows concerning the oath. The oath is a confirmation among those who are quarrelling or making promises. In the law it is commanded that it should be done only in the name of God, truthfully and not falsely. Christ, who teaches the perfection of the law, forbids his [followers] all swearing, whether true or false; neither by heaven nor by earth, neither by Jerusalem nor by our head; and that for the reason which he goes on to give: 'For you cannot make one hair white or black.' You see, thereby all swearing is forbidden. We cannot perform what is promised in the swearing, for we are not able to change the smallest part of ourselves [Matthew 5:34–37]. . . .

Martin Luther, *The Small Catechism*
(1529)

After the Diet of Worms in 1521 Luther was in great danger. Some of his supporters arranged for him to be kidnapped on his journey home and kept out of harm's way in a castle called the Wartburg. While there, he began his translation of the Bible into German. The *Luther Bible* is of major cultural as well as religious significance. Apart from bringing the Bible to the common people it helped to mould the German language into its present form. Its influence can be compared to that of Shakespeare or the Authorized Version on the English language.

In the 1520s Luther and his followers set out to rebuild the church in Saxony on Reformation principles. In 1527 Luther and Melanchthon spent some time on a visitation of rural churches and were concerned by what they saw, especially the ignorance of basics such as the Ten Commandments, the Creed and the Lord's Prayer. They were also concerned about the dangers of preaching the forgiveness of sins without repentance. This leads people astray as they will think that they are already forgiven and lapse into a false sense of security without the fear of God. They are to be taught that there is no saving faith without repentance, contrition and the fear of God. Those who think that faith suffices on its own without these others are to be told that such arrogance and carnal security is worse than all of the earlier errors under the papacy.

Moved in part by these concerns, Luther wrote two catechisms, both in 1529. The *Large Catechism* is a substantial work, based on sermons that Luther had previously preached. The *Small Catechism* is much simpler, covering the basic points briefly. (The extracts below comprise nearly half of the whole.) As was normal for catechisms, it is based on the Ten Commandments, the Apostles' Creed, the Lord's Prayer and the sacraments. Other material was later added. Both catechisms are among the Lutheran confessions which, together with the *Formula of Concord* (see pages 269–73), make up the *Book of Concord*.

Part One: The Ten Commandments: The Simple Way a Father Should Present Them to His Household

The Conclusion to the Commandments
Q. What does God say to us about all these commandments?

A. This is what he says: 'I am the Lord Your God. I am a jealous God. I plague the grandchildren and great-grandchildren of those who hate me with their ancestor's sin. But I make whole those who love me for a thousand generations.' [Exodus 20:5–6]

Q. What does it mean?

A. God threatens to punish everyone who breaks these commandments. We should be afraid of his anger because of this and not violate such commandments. But he promises grace and all good things to those who keep such commandments. Because of this, we, too, should love him, trust him, and willingly do what his commandments require.

Part Two: The Creed: The Simple Way a Father Should Present it to His Household

I. The First Article: On Creation

> *I believe in God the Almighty Father, Creator of Heaven and Earth.*

Q. What does this mean?

A. I believe that God created me, along with all creatures. He gave to me: body and soul, eyes, ears and all the other parts of my body, my mind and all my senses and preserves them as well. He gives me clothing and shoes, food and drink, house and land, wife and children, fields, animals and all I own. Every day he abundantly provides everything I need to nourish this body and life. He protects me against all danger, shields and defends me from all evil. He does all this because of his pure, fatherly and divine goodness and his mercy, not because I've earned it or deserved it. For all of this, I must thank him, praise him, serve him and obey him. Yes, this is true!

II. The Second Article: On Redemption

> *And in Jesus Christ, his only Son, our Lord, Who was conceived by the Holy Spirit, born of the Virgin Mary, suffered under Pontius Pilate, was crucified, died and was buried, descended to Hell, on the third day rose again from the dead, ascended to Heaven and sat down at the right hand of God the Almighty Father. From there he will come to judge the living and the dead.*

Q. What does this mean?

A. I believe that Jesus Christ is truly God, born of the Father in eternity and also truly man, born of the Virgin Mary. He is my Lord! He redeemed me, a lost and condemned person, bought and won me from all sins, death and the authority of the devil. It did not cost him gold or silver, but his holy, precious blood, his innocent body – his death! Because of this, I am his very own, will live under him in his kingdom and serve him righteously, innocently and blessedly forever, just as he is risen from death, lives and reigns forever. Yes, this is true!

III. The Third Article: On Becoming Holy

I believe in the Holy Spirit, the holy Christian church, the community of the saints, the forgiveness of sins, the resurrection of the body, and an everlasting life. Amen.

Q. What does this mean?
A. I believe that I cannot come to my Lord Jesus Christ by my own intelligence or power. But the Holy Spirit called me by the Gospel, enlightened me with his gifts, made me holy and kept me in the true faith, just as he calls, gathers together, enlightens and makes holy the whole church on earth and keeps it with Jesus in the one, true faith. In this church, he generously forgives each day every sin committed by me and by every believer. On the last day, he will raise me and all the dead from the grave. He will give eternal life to me and to all who believe in Christ. Yes, this is true!

Part Three: The Lord's Prayer, The Our Father: The Simple Way a Father Should Present it to His Household

I. Introduction: 'Our Father, who is in Heaven.'
Q. What does this mean?
A. In this introduction, God invites us to believe that he is our real Father and we are his real children, so that we will pray with trust and complete confidence, in the same way beloved children approach their beloved Father with their requests.

II. The First Request: 'May your name be holy.'
Q. What does this mean?
A. Of course, God's name is holy in and of itself, but by this request, we pray that he will make it holy among us, too.
Q. How does this take place?
A. When God's Word is taught clearly and purely, and when we live holy lives as God's children based upon it. Help us, Heavenly Father, to do this! But anyone who teaches and lives by something other than God's Word defiles God's name among us. Protect us from this, Heavenly Father!

III. The Second Request: 'Your Kingdom come.'
Q. What does this mean?

A. Truly God's Kingdom comes by itself, without our prayer. But we pray in this request that it come to us as well.

Q. How does this happen?

A. When the Heavenly Father gives us his Holy Spirit, so that we believe his holy Word by his grace and live godly lives here in this age and there in eternal life. . . .

VI. The Fifth Request: 'And forgive our guilt, as we forgive those guilty of sinning against us.'

Q. What does this mean?

A. We pray in this request that our Heavenly Father will neither pay attention to our sins nor refuse requests such as these because of our sins and because we are neither worthy nor deserve the things for which we pray. Yet he wants to give them all to us by his grace, because many times each day we sin and truly deserve only punishment. Because God does this, we will, of course, want to forgive from our hearts and willingly do good to those who sin against us.

VII. The Sixth Request: 'And lead us not into temptation.'

Q. What does this mean?

A. God tempts no one, of course, but we pray in this request that God will protect us and save us, so that the devil, the world and our bodily desires will neither deceive us nor seduce us into heresy, despair or other serious shame or vice, and so that we will win and be victorious in the end, even if they attack us. . . .

Part Four: The Sacrament of Holy Baptism: The Simple Way a Father Should Present it to His Household

I. Q. What is baptism?

A. Baptism is not just plain water, but it is water contained within God's command and united with God's Word.

Q. Which Word of God is this?

A. The one which our Lord Christ spoke in the last chapter of Matthew: 'Go into all the world, teaching all heathen nations, and baptizing them in the name of the Father, the Son and of the Holy Spirit' [28:19].

II. Q. What does baptism give? What good is it?

A. It gives the forgiveness of sins, redeems from death and the devil, gives eternal salvation to all who believe this, just as God's words and promises declare.

Q. What are these words and promises of God?

A. Our Lord Christ spoke one of them in the last chapter of Mark: 'Whoever believes and is baptized will be saved; but whoever does not believe will be damned' [16:16].

III. Q. How can water do such great things?

A. Water doesn't make these things happen, of course. It is God's Word, which is with and in the water. Because, without God's Word, the water is plain water and not baptism. But with God's Word it is a baptism, a grace-filled water of life, a bath of new birth in the Holy Spirit, as St Paul said to Titus in the third chapter: 'Through this bath of rebirth and renewal of the Holy Spirit, which he poured out on us abundantly through Jesus Christ, our Saviour, that we, justified by the same grace are made heirs according to the hope of eternal life. This is a faithful saying' [3:5–8].

IV. Q. What is the meaning of such a water baptism?

A. It means that the old Adam in us should be drowned by daily sorrow and repentance, and die with all sins and evil lusts, and, in turn, a new person daily come forth and rise from death again. He will live forever before God in righteousness and purity.

The Augsburg Confession (1530)

In 1530 the emperor, Charles V, called a national assembly (or 'diet') to meet at Augsburg. His desire was to negotiate with the Protestants and, if possible, to end the dispute. He wanted a united Germany the better to be able to fend off the Turkish armies invading Eastern Europe. Melanchthon drew up a Protestant confession of faith, based partly on some earlier writings of Luther. The finished product had the approval of Luther, who was unable to be present at the diet because he had been excommunicated. On 25 June it was read to the emperor at Augsburg – thus becoming known as the *Augsburg Confession.* Its tone and language was deliberately moderate, in the hope that the emperor might recognize Protestantism.

Charles commissioned some Roman Catholic theologians to refute the confession and their work was read in August. Melanchthon then wrote an *Apology [Defence] of the Augsburg Confession*, which was presented to the emperor in September – but he refused to accept it. The following year the *Augsburg Confession* was published in Latin and in German and a revised version of the *Apology* was also published.

The *Augsburg Confession* is in two parts. The first part consists of twenty-one articles setting out Lutheran beliefs. Some of these follow traditional Catholic doctrine (as on God, original sin, baptism); others are distinctively Lutheran (as on justification, the Lord's Supper, good works). The second part consists of seven articles about abuses which have been corrected in the Lutheran churches (such as the withholding of the cup from the laity in the holy communion or forbidding the clergy to marry).

In 1540 Melanchthon published a revised edition of the confession. The most significant change was in the tenth article which now stated that 'the body and blood of Christ are truly exhibited with the bread and wine to those partaking in the Lord's Supper'. This comes close to the position of Bucer and was approved by Calvin, as in his *Short Treatise on the Lord's Supper* (see pages 222–25). Luther was grieved, but said nothing. After his death, Melanchthon came increasingly under fire from hard-line Lutherans.

The 1531 editions of the *Augsburg Confession* and the *Apology* are among the Lutheran confessions which, together with the *Formula of Concord* (see pages 269–73), make up the *Book of Concord*. The extracts below are taken from the first Latin edition. The *Augsburg Confession* is the most basic of the Lutheran confessions and has also been influential outside of Lutheranism. In recent years even Roman Catholic theologians have come to recognize many positive features in the confession.

Article 4: Justification

Our churches also teach that people cannot be justified before God by their own strength, merits, or works, but are freely justified for Christ's sake, through faith, when they believe that they are received into favour, and that their sins are forgiven for the sake of Christ, who by his death has made satisfaction for our sins. This faith God reckons as righteousness in his sight. (Romans 3 and 4.)

Article 6: New Obedience

Our churches also teach that this faith is bound to bring forth good fruits and that it is necessary to do good works commanded by God, because of God's will, but that we should not rely on those works to merit justification before God. For remission of sins and justification are apprehended by faith, as also the voice of Christ attests, 'When you have done all these things say, "We are unprofitable servants"' [Luke 17:10]. The same is also taught by the Fathers. For [Pseudo-] Ambrose says, 'It is ordained of God that he who believes in Christ is saved without works by faith alone, freely receiving remission of sins.'

Article 20: Faith and Good Works

Our teachers are falsely accused of forbidding good works. For their published writings on the Ten Commandments and others on similar themes, bear witness that they have taught to good purpose about all manners and duties of life, as to what manners of life and what works are pleasing to God in every calling. Preachers previously taught but little on these matters, instead urging only childish and needless works, such as particular holy days, particular fasts, brotherhoods, pilgrimages, services in honour of saints, rosaries, monasticism, and such like. Since our adversaries have been admonished about these things, they are now unlearning them, and do not preach these unprofitable works as much as before. They are even beginning to mention faith, about which there was previously a marvellous silence. They teach that we are not justified by works only, but conjoin faith with works, saying that we are justified by faith and works. This teaching is more tolerable than the former one and can offer more consolation than their old teaching.

Seeing, therefore, that teaching about faith, which ought to be the chief teaching in the church, remained unknown for so long (as everyone must grant that about the righteousness of faith there was a profound silence in their sermons, while in the churches only the teaching of works was treated) our teachers have instructed the churches about faith as follows:

First of all we teach that our works cannot reconcile God or merit forgiveness of sins and grace, but that we obtain this only by faith when we believe that we are received into favour for the sake of Christ, who alone has been appointed to be Mediator and propitiation through whom the Father is reconciled

[1 Timothy 2:5–6]. Whoever, therefore, trusts that he merits grace by works despises the merit and grace of Christ and seeks a way to God without Christ through human strength, although Christ has said of himself, 'I am the Way, the Truth and the Life' [John 14:6].

This teaching about faith is treated everywhere by Paul, as in Ephesians 2:8–9: 'By grace you have been saved through faith, and this is not because of works,' etc. Lest any one should craftily say that we have invented a new interpretation of Paul, this entire matter is supported by testimonies of the [Early Church] Fathers. . . .

Although this teaching is despised by the inexperienced, nevertheless God-fearing and anxious consciences find by experience that it offers the greatest consolation, because consciences cannot be set at rest through any works, but only by faith, when they are convinced that God is reconciled for the sake of Christ. As Paul teaches, 'Being justified by faith, we have peace with God' [Romans 5:1]. This whole teaching is to be referred to that struggle of the terrified conscience and cannot be understood apart from that struggle. That is why those who are inexperienced and profane, dreaming that Christian righteousness is no more than civil and philosophical righteousness, judge this matter badly.

Previously consciences were plagued by teaching about works and heard no consolation from the Gospel. Some were driven by conscience into the desert, into monasteries, where they hoped to merit grace by a monastic life. Some also devised other works to merit grace and make satisfaction for sins. Hence there was a very great need to deal with and restore this teaching about faith in Christ, so that anxious consciences should not be left without consolation but know that grace and forgiveness of sins are apprehended by faith in Christ.

People are also admonished that the term 'faith' in this context does not signify merely historical knowledge (as found in the ungodly and the devil) but signifies a faith which believes not merely the history but also the effect of the history – namely this Article [of the Creed]: the forgiveness of sins – that is, that through Christ we have grace, righteousness and forgiveness of sins.

Whoever knows that he has a Father gracious to him through Christ, truly knows God, knows that God cares for him and calls upon God. In short, he is not without God, as are the heathen. For devils and the ungodly are not able to believe this article of the forgiveness of sins, so they hate God as an enemy, do not call upon him and expect no good from him. Augustine also admonishes his readers about the word 'faith', teaching that in the Scriptures the term 'faith' is to be understood not as knowledge (such as is in the ungodly) but as confidence which consoles and encourages the terrified mind.

Furthermore, we teach the need to do good works – not that we should trust to merit grace by them, but because it is the will of God. It is only by faith that forgiveness of sins and grace are apprehended. And because the Holy Spirit is received through faith, hearts are renewed and endowed with new affections, so as to be able to bring forth good works. For [Pseudo-]Ambrose says, 'Faith is the mother of the good will and the righteous deed.' Without the Holy Spirit human powers are full of ungodly affections and are too weak to do works which are good in God's sight. Besides, they are in the power of the devil who impels men to divers sins, ungodly opinions and open crimes. This can be seen in the philosophers, who tried to live honest lives but could not succeed, being defiled with many open crimes. Such is the feebleness of man when he governs himself by human strength alone, without faith or the Holy Spirit.

Hence it may be readily seen that this teaching should not be accused of prohibiting good works, but rather commended for showing us how we can do good works. For without faith human nature cannot possibly do the works of the First or of the Second Commandment. Without faith it does not call upon God, expect anything from God or bear the cross, but seeks and trusts in human help. And thus all kinds of lusts and human devices rule in the heart when there is no faith and trust in God – which is why Christ said, 'Apart from me you can do nothing' [John 15:5]; and the church sings:

Without your divine favour,
There is nothing found in man,
Naught in him is harmless.

Ulrich Zwingli,
Exposition of the Faith (1531)

Ulrich Zwingli is the founder of Swiss Protestantism and the first of the Reformed theologians. He was born on New Year's Day 1484, fifty-two days after Luther, at Wildhaus, some forty miles from Zurich. In 1506 Zwingli was appointed parish priest at Glarus. While there he began to attack the mercenary trade. At this time Swiss soldiers were in great demand as mercenaries and it was a lucrative source of income, much like Swiss banking today. Zwingli came to see the practice as immoral and began to preach against it. This did not go down well at Glarus, so in 1516 Zwingli moved to become parish priest at Einsiedeln – then, as now, a popular centre of devotion to the Virgin Mary. While at Glarus and Einsiedeln, Zwingli read widely and it was during this time that the foundations of his Reformed beliefs were laid – largely, but not entirely, independently of Luther. In particular, he came to realize the supreme and final role of Scripture. In 1518 Zwingli became parish priest at the Grossmünster (Great Cathedral) at Zurich. There he began to preach systematically through whole books of the Bible. This practice was common in the Early Church, but in Zwingli's time it came as a radical innovation.

At Zurich Zwingli gradually introduced reform, at first with the approval of the Roman Catholic authorities. In 1522 he produced the first of his many Reformation writings, which helped to spread his ideas widely through Switzerland. The Reformation in Zurich was largely complete by 1525, when the mass was abolished, to be replaced by a simple communion service. That year Zwingli composed a *Commentary on True and False Religion*, dedicated to King Francis I of France, in which he contrasts biblical truth with Roman error. Other Swiss cantons also decided for the reform and Zwingli's goal of a united evangelical Switzerland looked possible. To this end he formed an alliance of evangelical cantons, but the Roman Catholic cantons felt threatened and formed a rival alliance. The outcome was war, in 1529. After a lull, fighting broke out again in 1531 and Zwingli was himself killed on the battlefield, at Kappel. Zwingli's early death ended his leadership of the Swiss Reformation and prevented him from writing a major systematic exposition of Reformed theology. That task was left to Calvin, with the result that Reformed Protestantism is known as Calvinism, not Zwinglianism. But if the building was left to others and if Zwingli was to a large extent forgotten, the fact remains that it was he who laid the foundations of Swiss Protestantism and Reformed theology.

One of Zwingli's first writings was his *Clarity and Certainty of God's Word*, published in 1522. Here Zwingli propounded the fundamental Protestant principle of the final authority of Scripture. God's Word is clear – but this does not mean that it cannot be misunderstood. If we come to the Bible with our own opinions and interpretation and seek to force it into that mould, we will not hear its message. But when God speaks to his children, his word brings its own clarity with it. Then we can understand it without any human instruction – not because of our own understanding but because the Holy Spirit illuminates us and enables us to see God's word in its own light. We must avoid the error of subjecting the word of God to an infallible human interpreter, such as the pope or a council. Certainty comes not from human learning nor from church authority but from humbly listening to God himself.

But Zwingli learned the hard way that sincerely seeking to hear God's word did not necessarily end all disagreement. He found himself engaged in controversy with two other reform groups over the nature of the sacraments. First, there were those at Zurich who wanted a more radical reform. They were not satisfied with a Reformed state church but wanted a voluntary church of committed Christians, to be entered by adult baptism. At first Zwingli and these radicals had much in common, but by 1525 matters had come to a head and the Zurich city council, with Zwingli's approval, acted against them. In the same year Zwingli wrote his *Baptism, Rebaptism and the Baptism of Infants*. In it he defended infant baptism, on the basis that it is the sign of the covenant and the covenant embraces the whole family and not just the individual. But while he maintained the practice of infant baptism, Zwingli (unlike Luther) broke with the Catholic belief that baptism bestows (even on infants) new birth and the forgiveness of sins. He came to see baptism as primarily an outward sign of our faith.

The second controversy was with Luther, over the presence of Jesus Christ in the Lord's Supper. Luther rejected the Roman doctrine of transubstantiation, but continued to believe in the real presence of Christ's body and blood 'in, with and under' the bread and the wine. Zwingli was won away from this belief in 1524 and rejected the doctrine of real presence, maintaining that the bread and the wine are merely symbols of Christ's body and blood. The Lord's Supper is a thanksgiving memorial in which we look back to the work of Jesus Christ on the cross. It is also a fellowship meal in which the body of Christ is present – in the form of the congregation. These views Zwingli set out in his *Clear Exposition of Christ's Last Supper* (1526). Zwingli argued powerfully against a physical presence of Christ's body in the Lord's Supper, but he did not altogether escape the danger of reducing it to a mere memorial. His contribution was primarily the negative work of criticizing the old. It was left to others, especially Bucer and Calvin, to build a more positive doctrine of the Supper on that foundation – though some have argued that Zwingli began to move in that direction in his last work.

Zwingli's last work was his *Exposition of the Faith*. He was seeking a military alliance with France and was advised that the king, Francis I, had theological and social reservations about the Zurich Reformation. In response to this Zwingli composed his *Exposition of the Faith*, which was sent to Francis in the summer of 1531. Zwingli did not live to publish it but this was undertaken in 1536 by his successor Bullinger. Like the *Confession of Faith* that he wrote the previous year for the emperor Charles V, the

Exposition was both a statement of faith and an apology or defence of his beliefs against misrepresentations, especially the taint of Anabaptism. Because of the controversies in which he had been embroiled, he devoted over a third of the work to the question of the sacraments. Both works, which overlap to some extent, summarize Zwingli's mature thought briefly, building on the more solid earlier accounts such as his *Commentary on True and False Religion*.

[Chapter 1] We know that this God is good by nature, for whatever he is he is by nature. But goodness is both mercy and justice. Deprive mercy of justice, and it is no longer mercy, but indifference or timidity. But fail to temper justice by kindness and forbearance and at once it becomes the greatest injustice and violence. Therefore when we confess that God is good by nature, we confess that he is both loving, kind and gracious, and also holy, just and impassible. But if he is just and righteous, necessarily he must abhor all contact with evil. Hence it follows that we mortals cannot have any hope of fellowship or friendship with him, since we are not only guilty of sin, but actually participate in it. On the other hand, if he is good, he must necessarily temper every resolve and act with equity and grace.

It was for this reason that he clothed his only Son with flesh, not merely to reveal to, but actually to bestow upon, the whole earth both salvation and renewal. For inasmuch as his goodness, that is, his justice and mercy, is impassible, that is, steadfast and immutable, his justice required atonement, but his mercy forgiveness, and forgiveness newness of life. Clothed therefore with flesh, for according to his divine nature he cannot die, the Son of the Most High King offered up himself as a sacrifice to placate irrevocable justice and to reconcile it with those who because of their consciousness of sin dared not enter the presence of God on the ground of their own righteousness. He did this because he is kind and merciful, and these virtues can as little permit the rejection of his work as his justice can allow escape from punishment. Justice and mercy were conjoined, the one furnishing the sacrifice, the other accepting it as a sacrifice for all sin.

[Chapter 5] Even under the guise of piety we ought not to ascribe either to the Supper or to baptism anything that might jeopardize religion and truth. But does that mean that the sacraments have no virtue or power at all?

The first virtue: they are sacred and venerable things instituted and received by the great High Priest Christ himself. For not only did he institute baptism, but he himself received it. And he not only commanded us to celebrate the Supper, but he himself celebrated it first.

The second virtue: they testify to historical facts. . . . If baptism proclaims symbolically the death and resurrection of Christ, it follows that these events did actually take place.

The third virtue: they take the place, the name, of that which they signify. . . . The body of Christ and all that happened in relation to it cannot be exhibited to us, but its place is taken by the bread and wine which we consume instead.

Fourth: they represent high things. . . . We do not value them according to their intrinsic worth, but according to the greatness of that which they represent. . . .

The fifth virtue is the analogy between the signs and the things signified. In the Supper there is a twofold analogy. The first is to Christ. . . . The second analogy is to ourselves. . . .

The sixth: the sacraments augment faith and are an aid to it. . . . In the Supper the four most important senses, indeed all the senses, are at once released and redeemed from the desires of the flesh and placed under the obedience of faith. With the hearing it is no longer the music of strings and the harmony of varied sounds that we hear, but the heavenly voice: [Zwingli quotes John 3:16]. . . . With the sight we see the bread and wine which in Christ's stead signify his goodness and favourable disposition. . . . With the sense of touch we take the bread into our hands and in signification it is no longer bread but Christ. And there is also a place for taste and smell in order that we may taste and see how good the Lord is and how blessed is the man that trusts in him. . . . Thus the sacraments assist the contemplation of faith and conjoin it with the strivings of the heart, which is something that could not happen to the same degree or with the same harmony apart from the use of the sacraments. . . .

The seventh virtue of the sacraments is that they act as an oath of allegiance.

[Chapter 9] There are those who unjustly slander us as though we prohibited good works. . . . Since faith is inspired by the Holy Spirit, how can it be slothful or inactive when the Spirit himself is unceasing in his activity and operation? Where there is true faith, works necessarily result, just as fire necessarily brings with it heat. But where faith is lacking, works are not true works but only a futile imitation of works.

John Calvin, *Institutes of the Christian Religion* (1539)

John Calvin was born in 1509 at Noyon, in northern France. He studied at Paris, Orleans and Bruges universities and became an admirer of Erasmus and Humanism. He himself produced in 1532 a work of humanist scholarship (a commentary on the Roman philosopher Seneca's *Clemency*), which failed to make as much impact as he had hoped. At about this time Calvin was converted: 'God by a sudden conversion subdued and brought my mind to a teachable frame.' He immediately devoted himself to theological study.

In 1533 Calvin was associated with a mildly Protestant speech given by the new rector of Paris university, Nicholas Cop, and had to leave town in a hurry. The following year a number of 'placards' attacking the Roman mass were posted round Paris, enraging the king, Francis I, who launched a vigorous onslaught on the Evangelicals. Calvin left France and settled in Basel, to study and to write. By the summer of 1535 he had finished the first edition of his *Institutes*. But his life of peaceful scholarship was to be short. In 1536 he was forced by a local war to make a detour through Geneva, which had just accepted the Reformation. Calvin planned to stop for one night only but Farel, the leader of the Genevan Reformers, prevailed upon him to stay.

The city council noted the employment of 'that Frenchman'. Calvin's ministry in Geneva lasted until his death in 1564, though not without interruption. In 1538 a row over the issue of church government led to his exile and he withdrew to Basel, to resume his studies. But again this was not to be. Martin Bucer persuaded him to come to Strassburg to minister to the small congregation of French refugees in this German city. There he stayed until 1541, profiting from the contact with other Reformers, especially Bucer. But while Calvin was at Strassburg, the church at Geneva was going from bad to worse and eventually Calvin was prevailed upon to return. There followed a long and bitter struggle in which Calvin fought for the spiritual independence of the Genevan church and for the imposition of a rigorous discipline. For many years Calvin had to face intense opposition from the magistrates, but eventually his opponents were discredited and there was a pro-Calvin city council. In the final years of his life he was highly respected, though his wishes were not always obeyed.

Calvin is best known for his *Instruction in the Christian Religion* (commonly called the *Institutes*). This work went through four major editions in Calvin's lifetime. The first edition was of pocketbook length and appeared in 1536. There were six chapters, the first four of which followed the pattern of Luther's catechisms. At the last minute Calvin added a lengthy dedication to King Francis I, who was harrying the French Evangelicals and branding them as Anabaptists. Calvin presented his work to the king as an apology or defence of evangelical doctrine. He substantially rewrote it for the second edition, which appeared in 1539 and was three times the length of the first. The next, in 1543, was not much longer, but reflected the influence of Bucer and the stay at Strassburg. Finally, the definitive edition was published in 1559, about five times the length of the first. Calvin stated that he 'never felt satisfied until the work was arranged in the order in which it now appears'. Alongside these Latin editions there were French translations, mostly by Calvin himself. The *Institutes* was not simply a theological treatise – it was a 'sum of piety' (1536 title page) for the edification of the people of France. The French editions are important for the history of the developing French language as no work of such weight had previously appeared in French.

Calvin's *Institutes* is still widely read today, more so than any other major theological work that old. This is in part because of Calvin's great success in his aim of 'lucid brevity', of covering a topic briefly while yet expressing clearly what he had to say. That makes his writing easier to read than most comparable works. It is also in part because of his great theological skills, which are appreciated even by those who may differ from him on particular doctrines, be that infant baptism or predestination.

Five brief chapters of the final work are devoted to the theme of the Christian life. These concern the imitation of Christ, which Calvin sees as the basic principle, which is worked out in self-denial and daily bearing the cross (Luke 9:23). He also writes of the need to meditate on the future life, after the grave, and the way in which we should make use of this world in the light of that hope. The teaching of these chapters is deeply influenced by the spirituality of the Modern Devotion, found supremely in *The Imitation of Christ* (see pages 186–89) by Thomas à Kempis. Calvin builds upon this tradition, but applies it to all Christians (not just those living in community) and also moderates Thomas's asceticism, which was in danger of denying that the good things of this life are gifts from God for us to enjoy. Calvin evidently felt that this material was of especial importance as in 1550 he published this section from his *Institutes* separately. Almost all of the material in these chapters was first introduced into the 1539 edition of the *Institutes*. The extracts below are from the 1539 edition, though for convenience the references given are to the definitive 1559 edition.

─────────────────────

3:6:4. Doctrine is an affair not of the tongue, but of the life. It is not apprehended by the intellect and memory alone, like other branches of learning, but is received only when it possesses the whole soul and finds its seat and habitation in the inmost recesses of the heart. Let [hypocrites], therefore, either cease to insult God by boasting that they are what they are not, or let them show themselves disciples not unworthy of their divine Master. We have given the priority to the doctrine in which our religion is contained since our salvation commences by [believing] it, but it must move on [from our head] into our heart, pass on into conduct and thus transform us into itself so as not to prove unfruitful. Philosophers are rightly offended by those who, while professing an art which ought to be the mistress of their conduct, convert it into mere loquacious sophistry – and they expel them from their company in disgrace. With how much better reason shall we detest those flimsy sophists who are contented to let the Gospel merely play upon their lips – when its efficacy ought to penetrate the inmost affections of the heart, fix its seat in the soul and pervade the whole man a hundred times more than the frigid discourses of philosophers?

3:6:5. I do not insist that the life of the Christian shall breathe nothing but the perfect Gospel, though this is to be desired and ought to be attempted. I do not insist so strictly on evangelical perfection as to refuse to acknowledge as a Christian anyone who has not yet attained it. That would exclude everyone from the church, since there is no one who is not far removed from such perfection, while many who have made but little progress would be undeservedly rejected. What then? Let us set this [perfection] before our eyes as the target at which we should constantly aim. Let it be regarded as the goal towards which we should run. For you cannot divide the matter with God, undertaking only part of what his Word enjoins and omitting the rest at your pleasure. For, in the first place, God consistently commands integrity as the principal part of worshipping him. By integrity he means real singleness of mind, devoid of gloss and fiction, the opposite of a double mind.

But in this earthly prison of the body no one has sufficient strength to hasten in his course with proper alacrity, while the greater number are so oppressed with weakness that they make little progress, hesitating, halting and even crawling along the ground. So let every one of us go as far as our humble ability enables us, and press on with the journey we have begun. No one will travel so badly as not to make some degree of daily progress. Let us, therefore, never cease to do this, so that we may daily advance in the way of the Lord. And let us not despair because of the slender measure of success. However meagre the success may be compared with our wish, our labour is not lost when today is better than yesterday – provided with true singleness of mind we keep our aim and aspire to the goal, not flattering ourselves nor excusing our vices but making it our constant endeavour to improve, until we attain to goodness itself. If during the whole course of our life we seek this and follow it, we shall in due course attain it when we are relieved from the infirmity of the flesh and admitted to full fellowship with God.

3:10:4. There is no surer or quicker way [to control immoderate desires] than by despising the present life and longing for heavenly immortality. Two rules follow from this: that those who make use of this world should be no more affected by it than if they had not used it, those who marry than if they had not, those who buy than if they had not, as Paul teaches [1 Corinthians 7:29–31]. Secondly, we must learn both to be peaceful and patient in enduring poverty and to exercise moderation in enjoying abundance. He who makes it his rule to use this world as though not using it eliminates all gluttony in regard to food and drink, all effeminacy, ambition, pride, excessive display and austerity, in regard to his table, his house and his clothes. He also removes every care and affection which might divert or hinder him from aspiring to the heavenly life and cultivating spiritual interests. Cato put it well: 'Luxury causes many cares and produces great carelessness as to virtue.' There is an old proverb: 'Those who are much occupied with the care of the body usually give little care to the soul.' Therefore while Christian freedom in external matters is not to be tied to strict rules, it is however subject to this law: we must indulge ourselves as little as possible and make it our constant aim not only to curb luxury but to cut off all show of superfluous wealth and carefully beware of turning helps into hindrances.

3:10:5. Another rule is that those in narrow and straitened circumstances should learn to bear their wants patiently, lest they acquire an immoderate desire for material things. Those who use outward things with moderation have made no little progress in the school of Christ. . . . Scripture, moreover, has a third rule for controlling the use of earthly blessings. . . . For it declares that they have all been given us by the kindness of God and when we make use of them we are to regard them as things given on trust, for which we must one day render account. We must therefore handle them as though we constantly heard the words sounding in our ears, 'Give an account of your stewardship' [Luke 16:2]. At the same time let us remember who it is that requires this account – he who highly commends abstinence, sobriety, frugality and moderation and also abominates luxury, pride, ostentation and vanity. He has with his own lips already condemned all those pleasures which distract the heart from chastity and purity or darken the intellect and he approves of no management of possessions which is not combined with love.

John Calvin, *Short Treatise on the Lord's Supper* (1541)

With some justice Calvin claimed, 'I have a natural love of brevity.' Yet he was one of the most prolific writers in the history of the church. His output would have been remarkable for a full-time scholar – yet Calvin fitted it into a schedule that would have exhausted two lesser men. Apart from his many responsibilities at Geneva, he was the most important leader of the international network of Reformed churches. His letters fill many large volumes and a list of their recipients would read like a *Who's Who* of Reformation Europe.

It has been mistakenly said that Calvin was a man of one book, the *Institutes*. In fact the central focus of his ministry was the exposition of the Bible. This took three main forms:

● Calvin preached regularly throughout his time at Geneva. From 1549 his sermons were recorded in shorthand. A number were published in the sixteenth century, but the majority remained in the Genevan library in shorthand form. Incredibly, these were sold off by weight in 1805 and three quarters of them are lost. Those which survive are now being published.

● Calvin also lectured at the Academy in Geneva. He taught not systematic theology but Old Testament. Many of what are today called his Old Testament commentaries are in fact transcriptions of these lectures. All of the prophetical books except for Isaiah and Ezekiel 21–48 are covered in this way.

● Calvin wrote commentaries on many of the books of the Bible. Starting with Romans in 1540, by 1555 he had covered the entire New Testament except for 2 and 3 John and Revelation. From the Old Testament he produced commentaries on the Pentateuch, Joshua, Psalms and Isaiah. These commentaries were often based on earlier sermons or lectures. Calvin's commentaries are among the very few written before the nineteenth century which are still of value for understanding the meaning of the text (as opposed to those which might be read today for edification rather than for the light that they shed on the text of the Bible). He is the only writer ever to belong without question both to the first rank of theologians and to the first rank of commentators.

● Calvin also wrote many polemical treatises. Several of these were directed against Anabaptism. More important were his attacks on Roman Catholicism. In 1539, after Calvin had been exiled from Geneva, Cardinal Sadolet wrote to the Genevans urging them to return to the Roman fold. The letter was forwarded to Calvin who wrote a *Reply to Sadolet* which is one of his best works. He also published the *Acts* of the early sessions of the Council of Trent – with an *Antidote*. Calvin was capable of satire as biting as any of Erasmus, as can be seen from his *Admonition in which it is shown how advantageous for Christendom would be an inventory of the bodies and relics of saints*. Calvin also found himself forced against his will to write against Lutherans. Two Lutheran pastors, Westphal and Hesshusius, attacked his doctrine of the Lord's Supper and Calvin responded. Eventually he abandoned the controversy, which had grieved him because he saw himself as a disciple of Luther.

Not all of Calvin's treatises were polemical. One of the finest is a *Short Treatise on the Lord's Supper*, which sets out his teaching in a conciliatory fashion, as the middle way between Zwingli and Luther. This he wrote in 1540, while at Strassburg, in French as it was intended to be read by lay folk. It was not published until the following year, in Geneva. Calvin adopts the standard approach of those occupying a middle position. He argues that each side had some element of the truth but erred in failing to listen to the other side. He portrays his own middle way as incorporating the positive features of both sides. He agreed with Zwingli that Christ's body and blood are ascended into heaven and not to be found on earth; he agreed with Luther that the Lord's Supper is more than a mere memorial and that we feed on Christ in it. In adopting this middle way Calvin was following the approach of Martin Bucer, with whom he had close contact during his years at Strassburg (1538–41).

_____

3. As the life into which [God] has begotten us again is spiritual, so also must the food be spiritual, in order to preserve and strengthen us. For we should understand that he has not only called us one day to possess his heavenly inheritance, but that by hope he has already in some measure installed us in possession; that he has not only promised us life, but already transferred us into it, delivering us from death – when by adopting us as his children he begot us again by immortal seed, his Word imprinted on our hearts by the Holy Spirit.

4. What is needed to maintain us in this spiritual life is not to feed our bodies with fading and corruptible food, but to nourish our souls on the best and most precious diet. Now all Scripture tells us that the spiritual food by which our souls are maintained is that same Word by which the Lord has regenerated us. But it frequently adds the reason – that in it Jesus Christ, our only life, is given and administered to us. For we must not imagine that there is life anywhere than in God. But just as God has placed all fullness of life in Jesus, in order to communicate it to us by his means, so he ordained his Word as the instrument by which Jesus Christ, with all his graces, is dispensed to us. Still it always remains

true that our souls have no other pasture than Jesus Christ. Our heavenly Father, therefore, in his care to nourish us gives us no other [pasture], but rather recommends us to take our fill there as a refreshment amply sufficient, with which we cannot dispense and beyond which no other can be found.

5. We have already seen that Jesus Christ is the only food by which our souls are nourished. But as it is distributed to us by the Word of the Lord, which he has appointed an instrument for that purpose, that Word is also called bread and water. Now what is said of the Word applies as well to the sacrament of the Supper, by means of which the Lord leads us to communion with Jesus Christ. For seeing we are so weak that we cannot receive him with true heartfelt trust when he is presented to us by simple teaching and preaching, the Father of mercy, not disdaining to condescend in this matter to our infirmity, has been pleased to add to his Word a visible sign, by which he might represent the substance of his promises, to confirm and fortify us by delivering us from all doubt and uncertainty. Since, then, to say that we have communion with the body and the blood of Jesus Christ is something so mysterious and incomprehensible, and we on our part are so rude and gross that we cannot understand the least things of God, it was of importance that we should be given to understand it as far as our capacity could admit.

6. Our Lord, therefore, instituted the Supper [for three reasons]. First, in order to sign and seal in our consciences the promises contained in his gospel concerning our being made partakers of his body and blood, and to give us certainty and assurance that our true spiritual nourishment lies there, so that having such an earnest we might entertain a right reliance on salvation. Secondly, in order to exercise us in recognizing his great goodness toward us, and thus lead us to laud and magnify him more fully. Thirdly, in order to exhort us to all holiness and innocence inasmuch as we are members of Jesus Christ, and especially to exhort us to union and brotherly love as we are expressly commanded. When we have well considered these three reasons, to which the Lord had respect in ordaining his Supper, we shall be able to understand both what benefit accrues to us from it, and what is our duty in order to use it properly.

9. Here, then, is the singular consolation which we derive from the Supper. It directs and leads us to the cross of Jesus Christ and to his resurrection, to assure us that whatever iniquity there may be in us, the Lord nevertheless recognizes and accepts us as righteous; whatever material of death may be in us, he nevertheless gives us life; whatever misery may be in us, he nevertheless fills us with all felicity. Or to explain the matter more simply, as in ourselves we are devoid of all good and have not one particle of what might help to procure salvation, the Supper is an

attestation that, having been made partakers of the death and passion of Jesus Christ, we have every thing that is useful and salutary to us.

10. We can therefore say that in it the Lord displays to us all the treasures of his spiritual grace, inasmuch as he makes us associates of all the blessings and riches of our Lord Jesus. Let us recollect, then, that the Supper is given us as a mirror in which we may contemplate Jesus Christ crucified in order to deliver us from condemnation, and raised again in order to procure for us righteousness and eternal life. It is indeed true that this same grace is offered us by the gospel, yet as in the Supper we have more ample certainty and fuller enjoyment of it, with good cause do we recognize this fruit as coming from it.

11. But as the blessings of Jesus Christ do not belong to us at all unless he be previously ours, it is necessary first of all that he be given us in the Supper, in order that the things which we have mentioned may be truly accomplished in us. For this reason I am wont to say that the substance of the sacraments is the Lord Jesus, and the efficacy of them the graces and blessings which we have by his means. Now the effect of the Supper is to confirm to us the reconciliation which we have with God through our Saviour's death and passion; the washing of our souls which we have in the shedding of his blood; the righteousness which we have in his obedience; in short, the hope of salvation which we have in all that he has done for us. It is necessary, then, that the substance should be conjoined with these, otherwise nothing would be firm or certain. Hence we conclude that two things are presented to us in the Supper – Jesus Christ as the source and substance of all good and, secondly, the fruit and efficacy of his death and passion. This is implied in the words which were used. For after commanding us to eat his body and drink his blood, he adds that his body was delivered for us and his blood shed for the remission of our sins. Hereby he intimates, first, that we ought not simply to communicate in his body and blood without any other consideration, but in order to receive the fruit derived to us from his death and passion; secondly, that we can attain the enjoyment of such fruit only by participating in his body and blood from which it is derived.

Ignatius Loyola, *Spiritual Exercises*
(1548)

Iñigo López was born in the early 1490s into a noble family at Loyola, just south of the Pyrenees. He became a courtier, caring little for the things of God, but was brought to a halt at the siege of Pamplona in 1521, when his leg was mangled by a cannon ball. Ignatius was laid up for a considerable period and turned to read an account of the life of Christ and the lives of the saints. This led to his conversion and resolve to follow Jesus Christ. When his leg was better he made a pilgrimage to the monastery of Montserrat, near Barcelona, where he made his general confession and exchanged clothes with a beggar. He then spent a year of solitude and prayer at Manresa. During this time he underwent deep spiritual experiences and drew up the first draft of his *Spiritual Exercises.* Thomas à Kempis's *The Imitation of Christ* (see pages 186–89) influenced him deeply at this stage. After visiting Rome and Jerusalem he returned to study in Spain (1524–28) and at Paris (1528–35).

     In 1534 Ignatius and six companions took vows of poverty and celibacy. In 1537 they went to Rome and offered their services to the pope. They won support from some of the leading figures at Rome and in 1540 Pope Paul III sanctioned the Society of Jesus. Ignatius became the first General of the Jesuits and organized the order. He drew up its *Constitutions* from 1547 to 1550 and made further improvements until his death in 1556. The Jesuits had three major aims: to reform the church from within (by education especially); to fight heresy (especially Protestantism); to preach the gospel to the pagan world. In addition to the three normal vows of poverty, celibacy and obedience, some Jesuits took a fourth: going without delay wherever the pope might order for the salvation of souls. The Jesuits included some of the greatest figures of the Catholic Reformation, such as the missionary Francis Xavier and the theologian Robert Bellarmine.

     Ignatius's greatest work is his *Spiritual Exercises*, one of the major spiritual classics, which he began to write in 1522 and published in 1548. The *Spiritual Exercises* was designed not as a book to be read for spiritual edification but as a guide for people leading other Christians in spiritual growth. They have been described as a summary in simplified form of Ignatius's own experience from his conversion on his sick bed to his time in Paris. The aim is to take the disciple systematically through the process of Ignatius's conversion in order to produce the same effect. The goal is to discover God's will for one's life, and to dedicate oneself completely to the service of Jesus Christ – ideally as a Jesuit. The exercises are designed to last four weeks, though each 'week' may be shorter or longer than seven days.

● The emphasis of week one is on the purgation of sin. 'Retreatants' are to examine their consciences and confess their faults. They are to meditate on the realities of sin and hell, be thankful that they have been spared this fate until now and resolve to forsake sin.

● The emphasis of week two is on the kingdom of Jesus Christ. The retreatant meditates on the main events of Jesus' life from his birth to his entry into Jerusalem on Palm Sunday. The aim of the week is to resolve to serve under the standard of Jesus Christ, rather than that of the devil. At this stage there may come the resolve to turn one's back on the world and embrace the 'religious' life, especially as a Jesuit.

● In the third week the retreatant meditates on the passion of Jesus Christ.

● In the fourth week the retreatant meditates on the risen Jesus Christ.

Ignatius's *Spiritual Exercises* have been hugely influential. It has been estimated that in the four centuries following 1548 a new edition of the *Exercises* came out on average once a month. They are still widely used today for leading retreats, especially but not exclusively by Roman Catholics. While they are a product of their time there is much that is just as relevant today. Relatively few will suffer today from the scruples described below, but the opposite danger of a lax conscience is very powerful.

345–51. Toward Perceiving and Understanding Scruples and the Enticements of Our Enemy the Following Notes are Helpful

The First Note. People commonly apply the word scruple to something which comes from our own judgment and free will, for example, when I take something that is not sinful and freely build it up into a sin. This happens, for example, if someone accidentally steps on a cross made by straws and afterward forms the judgment that he or she has sinned. This, strictly speaking, is an erroneous judgment and not a scruple in the proper sense of the term.

The Second Note. After I have stepped on that cross, or after I have thought or said or done something else similar, there comes to me from without the thought that I have sinned; but on the other hand I think I have not sinned. However, in all this I feel disturbed, that is, at one moment I doubt and at another I do not. This is a scruple in the proper sense of the term, and a temptation brought on by the enemy.

The Third Note. The first scruple, that described in the first note, should be strongly abhorred, since it is totally error. But the second, described in the second note, can for a limited period of time be profitable to a person performing spiritual exercises. For it greatly purifies and cleanses a soul, and separates it far from every semblance of sin, in accordance with Gregory's maxim: 'It is characteristic of good souls to see a fault where none exists.'

The Fourth Note. The enemy considers attentively whether one has a lax or a delicate conscience. If a conscience is delicate, the enemy strives the harder to make it delicate even to an extreme, in order to trouble it more and eventually thwart it. For example, if he sees that a person does not consent to any sin, whether mortal or venial or even merely an appearance of deliberate sin, since he cannot make the person fall into what even appears sinful, he brings him or her to judge as sinful something in which no sin exists; for example, in some unimportant word or thought. But if a person has a lax conscience, the enemy works to make it still more lax. For example, if a soul makes little or nothing of venial sins, he tries to bring it to similar unconcern about mortal sins; and if previously it did have some concern about them, he now tries to make the concern less or to banish it.

The Fifth Note. A person who desires to make progress in the spiritual life ought always to proceed in a manner contrary to that of the enemy. In other words, if the enemy seeks to make a soul lax, it should try to make itself more sensitive. In the same way, if the enemy seeks to make a soul too sensitive, in order to entice it to an extreme, the soul should endeavour to establish itself staunchly in a correct mean and thus arrive at complete peace.

The Sixth Note. Sometimes a good soul of this type wishes to say or do something which, in conformity with the church or the mind of our superiors, contributes to the glory of God our Lord. But it gets a thought or temptation from without not to say or do it. Specious reasons of vainglory or other similar things are brought up. In such a case we ought to raise our minds to our Creator and Lord; and if we see that it is for his due service, or at least not opposed to it, we ought to act diametrically against the temptation. We should reply as St Bernard: 'I did not begin because of you, and neither will I desist for you.'

Heinrich Bullinger, *Decades* (1549–51)

Johann Heinrich Bullinger was born in 1504 in Bremgarten, a small town not far from Zurich, where his father was the parish priest. Having started school locally in 1509, he left home in 1516 for a school at Emmerich where he was educated according to the principles of Renaissance Humanism. In 1519 he moved on to the University of Cologne where traditional scholastic theology was still taught, along the lines of Thomas Aquinas and Duns Scotus, but Bullinger retained his interest in the humanist approach. Stimulated by the controversy over Luther, whose books were burned at Cologne, he turned to theology and especially the study of the Early Church Fathers. This turned him away from the medieval scholastics to Luther. By 1522 he had decided definitively for the Reformation.

Bullinger returned to Bremgarten and continued to study the Fathers, as well as Luther and Melanchthon. In 1523 he became head teacher at the school of the Cistercian monastery at Kappel, introducing humanist and Reformed ideas. In due course the mass was replaced by a Protestant service and many of the monks became Reformed ministers.

In 1523 Bullinger met Zwingli and Leo Jud at Zurich. He found that he agreed with Zwingli on many matters, especially his rejection of the real presence of Christ in the Lord's Supper, and their relationship deepened. Bullinger joined Zwingli in disputations with the Anabaptists in 1525, through which he developed his covenant theology, and also accompanied him to the disputation with Roman Catholics at Bern in 1528, where he met other Reformers such as Bucer. That year Bullinger became part-time pastor of a village near Kappel. The following year he became the Reformer of Bremgarten, where his father had belatedly embraced the Reformation earlier that year and had helped to initiate reform in his parish. Heinrich carried on the work and brought it to fruition that summer, when he also married a former nun, by whom he had eleven children.

In October 1531 Zwingli was defeated and killed on the battlefield at Kappel. One of the terms of the ensuing peace treaty was Bullinger's exile from Bremgarten. He set out for Zurich in November that year and was soon being sought out for church office in Basel and Bern as well as Zurich. He opted for the last of these and in December took over Zwingli's role as chief minister of the city, where he was to remain until his death in 1575.

Zwingli's death raised the issue of the relative authority of the pastors and the magistrates. Bullinger reached an agreement with the city council which guaranteed the freedom of the pastors to preach God's Word in its fullness, but also laid down that the pastors should not meddle in the affairs of the magistracy. He saw moral discipline as the task of the magistrate and resisted Leo Jud's attempt to introduce a church court with the power of excommunication. The city council also had ultimate control over church finances and a major role in the Synod that was responsible for the hire and discipline of clergy.

Bullinger was involved in ongoing controversy with both Anabaptists and Lutherans. He also played an important role in the development of Reformed theology and church life. He co-authored the *First Helvetic Confession* of 1536 and thirty years later wrote the fuller *Second Helvetic Confession*, one of the most influential of the Reformed confessions which was accepted far beyond Switzerland. He was concerned to promote unity between Reformed Christians and had close relations with Calvin, with whom he did not agree on all points. He was out of sympathy with the Genevan approach to church discipline. Although he shared with Calvin a commitment to the Augustinian doctrine of unconditional election, he was not happy to go beyond this to talk of positive predestination to damnation. Most importantly, they reached a common agreement on the Eucharist, the 1549 Zurich Agreement. This was the fruit of some years of negotiations and involved an element of compromise on both sides. Bullinger also helped to develop the idea of a conditional covenant between God and his people, one that was to be very influential within later Reformed theology.

Bullinger was a prolific author leaving behind many published works. He wrote New Testament commentaries, doctrinal treatises and polemical works against Anabaptists and Lutherans especially. His collected correspondence includes more than twelve thousand letters to and from him.

Bullinger had a significant role to play in the English Reformation. During the reign of Catholic Queen Mary (1553–1558) Zurich played host to a number of leading Protestant exiles. These maintained their contact with Bullinger after their return to take up positions of leadership in the Elizabethan church and their correspondence was published as *The Zurich Letters*. Bullinger's *Decades*, a selection of fifty sermons on Christian doctrine, became a standard theological textbook in Elizabethan England.

The *Decades* were published in Latin in four volumes between 1549 and 1551 and an English translation went through a number of editions during Elizabeth's reign. They were designed as a theological resource for pastors in sermon preparation. The sermons are divided into five 'decades' of ten sermons each, but this is for convenience rather than reflecting the structure of the subject matter. Between them the sermons cover a wide range of Christian doctrine, including the standard contents of a catechism: the Apostles' Creed, the Ten Commandments, the Lord's Prayer and the sacraments.

Fourth Decade, Sermon 2: Repentance and the Causes Thereof

Repentance is an unfeigned turning to God by which, having a sincere fear of God and being humbled, we acknowledge our sins and so, by putting to death our old self, are freshly renewed by the Spirit of God. . . .

First we say, that repentance is an unfeigned turning unto God. For I will later show that there are two sorts of repentance, feigned and unfeigned. . . . We have all turned away from the true, just and good God and from his holy will to the devil and our own corrupt affections. And therefore we must turn again from the devil and from our old wicked life and will to the living God and his most holy will and pleasure.

There is no one too blind to see that to stir us up to repentance we need the preaching or teaching of the truth – to teach us who is the God to whom we must be turned, what is the goodness and holiness to which we must be turned, who is the devil and what is the evil and wickedness from which we must be turned, and lastly what it is that must be amended in our mind and life and how it must be altered and amended. The prophets and apostles of the Lord, when exhorting people to repentance, labour hard and persevere in describing God's nature, goodness, righteousness, truth and mercy; in expounding the laws and offices of human life; and in accusing and heaping up the sins of men; to which they add the grievous and horrible signs of God's just judgments. This is found abundantly throughout the prophets' writings. There are some who even today bid us preach the law to those whom we would lead unto repentance. While I do not oppose this opinion but like it very well, I nevertheless counsel them that the preaching of the gospel itself attributes to men their sins and grievously accuses them. . . .

Repentance is preached unto us in vain unless, by fear and trembling formed in our minds, we reverently dread the wrath and judgment of Almighty God conceived against us because of our sins and wickednesses. Now this fear is outwardly stirred in us by the external preaching or discipline of the minister – but that external teaching has no efficacy on its own unless we be moved inwardly, in our hearts, by the Holy Spirit of our heavenly Father. Therefore Jeremiah cries out in his Lamentations: 'Turn us, O Lord, and we shall be turned' [5:21]. . . . Therefore when our ears are pierced by the Word of God and our hearts touched by his Holy Spirit, we shall unfeignedly reverence and dread the Lord like true penitents.

In addition, being humbled before the most just and holy God, whom with our sins we so much offend and provoke to wrath and indignation, we confess the justice of his judgment against us and freely acknowledge all the sins and iniquities that in the Word of God are attributed to us. . . .

I speak now of the sincere fear of God, for we confess that there are two sorts of fear of God, sincere and insincere. The sincere fear of God is seen in the faithful and is a godly reverence consisting in the love and honour of God. . . . Therefore the sincere fear of God in the repentant is not the servile dread of punishment, but an anxious inclination mixed with love and honour for God. . . . Penitents not only fear God – because they know, being taught by the Spirit of God, that they have committed sins for which they deserve to be forsaken by the

Lord – but also love him as their merciful Father and are therefore sorry with all their hearts for the sins they have committed and most ardently desire above all else to be reconciled again to their merciful God and loving Father.

This sincere fear of God is joined with grief or sorrow, which is conceived by the Spirit of God for our sins that we commit. St Paul mentions two sorts of sorrow. 'Godly sorrow brings a repentance not to be repented of, but worldly sorrow brings death' [2 Corinthians 7:10]. . . . The godly are greatly grieved because they so often and so foully offend so good a God and gracious Father. . . .

Worldly grief is the sorrow of such as do not know God and are without faith and true love of God – of such as submit to the burden of sorrow, adversities and their sins. Insincere fear of God is similar. For the wicked (like their chief the devil) fear God not as a father, whom they are sorry to offend and to whom they desire to be reconciled, but as a tormentor because they know he will revenge their evil deeds. Therefore with Judas they run to the rope. There is in them no love of God, no honour, no good-will, no reverence but mere hatred of God, horror, and utter desperation. The apostle and evangelist John denied that such fear is found in love, saying that 'perfect love casts out all fear' [1 John 4:18]. I am referring not to that fear of the Lord that is the beginning of wisdom [Proverbs 9:10] but to that of which I have been speaking, the fear that is found in the devil and wicked men. . . .

To summarize what I have said concerning repentance, let us hold that repentance is a turning to God which, although he stirs it up in us by his Word and other means, is notwithstanding so fashioned in us by the Holy Ghost especially, that with fear and love we fear our just God and merciful Lord from whom we have turned away, being sorry now with our whole hearts that we ever offended so gracious a Father by our sins. Being humbled before his eternal and most sacred majesty, we acknowledge the sins that are attributed to us by the Word of God; indeed we acknowledge that there is no integrity or soundness in us and heartily desire to be reconciled with God again. Since that reconciliation can only be made by the sole Mediator, the Lord Christ Jesus, by faith we lay hold of him in whom we, being acquitted of all our sins, are reckoned by God to be righteous and holy. Whoever sincerely acknowledges this benefit cannot but choose to hate sin and put to death the old self.

Martin Bucer,
The Kingdom of Christ (1550)

Martin Bucer was born in 1491 at Schlettstadt (modern-day Sélestat) in Alsace. At the age of fifteen he became a Dominican friar. He was trained in the theology of Thomas Aquinas and also came under the influence of Erasmus's Humanism. In 1518 he attended the General Chapter of the Augustine friars at Heidelberg where Luther was speaking and became an instant convert. A few years later, in 1523, he settled in Strassburg. The Reformation had already been introduced there by Matthew Zell and a number of Reformers were to live there for a shorter or longer period – John Calvin, Wolfgang Capito, Kaspar Hedio, Peter Martyr, Jakob and John Sturm. But it was Bucer who became the leading Reformer of Strassburg.

Strassburg became a major centre of the Reformation. In many ways it set an example for others to follow. Its educational reforms, pioneered by John Sturm especially, with the support of Bucer, were copied all round Europe. Bucer was also concerned for pastoral care as well as reform of doctrine. His *True Pastoral Care* is one of the most important sixteenth-century works on that subject. Bucer also saw the need for discipline in the church and sought to introduce it at Strassburg. In 1546 he proposed the introduction of small groups within the congregation, for spiritual edification. In the following century this may well have helped to inspire Spener to write his *Holy Desires* (see pages 332–35). But in 1546 Strassburg was forced to surrender to the army of the (Roman Catholic) emperor and had to accept the Interim settlement of religion that he imposed. Bucer refused to compromise in this way and accepted an invitation to become Regius professor of divinity at Cambridge. He died there in 1551. After the collapse of the Interim settlement, Strassburg became militantly Lutheran, and Bucer was no longer honoured there.

Much of Bucer's efforts were directed to the cause of church unity. Like Erasmus he disliked division and strife, and like Melanchthon he was often felt to be too conciliatory and was therefore mistrusted. Bucer was enthusiastic in the search for reconciliation between Protestants and Roman Catholics. From 1530 there was a series of colloquies aimed at uniting the two parties in Germany. The Colloquy of Regensburg, in 1541, came nearest to success, agreement being reached on the doctrine of justification by faith. The discussions were based on the *Regensburg Book*, a document previously drawn up in secret by Bucer and the moderate Catholic Johann Gropper.

Bucer also sought to win over the Anabaptists. All over Europe they were savagely persecuted, but in Strassburg they were treated kindly. Bucer debated with them and many were won over to his way, one of whom was to become Calvin's wife. This was not a purely one-way process. Bucer listened as well as argued and was willing to learn. His concern for church discipline sprang at least in part from his debates with the Anabaptists.

Bucer also sought to heal the rift within the Protestant camp. The dispute over Christ's presence in the Lord's Supper had split the Reformers into two opposing camps – the Lutherans and the Swiss. When Bucer was first confronted with the case for seeing the bread and the wine as mere symbols, he sought to defend the doctrine of Christ's real presence. Eventually, however, he concluded that this was not possible from the Bible alone and so he moved into the Swiss camp. But in 1528, after the controversy was well under way, he came to the conclusion that the Swiss had misunderstood Luther, that Luther did not in fact teach a local presence of Christ's body and blood in the bread and wine. He then decided that the two parties could be drawn together and sought a mediating position between them. Bucer's own attempts to establish a firm 'centre party' between the Lutherans and the Zwinglians met with only limited success. His most solid achievement was the recruitment of Calvin to the cause, as can be seen from the latter's *Short Treatise on the Lord's Supper* (see pages 222–25).

Bucer left no organized group behind him and until recently he has been largely neglected. But in fact his influence has been considerable, in two directions. Bucer's greatest influence has been through John Calvin, who spent the years 1538 to 1541 at Strassburg. During this time Bucer was able to influence his thinking in a number of key areas. He has been called, with pardonable exaggeration, the father of Calvinism. During his exile in England Bucer was able to influence the course of the English Reformation, especially through Thomas Cranmer. Bucer's hand can be seen in Cranmer's 1549 and 1552 editions of *The Book of Common Prayer* (see pages 237–41).

Bucer's last book, written at Cambridge during 1550, was his *Kingdom of Christ*, a blueprint for a Christian England addressed to Edward VI. Because Bucer died early in 1551 it was not published until 1557, in Basel. German and French translations followed the next year. Ironically, an English translation did not appear until 1969, although in 1644 John Milton published a translation of a lengthy section on divorce. Bucer's death delayed its publication and Edward's death in 1553 ended hopes for its implementation, though some of its proposals had already been enacted.

The Kingdom of Christ is in two books, the first devoted to a biblical theology of the Kingdom of Christ and the second to practical proposals for its implementation in England, expressed in fourteen specific laws. For Bucer, unlike Luther, the Kingdom of Christ relates to all areas of life. His proposals encompass not just church life but also issues of the economy and government. He was concerned to end the scourge of unemployment, through better training of labourers and through a proper development of the wool trade. Bucer also, unlike Luther, held that secular politics should be based on specifically Christian principles, arguing that all of the laws of the land should be based upon the two great commandments to love God and one's neighbour (2:56).

Bucer's proposals for poor relief are radical. Begging is to be outlawed – not because of lack of concern for the poor but in order for there to be *effective* poor relief. This is to be administered by the deacons of the church. They are to ascertain who is in genuine need and to meet their needs. Able-bodied persons who are too lazy to work are not to be supported. Bucer strongly discourages individuals from giving directly to the needy, primarily because they are likely to give to the wrong people. 'Just as the wicked are never satisfied, and beggary knows neither moderation nor limit, so also reputable and prudent men dissimulate and conceal their need and judge whatever is provided for them by the churches to be too much' (2:14).

Some of Bucer's proposals are amazingly modern, with the provision of a comprehensive safety net for the poor, with steps to restore full employment and with the goal of universal education. There are even plans for the recycling of waste products (2:49)! At the same time they avoid one of the pitfalls of modern welfare states in that they take care not to end up by rewarding irresponsible behaviour.

1:14. A fourth common observance of all the churches, and one proper to the Kingdom of Christ, is the care of the poor and needy. For the Lord expressly forbids his people to allow anyone among them to be in need. . . . Since, then, it is manifest that God has gravely forbidden his people to allow anyone among them to beg, and has established that care for the poor should be exercised by certain approved men in the church, that the alms of the faithful may be distributed to needy individuals in proportion to the need of each, all those undoubtedly pray thoughtlessly, 'Thy kingdom come,' who do not extend every effort for this method of caring for the poor to be restored which the Lord himself commanded and the Holy Spirit established in the Early Church. . . .

When each person wishes to distribute his own alms for himself, there is violated, first of all, the institution of the Holy Spirit and the legitimate communion of the saints. Secondly, alms due to the least of Christ's brethren, and therefore to Christ himself, are more often given to the unworthy than the worthy. Nor can every single individual know and investigate each of the poor who happen to encounter him; for those who are least worthy are much better instructed at begging, indeed extorting, the alms which should be dispensed to the poor alone. Furthermore, when everyone gives alms by his own hand, it is with great difficulty that he will exclude from his heart a desire for the appreciation and praise of men; and when he receives this empty reward from men, a real and sure one is not to be expected from God. Finally, since it is obvious that those who voluntarily give themselves over to beggary are prone to every crime, what else do those people who foster them do but sustain and support very harmful pests of society.

2:14. [The deacons'] duty and office is contained under these headings: First, they should investigate how many really indigent persons live in each church for whom it is equitable for the church to provide the necessities of life. For the churches of Christ must exclude from their communion those who, when they can sustain themselves by their own powers, neglect this and live inordinately, accepting borrowed food; it certainly is not the duty of the church to foster such people in their godless idleness. Against these, therefore, the saying should prevail: 'Whoever does not work, let him not eat' [2 Thessalonians 3:10]. . . .

Even if someone is well acquainted with his needy neighbours and knows their ways, nevertheless, in order that others may not also wish by his example themselves to dispense their alms and very often to those who are little known or investigated (in view of the fact that those who are least worthy of alms are accustomed to beg them all the more imprudently and deviously), it is far better for everyone to send those whom he encounters in need of help, however well he knows them to be good and virtuous, to the deacons of the church, so that they may obtain from these what they need. . . .

This, however, is also within the competence of the deacons, that they take into consideration not only the need of various persons but also their faintness of heart, and that with prudence and liberality they offer assistance in such a way that in no case they add the affliction of shame to the affliction of poverty, and that they do not reduce those whom the Lord previously blessed with ease and comfort to an unbearable harshness of diet and dress, even though this may be satisfactory to other men who have been accustomed to this according to their living conditions.

2:48. The children of citizens of the lower classes should learn the art of reading and writing and the fundamentals of our religion at a tender age, when they cannot yet be used for other tasks. . . . But when the boys have learned the writings and the catechism of our religion, those directors of youth education must find out which of the boys have talents for acquiring greater learning and arrange that boys of this kind are instructed more liberally in literature, languages, and the fine arts and thus better prepared for a fuller service to church and state. They may be left in the schools in which they are or sent to others where better teaching is available, at the expense of their parents if the Lord has given them abundance, otherwise at the expense of the church.

Thomas Cranmer,
The Book of Common Prayer (1552)

Thomas Cranmer was born in 1489, in Nottinghamshire. He studied at Jesus College, Cambridge, where he became a fellow in 1511. In the early 1520s he was among a group of young scholars who met in the White Horse Inn at Cambridge to discuss Erasmus's Greek New Testament. It was the 'king's matter' which propelled Cranmer into public life. Henry VIII desperately needed a male heir for the stability of the realm. England had only recently emerged from the period of turmoil known as the Wars of the Roses. It was essential that the succession be unquestioned. The queen, Catherine, had produced only one surviving child – Mary. To complicate matters, Catherine had been married to Henry's older brother Arthur before his early death, which meant that her marriage to Henry was contrary to Leviticus 20:21. Henry wanted an annulment of the marriage on these grounds, seeing the lack of a male heir as God's judgment on an unlawful union. (Leviticus 20:21 actually mentions childlessness.) Normally there would have been no problems, but the pope was being controlled by the emperor Charles V – who happened to be Catherine's nephew, and so was opposed to the annulment. In 1529 Cranmer put forward the bright idea of consulting the universities for their judgment. Henry heard of this and sent Cranmer on a tour of the European universities.

At this time the 'Reformation Parliament' (1529–36) put through a series of laws gradually severing all links between the English Church and Rome. This culminated in the Act of Supremacy in 1534 which declared the sovereign to be 'the only Supreme Head in earth of the Church of England'. In the meantime, the archbishop of Canterbury had died in 1532 and Henry had appointed a reluctant Cranmer to replace him. Cranmer fitted the post admirably, for two reasons: he believed sincerely in the authority of the 'godly prince' over the church (i.e. it was not merely a tactical position), and his views moved gradually in the direction of Protestantism, at about the right speed for the royal will. But this belief was to bring Cranmer to the greatest crisis of his life, at the end.

During the later years of Henry's reign there was a constant power struggle between the conservative Catholic faction and those desiring Protestant reform. At first Cranmer gained some notable victories: the publication and installation in every parish church of an English Bible (drawing heavily on Tyndale's translation [see pages 198–201]) and the publication in 1536 of *Ten Articles* which leaned gently in a Lutheran direction. But in 1539 there was a Catholic reaction with the publication of *Six Articles* of an anti-Protestant nature, which Cranmer opposed. The following year, his ally Thomas Cromwell fell from favour and was beheaded. Cranmer's enemies tried to topple him too, but Henry, who respected him, always protected him.

When Edward VI succeeded Henry in 1547, the time was ripe for real reform with Cranmer at the forefront. In 1549 the first English prayer book was published. This was a Protestant work, but carefully written so as not to cause unnecessary offence to traditional Catholics. The Holy Communion 'commonly called the masse' still looked very much like the old mass to the uninitiated. The Catholic party exploited this fact to interpret it in a traditional sense. Because of this and in the light of suggestions from Peter Martyr and Bucer (who had become professors at Oxford and Cambridge at Cranmer's invitation), a revised prayer book was introduced in 1552: *The Boke of Common Prayer and Administracion of the Sacramentes and other Rites and Ceremonies in the Churche of England*. In some ways there were few changes, but the ambiguities of 1549 were gone and the result was an unequivocally Protestant work. As a leading scholar with Catholic sympathies has put it, this prayer book 'is not a disordered attempt at a catholic rite, but the only effective attempt ever made to give liturgical expression to the doctrine of "justification by faith alone"'.

The 1552 edition was the last to involve Cranmer, but two other major editions were to follow within just over a century. After the accession of Elizabeth I on Mary's death the *Book of Common Prayer* was reissued in 1559. There were very few changes between 1552 and 1559 but, in order not to antagonize her Roman Catholic subjects more than necessary, Elizabeth removed one prayer from the Litany: 'From the tyranny of the bishop of Rome and al hys detestable enormities . . . Good Lorde, delyver us'! The prayer book fell out of use during the year's of Cromwell's Commonwealth but after the accession of Charles II it was restored, in the new 1662 version, which reigned supreme in Anglicanism for three hundred years. There are relatively few differences between the 1552, 1559 and 1662 editions. Over the centuries the *Book of Common Prayer* has moulded Anglican worship. Its recent successors use more 'accessible' language, but lack the majesty, grandeur and theological depth of Cranmer.

The reign of Edward also saw doctrinal reform. In 1547 a *Book of Homilies* was published, many of them being written by Cranmer. These were evangelical sermons to be read in parishes where there was no qualified preacher. In 1553 Cranmer and Ridley (bishop of London) produced *Forty-two Articles*, which were later modified to become the *Thirty-nine Articles* (see pages 264–68).

Edward died young in 1553 and was succeeded by Mary, a zealous Roman Catholic. She set about dismantling the Edwardian Protestant settlement. At first she moved cautiously, but in 1555 the burning of Protestant heretics began. A number of bishops were burnt, including Latimer and Ridley in October 1555, witnessed by Cranmer. The government worked hard to persuade him to recant his Protestant beliefs. In particular, they exploited his belief in the sovereign's authority over the church – his sovereign was now ordering him to revert to Roman Catholicism. Under extreme psychological pressure Cranmer gave way and recanted. But then Mary made a great mistake. It was not the practice to burn heretics who recanted, but Mary was determined to have her revenge and ordered that he should be burnt. It was arranged that Cranmer would publicly renounce Protestantism at his execution – but instead he renounced his recantation and reaffirmed his Protestant convictions in full. He was rushed to the stake, where he held his right hand (which had signed the recantation) in the flames until it was burnt. The full account is given by John Foxe in his *Book of Martyrs* (see pages 259–63), which ensured that the witness of Cranmer and others would not be forgotten.

The Order for Morning Prayer

DEARLY beloved brethren, the Scripture moveth us in sundry places, to acknowledge and confess our manifold sins and wickedness, and that we should not dissemble nor cloak them before the face of almighty God our heavenly father, but confess them with an humble, lowly, penitent and obedient heart: to the end that we may obtain forgiveness of the same by his infinite goodness and mercy. And although we ought at all times humbly to knowledge our sins before God: yet ought we most chiefly so to do, when we assemble and meet together, to render thanks for the great benefits that we have received at his hands, to set forth his most worthy praise, to hear his most holy word, and to ask those things which be requisite and necessary, as well for the body as the soul. Wherefore I pray and beseech you, as many as be here present, to accompany me with a pure heart and humble voice, unto the throne of the heavenly grace, saying after me.

A general confession, to be said of the whole congregation after the minister, kneeling:

ALMIGHTY and most merciful father, we have erred and strayed from thy ways, like lost sheep. We have followed too much the devices and desires of our own hearts. We have offended against thy holy laws. We have left undone those things which we ought to have done, and we have done those things which we ought not to have done, and there is no health in us: but thou, O Lord, have mercy upon us miserable offenders. Spare thou them, O God, which confess their faults. Restore thou them that be penitent, according to thy promises declared unto mankind, in Christ Jesu our Lord. And grant, O most merciful father, for his sake, that we may hereafter live a godly, righteous, and sober life, to the glory of thy holy name. Amen.

The absolution to be pronounced by the minister alone.

ALMIGHTY God, the Father of our Lord Jesus Christ, which desireth not the death of a sinner, but rather that he may turn from his wickedness and live: and hath given power and commandment to his ministers, to declare and pronounce to his people being penitent, the absolution and remission of their sins: he pardoneth and absolveth all them which truly repent, and unfeignedly believe his holy gospel. Wherefore we beseech him to grant us true repentance and his Holy Spirit, that those things may please him, which we do at this present, and that the rest of our life hereafter, may be pure and holy: so that at the last we may come to his eternal joy, through Jesus Christ our Lord. Amen.

The Order of the Ministration of the Holy Communion

Then shall the Priest, kneeling down at God's board, say in the name of all them that shall receive the Communion, this prayer following.

WE do not presume to come to this thy table (O merciful Lord) trusting in our own righteousness, but in thy manifold and great mercies: we be not worthy, so much as to gather up the crumbs under thy table: but thou art the same Lord whose property is always to have mercy: grant us therefore (gracious Lord) so to eat the flesh of thy dear son Jesus Christ, and to drink his blood, that our sinful bodies may be made clean by his body, and our souls washed through his most precious blood, and that we may evermore dwell in him, and he in us. Amen. . . .

Then shall the minister first receive the Communion in both kinds himself, and next deliver it to other ministers, if any be there present (that they may help the chief minister) and after to the people in their hands kneeling.
And when he delivereth the bread, he shall say.

TAKE and eat this, in remembrance that Christ died for thee, and feed on him in thy heart by faith, with thanksgiving.

And the Minister that delivereth the cup, shall say.

DRINK this in remembrance that Christ's blood was shed for thee, and be thankful.

Then shall the Priest say the Lord's prayer, the people repeating after him every petition. After shall be said as followeth.

O LORD and heavenly father, we thy humble servants entirely desire thy fatherly goodness, mercifully to accept this our Sacrifice of praise and thanksgiving: most humbly beseeching thee to grant, that by the merits and death of thy son Jesus Christ, and through faith in his blood, we and all thy whole church may obtain remission of our sins, and all other benefits of his passion. And here we offer and present unto thee, O Lord, our selves, our souls and bodies, to be a reasonable, holy, and lively sacrifice unto thee: humbly beseeching thee, that all we which be partakers of this holy Communion, may be fulfilled with thy grace and heavenly benediction. And although we be unworthy through our manifold sins to offer unto thee any Sacrifice: Yet we beseech thee to accept this our bounden duty and service, not weighing our merits, but pardoning our offences, through Jesus Christ our Lord; by whom, and with whom, in the unity of the Holy Ghost, all honour and glory be unto thee, O father almighty, world without end. Amen.

Menno Simons,
The Cross of the Saints (c. 1554)

Menno Simons was born in Friesland, in the north of the Netherlands, in 1496 or 1497. In 1524 he became a priest, but before long he began to doubt the doctrine of transubstantiation. He then turned to the Bible (for the first time) and came to the conclusion that the Roman teaching was false – but stayed in his post. Some time later he heard of an Anabaptist nearby who was martyred for his rejection of infant baptism. 'It sounded very strange to me to hear of a second baptism. I examined the Scriptures diligently and pondered them earnestly, but could find no report of infant baptism.' He then turned to the early Fathers and Reformers, but found no coherent scriptural defence of infant baptism. He concluded that 'we were deceived in regard to infant baptism' – but did nothing about it. So far he had had no direct contact with Anabaptists.

In 1534 the city of Münster was taken over by some of the wilder revolutionary Anabaptists. They saw it as the New Jerusalem prophesied in Revelation. Polygamy was introduced, on the basis of the Old Testament. Roman Catholics and Protestants united to besiege the city, which fell in 1535. There was a bloodbath. The affair of Münster served to discredit the Anabaptist cause for some time. But, ironically, Münster marked the end of revolutionary Anabaptism. From now on it was the pacifist evangelical Anabaptism which predominated – and inherited the reputation of Münster.

Menno saw the effects of Münster and the persecution of the scattered and leaderless Anabaptist brethren. His conscience smote him for his hypocritical life of outward conformity to Rome. He began openly to preach what he believed and after nine months, in 1536, left home to become a wandering Anabaptist preacher. For eighteen years he travelled constantly – nowhere was safe for him. But in 1554 he was able to settle on the estate of a sympathetic nobleman in Holstein, northern Germany. Here he was able to write and to publish his works in peace, until his death in 1561.

Menno became the leader of the Anabaptist movement in Holland and north-west Germany. He organized independent congregations with their own leaders. In due course his followers came to be known as Mennonites. The movement grew in (relatively) tolerant Holland. Over the centuries, other Anabaptist groups have also come to be called Mennonites. In the eighteenth century the Mennonites spread to Russia, at the invitation of Catherine the Great. Later, persecution in Russia caused migration to North America, especially in 1873–82 and 1923–30. Today there are some 1,200,000 Mennonites (baptized believers) spread throughout the world.

Menno held to the evangelical Anabaptist position, as set out in *The Schleitheim Confession* (see pages 202–04). He opposed the revolutionary Anabaptists, holding to a firmly pacifist position, as do most Mennonites today. He also opposed the 'spiritualist' Anabaptists, who relied on the 'inner light' for special private revelations. Menno sought to base his teaching on the Bible alone. Like the Reformers, he held that Scripture alone is the supreme and final norm for all doctrine. But he did not follow the Reformers in the deep respect that they retained for the writings of the Early Church Fathers (while insisting that they must be tested by Scripture).

Menno Simons was one of the very few Anabaptist leaders to exercise a lengthy ministry (twenty-five years), to write extensively (his *Complete Writings* contains more than a thousand large pages) and to leave behind him an organized movement. The Mennonites today have much in common with the Baptists, but they are noted for their stress on radical discipleship, including pacifism.

One of Menno's finest works is his *The Cross of the Saints* or, to give the full title of the original, *A Comforting Admonition Concerning the Sufferings, the Cross, and the Persecution of the Saints Because of the Word of God and his Testimony*. It was written in about 1554 to encourage Anabaptists facing persecution. He points to who the persecutors are, why they persecute and what excuses they give. At greater length he shows that persecution was the lot of the faithful in both Old and New Testaments and that believers today should expect nothing else. The finest part of the book is the fifth section, in which Menno portrays persecution and cross-bearing not as a negative evil but as a blessing sent by God for the purpose of our salvation. In the short term it 'seems to the flesh grievous, harsh, and severe', but it is to be welcomed because of the fruit that it brings for eternity.

---

1. [Who the Persecutors Are]

Worthy and faithful brethren in the Lord, note well – such a blind, naked, poor, miserable, and senseless people it is (in divine things) who so bitterly persecute and destroy you without mercy on account of your faith. Therefore the true and chosen children of God must not, no matter how heavily the cross may be laid on them by these people, be angry over them, but sincerely pity them and sigh sorely for their poor souls with all meekness and fervour after the example of Christ and Stephen, praying over their raging and cursed folly and blindness – for they know not what they do. . . .

2. [Why They Persecute the Saints]

I consider it a fine, mollifying ointment, and an easing of our misery and griefs, if we will but reflect upon the real reason why our persecutors hate us so and deprive us so grievously of name and fame, of prosperity, property, and life. . . . In short, it is because we in good faith set forth before them the sure and infallible truth of God, the true light and the highway to eternal life, and in this way warn and frighten them as much as we may, with doctrine and life, from eternal death in hell and the wrath of God. . . .

3. [Biblical Examples]

You see, brethren, every Christian should be prepared for this. For this is the real reward and crown of this world with which it has paid off, rewarded, and honoured all true servants of God who have set before them in pure love the kingdom, the Word, and the will of God. Thus it has rewarded those who have called to repentance and reformation; those who have rendered many kindnesses, services, and favours; those who with every kind of holiness, righteousness, truth, and the fear and love of God, have like the golden candlestick thrown off light in the Lord's tabernacle, and have flourished and blossomed like a fruitful olive tree in the house of God. Everyone who ponders well these and similar histories and narratives of the pious men of God will undoubtedly not lose courage, but in all his miseries, crosses, and sufferings, will by God's grace surely remain standing, and will abide pious and strong to the end. . . .

4. [Excuses of the Persecutors]

We will now proceed in the name of the Lord to show with few words what feeble and unbecoming excuses are advanced by those who persecute us, excuses which cannot stand before God any more than stubble and sulphur before fire, but wherewith they think to excuse themselves and prove that they are doing right in so molesting and harming the pious. . . . In the first place, those who persecute us say that we are like those of Münster were and that we are not obedient to the magistrates. . . . In the second place, we are with great severity but without cause accused by those who persecute us of being headstrong, self-willed, and impossible persons who consistently refuse to be taught or instructed. . . . In the third place, those who persecute us try to justify themselves by saying that it is right that we are persecuted since we mislead many people sadly, and lead them to destruction. . . . In the fourth place, those who persecute us also accuse us with great bitterness because we separate ourselves from their doctrines, sacraments, church service, and from the carnal life, and in such things do not feel free to have to do with them. They say that by so doing we condemn them and consign them to hell. . . .

5. [The Blessings of Cross-Bearing]

For this cause, dear brethren and sisters in the Lord, do not reject the chastening and instruction of your dear Father, but receive the admonition of his faithful love with great joy. Thank him that through his fatherly goodness he has chosen you to be his dear children in Christ Jesus, and has called you by his powerful Word. Thank him that he has enlightened you with the Holy Spirit in order that through the medicine and remedy of the cross of Christ he may restore to health your poor, weak, mortal flesh, subject to so many harmful and destructive ailments of concupiscence, and has diverted it from the lusts and loves of the world in order that you in this way may be made partakers of the burden of Christ and conformed unto his death, and so attain unto the resurrection of the dead. . . .

6. [Promises for Those Bearing the Cross]

Finally, I beseech and exhort you, consider with all diligence what it is that is promised to all soldiers and conquerors in Christ in the world to come; namely, an eternal kingdom that does not pass, the crown of honour, and the life that will remain forever.

Philip Melanchthon, *Loci Communes* (1555)

Philip Melanchthon was born in 1497 in southern Germany. He was the great nephew of John Reuchlin (1455–1522), a leading German Humanist and the foremost Christian Hebrew scholar of his day. Melanchthon studied at Heidelberg and Tübingen universities, completing his studies at an unusually early age. While at Tübingen he came under humanist influence and became a lifelong admirer of Erasmus. On Reuchlin's recommendation he was appointed professor of Greek at Wittenberg university in 1518. Here he was influenced by Luther and drawn into the Reformation camp. In 1519 he joined the theology faculty, though without ever leaving the arts faculty.

Melanchthon was Luther's closest friend, though their temperaments were strikingly different – Melanchthon was a somewhat timid, moderate and conciliatory humanist scholar. Furthermore, there were marked differences in their theological approaches, as Luther's disciples later observed. This did not obstruct their warm friendship, although it did give rise to some theological differences.

Melanchthon was the author of *The Augsburg Confession* (see pages 210–13), the most important Lutheran confession of faith, which was read to the emperor Charles V at Augsburg in 1530. Charles commissioned some Roman Catholic theologians to refute the confession and their work was read in August. Melanchthon then wrote an *Apology [Defence] of the Augsburg Confession*, which was presented to the emperor in September.

Melanchthon's main theological work was his *Loci Communes* (or *Common Places*, a standard title for a book that tackled a series of standard theological themes). This first appeared in 1521 and was the first Protestant attempt at a systematic theology. It went through many editions, those of 1521, 1535 and 1555 being the most important. There were German translations of the different editions. At the beginning of the 1521 edition Melanchthon sets out his approach:

> *We do better to adore the mysteries of deity than to investigate them. What is more, these matters cannot be probed without great danger, and even holy men have often experienced this. . . . Therefore, there is no reason why we should labour so much on those exalted topics, such as 'God', 'the unity and trinity of God', 'the mystery of creation' and 'the manner of the incarnation'. What, I ask you, did the Scholastics accomplish during the many ages they were examining only these points? . . . But as for one who is ignorant of the other fundamentals, namely 'the power of sin', 'the law' and 'grace', I do not see how I can call him a Christian.*

For from these things Christ is known, since to know Christ means to know his benefits and not, as they [the Scholastics] teach, to reflect upon his natures and the modes of his incarnation. For unless you know why Christ put on flesh and was nailed to the cross, what good will it do you to know merely the history about him? . . . Christ was given us as a remedy and, to use the language of Scripture, a saving remedy. It is therefore proper that we know Christ in another way than that which the Scholastics have set forth.

At this stage it was Melanchthon's aim to rescue theology from philosophical distortions and to give it a firmly scriptural basis. He considered that the early Fathers had been misled by Platonism and the Scholastics by Aristotle. 'For just as we in these latter times of the church have embraced Aristotle instead of Christ, so immediately after the beginnings of the church Christian doctrine was weakened by Platonic philosophy.' But later Melanchthon revised his opinion of Aristotle and even encouraged the study of him in German universities. Melanchthon also came to a deeper appreciation of the Early Church Fathers. Scripture remained the sole infallible norm, but the consensus of the early Fathers was worthy of great respect.

When controversy arose between Luther and Zwingli over the real presence, Melanchthon sided with Luther. Indeed, at the Marburg Colloquy in 1529 it was Melanchthon who, uncharacteristically, remained intransigent and held Luther firm. In a letter written that year to Oecolampadius (the Reformer of Basel, and a friend of Zwingli) he argued for the real presence on the grounds that it was scriptural, that it was taught by the early Fathers and that it was fitting and reasonable. But Oecolampadius managed to persuade him that the early Fathers did not all support Luther's position. This caused Melanchthon to move away from Luther's doctrine of the real presence. In 1540 he published a revised version of *The Augsburg Confession*, in which the reference to Christ's body and blood being 'truly present' was changed to 'truly exhibited'. The definitive 1555 *Loci Communes* also avoided the language of real presence. Instead Melanchthon taught that:

With this bread and wine [Jesus Christ] gives his body and blood to us and thereby attests that he accepts us, makes us his members, grants us forgiveness of sins and that he has purified us with his blood and will abide in us. . . . The living Son of God, Jesus Christ, our Saviour, is truly present and active in this participation, attesting through it that he will abide in us. (22)

This statement was acceptable to Calvin, for instance. Luther was grieved by Melanchthon's change, but did not oppose him openly. Melanchthon claimed that shortly before his death, Luther admitted that he had gone too far on the issue of the real presence but said that he could not now modify his position, because all of his teaching might be brought into disrepute. It is hard to know how to evaluate such a claim, as Melanchthon could not be said to be impartial in this matter.

In 1546 much of Lutheran Germany, including Wittenberg, was overrun by the armies of the emperor, Charles V. Charles tried to impose an interim settlement on the Lutheran territories, which involved considerable compromise of Lutheran doctrine. Melanchthon vacillated – he would not accept the Interim but he was prepared to compromise and to make some concessions. The result was that he came under fire from both sides. He had the misfortune of being a moderate in an age which was becoming increasingly intransigent and hard line. This was the beginning of the attacks on Melanchthon by those who considered that he had betrayed the heritage of Luther. These attacks continued until his death in 1560 and beyond, leading to the condemnation of many of his ideas in *The Formula of Concord* (see pages 269–73). But Melanchthon was not out of favour with everyone, and he has come to be known as the 'Teacher of Germany' for his considerable achievements in educational reform.

Chapter 13 [1555 edition]. Why say that we have forgiveness of sins and are justified *only* through faith? Surely many virtues must accompany faith, repentance and sorrow for sins, belief, good resolution, and hope.

Answer: The exclusive *sola* [alone] or *gratis* [freely] must be fully maintained, as will be explained later more adequately. It shuts out *all our merit*; it teaches that we receive forgiveness of sins and are justified *for the sake of Christ alone*, that is, we are pleasing to God, and the heart must receive this with faith. This great grace is given through the knowledge of Christ, as Isaiah says [53:11]. This knowledge is the faith about which we speak. Here an order is established by God that makes a distinction between God's children and others. The children of God are those who thus recognize Christ and accept him with faith. There must be an *application* of the grace of Christ; and this *application* occurs through faith, and faith results from preaching, contemplation of the gospel, and the sacraments.

And it is true. . . that where true faith is, there at the same time are many virtues. However, they are not meritorious; they are not *causae justificationis* [causes of justification]; they are not reasons why God accepts us. They result from faith; as indicated above, we receive grace and gift. As the sun has both light and the power to warm, and the two cannot be separated, so wherever there is true faith, a recognition of God's mercy, there also is love, invocation of God, and hope, and a will which willingly subjects itself to God and is obedient. These accompany faith as light and heat accompany a fire. Nevertheless, there is no merit in these virtues. Merit lies only in the faith by which we receive forgiveness of our sins, and is received *for the sake of the Christ*. This we receive in the Word and through the Word; the Lord Christ is active through the gospel.

Why must we firmly maintain the exclusive: *fide sola* [by faith alone] or *gratis* [freely]?

Answer: For five reasons. The first, so that Christ may be given his special honour, for *his* obedience *alone* is merit for us. On his account God is willing to forgive us our sins, receive us graciously, and make us heirs of eternal blessedness; and *our* wretched deeds, sufferings, and works do not merit this exalted grace.

The second reason is that God in his great mercy wants the grace which he has offered to men in his promise to stand certain, firm, and immovable, for the promise is called an eternal testament. This comfort is certain if it is grounded *only on the Son of God* and *not* on our merit. For this reason we say, *only* through faith may the heart be assured that God is gracious, for the sake of Christ. If this depended on our merit, it would not only be uncertain, but the promise would be empty, for in this wretched life we always have much sin, ignorance, and transgression. *Paul* says, 'Therefore, *out of faith, without merit on our part*, the promise remains firm' [e.g. Romans 4:13–16].

The third reason is that there is no other means whereby we acknowledge and accept the Lord Christ and his grace except by *faith alone*. . . . Faith hears the preaching of the gospel, in which Christ and his grace are conveyed to us, and faith accepts. . . .

The fourth reason: so that the distinction between law and the gospel may be clear. The law says that when we are as the law commands, then we are justified. But no man, with the exception of our Lord and Saviour Christ, is as the law teaches. But when we *believe on the Son of God*, we have forgiveness of sins, and we are pleasing to God *for the sake of Christ*, freely, without any merit on our part, although our sinful nature is very unlike the law.

The fifth reason: so that we may be able to call on God. Without this Mediator, the Son of God, we could not approach God. If invocation depended upon our merit, then the heart would flee from God. Therefore, the Lord says, we are to invoke in *his* name, that is, *in the faith* that he is the Mediator and High Priest who bears our prayer before God and that we are heard *for the sake of his merit*.

John Knox, *The Scots Confession*
(1560)

John Knox was born around 1513 at Haddington, not far from Edinburgh. He was educated at St Andrews university and was subsequently ordained. At the age of about thirty he was won over to Protestantism. He was deeply impressed by his contemporary George Wishart, who preached the gospel fearlessly and paid for it by being burnt at the stake at St Andrews in 1546. For the next thirteen years Knox travelled widely. He spent nineteen months as a French galley slave, after taking part in an abortive revolt at St Andrews. He was in England during the latter part of the reign of Edward VI and took part in the final stages of preparing Cranmer's 1552 *The Book of Common Prayer* (see pages 237–41).

When Mary became queen in 1553 he fled to continental Europe. For a time he was pastor of the English exile congregation at Frankfurt, where he became embroiled in controversy. Knox and others had gone beyond the *Book of Common Prayer*, introducing a more thoroughly Reformed pattern of worship. But the more conservative exiles in other European cities were displeased and sent Richard Cox and others to put Knox right. They remonstrated with him, saying that 'they would have the face of an English church'. Knox replied, 'The Lord grant it to have the face of Christ's church.' This conflict was the precursor of the Puritan controversies during the reign of Elizabeth I, with some wanting to preserve the *Book of Common Prayer* and others wanting a fuller Reformation in line with the Reformed churches in continental Europe. Cox managed to have Knox expelled from Frankfurt (by drawing attention to his radical political views) and Knox went to Geneva. He was an ardent admirer of Calvin's Geneva, declaring it to be 'the most perfect school of Christ that ever was in the earth since the days of the apostles. In other places I confess Christ to be truly preached. But manners and religion to be so sincerely reformed, I have not yet seen in any other place.' While there he wrote his infamous *First Blast of the Trumpet against the Monstrous Regiment [Reign] of Women* (1558). This attack on female rulers was aimed at Mary Tudor, queen of England, but in 1558 Elizabeth came to the English throne and did not take kindly to Knox's work.

In 1559 Knox returned to Scotland, where he helped to reform the church. With others he drafted the *Book of Discipline* (1561) and the *Book of Common Order* (1564). He was also the most important of the 'Six Johns' (six Scots Reformers named John) who in four days in August 1560 drew up the *Scots Confession*. This confession of faith was ratified by the Scots Parliament as 'doctrine grounded upon the infallible Word of God' and became the confession of the Scots Reformed Kirk until in 1647 *The Westminster*

Confession of Faith was adopted (see pages 301–305). It differs from Calvin's approach in one significant point. The notes or criteria of the true church include (with Calvin) 'the true preaching of the Word of God' and 'the right administration of the sacraments of Christ Jesus'. But there is a third note in the Scots Confession, 'ecclesiastical discipline uprightly ministered'. Calvin had taken care not to include this as it opens the door for people to reject the Protestant state church on the ground that they do not consider its discipline rigorous enough.

Knox's second blast against the monstrous regiment of women was his sustained opposition to Mary Stuart (Mary Queen of Scots) from her accession to the throne in 1560 until her flight to England in 1568. He pushed through the Scottish reformation despite her resistance. He wrote a major *History of the Reformation of Religion within the Realm of Scotland*, which did not appear in full until 1644. Knox died in 1572.

Chapter 9: Christ's Death, Passion and Burial

That our Lord Jesus offered himself a voluntary sacrifice unto his Father for us, that he suffered contradiction of sinners, that he was wounded and plagued for our transgressions, that he, the clean innocent Lamb of God, was condemned in the presence of an earthly judge, that we should be absolved before the judgment seat of our God; that he suffered not only the cruel death of the cross, which was accursed by the sentence of God, but also that he suffered for a season the wrath of his Father which sinners had deserved. But yet we avow that he remained the only, well beloved and blessed Son of his Father even in the midst of his anguish and torment which he suffered in body and soul to make full atonement for the sins of his people. From this we confess and avow that there remains no other sacrifice for sin; if any affirm so, we do not hesitate to say that they are blasphemers against Christ's death and the everlasting atonement thereby purchased for us.

Chapter 13: The Cause of Good Works

The cause of good works, we confess, is not our free will, but the Spirit of the Lord Jesus, who dwells in our hearts by true faith, brings forth such works as God has prepared for us to walk in. For we most boldly affirm that it is blasphemy to say that Christ abides in the hearts of those in whom is no spirit of sanctification. Therefore we do not hesitate to affirm that murderers, oppressors, cruel persecutors, adulterers, filthy persons, idolaters, drunkards, thieves and all workers of iniquity have neither true faith nor anything of the Spirit of the Lord Jesus, so long as they obstinately continue in wickedness. For as soon as the Spirit of the Lord Jesus, whom God's chosen children receive by true faith, takes possession of the heart of any man, so soon does he regenerate and renew him, so that he begins to hate what before he loved and to love what he hated before. Thence comes that continual battle which is between the flesh and Spirit in God's children, while the flesh and the natural man, being corrupt, lust for things pleasant and delightful to themselves, are envious in adversity and proud in prosperity, and every moment prone and ready to offend the majesty of God. But the Spirit of God, who bears witness to our spirit that we are the sons of God, makes us resist filthy pleasures and groan in God's presence for deliverance from this bondage of corruption, and finally to triumph over sin so that it does not reign in our mortal bodies. Other men do not share this conflict since they do not have God's Spirit, but they readily follow and obey sin and feel no regrets, since they act as the devil and their corrupt nature urge. But the sons of God fight against sin; sob and mourn when they find themselves tempted to do evil; and, if they fall, rise again with earnest and unfeigned repentance. They do these things, not by their own power, but by the power of the Lord Jesus, apart from whom they can do nothing.

Chapter 15: The Perfection of the Law and the Imperfection of Man

We confess and acknowledge that the Law of God is most just, equal, holy and perfect, commanding those things which, when perfectly done, can give life and bring man to eternal felicity; but our nature is so corrupt, weak and imperfect that we are never able perfectly to fulfil the works of the Law. Even after we are reborn, if we say that we have no sin we deceive ourselves and the truth of God is not in us. It is therefore essential for us to lay hold on Christ Jesus, in his righteousness and his atonement, since he is the end and consummation of the Law and since it is by him that we are set at liberty so that the curse of God may not fall upon us, even though we do not fulfil the Law in all points. For as God the Father beholds us in the body of his Son Christ Jesus, he accepts our imperfect obedience as if it were perfect and covers our works, which are defiled with many stains, with the righteousness of his Son. We do not mean that we are so set at liberty that we owe no obedience to the Law – for we have already acknowledged its place – but we affirm that no man on earth, with the sole exception of Christ Jesus, has given, gives or shall give in action that obedience to the Law which the Law requires. When we have done all things we must fall down and unfeignedly confess that we are unprofitable servants. Therefore, whoever boasts of the merits of his own works or puts his trust in works of supererogation, boasts of what does not exist, and puts his trust in damnable idolatry.

Chapter 18: The Notes by Which the True Kirk Shall Be Determined from the False, and Who Shall Be Judge of Doctrine

Since Satan has laboured from the beginning to adorn his pestilent synagogue with the title of the Kirk of God, and has incited cruel murderers to persecute, trouble and molest the true Kirk and its members, as Cain did to Abel, Ishmael to Isaac, Esau to Jacob and the whole priesthood of the Jews to Christ Jesus himself and his apostles after him – so it is essential that the true Kirk be distinguished from the filthy synagogues by clear and perfect notes lest we, being deceived, receive and embrace, to our own condemnation, the one for the other. The notes, signs and assured tokens whereby the spotless bride of Christ is known from the horrible harlot, the false Kirk, we state, are neither antiquity, usurped title, lineal succession, appointed place, nor the numbers of men approving an error. For Cain was before Abel and Seth in age and title; Jerusalem had precedence above all other parts of the earth, for in it were priests lineally descended from Aaron, and greater numbers followed the scribes, pharisees and priests than unfeignedly believed and followed Christ Jesus and his doctrine . . . and yet no man of judgment, we suppose, will hold that any of the forenamed were the Kirk of God. The notes of the true Kirk, therefore, we believe, confess and avow to be: first, the true preaching of the Word of God, in which God has revealed himself to us, as the writings of the prophets and apostles declare; secondly, the right administration of the sacraments of Christ Jesus, with which must be associated the Word and promise of God to seal and confirm them in our hearts; and lastly, ecclesiastical discipline uprightly ministered, as God's Word prescribes, whereby vice is repressed and virtue nourished. Then wherever these notes are seen and continue for any time, be the number complete or not, there, beyond any doubt, is the true Kirk of Christ, who, according to his promise, is in its midst.

The Heidelberg Catechism (1563)

In 1559 the Palatinate, one of the German states, acquired a new ruler, the elector Frederick III. He wished to advance the Reformed faith there. To this end, he commissioned a catechism, for use in the churches and the schools. This was written in 1562 by a number of theologians from Heidelberg university, principally Zacharias Ursinus and Kaspar Olevianus, both still in their twenties. The following year it was approved by the synod of Heidelberg and published. That same year it was also translated into Latin and other languages. It is one of the most popular of the Reformation catechisms and has been widely distributed. It has been said to combine the intimacy of Luther, the charity of Melanchthon and the fire of Calvin.

The text comprises 129 questions and answers. These are divided into 52 Sundays, so that the catechism can be fitted into a year's programme. After two introductory questions the catechism is divided into three parts, corresponding to the three parts of Romans 7:24–25: 'What a wretched man I am! Who will rescue me from this body of death? Thanks be to God – through Jesus Christ our Lord!': that is to say, our sin and misery (questions 3–11); redemption from sin and its consequences (questions 12–85); our response of gratitude (questions 86–129). The answers are given in the first person singular and the catechism has a warm personal tone which has helped to guarantee its abiding popularity.

Question 1. What is your only comfort in life and death?
Answer. That I belong – body and soul, in life and in death – not to myself but to my faithful Saviour, Jesus Christ, who at the cost of his own blood has fully paid for all my sins and has completely freed me from the dominion of the devil; that he protects me so well that without the will of my Father in heaven not a hair can fall from my head; indeed, that everything must fit his purpose for my salvation. Therefore, by his Holy Spirit, he also assures me of eternal life, and makes me wholeheartedly willing and ready from now on to live for him.

Question 2. How many things must you know that you may live and die in the blessedness of this comfort?
Answer. Three. First, the greatness of my sin and wretchedness. Second, how I am freed from all my sins and their wretched consequences. Third, what gratitude I owe to God for such redemption.

Question 3. Where do you learn of your sin and its wretched consequences?
Answer. From the Law of God.

Question 4. What does the Law of God require of us?
Answer. Jesus Christ teaches this in a summary in Matthew 22:37–40: 'You shall love the Lord your God with all your heart, and with all your soul, and with all your mind. This is the great and first commandment. And a second is like it, you shall love your neighbour as yourself. On these two commandments depend all the law and the prophets.'

Question 5. Can you keep all this perfectly?
Answer. No, for by nature I am prone to hate God and my neighbour.

Question 12. Since, then, by the righteous judgment of God we have deserved temporal and eternal punishment, how may we escape this punishment, come again to grace, and be reconciled to God?
Answer. God wills that his righteousness be satisfied; therefore, payment in full must be made to his righteousness, either by ourselves or by another.

Question 13. Can we make this payment ourselves?
Answer. By no means. On the contrary, we increase our debt each day.

Question 14. Can any mere creature make the payment for us?
Answer. No one. First of all, God does not want to punish any other creature for man's debt. Moreover, no mere creature can bear the burden of God's eternal wrath against sin and redeem others from it.

Question 15. Then, what kind of mediator and redeemer must we seek?
Answer. One who is a true and righteous man and yet more powerful than all creatures, that is, one who is at the same time true God.

Question 16. Why must he be a true and righteous man?
Answer. Because God's righteousness requires that man who has sinned should make reparation for sin, but the man who is himself a sinner cannot pay for others.

Question 17. Why must he at the same time be true God?
Answer. So that by the power of his divinity he might bear as a man the burden of God's wrath, and recover for us and restore to us righteousness and life.

Question 18. Who is this mediator who is at the same time true God and a true and perfectly righteous man?

Answer. Our Lord Jesus Christ, who is freely given to us for complete redemption and righteousness.

Question 19. Whence do you know this?
Answer. From the holy gospel, which God himself revealed in the beginning in the Garden of Eden, afterward proclaimed through the holy patriarchs and prophets and foreshadowed through the sacrifices and other rites of the Old Covenant, and finally fulfilled through his own well-beloved Son.

Question 20. Will all men, then, be saved through Christ as they became lost through Adam?
Answer. No. Only those who, by true faith, are incorporated into him and accept all his benefits.

Question 21. What is true faith?
Answer. It is not only a certain knowledge by which I accept as true all that God has revealed to us in his Word, but also a wholehearted trust which the Holy Spirit creates in me through the gospel, that, not only to others, but to me also God has given the forgiveness of sins, everlasting righteousness and salvation, out of sheer grace solely for the sake of Christ's saving work.

Question 56. What do you believe concerning 'the forgiveness of sins'?
Answer. That, for the sake of Christ's reconciling work, God will no more remember my sins or the sinfulness with which I have to struggle all my life long; but that he graciously imparts to me the righteousness of Christ so that I may never come into condemnation.

Question 59. But how does it help you now that you believe all this? [The Creed]
Answer. That I am righteous in Christ before God, and an heir of eternal life.

Question 60. How are you righteous before God?
Answer. Only by true faith in Jesus Christ. In spite of the fact that my conscience accuses me that I have grievously sinned against all the commandments of God, and have not kept any one of them, and that I am still ever prone to all that is evil, nevertheless, God, without any merit of my own, out of pure grace, grants me the benefits of the perfect expiation of Christ, imputing to me his righteousness and holiness as if I had never committed a single sin or had ever been sinful, having fulfilled myself all the obedience which Christ has carried out for me, if only I accept such favour with a trusting heart.

Question 61. Why do you say that you are righteous by faith alone?
Answer. Not because I please God by virtue of the worthiness of my faith, but because the satisfaction, righteousness, and holiness of Christ alone are my righteousness before God, and because I can accept it and make it mine in no other way than by faith alone.

Question 62. But why cannot our good works be our righteousness before God, or at least a part of it?
Answer. Because the righteousness which can stand before the judgment of God must be absolutely perfect and wholly in conformity with the divine Law. But even our best works in this life are all imperfect and defiled with sin.

Question 63. Will our good works merit nothing, even when it is God's purpose to reward them in this life, and in the future life as well?
Answer. This reward is not given because of merit, but out of grace.

Question 64. But does not this teaching make people careless and sinful?
Answer. No, for it is impossible for those who are ingrafted into Christ by true faith not to bring forth the fruit of gratitude.

Question 86. Since we are redeemed from our sin and its wretched consequences by grace through Christ without any merit of our own, why must we do good works?
Answer. Because just as Christ has redeemed us with his blood he also renews us through his Holy Spirit according to his own image, so that with our whole life we may show ourselves grateful to God for his goodness and that he may be glorified through us; and further, so that we ourselves may be assured of our faith by its fruits and by our reverent behaviour may win our neighbours to Christ.

Question 87. Can those who do not turn to God from their ungrateful, impenitent life be saved?
Answer. Certainly not! Scripture says, 'Surely you know that the unjust will never come into possession of the kingdom of God. Make no mistake: no fornicator or idolater, none who are guilty either of adultery or of homosexual perversion, no thieves or grabbers or drunkards or slanderers or swindlers, will possess the kingdom of God' [1 Corinthians 6:9–10].

Question 88. How many parts are there to the true repentance or conversion of man?
Answer. Two: the dying of the old self and the birth of the new.

Question 89. What is the dying of the old self?
Answer. Sincere sorrow over our sins and more and more to hate them and to flee from them.

Question 90. What is the birth of the new man?
Answer. Complete joy in God through Christ and a strong desire to live according to the will of God in all good works.

Question 91. But what are good works?
Answer. Only those which are done out of true faith, in accordance with the Law of God, and for his glory, and not those based on our own opinion or on the traditions of men.

Question 114. But can those who are converted to God keep these commandments perfectly?
Answer. No, for even the holiest of them make only a small beginning in obedience in this life. Nevertheless, they begin with serious purpose to conform not only to some, but to all the commandments of God.

Question 115. Why, then, does God have the ten commandments preached so strictly since no one can keep them in this life?
Answer. First, that all our life long we may become increasingly aware of our sinfulness, and therefore more eagerly seek forgiveness of sins and righteousness in Christ. Second, that we may constantly and diligently pray to God for the grace of the Holy Spirit, so that more and more we may be renewed in the image of God, until we attain the goal of full perfection after this life.

John Foxe, *Book of Martyrs*
(1563)

John Foxe was born at Boston, in Lincolnshire, in 1516. He went as a student to Brasenose College, Oxford and from 1539 to 1545 was a fellow of Magdalen College. While there he developed Protestant views. After Oxford he took two posts as a private tutor until Mary came to the throne, when he fled with his wife to the Continent, spending time at Frankfurt and Basel.

Foxe used his exile to develop a comprehensive martyrology, an account of Christian martyrdoms from the time of the apostles, especially those of recent years. The first edition was published in Basel in 1559, in Latin. Having achieved this Foxe returned to England and in 1560 was ordained. High office in the Church of England was closed to him because he was unwilling to conform to all of the prescribed rituals, such as wearing the surplice. He was, however, eventually given the prebendary of Shipton, in the cathedral of Salisbury, which provided him with an income. Foxe used this to enable him to develop his martyrology further.

The first edition in English appeared in 1563 under the title *Actes and Monuments of these Latter and Perillous Dayes touching Matters of the Church, wherein ar Comprehended and Described the Great Persecutions and Horrible Troubles, that have been Wrought and Practised by the Romishe Prelates*. It is usually referred to simply as Foxe's *Book of Martyrs*. Further editions were published in 1570, 1576 and 1583, each being larger than the previous one. The final version was divided into twelve books and was most recently published in eight fat volumes. Of the twelve books, six cover the period of the Reformation, three of these covering Mary's reign (1553–58). Foxe died in 1587 in his seventieth year.

Foxe's *Book of Martyrs* was hugely influential and at one point a copy was placed in every cathedral church in England. As the 1563 title indicates, a major theme was portrayal of the Roman Catholic Church as the persecuting church, a theme for which there was no shortage of evidence at the time. Foxe helped to immortalize the achievements of the Protestant martyrs. When Mary came to the throne Protestantism was not particularly popular. But by an unwise and unpopular alliance with Spain and by the executions, Mary burnt Protestantism into the English consciousness and earned the title 'Bloody Mary'. The courageous martyrdoms of Latimer, Ridley, Cranmer and some two hundred others won the hearts of the people for Protestantism in a way that the legislation of Edward's reign could not have achieved. Foxe ensured that the lesson would not be forgotten.

Foxe's historical reliability was for a time questioned, but research has vindicated the substantial accuracy of his account. If he can be faulted it would be for his evidently partisan stance (in common with all of that time) and in some of the things that he fails to mention.

———————————————

[During his three-year imprisonment] the doctors and divines of Oxford busied themselves all that ever they could about master Cranmer, to have him recant, essaying by all crafty practices and allurements they might devise, how to bring their purpose to pass. And to the intent they might win him easily, they had him to the dean's house of Christ's church in the said university, where he lacked no delicate fare, played at the bowls, had his pleasure for walking, and all other things that might bring him from Christ. . . .

[Cranmer recants, as follows:]

> I, Thomas Cranmer, late archbishop of Canterbury, do renounce, abhor, and detest all manner of heresies and errors of Luther and Zwingli, and all other teachings which be contrary to sound and true doctrine. And I believe most constantly in my heart, and with my mouth I confess one holy and Catholic Church visible, without the which there is no salvation; and thereof I acknowledge the bishop of Rome to be supreme head in earth, whom I acknowledge to be the highest bishop and pope, and Christ's vicar, unto whom all Christian people ought to be subject. . . .

The queen, having now gotten a time to revenge her old grief, received his recantation very gladly; but of her purpose to put him to death, she would nothing relent. . . .

Soon after, about nine of the clock, the lord Williams, sir Thomas Bridges, sir John Brown, and the other justices, with certain other noblemen that were sent of the queen's council, came to Oxford with a great train of waiting men. Also of the other multitude on every side (as is wont in such a matter) was made a great concourse, and greater expectation. For first of all, they that were of the pope's side were in great hope that day to hear something of Cranmer that should stablish the vanity of their opinion: the other part, which were endued with a better mind, could not yet doubt, that he who by continual study and labour for so many years, had set forth the doctrine of the gospel, either would or could now in the last act of his life forsake his part. . . .

In this so great frequency and expectation, Cranmer at length cometh from the prison of Bocardo unto St Mary's Church (the chief church in the university), because it was a foul and rainy day. . . . There was a stage set over against the pulpit, of a mean height from the ground, where Cranmer had his standing, waiting until Cole made him ready to his sermon.

[Cole preaches]

Cole, after he had ended his sermon, called back the people that were ready to depart, to prayers. 'Brethren,' said he, 'lest any man should doubt of this man's earnest conversion and repentance, you shall hear him speak before you; and therefore I pray you, master Cranmer, that you will now perform that you promised not long ago, namely, that you would openly express the true and undoubted profession of your faith, that you may take away all suspicion from men, and that all men may understand that you are a catholic indeed.'

'I will do it,' said the archbishop, 'and that with a good will,' who by and by rising up and putting off his cap, began to speak thus unto the people:

> I desire you, well-beloved brethren in the Lord, that you will pray to God for me, to forgive me my sins, which above all men, both in number and greatness, I have committed. But among all the rest, there is one offence which most of all at this time doth vex and trouble me, whereof in process of my talk you shall hear more in its proper place.

And then, putting his hand in his bosom, he drew forth his prayer, which he recited to the people . . . And then he rising, said:

> Every man, good people, desireth at the time of his death to give some good exhortation that others may remember the same before their death, and be the better thereby: so I beseech God grant me grace, that I may speak something at this my departing, whereby God may be glorified, and you edified. . . .
>
> And now forasmuch as I am come to the last end of my life, whereupon hangeth all my life past, and all my life to come, either to live with my master Christ for ever in joy, or else to be in pain for ever with wicked devils in hell, and I see before mine eyes presently, either heaven ready to receive me, or else hell ready to swallow me up; I shall therefore declare unto you my very faith how I believe, without any colour or dissimulation: for now is no time to dissemble, whatsoever I have said or written in time past.
>
> First, I believe in God the Father Almighty, Maker of heaven and earth, etc. And I believe every article of the Catholic faith, every word and sentence taught by our Saviour Jesus Christ, his apostles and prophets, in the New and Old Testament.
>
> And now I come to the great thing which so much troubleth my conscience, more than any thing that ever I did or said in my whole life, and that is the

setting abroad of a writing contrary to the truth, which now here I renounce and refuse, as things written with my hand contrary to the truth which I thought in my heart, and written for fear of death and to save my life, if it might be; and that is, all such bills or papers which I have written or signed with my hand since my degradation, wherein I have written many things untrue. And forasmuch as my hand offended, writing contrary to my heart, my hand shall first be punished for it; for may I come to the fire it shall be first burned.

And as for the pope, I refuse him as Christ's enemy, and Antichrist, with all his false doctrine.

Here the standers-by were all astonished, marvelled, were amazed, did look one upon another, whose expectation he had so notably deceived. Some began to admonish him of his recantation, and to accuse him of falsehood. Briefly, it was a world to see the doctors beguiled of so great a hope. I think there was never cruelty more notably or better in time deluded and deceived; for it is not to be doubted but they looked for a glorious victory and a perpetual triumph by this man's retractation; who, as soon as they heard these things, began to let down their ears, to rage, fret, and fume; and so much the more, because they could not revenge their grief – for they could now no longer threaten or hurt him. For the most miserable man in the world can die but once; and whereas of necessity he must needs die that day, though the papists had been never so well pleased, now, being never so much offended with him, yet could he not be twice killed of them. . . .

And when he began to speak more of the sacrament and of the papacy, some of them began to cry out, yelp and bawl, and specially Cole cried out upon him, 'Stop the heretic's mouth and take him away.'

And then Cranmer being pulled down from the stage, was led to the fire. . . .

But when he came to the place where the holy bishops and martyrs of God, Hugh Latimer and Nicholas Ridley, were burnt before him for the confession of the truth, kneeling down, he prayed to God; and not long tarrying in his prayers, putting off his garments to his shirt, he prepared himself to death. . . .

Then was an iron chain tied about Cranmer, whom when they perceived to be more steadfast than that he could be moved from his sentence, they commanded the fire to be set unto him.

And when the wood was kindled, and the fire began to burn near him, stretching out his arm, he put his right hand into the flame, which he held so steadfast and immovable (saving that once with the same hand he wiped his face), that all men might see his hand burned before his body was touched. His body did so abide the burning of the flame with such constancy and steadfastness, that standing always in one place without moving his body, he seemed to move no more than the stake to which he was bound; his eyes were lifted up to heaven, and oftentimes he repeated 'this unworthy right hand,' so long as his voice would suffer him; and using often the words of Stephen, 'Lord Jesus, receive my spirit,' in the greatness of the flame, he gave up the ghost.

The Thirty-nine Articles (1571)

The *Thirty-nine Articles* of the Church of England form its principal confession of faith and are found in *The Book of Common Prayer* (see pages 237–41). They began their life in 1553, during the reign of Edward VI, when Cranmer and Ridley drew up *Forty-two Articles*. In 1563, after the restoration of Protestantism by Elizabeth I, Archbishop Matthew Parker revised them, producing the *Thirty-nine Articles*, the Latin text of which was approved by the Convocation (of the clergy) that year. The Queen made some minor changes, adding the first clause of Article 20 and removing Article 29. In 1571 a compromise was reached, the addition to Article 20 being accepted and Article 29 being restored. That year the revised Latin text with English translation was published with the Queen's authority. The present preface (by Charles I) dates from 1628. In 1801 the American Episcopal churches produced their own minor revision.

Despite attempts to prove the contrary, of which the boldest was by John Henry Newman's infamous *Tract 90* (1841), the *Articles* clearly teach a moderate form of Calvinism, with Lutheran influence apparent at some points. If they present a *via media* or middle path it is the same one that all the Reformers sought – a middle way between the errors of Roman Catholicism and Anabaptism. Until the nineteenth century all the clergy were required to give assent to the *Articles*, as were those wishing to take degrees at Oxford and Cambridge until 1871. Since 1865 a looser form of assent has been required of the clergy alone.

The language of the *Articles* is somewhat antiquated and demands some effort from the modern reader. This effort will be richly rewarded as they summarize the teaching of the Reformation clearly and succinctly. In the extracts below the original spelling and punctuation, but not capitalization, are preserved.

---

6. Of the Sufficiency of the Holy Scriptures for Salvation

Holy Scripture containeth all things necessary to salvation: so that whatsoever is not read therein, nor may be proved thereby, is not to be required of any man, that it should be believed as an article of the faith, or be thought requisite or necessary to salvation. In the name of the Holy Scripture we do understand those canonical books of the Old and New Testament, of whose authority was never any doubt in the church. . . . And the other [Old Testament Apocryphal] books (as Hierome saith) the church doth read for example of life and instruction of manners; but yet doth it not apply them to establish any doctrine. . . .

8. Of the Creeds

The three creeds, Nicene Creed, Athanasius's Creed, and that which is commonly called the Apostles' Creed, ought thoroughly to be received and believed: for they may be proved by most certain warrants of Holy Scripture.

9. Of Original or Birth Sin

Original sin standeth not in the following of Adam. . . but it is the fault and corruption of the nature of every man, that naturally is engendered of the offspring of Adam; whereby man is very far gone from original righteousness, and is of his own nature inclined to evil, so that the flesh lusteth always contrary to the spirit; and therefore in every person born into this world, it deserveth God's wrath and damnation. And this infection of nature doth remain, yea in them that are regenerated; whereby the lust of the flesh . . . is not subject to the law of God. And although there is no condemnation for them that believe and are baptized, yet the apostle doth confess, that concupiscence and lust hath of itself the nature of sin.

10. Of Free Will

The condition of man after the fall of Adam is such, that he cannot turn and prepare himself, by his own natural strength and good works, to faith, and calling upon God. Wherefore we have no power to do good works pleasant and acceptable to God, without the grace of God by Christ preventing us, that we may have a good will, and working with us, when we have that good will.

11. Of the Justification of Man

We are accounted righteous before God, only for the merit of our Lord and Saviour Jesus Christ by faith, and not for our own works or deservings: wherefore, that we are justified by faith only is a most wholesome doctrine, and very full of comfort. . . .

12. Of Good Works

Albeit that good works, which are the fruits of faith, and follow after justification, cannot put away our sins, and endure the severity of God's judgment; yet are they pleasing and acceptable to God in Christ, and do spring out necessarily of a true and lively faith; insomuch that by them a lively faith may be as evidently known as a tree discerned by the fruit.

14. Of Works of Supererogation

Voluntary works besides, over and above, God's commandments, which they call works of supererogation, cannot be taught without arrogancy and impiety: for by them men do declare, that they do not only render unto God as much as they are bound to, but that they do more for his sake, than of bounden duty is required: whereas Christ saith plainly, 'When ye have done all that are commanded to you, say, We are unprofitable servants' [Luke 17:10].

17. Of Predestination and Election

Predestination to life is the everlasting purpose of God, whereby (before the foundations of the world were laid) he hath constantly decreed by his counsel secret to us, to deliver from curse and damnation those whom he hath chosen in Christ out of mankind, and to bring them by Christ to everlasting salvation, as vessels made to honour. Wherefore, they which be endued with so excellent a benefit of God, be called according to God's purpose by his Spirit working in due season: they through grace obey the calling: they be justified freely: they be made sons of God by adoption: they be made like the image of his only-begotten Son Jesus Christ: they walk religiously in good works, and at length, by God's mercy, they attain to everlasting felicity. . . .

19. Of the Church

The visible church of Christ is a congregation of faithful men, in which the pure Word of God is preached, and the sacraments be duly ministered according to Christ's ordinance, in all those things that of necessity are requisite to the same.

As the church of Jerusalem, Alexandria, and Antioch, have erred; so also the church of Rome hath erred, not only in their living and manner of ceremonies, but also in matters of faith.

20. Of the Authority of the Church

The church hath power to decree rites or ceremonies, and authority in controversies of faith: and yet it is not lawful for the church to ordain anything that is contrary to God's Word written, neither may it so expound one place of Scripture, that it be repugnant to another. Wherefore, although the church be a witness and a keeper of Holy Writ, yet, as it ought not to decree any thing against the same, so besides the same ought it not to enforce any thing to be believed for necessity of salvation.

24. Of Speaking in the Congregation in Such a Tongue as the People Understandeth

It is a thing plainly repugnant to the Word of God, and the custom of the primitive church, to have publick prayer in the church, or to minister the sacraments, in a tongue not understood of the people.

25. Of the Sacraments

Sacraments ordained of Christ be not only badges or tokens of Christian men's profession, but rather they be certain sure witnesses, and effectual signs of grace, and God's good will towards us, by the which he doth work invisibly in us, and doth not only quicken, but also strengthen and confirm our faith in him.

There are two sacraments ordained of Christ our Lord in the gospel, that is to say, baptism, and the Supper of the Lord.

Those five commonly called sacraments, that is to say, confirmation, penance, orders, matrimony, and extreme unction, are not to be counted for sacraments of the gospel, being such as have grown partly of the corrupt following of the apostles, partly are states of life allowed in the Scriptures; but yet have not like nature of sacraments with baptism, and the Lord's Supper, for that they have not any visible sign or ceremony ordained of God.

The sacraments are not ordained of Christ to be gazed upon, or to be carried about, but that we should duly use them. And in such only as worthily receive the same they have a wholesome effect or operation: but they that receive them unworthily purchase to themselves damnation, as Saint Paul saith [1 Corinthians 11:29].

27. Of Baptism

Baptism is not only a sign of profession, and mark of difference, whereby Christian men are discerned from others that be not christened, but it is also a sign of regeneration or new birth, whereby, as by an instrument, they that receive baptism rightly are grafted into the church; the promises of the forgiveness of sin, and of our adoption to be the sons of God by the Holy Ghost, are visibly signed and sealed; faith is confirmed, and grace increased by virtue of prayer unto God. The baptism of young children is in any wise to be retained in the church, as most agreeable with the institution of Christ.

28. Of the Lord's Supper

The Supper of the Lord is not only a sign of the love that Christians ought to have among themselves one to another; but rather it is a sacrament of our redemption by Christ's death: insomuch that to such as rightly, worthily, and with faith, receive the same, the bread which we break is a partaking of the body of Christ; and likewise the cup of blessing is a partaking of the blood of Christ.

Transubstantiation (or the change of the substance of bread and wine) in the Supper of the Lord, cannot be proved by Holy Writ; but is repugnant to the plain words of Scripture, overthroweth the nature of a sacrament, and hath given occasion to many superstitions.

The body of Christ is given, taken, and eaten, in the Supper, only after an heavenly and spiritual manner. And the mean whereby the body of Christ is received and eaten in the Supper is faith.

The sacrament of the Lord's Supper was not by Christ's ordinance reserved, carried about, lifted up, or worshipped.

The Formula of Concord (1577)

After Luther's death, Lutheranism lacked a single authoritative leader. Melanchthon was in many ways the natural candidate to succeed Luther, but many deeply distrusted him and saw him as the betrayer of Luther. Lutheranism was divided into several parties which differed violently over key doctrines. At one stage the professors at Königsberg were taking guns into their lectures, so heated was the debate! At the 1557 Colloquy of Worms (with the Roman Catholics) the Lutherans were embarrassed by the public exposure of their divisions. The controversies continued and attempts were made to resolve the disputed points. In the 1570s a number of confessions were produced and in 1577 some of these were drawn together to form the *Formula of Concord,* which won the approval of many of the German Lutheran states. In 1580, fifty years to the day from the reading of *The Augsburg Confession* to the emperor (see pages 210–13), the *Book of Concord* was published. This contains: the three ancient creeds (the Apostles', Nicene and Athanasian Creeds [see pages 115–17]), the *Augsburg Confession* and Melanchthon's *Apology* [Defence] of it, Luther's *Smalcald Articles* (1537), Melanchthon's treatise on *The Power and Primacy of the Pope* (1537), Luther's *Small* and *Large Catechisms* (both 1529 – see pages 205–209) and *The Formula of Concord.*

    The Formula of Concord defined the Lutheran position on a wide range of issues, thus creating a precise Lutheran orthodoxy. But the *Book of Concord* did not meet with the approval of all Lutherans. The (Lutheran) king of Denmark was so disgusted that he threw his copy into the fire and it has never been adopted by the Danish church. A number of German Lutheran states also refused to accept it and some of these later joined the Reformed camp.

    The Formula of Concord is divided into two parts. First, 'An Epitome [Summary] of the Articles in Controversy among the Theologians of the *Augsburg Confession*, Expounded and Settled in a Christian Way, according to the Direction of God's Word, in the Following Recapitulation'. This comprises an introduction and twelve articles, covering the disputed points. Second, there is a 'Solid Declaration', some four times as long, which covers the same points in more detail. While for the first ten articles the *Formula* starts with issues of controversy between Lutherans, it also gives a more general exposition of the doctrine concerned and engages with the views of non-Lutherans, especially Roman Catholic and Reformed. The articles are as follows:

Introduction: Scripture as sole rule and norm for doctrine.

1) *Original Sin*: even as fallen we remain God's creatures, though corrupted by sin.

2) *Free Will*: prior to rebirth human free will is not able to assent to God's grace.

3) *The Righteousness of Faith*: Christ is our righteousness in his human and divine natures.

4) *Good Works*: salvation is not by works, but they necessarily follow conversion.

5) *Law and Gospel*: the distinction between the two is to be maintained.

6) *Third Function of the Law*: obedience to the law of God is part of the Christian life.

7) *Lord's Supper*: Christ's body and blood are given to all who receive the bread and wine.

8) *Person of Christ*: his humanity shares divine properties, so can be present in the Supper.

9) *Christ's Descent into Hell*: speculation on the question is to be avoided.

10) *'Adiaphora'*: the Church has freedom in 'indifferent matters' where Scripture is silent.

11) *God's Foreknowledge and Election*: knowing that God has chosen us is a great comfort.

12) *Non-Lutheran 'Factions and Sects'*: rejection of errors of Anabaptists and others.

The *Formula of Concord* is one of the most important of the Reformation confessions of faith and is still held by many Lutherans worldwide. It is a carefully drafted document that sets out to clarify a number of disputed points. The third and fourth articles, on the righteousness of faith and good works, express what had become the generally accepted Protestant doctrine of justification by faith, held by the Reformed as well as by Lutherans.

---

3. The Righteousness of Faith Before God

Affirmative Theses

2. We believe, teach and confess that our righteousness before God consists in the fact that God forgives us our sins out of pure grace, without any work, merit, or worthiness of ours (past, present or future); that he gives and reckons to us the righteousness of Christ's obedience; and that on account of this righteousness we are received into grace by God, and regarded as righteous.

3. We believe, teach and confess that faith alone is the means and instrument by which we lay hold of Christ and (in Christ) of that righteousness which avails before God. For Christ's sake this faith is reckoned to us as righteousness [Romans 4:5].

4. We believe, teach and confess that this faith is not a bare knowledge of the narratives about Christ, but a gift of God by which we come to the right knowledge of Christ as our Redeemer in the word of the gospel, and trust in him that for the sake of his obedience alone we have the forgiveness of sins by grace, are regarded as holy and righteous by God the Father, and are eternally saved.

5. We believe, teach and confess that, according to the usage of Holy Scripture, the word 'justify' in this article means 'absolve', that is 'declare free from sins'. 'He that justifies the wicked and he that condemns the innocent are both an abomination to the Lord' [Proverbs 17:15]. Also, 'Who shall bring any charge against God's elect? It is God that justifies' [Romans 8:33]. . . .

6. We also believe, teach and confess that although many weaknesses and defects cling to those who truly believe and are born again, even to the grave, they must not on that account doubt either their righteousness, which is reckoned to them by faith, or the salvation of their souls. They must regard it as certain that they have a gracious God for Christ's sake, according to the promise and Word of the holy Gospel.

7. We believe, teach and confess that for the preservation of the pure doctrine concerning the righteousness of faith before God it is necessary to urge with special diligence the 'exclusive terms' – i. e. the following words of the holy Apostle Paul, which entirely separate the merit of Christ from our works and give the honour to Christ alone. The holy Apostle Paul writes: 'by grace', 'without merit', 'without law', 'without works', 'not of works'. What all these words together amount to is that we are justified and saved alone by faith in Christ. [Ephesians 2:8; Romans 1:17, 3:24, 4:3ff.; Galatians 3:11; Hebrews 11]

8. We believe, teach and confess that, although the contrition that precedes and the good works that follow [justification] do not belong to the article of justification before God, yet one is not to imagine a faith of such a kind as can exist and abide with, and alongside of, a wicked intention to sin and to act against one's conscience. But after man has been justified by faith, then a true living faith works through love [Galatians 5:6]. Thus good works always follow justifying faith and are surely found with it, if it be true and living, since faith is never alone but always has with it love and hope.

4. Good Works

Affirmative Theses
The Pure Doctrine of the Christian Churches concerning this Controversy

For the thorough statement and decision of this controversy our doctrine, faith and confession is:

1. That good works certainly and without doubt follow true faith (if it is a living and not a dead faith) like fruits of a good tree.

2. We also believe, teach and confess that good works should be entirely excluded both from the question of salvation and from the article of justification before God. The apostle bears clear witness to this: 'David also describes the blessedness of the one to whom God reckons righteousness without works: "Blessed is the man to whom the Lord will not reckon sin"' [Romans 4:6–8]. Again: 'By grace you are saved through faith; and that not of yourselves, it is the gift of God; not by works, lest any one should boast' [Ephesians 2:8–9].

3. We also believe, teach and confess that all people, but those especially who are born again and renewed by the Holy Spirit, are obliged to do good works.

4. In this sense to use the words 'necessary', 'shall', and 'must' also with respect to the regenerate is correct, Christian and in no way contrary to the form of sound words and speech.

5. Nevertheless, when used of the regenerate the words 'necessity' and 'necessary' are to be understood not of coercion but only of the due obedience which true believers, so far as they are regenerate, render not from coercion or the compulsion of the law but from a voluntary spirit, because they are 'no longer under the law but under grace' [Romans 6:14].

6. Accordingly, we also believe, teach and confess that when it is said: 'The regenerate do good works from a free spirit', this is not to be understood as though the regenerate have the option to do or not to do good as they wish and that they can still retain their faith if they deliberately persist in sin.

7. This is not to be understood otherwise than as the Lord Christ and his apostles explain it – that the liberated spirit does works not from fear of punishment, like a slave, but from love of righteousness, like a child [Romans 8:15].

8. However, this spontaneity is not perfect in the elect children of God, but burdened with great weakness, as St Paul complains of himself in Romans [7:14–25] and Galatians [5:17].

9. Nevertheless, for the sake of the Lord Christ, the Lord does not reckon this weakness against his elect, as it is written: 'Therefore there is now no condemnation for those who are in Christ Jesus' [Romans 8:1].

10. We also believe, teach and confess that it is not works that preserve faith and salvation in us, but the Spirit of God alone, through faith. Good works are evidences of the Spirit's presence and indwelling.

Teresa of Avila, *The Interior Castle*
(1577)

Teresa de Cepeda y Ahumada was born in 1515 at Avila, into an old Spanish family. In 1528 her mother died. At about this time her childhood piety began to evaporate and she developed an interest in books of chivalry and began to think of marriage. But in 1531 her father entrusted her to an Augustinian convent for her education and while there she felt a call to the monastic life. Her father was reluctant, so in 1535 she ran away from home and joined the Carmelite monastery of the incarnation at Avila. But entering a religious order did not solve all her spiritual problems. She had difficulties with her spiritual life and with prayer until, in 1554, she had a deeper experience of conversion. First, she was deeply moved by the sight of a statue of Jesus Christ after he had been scourged. 'I felt so keenly aware of how poorly I thanked him for those wounds that, it seems to me, my heart broke. Beseeching him to strengthen me once and for all that I might not offend him, I threw myself down before him with the greatest outpouring of heart.' (*Life* 9:1) This led her to place all her trust in God. At that time she also read Augustine's *Confessions* (see pages 91–94), and was encouraged by the examples there of God's grace. 'By considering the love [God] bore me, I regained my courage, for I never lost confidence in his mercy – in myself I lost it many times' (*Life* 9:7).

After this deeper conversion, Teresa progressed rapidly in the life of prayer. But there were problems. At first her confessors believed that her unusual experiences came not from God but from the devil. One of her confessors asked her to write an account of her spiritual experiences, which she did in her *Life*. The first draft was completed in 1562. A few years later Teresa revised it and extended it to include the period to 1565.

At about the same time, Teresa wrote *The Way of Perfection*, on the life of prayer. The first draft was completed by 1566 and it was revised soon afterwards for the benefit of the censors. Teresa comments on the Lord's Prayer and also writes in defence of 'mental prayer'. At this time many Spanish theologians were saying that ordinary folk should confine themselves to merely vocal prayer (reciting prayers without using the mind). Against them, Teresa stresses the importance of praying with the mind – but without despising vocal prayer. She rejects the idea that 'you are speaking with God while you are reciting the Our Father and at the same time in fact thinking of the world' [*The Way of Perfection* 22:1].

Teresa's third great work is her *Interior Castle*. This was written in the space of a few months in 1577, being addressed to her fellow nuns. It is Teresa's greatest book on prayer, where her mature teaching is set out systematically. The castle is a picture of the human soul, which is entered through the gate of prayer. There are seven dwelling places in the castle and God himself dwells in the seventh or innermost place. The purpose of the life of prayer is to progress through these seven dwelling places to God himself. The first three dwelling places are reached through 'acquired' prayer, something that is possible for all Christians by their own efforts, aided by God's grace. The four remaining dwelling places are entered through 'passive' or supernatural prayer – a gift of God. It comes directly from him and not through our own efforts. If the earlier stages of prayer can be compared to the labour of channelling water through irrigation canals, passive prayer can be compared to a spring of water surging up from the ground where it is needed. This is a gift of God given as he will.

● The first dwelling place is for those who have some desire for good and who pray occasionally, but who are still wrapped up in the world. These need to know themselves better and to see the ugliness of sin.

● The second dwelling place is for those who are willing to struggle against sin and to persevere in the life of prayer.

● The third dwelling place is for those who seek to avoid all sin, including 'venial' or lesser sins. They love their neighbours and practise asceticism, but are still held back by the love of wealth, honour and health.

● The fourth dwelling place is the place for passive or supernatural prayer. This begins with a passive experience of recollection, the prayer of quiet in the peace of God's presence.

● The fifth dwelling place is the place for the prayer of union with God. This stage can be compared to the state of being in love that precedes betrothal.

● The sixth dwelling place is the place for spiritual betrothal with God. This stage calls for great courage and fortitude as it involves many trials and much suffering. It also brings the prayer of rapture.

● The seventh dwelling place is the place for spiritual marriage or perfect union with God. Teresa herself reached this stage in 1572. It involves the vision of God the Trinity. The purpose of this experience is not leisurely retirement but a life of service in good works.

Teresa's book is a classic exposition of the stages of mystical prayer. It is unfortunate that Spanish translations of the Bible were forbidden so there is little biblical content in Teresa's work. Indeed, because of the obsessive caution of the Inquisition, many other spiritual writings were denied to her. This grieved her, but 'the Lord said to me: "Don't be sad, for I shall give you a living book"' (*Life* 26:5). It is the living book of her experience that is the strength of Teresa's works.

Teresa was not merely a contemplative. She also fought to reform her order and achieved considerable success despite battling constantly against ill health. By this time the Carmelites had relaxed some of their early strictness. Teresa wished to found a house where the primitive rule of 1209 could be observed strictly. After facing much opposition, she was able to do this in 1562, founding St Joseph's at Avila. From 1567 she set about founding other such houses throughout Spain and the new order came to be known as the Discalced (or 'barefoot') Carmelites. She encountered much opposition from the official 'Calced' Carmelites and from the suspicious church authorities – the papal nuncio in Spain called her a 'restless gadabout'! But she won an important ally in the person of John of the Cross (1542–91), who became the joint-founder of the Discalced Carmelites. He was also one of the greatest mystical writers, being known especially for his *Ascent of Mount Carmel* and *The Dark Night of the Soul* (see pages 278–81). Teresa died in 1582 and in 1970 was granted the title Doctor of the [Roman Catholic] Church.

5:3:7. Here in our religious life the Lord asks of us only two things: love of his Majesty [God] and love of our neighbour. These are what we must work for. By observing them with perfection, we do his will and so will be united with him. But how far, as I have said, we are from doing these two things for so great a God as we ought! May it please his Majesty to give us his grace so that we might merit, if we want, to reach this state that lies within our power.

5:3:8. The most certain sign, in my opinion, as to whether or not we are observing these two laws is whether we observe well the love of neighbour. We cannot know whether or not we love God, although there are strong indications for recognizing that we do love him; but we can know whether we love our neighbour. And be certain that the more advanced you see you are in love for your neighbour the more advanced you will be in the love of God, for the love his Majesty has for us is so great that to repay us for our love of neighbour he will in a thousand ways increase the love we have for him. I cannot doubt this.

5:3:9. It's important for us to walk with careful attention to how we are proceeding in this matter, for if we practise love of neighbour with great perfection we will have done everything. I believe that, since our nature is bad, we will not reach perfection in the love of neighbour if that love doesn't rise from love of God as its root. . . .

5:3:10. I am amused sometimes to see certain souls who think when they are at prayer that they would like to be humiliated and publicly insulted for God, and afterward they would hide a tiny fault if they could; or, if they have not committed one and yet are charged with it – God deliver us!

6:7:3. I know a person [i.e. herself] who, apart from wanting to die in order to see God, wanted to die so as not to feel the continual pain of how ungrateful she had been to one to whom she ever owed so much and would owe. Thus it didn't seem to her that anyone's wickedness could equal her own, for she understood that there could be no one else from whom God would have had so much to put up with and to whom he had granted so many favours. As for the fear of hell, such persons don't have any. That they might lose God, at times – though seldom – distresses them very much. All their fear is that God might allow them out of his hand to offend him, and they find themselves in as miserable a state as they were once before. In regard to their own suffering or glory, they don't care.

7:1:6. In this seventh dwelling place the union comes about in a different way: our good God now desires to remove the scales from the soul's eyes and let it see and understand, although in a strange way, something of the favour he grants it. When the soul is brought into that dwelling place, the Most Blessed Trinity, all three Persons, through an intellectual vision, is revealed to it through a certain representation of the truth. First there comes an enkindling in the spirit in the manner of a cloud of magnificent splendour; and these three Persons are distinct, and through an admirable knowledge the soul understands as a most profound truth that all three Persons are one substance and one power and one knowledge and one God alone. It knows in such a way that what we hold by faith, it understands, we can say, through sight – although the sight is not with the bodily eyes nor with the eyes of the soul, because we are not dealing with an imaginative vision. Here all three Persons communicate themselves to it, speak to it, and explain those words of the Lord in the Gospel: that he and the Father and the Holy Spirit will come to dwell with the soul that loves him and keeps his commandments [John 14:23].

John of the Cross,
The Dark Night of the Soul (1582–85)

Juan de Yepez y Alvarez was born in 1542 at Fontiveros in north-west Spain. At the age of twenty-one he entered the Carmelite monastery at Medina del Campo, near Valladolid. From 1564 to 1568 he was sent to study at Salamanca, where he met Teresa of Avila. She persuaded him not to leave the Carmelites for the (stricter) Carthusians but to join with her in attempts to reform the order. They were the joint-founders of the 'Discalced' (or 'barefoot') Carmelites, who restored the primitive rule of 1209. In 1568 John helped found the first house of Discalced friars at Duruelo. In 1570 he left to serve as rector of the newly founded Carmelite house of studies at Alcalá de Henares (by Madrid). Two years later he moved again, to become confessor of Teresa's Convent of the Incarnation at Avila.

Like Teresa, John faced persecution from the unreformed ('Calced') Carmelites and in 1577 he was seized and imprisoned in a Carmelite monastery at Toledo. While there he began to write his *Spiritual Canticle*. After nine months of imprisonment he escaped to the monastery of Calvario in the south of Spain, where he became prior. After a year he became rector of the Carmelite college at Baëza, from 1579 to 1581. The 1580s were busy years for John as he held a number of important positions in the new order. In 1590, however, he opposed two controversial moves by the Vicar General and at the Chapter the following year failed to be elected to any office. He was sent to the remote friary at La Peñuela in Andalusia and moves were taken to have him expelled from the order. Soon after he was taken ill and moved to Ubeda in order to receive treatment. There he was treated very harshly and died at the end of 1591. He was canonized in 1726 and declared a 'Doctor of the [Roman Catholic] Church' in 1926.

Despite a relative short life, with so many moves and so many different positions of responsibility within the order, and despite facing repeated persecution from other Carmelites, John is one of the greatest mystics in the history of the church. He wrote three poems with commentaries: *The Ascent of Mount Carmel* and *The Dark Night of the Soul* (which are two parts of a single work), *The Spiritual Canticle* and *The Living Flame of Love*. The theme of these works is the ascent of the soul to union with God. As with Teresa in her *The Interior Castle* (see pages 274–77), John's works are based heavily on his own experience as a contemplative. The ascent is via the 'dark night of the soul', the phrase for which John is best known. It culminates in a spiritual marriage in which the intellect is transformed into perfect faith, the memory into perfect hope and the will into perfect love.

Some time between 1579 and 1581 John drew a simple sketch of Mount Carmel, incorporating a summary of the steps to union with God. At the same time he wrote a poem on the theme, in eight verses of five lines each. His commentary on the poem is found in two works written between 1579 and 1585: *The Ascent of Mount Carmel* and the briefer *The Dark Night of the Soul,* which was intended by John to be the second part of *The Ascent.* Following a tradition of scholastic theology, John divided the human soul into two parts. The sensory part has the five senses plus phantasy and imagination; the spiritual part has three faculties: intellect, memory and will. *The Ascent* describes the 'Active Night of the Senses', which is the mortification of our appetites, and the 'Active Night of the Spirit', which is the journey in faith. The intellect reaches union with God in faith, the memory in hope and the will in love. *The Dark Night* goes on to describe the 'Passive Night of the Senses' and the 'Passive Night of the Spirit'. In the first of these he perceptively shows how the spiritual fervour of beginners is in danger of being corrupted by each of the seven deadly sins: pride, avarice, lust, anger, gluttony, envy and sloth.

How does John know about these things? In his Prologue he acknowledges that he has made use of experience and 'science' (secular learning) but his primary source is Scripture, through which the Holy Spirit speaks. (He also expresses his intention to be true to the teaching of the church, a wise precaution given the activities of the Inquisition in Spain at that time!) But are such works only of relevance to those who enjoy the mystical union with God described by John? His avowed aim was to write for all who are on the road to God, whatever stage they have reached. His teaching about the dark night of the soul has been a great encouragement to many who have found themselves going through difficult times.

1:7:1. As for the other two vices, spiritual envy and sloth, these beginners [on the spiritual way] also have many imperfections. In regard to envy, many of them will feel sad about the spiritual good of others and experience sensible grief in noting that their neighbour is ahead of them on the road to perfection, and they will not want to hear others praised. To learn of the virtues of others makes them sad; they cannot bear to hear others praised without contradicting and undoing these compliments as much as possible. Their annoyance grows because they themselves do not receive these plaudits and because they long for preference in everything. All of this is contrary to charity, which, as St Paul says, rejoices in goodness [1 Corinthians 13:6]. If any envy accompanies charity, it is a holy envy, saddened at not having the virtues of others, rejoicing that others have them, happy that all others are ahead of it in the service of God, since it is so wanting in his service.

1:7:2. Also regarding spiritual sloth, these beginners usually become weary in the more spiritual exercises and flee from them, since these exercises are contrary to sensory satisfaction. Since they are so used to finding delight in spiritual practices, they become bored when they do not find it. If they do not receive in prayer the satisfaction they crave – for after all it is fit that God withdraw this so as to try them – they do not want to return to it or at times they either give up prayer or go to it begrudgingly. Because of their sloth, they subordinate the way of perfection (which requires the denial of one's will and satisfaction for God's sake) to the pleasure and delight of their own will. As a result they strive to satisfy their own will rather than God's.

1:7:3. Many of these beginners want God to desire what they want, and become sad if they have to desire God's will. They feel an aversion toward adapting their will to God's. Hence they frequently believe that what is not their will, or that which brings them no satisfaction, is not God's will, and, on the other hand, that if they are satisfied, God is too. They measure God by themselves and not themselves by God, which is in opposition to his teaching in the Gospel: that he who loses his life for his sake will gain it, and he who desires to gain it will lose it [Matthew 16:25].

1:7:4. Beginners also become bored when told to do something unpleasant. Because they look for spiritual gratifications and delights, they are extremely lax in the fortitude and labour perfection demands. Like those who are reared in luxury, they run sadly from everything rough, and they are scandalized by the cross, in which spiritual delights are found. And in the more spiritual exercises their boredom is greater. Since they expect to go about in spiritual matters according to the whims and satisfactions of their own will, to enter by the narrow way of life, about which Christ speaks [Matthew 7:14], is saddening and repugnant to them.

2:1:1. If God intends to lead the soul on, he does not put it in this dark night of spirit immediately after its going out from the aridities and trials of the first purgation and night of sense. Instead, after having emerged from the state of beginners, it usually spends many years exercising itself in the state of proficients. In this new state, as one liberated from a cramped prison cell, the soul goes about the things of God with much more freedom and satisfaction of spirit and with more abundant interior delight than it did in the beginning before entering the night of sense. Its imagination and faculties are no longer bound to discursive meditation and spiritual solicitude, as was their custom. The soul readily finds in its spirit, without the work of meditation, a very serene, loving contemplation and spiritual delight. Nonetheless, since the purgation of the soul is not complete (the purgation of the principal part, that of the spirit, is lacking, and without it the sensory purgation, however strong it may have been, is incomplete because of a communication existing between the two parts of the soul which form only one *suppositum*), certain needs, aridities, darknesses and conflicts are felt. These are sometimes far more intense than those of the past and are like omens or messengers of the coming night of the spirit.

But they are not lasting, as they will be in the night that is to come. For after enduring the short period or periods of time, or even days, in this night and tempest, the soul immediately returns to its customary serenity. Thus God purges some individuals who are not destined to ascend to so lofty a degree of love as are others. He brings them into this night of contemplation and spiritual purgation at intervals, frequently causing the night to come and then the dawn so that David's affirmation might be fulfilled: 'He sends his crystal (contemplation) like morsels' [Psalm 147:17]. These morsels of dark contemplation, though, are never as intense as is that frightful night of contemplation we are about to describe, in which God places the soul purposely in order to bring it to the divine union.

Richard Hooker, *A Learned Discourse of Justification* (1586)

When Mary died, in 1558, Elizabeth I came to the throne of England. The following year there was a settlement of religion which was essentially a compromise. Elizabeth herself wanted a more conservative reform, one in which a number of 'Catholic' elements would remain, such as the use of the wedding ring and the wearing of surplices by the clergy. But she had a problem. The leading Roman Catholic clergy from Mary's reign were not prepared to accept any more flirtations with Protestantism. On the other hand, most of the leading Protestants had been abroad during the reign of Mary. They had been to places like Zurich and Geneva and most of them had come to desire a more radical reform than that of the 1552 *The Book of Common Prayer* from the end of Edward's reign (see pages 237–41). In the end the 1559 Elizabethan settlement approximated very closely to that of 1552. For Elizabeth, this was the upper limit – no more reform would be allowed (nor was it). But for most of her new bishops, this was the bottom line, a tolerable level of reform. They accepted it for fear that refusal would open the door to Roman (or even Lutheran) 'wolves'.

But not all of the leading Protestants were prepared to accept the Elizabethan settlement. There were some, especially those who had spent Mary's reign in Geneva, who agitated for further reform and sometimes went so far as to refuse to conform. They had learned at Geneva that it was not necessary for the church to be subservient to the state. They came to be known as Puritans. These were members of the Church of England who desired to see it more thoroughly reformed – there was no question of leaving it or allowing more than one church in the land. In response to Puritanism a new attitude began to appear within the Church of England towards the end of Elizabeth's reign. Some of its new leaders regarded the Elizabethan settlement not merely as an acceptable form of Protestantism but as an especially desirable form. Among these was Richard Hooker, who became the chief apologist for the Elizabethan settlement against Puritanism.

Richard Hooker was born in 1553 or 1554 near Exeter. In 1569 he went to Corpus Christi College, Oxford, where in due course he became a fellow. In 1585 he was appointed master of the Temple, in London, through the patronage of the archbishop of York, whose son he was tutoring. The Puritan Walter Travers was already reader at the Temple, but had been passed over for promotion to master because of his Puritan convictions. Travers continued preaching in the afternoons and Hooker preached in the mornings – with the result that 'the forenoon sermon spake Canterbury and the afternoon Geneva'. Hooker stepped down in 1591 becoming subdean of Salisbury Cathedral and taking a living at Boscomb in Wiltshire – although he probably never ministered there.

Ending absenteeism among the clergy was one of the Puritan reforms which Hooker opposed. In 1595 he became rector of St Mary's Church, Bishopsbourne, where he died in 1600.

Hooker's best-known work is his *The Laws of Ecclesiastical Polity*, a defence of the practices of the Church of England against Puritan objections. This comprises eight books, of which only the first five were published in his lifetime. It was not until 1661 or 1662 that all eight books were published. Hooker had no qualms about the role of the sovereign in the church. This was questioned by both the Roman Catholics (in the name of papal authority) and the Puritans (in the interests of scriptural authority and links with the international Reformed movement).

Hooker opposed Puritanism, but that does not mean that his doctrine was anything but Protestant. In 1586 he preached two sermons on Habakkuk 1:4, of which the first is relatively brief and unimportant. The second is much longer (45 pages) and is on the doctrine of justification. It was first published in 1612 with the title *A Learned Discourse of Justification, Works and How the Foundation of Faith is Overthrown*. The bulk of it is devoted to answering an important question: if the Gospel is about justification by faith alone, can those be saved who now or in earlier ages belong to the Roman Catholic Church which denies this doctrine? In an earlier sermon Hooker had stated: 'I doubt not but God was merciful to save thousands of our fathers living in popish superstitions, inasmuch as they sinned ignorantly.' He was criticized for this view and preached the present sermon in order to defend it.

Hooker's answer has a thoroughness that makes it of relevance far wider than the original question. He begins by setting out very clearly where the precise difference lies between the Protestant and Roman understandings of justification – what is held in common and where the differences lie. That the Roman view was seriously mistaken and 'doth bereave men of comfort, both in their lives, and at their deaths' (9) he had no doubt; that this meant that Roman Catholics could not have a true faith in Christ and be justified by this faith he denied. Hooker makes the important point that for many people what they believe in their heart and live out in their life may be sounder than the doctrine that they hold in their head. The reverse can, of course, equally be true.

---

29. Let us beware lest, if we make too many ways of denying Christ, we scarce leave any way for ourselves truly and soundly to confess him. Salvation only by Christ is the true foundation whereupon indeed Christianity stands. But what if I say, 'Ye cannot be saved only by Christ without this addition: Christ believed in heart, confessed with mouth, obeyed in life and conversation'? Because I add, do I therefore deny that which directly I did affirm? There may be an addition of explication which overthrows not but proves and concludes the proposition whereunto it is annexed. . . .

30. Now whereas the church of Rome adds works, we must note, further, that the adding of works is not like the adding of circumcision unto Christ. Christ came not to abrogate and take away good works; he did, to change circumcision, for we see that in place thereof he has substituted holy baptism. To say, 'Ye cannot be saved by Christ except ye be circumcised,' is to add a thing excluded, a thing not only not necessary to be kept, but necessary not to be kept by them that will be saved. On the other side, to say, 'Ye cannot be saved by Christ without works,' is to add things not only not excluded, but commanded as being in place and in their kind necessary, and therefore subordinated unto Christ even by Christ himself, by whom the web of salvation is spun: 'Except your righteousness exceed the righteousness of the scribes and Pharisees, ye shall not enter into the kingdom of heaven' [Matthew 5:20]. . . .

31. But we say our salvation is by Christ alone. Therefore howsoever or whatsoever we add unto Christ in the matter of salvation we overthrow Christ. Our case were very hard if this argument, so universally meant as it is proposed, were sound and good. We ourselves do not teach Christ alone excluding our own faith unto justification, Christ alone excluding our own works unto sanctification, Christ alone excluding the one or the other as unnecessary unto salvation. It is a childish cavil wherewith in the matter of justification our [Roman Catholic] adversaries do so greatly please themselves, exclaiming that we tread all Christian virtues under our feet and require nothing in Christians but faith, because we teach that faith alone justifies – whereas by this speech we never meant to exclude either hope and charity from being always joined as inseparable mates with faith in the man that is justified, or works from being added as necessary duties, required at the hands of every justified man, but to show that faith is the only hand which puts on Christ unto justification, and Christ the only garment which being so put on covers the shame of our defiled natures, hides the imperfections of our works, preserves us blameless in the sight of God, before whom otherwise the very weakness of our faith were cause sufficient to make us culpable, yea to shut us out from the kingdom of heaven, where nothing that is not absolute can enter.

How then is our salvation wrought by Christ alone? Is it our meaning that nothing is requisite to man's salvation but Christ to save, and he to be saved quietly without any more to do? No, we acknowledge no such foundation. As we have received, so we teach that besides the bare and naked work wherein Christ, without any other associate, finished all the parts of our redemption and purchased salvation himself alone, for conveyance of this eminent blessing unto us many things are required, as to be known and chosen of God before the foundation of the world, in the world to be called, justified, sanctified, after we have left the world to be received into glory: Christ in every one of these hath something which he works alone. Through him, according to the eternal purpose of God before the foundation of the world, born, crucified, buried, raised, etc., we were in a gracious acceptation known unto God long before we were seen of men. God knew us, loved us, was kind towards us in Christ Jesus; in him we were elected to be heirs of life.

Thus far God through Christ has wrought in such sort alone that ourselves are mere patients, working no more than dead and senseless matter, wood or stone or iron, does in the artificer's hand, no more than the clay when the potter appoints it to be framed for an honourable use. Nay, not so much. For the matter whereupon the craftsman works he chooses, being moved by the fitness which is in it to serve his turn; in us no such thing. Touching the rest, that which is laid for the foundation of our faith imports, further, that by him we be called, that we have redemption, remission of sins through his blood, health by his stripes, justice by him; that he does sanctify his church and make it glorious to himself; that entrance into joy shall be given us by him; yea, all things by him alone. Howbeit, not so by him alone as if in us, to our vocation, the hearing of the Gospel; in our justification, faith; to our sanctification, the fruits of the Spirit; to our entrance into rest, perseverance in hope, in faith, in holiness, were not necessary.

32. Then what is the fault of the church of Rome? Not that she requires works at their hands that will be saved, but that she attributes unto works a power of satisfying God for sin and a virtue to merit both grace here and in heaven glory. That this overthrows the foundation of faith I grant willingly; that it is a direct denial thereof I utterly deny.

William Perkins,
The Cases of Conscience (1606)

William Perkins was born in Warwickshire in 1558. In 1577 he went to Christ's College, Cambridge, where he became a fellow in 1584 until his marriage in 1594. Some time early in the 1580s he was converted from a loose life to serious godliness. He represents the moderate wing of Elizabethan Puritanism, the movement that sought further reform of the Church of England. In 1587 he was summoned before the vice-chancellor of the university to answer charges relating to one of his sermons. His answers revealed that he was uneasy about certain aspects of the prayer book (such as kneeling to receive communion), but that his belief in submission to lawful authority was strong enough to overcome these qualms. The 1580s saw an attempt by some Puritans to set up a shadow Presbyterian organization (with ministers and 'lay elders' gathered together into presbyteries) alongside the existing system of government by bishops. Perkins may well have sympathized with Presbyterianism, but he took care not to reveal any opinions on the matter – except that he strongly opposed any separation from the established church.

At this time the government was clamping down on Puritan nonconformity. Perkins felt that there were matters of greater importance than disputes over liturgy or church government. He shared the Puritan concern for deeper reform – but sought this through a deepening of personal spirituality and pastoral care, rather than through further legislation. Perkins's policy became widespread among the Puritans as they faced their inability to change the Elizabethan settlement. By devoting themselves to pastoral care and spirituality they made a deep mark on the nation – with lasting spiritual and political consequences for England, the New World and elsewhere.

From 1584 Perkins became lecturer (preacher) at Great St Andrew's Church in Cambridge, where he remained until his death in 1602. From this position he exercised a considerable influence over generations of undergraduates and thus set his mark on the Puritan movement of the seventeenth century, both in England and among the New England settlers. His extensive writings were no less influential and were reprinted many times in the first half of the seventeenth century. Where Richard Hooker defended the Church of England against Presbyterianism, Perkins defended it against Rome – as in his *Reformed Catholic*. 'By a Reformed Catholic I understand anyone that holds the same necessary heads of religion with the Roman Church, yet so as he pares off and rejects all errors in doctrine whereby the said religion is corrupted.' Perkins wrote theological works, especially on the doctrine of predestination. In 1595 or 1596 there was a controversy over predestination at Cambridge, where the doctrine was being questioned. Archbishop

Whitgift, a staunch anti-Puritan, approved nine *Lambeth Articles* which set out a strongly Calvinist doctrine of predestination. Perkins also wrote in defence of the doctrine.

Perkins is best known as a practical writer. Following the lead of Bucer, he stressed the importance of Christian experience. The concept of conversion became more prominent than it had been with the Reformers. With Perkins there begins an interest in the 'order of salvation' – the normal order of events in conversion and sanctification. Perkins's stress on conversion was to be influential on both Pietism (as with Spener) and Evangelicalism (as with the Wesleys).

The stress on personal experience led to the question of assurance – how can I know if I have a true saving experience of Jesus Christ? For most of the early Reformers, such as Luther, Melanchthon and Calvin, saving faith is a confidence that God has forgiven my sins in Christ and thus includes within itself assurance of salvation. But there was an alternative tradition, which came to fruition in seventeenth-century British Calvinism and found expression in *The Westminster Confession of Faith* (see pages 301–305). This viewed assurance as something clearly distinct from saving faith, meaning that believers had to seek assurance of salvation after their conversion. Where can this assurance be found? Many of the Puritans urged people to seek it by looking within themselves for the evidences of conversion. But as the hymn-writer put it, 'they who fain would serve thee best, are conscious most of wrong within', and the inevitable outcome was that many struggled long and hard to find assurance. The Puritans all agreed that assurance was possible for all believers, but the process of acquiring it became arduous. It thus becomes possible (and may even become normal) for those with saving faith to lack assurance. This has led in some Calvinist churches to a situation where assurance of salvation is rare and is even frowned upon – a reversal of the position of Luther and Calvin.

Perkins also introduced the art of casuistry (applying general ethical principles to specific cases of conscience) to Protestantism. In his time it was Roman Catholics (and especially Jesuits) who had devoted the most attention to this. A disciple of Perkins commented that in this matter Protestants were in a similar position to the Israelites who had to go down to the Philistines to have their tools sharpened [1 Samuel 13:19–20]! They drew on the medieval Dominican tradition of Thomas Aquinas and others, but developed it in a distinctively Protestant and Bible-based direction.

Perkins's greatest casuistical work was his *Cases of Conscience*. The first part of this was published in 1604 and the complete work appeared two years later as *The Whole Treatise of the Cases of Conscience*. It is divided into three books:

1. 'Man Simply Considered in Himself Without Relation to an Other.' This covers the nature of sin (and different grades of sin), conscience, how to be saved and how to reach assurance of salvation.

2. 'Man Standing in Relation to God.' This covers oaths and vows, baptism and the Lord's Supper, fasting and the Sabbath.

3. 'Man as he Stands in Relation to Man.' This is structured round the virtues of prudence (or wisdom), clemency (or moderation of anger), temperance (or moderation of appetite), liberality (especially almsgiving), justice (giving equity) and fortitude (maintaining equity).

Perkins discusses many vexed ethical dilemmas and brings to them a clear mind. For example, he sheds light on the relation between forgiveness and punishment. Victims of a crime should forgive the perpetrators. Does this mean that they should not seek for the crime to be punished? Can parents punish a child while forgiving him?

Book 1, chapter 5. What must a man do, that he may come into God's favour and be saved?

Section 1. In the working and effecting of man's salvation, ordinarily there are two special actions of God: the *giving of the first grace*, and after that the *giving of the second*. The former of these two works has ten several actions. (1) God gives man the outward means of salvation, specially the ministry of the Word, and with it he sends some outward or inward cross to break and subdue the stubbornness of our nature that it may be made pliable to the will of God. . . . (2) This done, God brings the mind of man to a consideration of the Law and therein generally to see what is good and what is evil, what is sin and what is not sin. (3) Upon a serious consideration of the Law, he makes a man particularly to see and know his own peculiar and proper sins, whereby he offends God. (4) Upon the sight of sin he smites the heart with a legal fear, whereby when man sees his sins he makes him to fear punishment and hell and to despair of salvation in regard of anything in himself.

Now these four actions are indeed no fruits of grace, for a reprobate may go thus far, but they are only *works of preparation* going before grace; the other actions which follow are effects of grace. (5) The fifth action of grace therefore is to stir up the mind to a serious consideration of the promise of salvation propounded and published in the gospel. (6) After this the sixth is to kindle in the heart some seeds or sparks of faith, that is a will and desire to believe, and grace to strive against doubting and despair. Now at the same instant, when God begins to kindle in the heart any sparks of faith, then also he justifies the sinner and withal begins the work of sanctification. (7) Then so soon as faith is put into the heart, there is presently a combat; for it fights with doubting, despair and distrust. And in this combat faith shows itself by fervent constant and earnest invocation for pardon; and after invocation follows a strength and prevailing of this desire. (8) Furthermore, God in mercy quiets and settles the conscience, as touching the salvation of the soul and the promise of life, whereupon it rests and stays itself.

(9) Next after this settled assurance and persuasion of mercy follows a stirring up of the heart to evangelical sorrow, according to God, that is a grief for sin because it is sin and because God is offended; and then the Lord works repentance, whereby the sanctified heart turns itself unto him. And though this repentance be one of the last in order, yet it shows itself first; as when a candle is brought into a room we first see the light before we see the candle, and yet the candle must needs be before the light can be. (10) Lastly, God gives a man grace to endeavour to obey his commandments by a new obedience. And by these degrees does the Lord give the first grace.

The second work of God tending to salvation is the giving of the second grace, which is nothing else but the continuance of the first grace given. For look as by creation God gave a being to man and all other creatures and then by his providence continued the same being, which was as it were a second creation; so in bringing a man to salvation God gives the first grace, for example, to believe and repent and then in mercy gives the second, to persevere and continue in faith and repentance to the end.

Book 3, chapter 3, question 1. How may a man carry himself, in respect of injuries and offences done to him?

. . . It is demanded, how a man should and ought to forgive an injury.

Answer. In forgiveness there be four things.

The first is forgiveness of *revenge*, that is of requiring evil for evil, either by thought, word or deed. This [forgiveness] must always be practised. For vengeance is not ours, but the Lord's, and great reason then that we should evermore forgive in regard of revenge and hatred. This the Apostle teaches when he says, 'Love is not provoked, it never thinks' (much less speaks or does) 'evil' [1 Corinthians 13:5].

The second is forgiveness of *private punishment*, which is when men return punishment for injuries done, in way of requital; and this must always take place with us, because as vengeance itself, so also punishment in way of revenge, is God's alone.

The third is forgiveness of *judgment*, when we judge an injury done to be an injury. This judgment we are not bound to forgive unto men. For we may with good conscience judge a sin and a wrong to be as they are. And yet notwithstanding, if a man make satisfaction for the wrong done, then there ought to be forgiveness even in regard of judgment.

The fourth is forgiveness of *satisfaction*. This we are not always bound to remit, but we may with good conscience always require satisfaction where hurt is done.

Francis de Sales,
Introduction to a Devout Life (1608)

Francis de Sales was born in 1567 into a noble family in Savoy, in the region round Lake Geneva, the eldest of thirteen children. He was academically gifted and was sent in 1582 to study in the University of Paris at the Jesuit college of Clermont, where he remained for six years. While at Paris, in 1586–87, Francis had an experience of conversion. He was concerned about the doctrine of predestination, at that time a subject of controversy within the Roman Catholic Church. Had God chosen him or might he be eternally lost? His response to this crisis was to surrender unconditionally to the mercy of God, leaving to God the question of his ultimate destiny. By thus renouncing anxious concern for his future destiny he found himself able to love God freely. As he himself put it:

> *Will I be deprived of the grace of the One who has so kindly let me experience his delights, and who has shown himself so loving to me? . . . However that may be, Lord, at the very least let me love you in this life if I am not able to love you in eternal life – for no one praises you in hell.*

The idea of 'disinterested love', that Christians should love God regardless of their own salvation, was popular in seventeenth-century France, but had its opponents. It was eventually condemned by Pope Innocent XII in 1699. In due course Francis, under the influence of the Jesuits, turned against the doctrine of predestination that he had learned from Augustine and Thomas Aquinas.

After Paris, his father sent him to the University of Padua to study law, with a view to a secular career. Francis managed to study some theology as well and in 1591 completed a doctorate in both civil and canon (church) law. On returning home Francis succeeded in persuading his father that a secular career was not for him and he was ordained in 1593, becoming an assistant to the bishop of Geneva. The following year he began his ministry among Catholics on the south shores of Lake Geneva. In 1602 he was appointed bishop of Geneva, in which post he remained until his death in 1622.

Francis wrote many letters, of which about a thousand remain, and a number of controversial writings against Protestantism. But only two works were published in his lifetime and it is because of these especially that he is highly regarded as a spiritual teacher. The first is his *Introduction to a Devout Life*, first published in 1608 and revised by Francis the following year. The second is his *Treatise on the Love of God*, published in 1616. This portrays God's union with humanity in Christ as not just the cure for sin but as the very purpose of creation.

The *Introduction to a Devout Life* was based on a number of Francis's earlier letters of spiritual direction. Like Ignatius's *Spiritual Exercises* (see pages 226–28) it is designed for those living in the world, not just for for those in a religious community. Francis's aim was to encourage a life of holiness amongst lay Catholics. There are five parts:

1. Reaching a firm resolution to lead a devout life;

2. Lifting up the soul to God in prayer and the sacraments;

3. Attaining the practice of virtue;

4. Resisting temptation;

5. Renewing and confirming the soul in devotion.

The *Introduction to a Devout Life* has always been recognized as a spiritual classic that offers much practical advice to those seeking to progress in the spiritual life.

5:3. Examination of the Soul as to its Progress in the Devout Life

. . . It is desirable to go through this [examination] in three days and two nights at the most, taking that season which you can best manage; for if you go through it at too distant intervals you will lose the depth of impression which ought to be made by this spiritual exercise. After each point of examination observe wherein you have failed and what is lacking to you and in what you have chiefly failed, so that you may be able to explain your troubles, get counsel and comfort and make fresh resolutions. . . . Everything must be done with a heart full of God's love, and an earnest desire for spiritual perfection. To begin this examination:

1. Place yourself in the presence of God.

2. Invoke the Holy Spirit and ask light of him so that you may know yourself, as Saint Augustine did, crying out 'Lord, teach me to know you and to know myself'; and Saint Francis, who asked 'Who are you, Lord, and who am I?' Resolve not to note any progress with any self-satisfaction or self-glorification, but give the glory to God alone, and thank him duly for it.

3. Resolve, too, that if you should seem to yourself to have made but little progress or even to have gone back, that you will not be discouraged, nor grow cool or indolent in the matter; but that, on the contrary, you will take fresh pains to humble yourself and conquer your faults, with God's help.

4. Then go on to examine quietly and patiently how you have conducted yourself towards God, your neighbour and yourself, up to the present time.

5:4. Examination of the Soul's Condition as Regards God

1. What is the aspect of your heart with respect to mortal sin? Are you firmly resolved never to commit it, come what may? And have you kept that resolution from the time you first made it? Therein lies the foundation of the spiritual life.

2. What is your position with respect to the commandments of God? Are they acceptable, light and easy to you? He who has a good digestion and healthy appetite likes good food and turns away from that which is bad.

3. How do you stand as regards venial sins? No one can help committing some such occasionally; but are there none to which you have any special tendency or, worse still, any actual liking and clinging?

4. With respect to spiritual exercises, do you like and value them? Or do they weary and vex you? To which do you feel most or least disposed – hearing or reading God's Word, meditating upon it, calling upon God, confession, preparing for communion and communicating, controlling your inclinations, etc.? What of all these is most repugnant to you? And if you find that your heart is not disposed to any of these things, examine into the cause, find out whence the disinclination comes.

5. With respect to God himself, does your heart delight in thinking of God, does it crave after the sweetness thereof? 'I remembered your everlasting judgments, O Lord, and received comfort,' says David [Psalm 119:52]. Do you feel a certain readiness to love him, and a definite inclination to enjoy his Love? Do you take pleasure in dwelling upon the immensity, the goodness, the tenderness of God? When you are immersed in the occupations and vanities of this world, does the thought of God come across you as a welcome thing? Do you accept it gladly, and yield yourself up to it, and your heart turn with a sort of yearning to him? There are souls that do so.

6. If a wife has been long separated from her husband, so soon as she sees him returning and hears his voice, however cumbered she may be with business or forcibly hindered by the pressure of circumstances, her heart knows no restraint but turns at once from all else to think upon him she loves. So it is with souls which really love God, however engrossed they may be. When the thought of him is brought before them they forget all else for joy at feeling his dear presence nigh, and this is a very good sign.

7. With respect to Jesus Christ as God and man, how does your heart draw to him? Honey bees seek their delight in their honey but wasps hover over stinking carrion. Even so pious souls draw all their joy from Jesus Christ and love him with an exceeding sweet love, but those who are careless find their pleasure in worldly vanities.

9. As to your tongue, how do you speak of God? Do you take pleasure in speaking his praise and singing his glory in psalms and hymns?

10. As to actions, have you God's visible glory at heart and do you delight in doing

whatever you can to honour him? Those who love God will love to adorn and beautify his house. Are you conscious of having ever given up anything you liked or of renouncing anything for God's sake? For it is a good sign when we deprive ourselves of something we care for on behalf of those we love. What have you ever given up for the love of God?

5:5. Examination of Your Condition as Regards Yourself
1. How do you love yourself? Is it a love which concerns this life chiefly? If so, you will desire to abide here for ever and you will diligently seek your worldly establishment. But if the love you bear yourself has a heavenward tendency you will long, or at all events you will be ready, to go hence whensoever it may please our Lord.
2. Is your love of yourself well regulated? For nothing is more ruinous than an inordinate love of self. A well-regulated love implies greater care for the soul than for the body, more eagerness in seeking after holiness than aught else, a greater value for heavenly glory than for any mean earthly honour. A well regulated heart much oftener asks itself, 'What will the angels say if I follow this or that line of conduct?' than 'What will men say?'
3. What manner of love do you bear to your own heart? Are you willing to minister to it in its maladies? For indeed you are bound to succour it and seek help for it when harassed by passion and to leave all else till that is done.
4. What do you imagine yourself worth in God's sight? Nothing, doubtless, nor is there any great humility in the fly which confesses it is nought, as compared with a mountain, or a drop of water, which knows itself to be nothing compared with the sea, or a cornflower or a spark as compared with the sun. But humility consists in not esteeming ourselves above other men and in not seeking to be esteemed above them. How is it with you in this respect?
5. In speech, do you never boast in any way? Do you never indulge in self-flattery when speaking of yourself?
6. In deed, do you indulge in anything prejudicial to your health – I mean useless idle pleasures, unprofitable night-watches, and the like?

5:6. Examination of the Soul's Condition as Regards Our Neighbour
Husband and wife are bound to love one another with a tender, abiding, restful love, and this tie stands foremost by God's order and will. And I say the same with respect to children and all near relations, as also friends in their respective degrees. But, generally speaking, how is it with you as concerning your neighbour? Do you love him cordially and for God's sake? In order to answer this fairly you must call to mind sundry disagreeable, annoying people – for it is in such cases that we really practise the love of God with respect to our neighbours, and still more towards them that do us wrong either by word or deed. Examine

whether your heart is thoroughly clear as regards all such and whether it costs you a great effort to love them. Are you quick to speak ill of your neighbours, especially of such as do not love you? Do you act unkindly in any way, directly or indirectly, towards them? A very little honest self-dealing will enable you to find this out.

Richard Sibbes, *The Bruised Reed and the Smoking Flax* (1630)

Richard Sibbes was born in rural Suffolk in 1577, the son of a wheelwright. Despite his humble origins his talents were noticed and it was arranged for him to study at St John's College, Cambridge, where he became a fellow in 1601. Shortly after this date he was converted through the preaching of William Perkins's successor at Great St Andrew's Church. In 1609 he was elected college preacher at St John's College and in 1610 he was appointed the lecturer at Holy Trinity Church in Cambridge. He was deprived of both of these posts in 1615, probably as part of the beginning crackdown on Puritan preachers. The following year, however, he was appointed preacher at Gray's Inn in London, the largest of the Inns of Court, a post that he held until his death in 1635. Further honours followed and in 1626 he became master of Catharine Hall at Cambridge (now St Catharine's College) and in 1633 he also became vicar of Holy Trinity Church, Cambridge. Izaac Walton (famous as the author of *The Compleat Angler*) wrote of Sibbes: 'Of this blest man, let this just praise be given, Heaven was in him, before he was in Heaven.'

While by no means lacking in theological skills, Sibbes did not devote much time to doctrinal or controversial writings. The focus of his preaching and writing was practical and applied pastoral theology. Best known of these writings is his *The Bruised Reed and the Smoking Flax*, which was published in 1630. This was an influential work through the reading of which the young Richard Baxter was converted. It takes its title from Matthew 12:20, where a prophecy of Isaiah is applied to Jesus: 'A bruised reed he will not break, and a smouldering wick he will not snuff out.' The context is the Puritan quest for assurance by looking within to see the evidences of sanctification. As preaching becomes more searching and as the individual comes to a greater realization of the extent of remaining sin, so assurance becomes more and more elusive.

Sibbes's aim in this context is twofold. On the one hand, he does not want to give assurance to those who are devoid of grace, to those who have no genuine faith or repentance. But on the other hand he is equally concerned not to deprive the feeble believer of assurance. In the newly converted 'there is but a little measure of grace, and that little mixed with much corruption which, as smoke, is offensive' (chapter 5). Christ will not snuff out this smoking wick and pastors should take care not to be stricter than he is. Also, Sibbes shrewdly observes that in such a climate some individual believers will be stricter with themselves than are the pastors, overlooking the evidences of God's working in their lives and dwelling only upon their defects. 'Gracious men oft complain that they have no grace, but they contradict themselves in their complaints. . . when the very complaint, springing from a displeasure against sin, shows that there is something in [them] opposite to sin' (chapter 11). Indeed, he continues, it is those who are the most spiritually alive who are the most aware of the corruption within. But this comfort is not meant to encourage any who might suppose that they can have Christ as Saviour without having him as their Lord, who 'divide Lord from Jesus, and so make a Christ of their own'. Christ 'so pardons as he will be obeyed as a king; he so takes us to be his spouse as he will be obeyed as a husband. The same Spirit that convinces us of the necessity of his righteousness to cover us, convinces us also of the necessity of his government to rule us' (chapter 19).

Chapter 10: Rules to try whether we be such as Christ will not quench

1. We must have two eyes, one to see imperfections in ourselves and others; the other to see what is good. . . . Those ever want comfort that are much in quarrelling with themselves, and through their infirmities are prone to feed upon such bitter things as will most nourish that distemper they are sick of. These delight to be looking on the dark side of the cloud only.
2. We must not judge of ourselves always according to present feeling; for in temptations we shall see nothing but smoke of distrustful thoughts. Fire may be raked up in the ashes, though not seen; life in the winter is hid in the root.
3. Take heed of false reasoning – as because our fire does not blaze out as others, therefore we have no fire at all – and by false conclusions come to sin against the commandment in bearing false witness against ourselves. . . . We must neither trust to false evidence, nor deny true; for so we should dishonour the work of God's Spirit in us, and lose the help of that evidence which would cherish our love to Christ and arm us against Satan's discouragements. Some are so faulty in this way, as if they had been hired by Satan, the 'accuser of the brethren' [Revelation 12:10], to plead for him in accusing themselves.
4. Know for a ground of this, that in the covenant of grace God requires the truth of grace, not any certain measure; and a spark of fire is fire as well as the whole element. Therefore we must look to grace in the spark as well as in the flame. . . . It is one thing to be wanting [i.e. lacking] in grace, and another thing to want grace altogether.
5. Grace sometimes is so little as is undiscernible to us; the Spirit sometimes has secret operations in us, which we know not for the present; but Christ knows. . . . In a gloomy day there is so much light whereby we may know it to be day, and not night; so there is something in a Christian under a cloud, whereby he may be discerned to be a true believer, and not a hypocrite.

Chapter 15: Of infirmities

God's children never sin with full will, because there is a contrary law of the mind, whereby the dominion of sin is broken, which always has some secret working against the law of sin. Notwithstanding there may be so much will in a sinful action, as may wonderfully waste our comfort afterward, and keep us long upon the rack of a disquieted conscience, God in his fatherly dispensation suspending the sense of his love. So much as we give way to our will in sinning, in such a measure of distance we set ourselves from comfort. Sin against conscience is as a thief in the candle, which wastes our joy, and thereby weakens our strength. We must know, therefore, that wilful breaches in sanctification will much hinder the sense of our justification.

Chapter 28: Be encouraged to go on cheerfully, with confidence of prevailing

Lord Jesus, thou hast promised not to quench the smoking flax, not to break the bruised reed; cherish thine own grace in me, leave me not to myself, the glory shall be thine. Let us not suffer Satan to transform Christ unto us, to be otherwise than he is to those that are his. . . . [Satan] will object (1) thou art a great sinner; we may answer, Christ is a strong Saviour; but he will object (2) thou hast no faith, no love; yes, a spark of faith and love; but (3) Christ will not regard that; yes, 'he will not quench the smoking flax'; but (4) this is so little and weak, that it will vanish and come to nought; nay, but Christ will cherish it, until he has brought judgment to victory. And thus much for our comfort we have already, that even when we first believed we overcame God himself, as it were, by believing the pardon of all our sins; notwithstanding the guilt of our own consciences and his absolute justice. Now having been prevailers with God, what shall stand against us if we can learn to make use of our faith? . . .

　Neither must we reason from a denial of a great measure of grace, to a denial of any at all in us; for faith and grace stand not in an indivisible point, so as he that hath not such and such a measure has none at all; but as there is a great breadth between a spark and a flame, so there is a great wideness between the least measure of grace and the greatest; and he that has the least measure, is within the compass of God's eternal favour; though he be not a shining light, yet he is a smoking wick, which Christ's tender care will not suffer him to quench.

George Herbert, *The Country Parson*
(1632)

George Herbert was born in 1593, the younger brother of Edward, Lord Herbert of Cherbury, who became one of the first English Deists. He was educated at Trinity College, Cambridge, where he went on to become a fellow. In 1619 or 1620 he was elected public orator of the university and looked set for a secular career, despite having embarked on study for a Bachelor of Divinity in 1616. He was elected as a member of the 1624 Parliament, but the disappointments of this experience appear to have caused him to turn his back on a secular career and later that year he was ordained deacon. He was influenced by his friend Nicholas Ferrar, the founder of the Little Gidding community. In 1626 he became a canon of Lincoln Cathedral, but he was not ordained priest until 1630, when he became rector of Fugglestone with Bemerton, on the outskirts of Salisbury, where he served until his death in 1633.

Herbert is famous for two works. He wrote many poems which he entrusted on his deathbed to Nicholas Ferrar, who published them the same year under the title *The Temple*. His other famous work is his *A Priest to the Temple, or the Country Parson: His Character and Rule of Holy Life*. This he completed in 1632 (the date of the Preface) but it was not published until 1652. It has become one of the classics of pastoral theology and contains much of abiding value although parts are dated. At that time the bulk of the population lived in the country, so Herbert's exhortations related to the majority of the clergy at the time. The clergy are to be willing to serve their flock as lawyers and doctors. As regards the latter, it is easy for a scholar to acquire the necessary skills by a little anatomy and by reading a couple of books (23)! Herbert emphasizes the importance of the parson's own life, in order that he may serve effectively as 'the deputy of Christ for the reducing of man to the obedience of God' (1). The Puritan movement was strong at the time but Herbert represents a different form of spirituality. He was very content with the Church of England as it was and the faithful public saying of Morning Prayer and Evening Prayer each day was very important for him. But Herbert was not a controversial figure and the Puritan Richard Baxter spoke approvingly of his spirituality.

3: The Parson's Life

The country parson is exceeding exact in his life, being holy, just, prudent, temperate, bold, grave in all his ways. And because the two highest points of life, wherein a Christian is most seen, are patience and mortification – patience in regard of afflictions; mortification in regard of lusts and affections and the stupefying and deading of all the clamorous powers of the soul – therefore he has thoroughly studied these, that he may be an absolute master and commander of himself, for all the purposes which God has ordained him. Yet in these points he labours most in those things which are most apt to scandalize his parish. And first, because country people live hardly – and therefore as feeling their own sweat and consequently knowing the price of money are offended much with any who by hard usage increase their travail – the country parson is very circumspect in avoiding all covetousness, neither being greedy to get, nor niggardly to keep, nor troubled to lose any worldly wealth, but in all his words and actions slighting and disesteeming it, even to a wondering that the world should so much value wealth, which in the day of wrath has not one dram of comfort for us. Secondly, because luxury is a very visible sin, the parson is very careful to avoid all the kinds thereof, but especially that of drinking, because it is the most popular vice; into which, if he come, he prostitutes himself both to shame and sin, and by having fellowship with the unfruitful works of darkness he disables himself of authority to reprove them. . . . Neither is it for the servant of Christ to haunt inns or taverns or alehouses to the dishonour of his person and office. . . . Thirdly, because country people (as indeed all honest men) do much esteem their word, it being the life of buying and selling and dealing in the world, therefore the parson is very strict in keeping his word, though it be to his own hindrance, as knowing that if he be not so he will quickly be discovered and disregarded, neither will they believe him in the pulpit whom they cannot trust in his conversation. As for oaths and apparel, the disorders thereof are also very manifest. The parson's yea is yea, and nay nay, and his apparel plain but reverend and clean, without spots or dust or smell, the purity of his mind breaking out and dilating itself even to his body, clothes and habitation.

7. The Parson Preaching

The country parson preaches constantly; the pulpit is his joy and his throne. . . . When he preaches he procures attention by all possible art: both by earnestness of speech (it being natural to men to think that where is much earnestness there is somewhat worth hearing), and by a diligent and busy cast of his eye on his auditors, with letting them know that he observes who marks and who not, and with particularizing of his speech now to the younger sort, then to the elder, now to the poor and now to the rich. 'This is for you' and 'This is for you'; for particulars ever touch and awake more than generals. . . . Sometimes he tells them stories and sayings of others, according as his text invites him, for them also men heed and remember better than exhortations, which though earnest yet often die with the sermon, especially with country people, which are thick and heavy and hard to raise to a point of zeal and fervency and need a mountain of fire to kindle them; but stories and sayings they will well remember. He often tells them that sermons are dangerous things, that none goes out of church as he came in, but either better or worse; that none is careless before his judge and that the word of God shall judge us. By these and other means the parson procures attention, but the character of his sermon is holiness; he is not witty or learned or eloquent, but holy. . . . [The character of holiness] is gained first by choosing texts of devotion, not controversy, moving and ravishing texts whereof the Scriptures are full. Secondly, by dipping and seasoning all our words and sentences in our hearts before they come into our mouths, truly affecting and cordially expressing all that we say, so that the auditors may plainly perceive that every word is heart-deep. . . . The parson exceeds not an hour in preaching, because all ages have thought that a competency and he that profits not in that time will less afterwards, the same affection which made him not profit before making him then weary, and so he grows from not relishing to loathing.

The Westminster Confession of Faith
(1647)

When Queen Elizabeth died in 1603 she was succeeded by James I, previously king of Presbyterian Scotland. During his reign there was a shift in attitude among the English bishops. While in the Elizabethan period episcopacy (government of the church by bishops) was defended on the grounds that it was desirable or at least tolerable, under James many began to argue that it was the one divinely ordained form of church government. Again, while under Elizabeth both the bishops and their Puritan critics shared a common Calvinist theology, many of the new bishops rejected it. They denied the doctrine of predestination and were therefore called Arminians, though their theology was very different from that of Arminius. They desired more ritual in church worship and saw regular participation in the sacraments as the way to salvation. So while under Elizabeth the Puritans differed from the establishment over questions of church government and ceremony, in the seventeenth century there was a much more serious theological divide. This worsened under James' son Charles I, who succeeded him in 1625. Charles strongly favoured the 'High Church' party and promoted them to positions of leadership. When someone, wishing to know more of their beliefs, asked what the Arminians held, the reply was 'all the best bishoprics and deaneries in England'!

William Laud became archbishop of Canterbury in 1633 and sought to impose High Church ways. Those who resisted were punished severely – many had their ears cut off. But in 1637 Charles and Laud made the mistake of seeking to impose *The Book of Common Prayer* (see pages 237–41) on Presbyterian Scotland. This provoked opposition which led in due course to the Civil War between Charles and Parliament. The result was the victory of Parliament and the execution of Laud and, eventually, of Charles himself. The Puritans by now would not accept anything less than radical change. Episcopacy was to be abolished 'root and branch'.

At first the initiative lay with the Presbyterians. The Scots wanted the Church of England to become like the Church of Scotland. To this end, Parliament convened the Westminster Assembly, which met in more than a thousand sessions from 1643 to 1649 and irregularly thereafter. The membership was overwhelmingly Presbyterian – many of those who were not Presbyterian left. The aim was to legislate for one common Presbyterian establishment of religion for the British Isles. To this end the assembly produced a *Directory for the Publick Worship of God*, designed to replace the *Book of Common Prayer*. They produced the *Shorter* and *Larger Catechisms*, which have acquired a status comparable to Luther's *Small* and *Large Catechism* (see pages 205–209). But their greatest achievement, completed in 1647, was the *Westminster Confession of Faith*,

a statement of seventeenth-century Reformed belief comparable in length and status to the Lutheran *Augsburg Confession* (see pages 210–13). The *Westminster Confession* was intended to replace the *Thirty-nine Articles* (see pages 264–68). It is a considerably longer document, and the moderate Calvinism of the *Articles* gave way
to a much stricter Calvinism.

The *Confession* reflects seventeenth-century British Calvinism which had developed in a number of ways from the teaching of early Reformed theologians like Calvin. For example, in the seventeenth century, 'Covenant Theology' became very popular within Calvinism. This meant taking the idea of the covenant as an organizing principle in theology. This approach is traced back to a significant work on the covenant by Heinrich Bullinger, whose *Decades* (see pages 229–32) were highly influential in Elizabethan England. A later development was the idea of a 'covenant of works' between God and Adam before the fall, contrasted with the 'covenant of grace' between God and the church. This idea was introduced by Zacharias Ursinus and Kaspar Olevianus, the authors of the *Heidelberg Catechism* (see pages 254–58). The Confession also taught, with most of the Puritans but against Luther and Calvin, that assurance of salvation is distinct from saving faith. This assurance is possible for all believers but obtaining it may involve a long and arduous search.

The *Westminster Confession* was not adopted by the Church of England, but it was widely accepted by the English-speaking Reformed churches. The Church of Scotland adopted it in 1647, in the place of the earlier *Scots Confession* drawn up by John Knox and others (see pages 250–53). It is one of the greatest confessions of the time and may be read with great profit even by those who do not agree with all that it says. One of its great strengths is the way in which subtle theological distinctions are expressed briefly in simple language. Much of the language is taken straight from Scripture and there are numerous biblical references, which are omitted in the extracts below.

Chapter 9: Of Free Will

1. God has endued the will of man with that natural liberty, that it is neither forced nor by any absolute necessity of nature determined to good or evil.

2. Man, in his state of innocency, had freedom and power to will and to do that which is good and well-pleasing to God; but yet mutably so that he might fall from it.

3. Man, by his fall into a state of sin, has wholly lost all ability of will to any spiritual good accompanying salvation; so as a natural man, being altogether

averse from that good and dead in sin is not able, by his own strength, to convert himself, or to prepare himself thereunto.

4. When God converts a sinner and translates him into the state of grace, he frees him from his natural bondage under sin and, by his grace alone, enables him freely to will and to do that which is spiritually good; yet so as that by reason of his remaining corruption, he does not perfectly, nor only, will that which is good, but does also will that which is evil.

5. The will of man is made perfectly and immutably free to good alone in the state of glory only.

Chapter 11: Of Justification

1. Those whom God effectually calls he also freely justifies: not by infusing righteousness into them, but by pardoning their sins and by accounting and accepting their persons as righteous; not for any thing wrought in them or done by them, but for Christ's sake alone; not by imputing faith itself, the act of believing, or any other evangelical obedience to them as their righteousness; but by imputing the obedience and satisfaction of Christ unto them, they receiving and resting on him and his righteousness by faith: which faith they have not of themselves; it is the gift of God.

2. Faith, thus receiving and resting on Christ and his righteousness, is the alone instrument of justification; yet is it not alone in the person justified, but is ever accompanied with all other saving graces and is no dead faith but works by love.

3. Christ, by his obedience and death, did fully discharge the debt of all those that are thus justified and did make a proper, real and full satisfaction to his Father's justice in their behalf. Yet inasmuch as he was given by the Father for them and his obedience and satisfaction accepted in their stead and both freely, not for any thing in them, their justification is only of free grace, that both the exact justice and rich grace of God might be glorified in the justification of sinners.

5. God does continue to forgive the sins of those that are justified; and although they can never fall from the state of justification, yet they may by their sins fall under God's Fatherly displeasure and not have the light of his countenance restored unto them, until they humble themselves, confess their sins, beg pardon and renew their faith and repentance.

Chapter 12: Of Adoption

All those that are justified God vouchsafes, in and for his only Son Jesus Christ, to make partakers of the grace of adoption: by which they are taken into the number and enjoy the liberties and privileges of the children of God; have his name put upon them; receive the Spirit of adoption; have access to the throne of grace with boldness; are enabled to cry, Abba, Father; are pitied, protected, provided for and chastened by him as by a father; yet never cast off but sealed to the day of redemption and inherit the promises, as heirs of everlasting salvation.

Chapter 13: Of Sanctification

1. They who are effectually called and regenerated, having a new heart and a new spirit created in them, are further sanctified, really and personally, through the virtue of Christ's death and resurrection, by his Word and Spirit dwelling in them; the dominion of the whole body of sin is destroyed, and the several lusts thereof are more and more weakened and mortified, and they more and more quickened and strengthened in all saving graces to the practice of true holiness, without which no man shall see the Lord.

2. This sanctification is throughout in the whole man, yet imperfect in this life; there abide still some remnants of corruption in every part: whence arises a continual and irreconcilable war, the flesh lusting against the Spirit and the Spirit against the flesh.

3. In which war, although the remaining corruption for a time may much prevail, yet through the continual supply of strength from the sanctifying Spirit of Christ, the regenerate part does overcome: and so the saints grow in grace, perfecting holiness in the fear of God.

Chapter 14: Of Saving Faith

1. The grace of faith, whereby the elect are enabled to believe to the saving of their souls, is the work of the Spirit of Christ in their hearts and is ordinarily wrought by the ministry of the Word: by which also, and by the administration of the sacraments and prayer, it is increased and strengthened.

2. By this faith, a Christian believes to be true whatsoever is revealed in the Word, for the authority of God himself speaking therein; and acts differently upon that which each particular passage thereof contains; yielding obedience to the commands, trembling at the threatenings, and embracing the promises of God for

this life and that which is to come. But the principle acts of saving faith are accepting, receiving and resting upon Christ alone for justification, sanctification and eternal life, by virtue of the covenant of grace.

3. This faith is different in degrees, weak or strong; may be often and many ways assailed and weakened, but gets the victory; growing up in many to the attainment of a full assurance through Christ, who is both the author and finisher of our faith.

Chapter 15: Of Repentance Unto Life

1. Repentance unto life is an evangelical grace, the doctrine whereof is to be preached by every minister of the gospel, as well as that of faith in Christ.

2. By it a sinner, out of the sight and sense, not only of the danger but also of the filthiness and odiousness of his sins as contrary to the holy nature and righteous law of God, and upon the apprehension of his mercy in Christ to such as are penitent, so grieves for and hates his sins as to turn from them all unto God, purposing and endeavouring to walk with him in all the ways of his commandments.

3. Although repentance be not to be rested in as any satisfaction for sin, or any cause of the pardon thereof, which is the act of God's free grace in Christ; yet is it of such necessity to all sinners that none may expect pardon without it.

4. As there is no sin so small but it deserves damnation; so there is no sin so great that it can bring damnation upon those who truly repent.

5. Men ought not to content themselves with a general repentance, but it is every man's duty to endeavour to repent of his particular sins particularly.

Richard Baxter,
The Saints' Everlasting Rest (1650)

Richard Baxter was born in 1615 at Rowton near Shrewsbury and at the age of fifteen was converted through reading Richard Sibbes's *The Bruised Reed and the Smoking Flax* (see pages 295–97). He was largely self-educated, with the help of various tutors. In 1638 he was ordained and the following year became master of the free Grammar School in Bridgnorth (Shropshire). Two years later Baxter began his ministry at Kidderminster, which did not end until 1660. With the outbreak of the Civil War, however, he absented himself for five years to serve as a chaplain to the Parliamentary army.

Baxter played a significant role in the recall of Charles II in 1660. Charles had solemnly promised religious toleration, a promise that he renounced once he had the throne. With the restoration of episcopacy Baxter was offered the see of Hereford, which he declined. In 1661 the 'Savoy Conference' was held in London at which the Puritans led by Baxter, hoped to secure sufficient modification of the *Book of Common Prayer* (see pages 237–41) to enable them to conform. The Royalist side was intransigent, however, and the Act of Uniformity in May 1662 led to the ejection from their pulpits of some two thousand Puritan clergy who were unable to conform. These included Baxter, who became one of the leaders of the Nonconformists. It was illegal for such to preach and Baxter was imprisoned more than once for doing so. He actively supported the 'Glorious Revolution' of 1689 which replaced the Catholic James II with William and Mary. He died two years later.

Baxter was opposed to unnecessary divisions in the church, taking as his motto the traditional saying, 'In necessary things, unity; in doubtful things, liberty; in all things, charity.' He was a prolific author. It has been estimated that he published more than twice the considerable output of John Owen, amounting to thirty to forty thousand closely printed pages of text. While most of the output was theological, he is famous today for two other works. *The Saints' Everlasting Rest* was a devotional work written in 1650. *The Reformed Pastor*, written in 1656, is a classic book on pastoral care. Baxter believed strongly in the value of private instruction of families to supplement the public ministry from the pulpit.

Countless books have been written on the theme of Christian discipleship. Far fewer have been written on the ultimate goal of that discipleship, the theme of *The Saints' Everlasting Rest*. This is a massive work of over 1,000 pages and in four parts. The first describes the rest awaiting the people of God; the second offers proofs for it, including lengthy digressions on the divine authority of Scripture; the third applies the doctrine of everlasting rest, both to the unconverted and the converted; the fourth part, the purpose of the whole work, is 'a directory of the getting and keeping of the heart in heaven' by heavenly meditation. As with many of Baxter's works, it is far too long and in 1758 an abridged version was produced, which is the form in which it has been most often published.

Part 1

1:1. It was not only our interest in God and actual fruition [enjoyment] of him, which was lost in Adam's covenant-breaking fall, but all spiritual knowledge of him and true disposition towards such a felicity. . . . When the Son of God comes with recovering grace and discoveries and tenders of a spiritual and eternal happiness and glory, he finds not faith in man to believe it. But as the poor man, that would not believe that any one had such a sum as a hundred pounds (it was so far above what he possessed) so man will hardly now believe there is such a happiness as once he had, much less as Christ has now procured.

2:1. The saints' rest, here in question, is the most happy estate of a Christian having obtained the end of his course; or it is the perfect endless fruition of God by the perfected saints, according to the measure of their capacity, to which their souls arrive at death, and both soul and body most fully after the resurrection and final judgment.

3:5. They that never knew they were without God, never yet enjoyed him; and they that never knew they were naturally and actually in the way to hell, did never yet know the way to heaven. . . . This is the sad case of many thousands and the reason why so few obtain this rest: they will not be convinced or made sensible that they are in point of title distant from it and in point of practice contrary to it. They have lost their God, their souls, their rest and do not know it, nor will they believe him that tells them so. Whoever travelled towards a place which he thought he was at already or sought for that which he knew not he had lost?

4. May we show what this rest contains, as well as what it presupposes? But, alas, how little know I of that whereof I am about to speak. Shall I speak before I know? But if I stay till I clearly know, I shall not come again to speak. . . . Therefore I will speak while I may that little, very little, which I do know of it rather than be wholly silent. The Lord reveal it to me, that I may reveal to you; and the Lord open some light, and show both you and me his inheritance.

4:1. There is contained in this rest a cessation from motion or action; not of all the action but of that which has the nature of a means and implies the absence of the end. When we have obtained the haven, we have done sailing. When the workman has his wages, it is implied he has done his work. When we are at our journey's end, we have done with the way.

4:2. This rest contains a perfect freedom from all the evils that accompanied us through our course. . . . There is not such a thing as grief and sorrow known there, nor is there such a thing as a pale face, a languid body, feeble joints, unable infancy, decrepit age, peccant humours, dolorous sickness, griping fears, consuming cares nor whatsoever deserves the name of evil. Indeed a gale of groans and sighs, a stream of tears, accompanied us to the very gates and there bid us farwell for ever. We did weep and lament when the world did rejoice, but our sorrow is turned into joy and our joy shall no man take from us.

4:3. This rest contains the highest degree of the saints' personal perfection, both of soul and body. . . . Were the glory ever so great and themselves not made capable of it by a personal perfection suitable thereto, it would be little to them. . . . The more perfect the sight is, the more delightful the beautiful object. The more perfect the appetite, the sweeter the food. The more musical the ear, the more pleasant the melody. The more perfect the soul, the more joyous those joys and the more glorious, to us, is that glory.

4:4. This rest contains, as the principal part, our nearest fruition of God, the chiefest good. And here, reader, wonder not if I be at a loss and if my apprehensions receive but little of that which is in my expressions. If to the beloved disciple . . . it did not appear what it shall be, but only in general, that 'when Christ shall appear we shall be like him' [1 John 3:2], no wonder if I know little. . . .

4:5. This rest contains a sweet and constant action of all the powers of the soul and body in this fruition of God. It is not the rest of a stone, which ceases from all motion when it attains the centre. . . . This body shall be so changed that it shall be no more flesh and blood, for that 'cannot inherit the kingdom of God', but 'a spiritual body' [1 Corinthians 15:50, 44]. . . . If grace make a Christian differ so much from what he was, that the Christian could say to his companion, 'I am not the man I was,' how much more will glory make us differ? . . .

4:6. Knowledge, of itself, is very desirable. . . . As far as the rational soul exceeds the sensitive, so far the delights of a philosopher, in discovering the secrets of nature, and knowing the mystery of sciences, exceed the delights of the glutton, the drunkard, the unclean and of all voluptuous sensualists whatsoever. So excellent is all truth. What, then, is their delight who know the God of truth?

4:7. The memory will not be idle, or useless, in this blessed work, if it be but by looking back to help the soul to value its employment. . . . From that height the saint can look behind him and before him. And to compare past with present things must needs raise in the blessed soul an inconceivable esteem and sense of its condition. To stand on that mount, whence we can see the Wilderness and Canaan both at once; to stand in heaven and look back on earth, and weigh them together in the balance of a comparing sense and judgment, how must it needs transport the soul, and make it cry out, 'Is this the purchase that cost so dear as the blood of God?' . . .

4:8. But O the full, the near, the sweet enjoyment is that of the affections, love and joy. . . . His love to thee will not be as thine was on earth to him, seldom and cold, up and down, mixed (as aguish bodies) with burning and quaking, with a good day and a bad. No, Christian, he that would not be discouraged by thine enmity, by thy loathsome, hateful nature, by all thy unwillingness, unkind neglects and churlish resistances; he that would neither cease nor abate his love for all these, can he cease to love thee, when he has made thee truly lovely? . . . No wonder if angels desire to pry into this mystery, and if it be the study of the saints here to know the height and breadth and length and depth of this love, though it passes knowledge – this is the saints' rest in the fruition of God by love.

4:9. The affection of joy has not the least share in this fruition. It is that which all the rest lead to and conclude in; even the inconceivable complacency which the blessed feel in their seeing, knowing, loving and being beloved of God. The delight of the senses here cannot be known by expressions, as they are felt – how much less this joy!

4:10. And it is not thy joy only; it is a mutual joy as well as a mutual love. Is there such joy in heaven at thy conversion, and will there be none at thy glorification? Will not the angels welcome thee thither and congratulate thy safe arrival? Yea, it is the joy of Jesus Christ; for now he has the end of his undertaking, labour, suffering, dying, when we have our joys, when he is 'glorified in his saints, and admired in all them that believe' [2 Thessalonians 1:10].

Jeremy Taylor, *The Rule and Exercises of Holy Dying* (1651)

Jeremy Taylor was born in 1613 at Cambridge and went on to study at Gonville and Caius College, of which he became a fellow in 1633. Shortly after, he preached at St Paul's Cathedral in London, which brought him to the attention of Archbishop William Laud. In 1635 Laud nominated him as a fellow of All Souls, Oxford and appointed him as his own chaplain. In 1638 Taylor became rector of Uppingham but left in 1642 to become a chaplain in the Royalist army. In 1645 he was captured and imprisoned briefly by the Parliamentarians after which he become chaplain to a noble family in Wales. His wife died in 1651 and he later remarried and settled with his new wife. In 1658 he became chaplain to another noble family, in the north-east of Ireland. During the years of Puritan rule he wrote a number of works and was twice imprisoned briefly because of indiscretions. After the Restoration of the monarchy and episcopacy he became bishop of Down and Connor, in Ireland, and vice-chancellor of Trinity College, Dublin. Although in 1647 he had written a book, *Liberty of Prophesying*, advocating religious tolerance, he was harsh and tyrannical in his treatment of the Presbyterians in his diocese. He died in 1667, shortly after the death of the last of his seven sons.

Taylor wrote a number of theological works, against Roman Catholicism and Presbyterianism, but he is famous today more for his devotional writings. A number of Taylor's sermons were published and he had the reputation of a great preacher. Among his best-known works are a pair: *The Rule and Exercises of Holy Living* (1650) and *The Rule and Exercises of Holy Dying* (1651). *Holy Living* has four chapters, on the means to a holy life, on Christian sobriety, on Christian justice and on the duties of religion. *Holy Dying* has five chapters. The first two are about preparing for a holy and blessed death, by considering one's mortality and by appropriate religious exercises. The next two are on the state of sickness, its temptations and the religious exercises appropriate to it. The final chapter offers the clergy guidance in the visitation of those who are sick or dying.

What relevance does *Holy Dying* have for today? Taylor writes of the ever-present danger of death. He was aware of how suddenly death could strike: 'when the [ancient Greek] poet Aeschylus was sitting under the walls of his house, an eagle hovering over his bald head mistook it for a stone, and let fall his oyster, hoping there to break the shell, but pierced the poor man's skull' (1:1)! He himself suffered the loss of his first wife and all seven of his sons. Such calamities do happen today, but almost exclusively in areas of the world hit by specific disasters. They seem remote to the average westerner – many of whom do not lose even a grandparent until they are young adults, do not lose a parent until they are middle aged and never suffer the loss of a child. Yet it remains as true today as in the seventeenth century that, together with taxes, death is the only certainty. The unpredictability of death also remains true. A premature death is far less likely – but still a real possibility. The biggest difference lies in the fact that mortality was then more readily accepted while today's westerners try to ignore it and are then shocked and scandalized when forced to confront it. Holy Dying can serve to remind us of the fact of death and also provide us with, as the title page puts it, 'the means and instruments of preparing ourselves and others respectively for a blessed death'.

Chapter 2. A General Preparation Towards a Holy and Blessed Death, by Way of Exercise

Section 1. Three Precepts preparatory to a Holy Death, to be practised in our whole Life

1. He that would die well must always look for death, every day knocking at the gates of the grave; and then the gates of the grave shall never prevail upon him to do him mischief. This was the advice of all the wise and good men of the world, who, especially in the days and periods of their joy and festival egressions, chose to throw some ashes into their chalices, some sober remembrances of their fatal period. Such was the black shirt of Saladine; the tombstone presented to the Emperor of Constantinople on his coronation day . . . These in fantastic semblances declare a severe counsel and useful meditation; and it is not easy for a man to be gay in his imagination, or to be drunk with joy or wine, pride or revenge, who considers sadly that he must, ere long, dwell in a house of darkness and dishonour, and his body must be the inheritance of worms, and his soul must be what he pleases, even as a man makes it here by his living good or bad.

I have read of a young hermit who, being passionately in love with a young lady, could not by all the arts of religion and mortification suppress the trouble of that fancy till at last, being told that she was dead and had been buried about fourteen days, he went secretly to her vault, and with the skirt of his mantle wiped the moisture from the carcass, and still at the return of his temptation laid it before him saying, 'Behold this is the beauty of the woman thou didst so much desire.' And so the man found his cure. And if we make death as present to us, our own death, dwelling and dressed in all its pomp of fancy and proper circumstances – if anything will quench the heats of lust, or the desires of money, or the greedy passionate affections of this world, this must do it. But withal, the frequent use of this meditation, by curing our present inordinations, will make death safe and friendly, and by its very custom will make, that the king of terrors shall come to us without his affrighting dresses; and that we shall sit down in the grave as we compose ourselves to sleep and do the duties of nature and choice. . . .

2. 'He that would die well must, all the days of his life, lay up against the day of death,' not only by the general provisions of holiness and a pious life indefinitely, but provisions proper to the necessities of that great day of expense, in which a man is to throw his last cast for an eternity of joys or sorrows, ever remembering that this alone well performed is not enough to pass us into paradise, but that alone, done foolishly, is enough to send us to hell, and the want of either a holy life or death makes a man to fall short of the mighty price of our high calling.

In order to this rule we are to consider what special graces we shall then need to exercise, and by the proper arts of the spirit, by a heap of proportioned arguments, by prayers and a great treasure of devotion laid up in heaven, provide beforehand a reserve of strength and mercy. Men in the course of their lives walk lazily and incuriously, as if they had both their feet in one shoe; and when they are passably revolved to the time of their dissolution they have no mercies in store, no patience, no faith, no charity to God or despite of the world, being without gust or appetite for the land of their inheritance, which Christ with so much pain and blood had purchased for them. When we come to die indeed, we shall be very much put to it to stand firm upon the two feet of a Christian, faith and patience. When we ourselves are to use the articles, to turn our former discourses into present practice, and to feel what we never felt before, we shall find it to be quite another thing to be willing presently to quit this life and all our present possessions for the hopes of a thing which we were never suffered to see, and such a thing of which we may fail so many ways, and of which, if we fail any, we are miserable for ever. Then we shall find how much we have need to have secured the Spirit of God and the grace of faith, by an habitual, perfect, unmovable resolution.

The same also is the case of patience, which will be assaulted with sharp pains, disturbed fancies, great fears, want of a present mind, natural weaknesses, frauds of the devil and a thousand accidents and imperfections. It concerns us therefore highly, in the whole course of our lives, not only to accustom ourselves to a patient suffering of injuries and affronts, of persecutions and losses, of cross accidents and unnecessary circumstances; but also by representing death as present to us, to consider with what arguments then to fortify our patience, and by assiduous and fervent prayer to God all our life long to call upon God to give us patience, and great assistances, a strong faith and a confirmed hope, the Spirit of God and his holy angels assistants at that time, to resist and to subdue the devil's temptations and assaults; and so to fortify our heart, that it break not into intolerable sorrows and impatience and end in wretchedness and infidelity.

But this is to be the work of our life, and not to be done at once, but as God gives us time, by succession, by parts and little periods. For it is very remarkable that God who gives plenteously to all creatures, he has scattered the firmament with stars, as a man sows corn in his fields, in a multitude bigger than the capacities of human order; he has made so much variety of creatures, and gives us great choice of meats and drinks, although any one of both kinds would have served our needs, and so in all instances of nature; yet in the distribution of our time God seems to be straighthanded, and gives it to us, not as nature gives us rivers, enough to drown us, but drop by drop, minute after minute, so that we never can have two minutes together, but he takes away one when he gives us another. This should teach us to value our time since God so values it and, by his so small distribution of it, tells us it is the most precious thing we have. Since, therefore, in the day of our death we can have still but the same little portion of this precious time, let us in every minute of our life, I mean in every discernible portion, lay up such a stock of reason and good works, that they may convey a value to the imperfect and shorter actions of our death-bed, while God rewards the piety of our lives by his gracious acceptation and benediction upon the actions preparatory to our deathbed.

3. He that desires to die well and happily, above all things, must be careful that he do not live a soft, a delicate, and voluptuous life; but a life severe, holy, and under the discipline of the cross, under the conduct of prudence and observation, a life of warfare and sober counsels, labour and watchfulness.

John Owen, *Temptation* (1658)

John Owen was born in 1616 near Oxford. He went to Queen's College, Oxford, but left in 1637 because of the religious changes introduced by Laud. In the 1640s he served as minister of two Essex churches, at Fordham and Coggeshall. At first his sympathies were Presbyterian, but he moved to an Independent position. He served as Cromwell's chaplain from 1649 to 1651, when he was appointed dean of Christ Church, Oxford. The following year Cromwell made him vice-chancellor of the university, a post he held till 1657. In 1660, with the restoration of the monarchy, he was expelled from Christ Church. He left Oxford for London and continued to preach and to write until his death in 1683.

Owen played a leading role in the English church during the years of Cromwell's rule as 'Lord Protector' (1653–58) He was one of the authors of a set of 'Humble Proposals', presented to Parliament in 1652. In 1654 these became the basis for Cromwell's settlement of religion, which was to allow Presbyterians, Independents and Baptists alike to be ministers of the parish churches. There was to be a board of 'Triers', composed of thirty-eight members, clergy and laity, whose duty it was to judge the fitness of candidates for service in a parish. The aim was that every parish should have a godly evangelical minister – be he Presbyterian, Independent or Baptist. Owen sat on this board. He also took a leading role at the Savoy Assembly, which met at the Savoy Palace in London in 1658. This was a Congregationalist or Independent gathering and produced the *Savoy Declaration of Faith* which, unlike the *Westminster Confession of Faith* (see pages 301–305), has never been widely used.

Owen was arguably the greatest theologian of the seventeenth-century Puritans. He was a prolific author and his works are printed in twenty-four large volumes. They fall into four groups:

● Owen wrote many controversial works against other groups – Arminians, Socinians (who denied the deity of Christ) and Roman Catholics. Perhaps the most famous of these is his *Death of Death in the Death of Christ* (1647), the classic defence of the doctrine of 'limited atonement'. Owen argued that the death of Christ does not merely make it *possible* for all to be saved, without actually guaranteeing the salvation of anyone. Rather, it makes the salvation of the elect (and them alone) not merely possible but certain.

● Owen wrote a number of doctrinal works. Of these the *Discourse on the Holy Spirit* has acquired some fame today because Owen was one of the earliest theologians to recognize that the human life of Jesus was lived in dependence upon the Holy Spirit, an idea now widely recognized.

● Owen also wrote practical works, of which three may be mentioned. In 1656 he published *The Mortification of Sin*, based on sermons preached at Oxford. At the urging of his friends he two years later published more sermon material, under the title *Temptation*. Finally, in 1667 he wrote a treatise on *Indwelling Sin in Believers*. These works contain much practical wisdom and those who are willing to grapple with the antiquated language and somewhat turgid style will be greatly rewarded.

● Owen wrote a massive *Exposition of the Epistle to the Hebrews* (1674), which occupies seven volumes.

Chapter 4: Particular cases proposed to consideration

When they are overtaken with a sin [many people] set themselves to repent of that sin, but do not consider the temptation that was the cause of it, to set themselves against that also to take care that they enter no more into it. Hence are they quickly again entangled by it, though they have the greatest detestation of the sin itself that can be expressed. He that would indeed get the conquest over any sin must consider his temptations to it, and strike at that root; without deliverance from thence, he will not be healed.

This is a folly that possesses many who have yet a quick and living sense of sin. They are sensible of their *sins*, not of their *temptations* – are displeased with the bitter fruit, but cherish the poisonous root. Hence, in the midst of their humiliations for sin, they will continue in those ways, those societies, in the pursuit of those ends which have occasioned that sin; of which more afterward.

Temptations have *several degrees*. Some arise to such a height, do so press on the soul, so cruciate and disquiet it, so fight against all opposition that is made to it, that it is a peculiar power of temptation that he is to wrestle withal. When a fever rages, a man knows he is sick, unless his distemper have made him mad. The lusts of men, as James [1:14] tells us, 'entice, draw away', and seduce them to sin; but this they do of themselves, without peculiar instigation, in a more quiet, even, and sedate manner. If they grow violent, if they hurry the soul up and down, give it no rest, the soul may know that they have got the help of temptation to their assistance.

Take an empty vessel and put it into some stream that is in its course to the sea, it will infallibly be carried thither, according to the course and speed of the stream; but let strong winds arise upon it, it will be driven with violence on every bank and rock, until being broken in pieces it is swallowed up of the ocean. Men's lusts will infallibly (if not mortified in the death of Christ) carry them into eternal ruin but oftentimes without much noise, according to the course of the stream of their corruptions; but let the wind of strong temptations befall them, they are hurried into innumerable scandalous sins and so, broken upon all accounts, are swallowed up in eternity. So is it in general with men; so in particular. Hezekiah had the root of pride in him always; yet it did not make him run up and down to show his treasure and his riches until he fell into temptation by the ambassadors of the king of Babylon. So had David; yet could he keep off from numbering the people until Satan stood up and provoked him and solicited him to do it. Judas was covetous from the beginning; yet he did not contrive to satisfy it by selling of his Master until the devil entered into him, and he thereby into temptation. The like may be said of Abraham, Jonah, Peter and the rest. So that when any lust or corruption whatever tumultuates and disquiets the soul, puts it with violence on sin, let the soul know that it has got the advantage of some outward temptation, though as yet it perceives not wherein, or at least is become itself a peculiar temptation by some incitation or provocation that has befallen it and is to be looked to more than ordinarily. . . .

In particular, a man begins to be in repute for piety, wisdom, learning or the like – he is spoken of much to that purpose; his heart is tickled to hear of it and his pride and ambition affected with it. If this man now, with all his strength, ply the things from whence his repute and esteem and glory amongst men do spring, with a secret eye to have it increased, he is entering into temptation; which, if he take not heed, will quickly render him a slave of lust. . . . So is it with many scholars. They find themselves esteemed and favoured for their learning. This takes hold of the pride and ambition of their hearts. Hence they set themselves to study with all diligence day and night – a thing good in itself; but they do it that they might satisfy the thoughts and words of men, wherein they delight: and so in all they do they make provision for the flesh to fulfil the lusts thereof. . . .

Let, then, a man know that when he likes that which feeds his lust, and keeps it up by ways either good in themselves or not downright sinful, he is entered into temptation. When by a man's state or condition of life, or any means whatever, it comes to pass that his lust and any temptation meet with occasions and opportunities for its provocation and stirring up, let that man know, whether he perceive it or not, that he is certainly entered into temptation. I told you before that to enter into temptation is not merely to be tempted, but so to be under the *power* of it as to be entangled by it. Now it is impossible almost for a man to have opportunities, occasions, advantages, suited to his lust and corruption, but he will be entangled. . . . Some men think to play on the hole of the asp and not be stung, to touch pitch and not be defiled, to take fire in their clothes and not be burnt; but they will be mistaken. If thy business, course of life, societies or whatever else it be of the like kind, do cast thee on such things, ways, persons, as suit thy lust or corruption, know that thou art entered into temptation; how thou wilt come out God only knows. Let us suppose a man that has any seeds of filthiness in his heart engaged, in the course of his life, in society, light, vain and foolish, what notice soever, little, great or none at all, it be that he takes of it, he is undoubtedly entered into temptation. So is it with ambition in high places; passion in a multitude of perplexing affairs; polluted corrupt fancy in vain societies and the perusal of idle books or treatises of vanity and folly. Fire and things combustible may more easily be induced to lie together without affecting each other, than *peculiar* lusts and *suitable* objects or occasions for their exercise.

Samuel Rutherford, *Letters* (1664)

Samuel Rutherford was born in 1600 into a farming family at Nisbet near Jedburgh in the Scottish Borders. In 1617 he went to study at Edinburgh University, graduating in 1621. Two years later he was appointed to teach Latin, on the basis of a competitive exam, but left that post in controversial circumstances and at around that time was converted. He studied theology and was ordained in 1627, serving as a parish minister at Anwoth near Kirkcudbright in Dumfries and Galloway. While there he suffered the loss in turn of his wife, mother and children. In 1636 he was deposed for nonconformity and for writing a book opposing Arminianism and was exiled during the king's pleasure to Aberdeen, at the other end of Scotland. While there he wrote many letters to his former parishioners and friends at Anwoth. In 1637 Charles I imposed an unpopular new prayer book on the Scottish church which led the next year to the signing by dissidents of a National Covenant and later to the abolition of episcopacy. So in the summer of 1638 Rutherford was free to return to Anwoth where he resumed his ministry for eighteen months. He then moved to St Andrews to become professor of divinity and married again shortly after.

In 1643 Rutherford went to London to serve as one of the five Scottish Commissioners at the Westminster Assembly, remaining for four years. He was involved in the production of the *Westminster Confession of Faith* (see pages 301–305) and the catechisms. His greatest work was his *Lex Rex, or the Law and the Prince; a Dispute for the Just Prerogatives of King and People* (1644). This was primarily a work of political science in which he argues for constitutional government by law rather than the arbitrary will of kings (such as Charles I) claiming to rule by divine right. The crown is given by the voluntary consent of the people.

On his return in 1647 Rutherford became principal of St Mary's College at St Andrews and in 1651 rector of the university. While he was in London the two children of his second marriage both died, but he was to have a further five children – only one of whom survived him. When the monarchy was restored in 1660 Rutherford was one of four leading Scottish Presbyterians marked out for execution. His *Lex Rex* was publicly burnt and he was deposed from all his offices. He was charged with high treason and summoned to appear before Parliament but was mortally ill. 'I have got summons already before a Superior Judge and Judicatory, and I behove to answer to my first summons, and ere your day come, I will be where few kings and great folk come.' He died early the next year.

Rutherford's letters were first published in 1644 under the title *Joshua Redivivus*. (He had pictured himself as a Joshua sent ahead to spy out the Promised Land and report back on the rich blessings available in Christ.) The collection grew in successive editions until in 1848 Andrew Bonar published a collection of 365 letters, which became standard.

Of this number, about two thirds are from the time at Aberdeen. Rutherford's *Letters* have come to be seen as a spiritual classic. Having himself suffered so many bereavements he was well equipped to offer comfort to others. His letters are also marked by a passion for the person of Christ.

Letter 226: To Lady Kilconquhar (Aberdeen, 8 August 1637)

. . . Oh, if the world did but know what a smell the ointments of Christ cast and how ravishing his beauty (even the beauty of the fairest of the sons of men) is, and how sweet and powerful his voice is, the voice of that one Well-beloved! Certainly, where Christ comes, he runs away with the soul's love so that it cannot be commanded. I would far rather look but through the hole of Christ's door, to see but the one half of his fairest and most comely face (for he looks like heaven!), suppose I should never win in to see his excellency and glory to the full, than to enjoy the flower, the bloom and chief excellency of the glory and riches of ten worlds. Lord, send me for my part but the meanest share of Christ that can be given to any of the indwellers of the New Jerusalem. But I know my Lord is no niggard; he can and it becomes him well to give more than my narrow soul can receive. If there were ten thousand thousand millions of worlds, and as many heavens full of men and angels, Christ would not be pinched to supply all our wants and to fill us all. Christ is a well of life, but who knows how deep it is to the bottom?

This soul of ours has love and cannot but love some fair one; and oh, what a fair One, what an only One, what an excellent, lovely ravishing One is Jesus! Put the beauty of ten thousand thousand worlds of paradises like the garden of Eden in one; put all trees, all flowers, all smells, all colours, all tastes, all joys, all sweetness, all loveliness in one. Oh what a fair and excellent thing would that be! And yet it would be less to that fair and dearest Well-beloved, Christ, than one drop of rain to the whole seas, rivers, lakes and fountains of ten thousand earths. Oh, but Christ is heaven's wonder and earth's wonder! What marvel that his bride says, 'He is altogether lovely!' [Song of Solomon 5:16]. Oh that black souls will not come and fetch all their love to this fair One!

Oh if I could invite and persuade thousands, and ten thousand times ten thousand of Adam's sons, to flock about my Lord Jesus and to come and take their fill of love! O pity for evermore that there should be such a one as Christ Jesus, so boundless, so bottomless and so incomparable in infinite excellency and sweetness, and so few to take him! Oh, oh, you poor dry and dead souls, why will you not come hither with your toom [empty] vessels and your empty souls to this huge and fair and deep and sweet well of life, and fill all your toom vessels? Oh that Christ should be so large in sweetness and worth, and we so narrow, so pinched, so ebb and so void of all happiness. And yet men will not take him! They lose their love miserably who will not bestow it upon this lovely One.

Letter 234: To James Lindsay (Aberdeen, 7 September 1637)

. . . I know that, as night and shadows are good for flowers, and moon-light and dews are better than a continual sun, so is Christ's absence of special use, and that it has some nourishing virtue in it, and gives sap to humility, and puts an edge on hunger, and furnishes a fair field to faith to put forth itself and to exercise its fingers in gripping it sees not what.

It is mercy's wonder, and grace's wonder, that Christ will lend a piece of the lodging and a back-chamber beside himself, to our lusts, and that he and such swine should keep house together in our soul. For suppose they couch and contract themselves into little room when Christ comes in and seem to lie as dead under his feet, yet they often break out again – and a foot of the old man, or a leg or arm nailed to Christ's cross looses the nail or breaks out again! And yet Christ, beside this unruly and misnurtured neighbour, can still be making heaven in the saints, one way or other. May I not say, 'Lord Jesus, what doest thou here?' Yet here he must be. But I will not lose my feet to go on into this depth and wonder; for free mercy and infinite merits took a lodging to Christ and us, beside such a loathsome guest as sin.

Sanctification and mortification of our lusts are the hardest part of Christianity. It is in a manner as natural to us to leap when we see the New Jerusalem as to laugh when we are tickled. Joy is not under command or at our nod, when Christ kisses. But oh! How many of us would have Christ divided into two halves, that we might take the half of him only! We take his office, Jesus and salvation; but 'Lord' is a cumbersome word, and to obey and work out our own salvation and to perfect holiness is the cumbersome and stormy northside of Christ; and that which we eschew and shift.

John Milton, *Paradise Lost* (1667)

John Milton was born in 1608. He was educated at Christ's College, Cambridge, and began to write poems from an early age. During the Civil War he wrote in favour of the Parliamentary cause and also defended the execution of Charles I. One of his best-known works is his *Areopagita* (1644) in which he argues for the freedom of the press from censorship. Although he supported the Parliamentary cause he was opposed to the intolerance of the Presbyterians who wished to impose a single Presbyterian church upon Britain and in 1646 he made the famous comment that 'new presbyter is but old priest writ large'. In 1649 he briefly held a government post, but in 1651 he became completely blind. It was in response to this experience that he wrote his best-known lines, which conclude his sonnet 'When I consider how my light is spent': 'Thousands at his bidding speed, and post o'er land and ocean without rest; they also serve who only stand and wait.'

With the Restoration of the monarchy in 1660 Milton was in considerable danger as an apologist for the execution of Charles I. But his friends managed to gain an amnesty for him and he spent his final years writing poetry. He died in 1674.

Milton's greatest work is undoubtedly his *Paradise Lost* which first appeared in 1667, though he revised it in 1674. In 1671 he wrote a briefer sequel in four books, *Paradise Regained*, which focusses especially on the temptations of Christ, and *Samson Agonistes* – but neither of these has quite the same quality as the earlier work. *Paradise Lost* is one of the great classics of English literature, an epic tale in twelve books, relating the Fall of Adam and Eve into sin, preceded by that of Satan and his angels, and ending with the promise of salvation and a summary of Old Testament history. Milton's aim is bold: 'that to the height of this great argument, I may assert eternal Providence, and justify the ways of God to men' (1:24–26).

But what of its theological value today? The poem is to be commended for portraying clearly the biblical pattern of Creation-Fall-Redemption. That is, it recognizes that God's creation is itself good, but that the creation of beings with free will brings the possibility of evil. This happens with the fall both of Satan and his angels and of human beings. God acts in history to bring salvation to the human race. This broad picture is in line with the scheme of biblical theology. But Milton's poem spans hundreds of pages and says much more than this. Where the Bible says almost nothing (but not nothing) about the fall of Satan and relatively little about the fall of Adam and Eve, Milton goes into considerable detail about both. This reflects both the fact that he was writing a literary drama and the fact that he was the heir of many centuries of theological speculation on the theme. In the era of modern science, theology should hold fast to the basic biblical framework of Creation-Fall-Redemption, but this will inevitably be understood in a different way from Milton.

[Satan's evil aims]

1:156. Whereto with speedy words the Arch-fiend replied.
        'Fallen Cherub, to be weak is miserable
        Doing or Suffering: but of this be sure,
        To do ought good never will be our task,
        But ever to do ill our sole delight,
        As being the contrary to his high will
        Whom we resist. If then his Providence
        Out of our evil seek to bring forth good,
        Our labour must be to pervert that end,
        And out of good still to find means of evil.'

[Satan's remarks on leaving Heaven for Hell]

1:249. 'Farewell happy Fields
        Where Joy for ever dwells: Hail horrors, hail
        Infernal world, and thou profoundest Hell
        Receive thy new Possessor: One who brings
        A mind not to be changed by Place or Time.
        The mind is its own place, and in itself
        Can make a Heaven of Hell, a Hell of Heaven.
        What matter where, if I be still the same,
        And what I should be, all but less than he
        Whom Thunder hath made greater? Here at least
        We shall be free; the Almighty hath not built
        Here for his envy, will not drive us hence:
        Here we may reign secure, and in my choice
        To reign is worth ambition though in Hell:
        Better to reign in Hell, than serve in Heaven.

[Adam and Eve as created and unfallen]

4:285. . . . this Assyrian Garden, where the Fiend
        Saw undelighted all delight, all kind
        Of living Creatures new to sight and strange:
        Two of far nobler shape erect and tall,
        Godlike erect, with native Honour clad
        In naked Majesty seemed Lords of all,
        And worthy seemed, for in their looks Divine
        The image of their glorious Maker shone,
        Truth, Wisdom, Sanctitude severe and pure,

Severe, but in true filial freedom placed;
Whence true authority in men; though both
Not equal, as their sex not equal seemed;
For contemplation he and valour formed,
For softness she and sweet attractive Grace,
He for God only, she for God in him:
His fair large Front and Eye sublime declared
Absolute rule; and Hyacinthine Locks
Round from his parted forelock manly hung
Clustering, but not beneath his shoulders broad:
She as a veil down to the slender waist
Her unadorned golden tresses wore
Dishevelled, but in wanton ringlets waved
As the Vine curls her tendrils, which implied
Subjection, but required with gentle sway,
And by her yielded, by him best received,
Yielded with coy submission, modest pride,
And sweet reluctant amorous delay.
Nor those mysterious parts were then concealed,
Then was not guilty shame, dishonest shame
Of nature's works, honour dishonourable,
Sin-bred, how have ye troubled all mankind
With shows instead, mere shows of seeming pure,
And banished from man's life his happiest life,
Simplicity and spotless innocence.
So passed they naked on, nor shunned the sight
Of God or Angel, for they thought no ill:
So hand in hand they passed, the loveliest pair
That ever since in love's embraces met,
Adam the goodliest man of men since born
His Sons, the fairest of her Daughters Eve.

[Satan speaks of his plans for the human race]
4:366. 'Ah gentle pair, ye little think how nigh
Your change approaches, when all these delights
Will vanish and deliver ye to woe,
More woe, the more your taste is now of joy;
Happy, but for so happy ill secured
Long to continue, and this high seat your Heaven
Ill fenced for Heaven to keep out such a foe
As now is entered; yet no purposed foe

To you whom I could pity thus forlorn
Though I unpitied: League with you I seek,
And mutual amity so strait, so close,
That I with you must dwell, or you with me
Henceforth; my dwelling haply may not please
Like this fair Paradise, your sense, yet such
Accept your Maker's work; he gave it me,
Which I as freely give; Hell shall unfold,
To entertain you two, her widest Gates,
And send forth all her Kings; there will be room,
Not like these narrow limits, to receive
Your numerous offspring; if no better place,
Thank him who puts me loath to this revenge
On you who wrong me not for him who wronged.
And should I at your harmless innocence
Melt, as I do, yet public reason just,
Honour and Empire with revenge enlarged,
By conquering this new World, compels me now
To do what else though damned I should abhor.'
So spake the Fiend, and with necessity,
The Tyrant's plea, excused his devilish deeds.

[Satan tempts Eve]
9:664.   [Eve] scarce had said, though brief, when now more bold
The Tempter, but with show of Zeal and Love
To Man, and indignation at his wrong,
New part puts on, and as to passion moved,
Fluctuates disturbed, yet comely, and in act
Raised, as of some great matter to begin.
As when of old some Orator renowned
In Athens or free Rome, where Eloquence
Flourished, since mute, to some great cause addressed,
Stood in himself collected, while each part,
Motion, each act won audience ere the tongue,
Sometimes in height began, as no delay
Of Preface brooking through his Zeal of Right.
So standing, moving, or to height upgrown
The Tempter all impassioned thus began.
'O Sacred, Wise, and Wisdom-giving Plant,
Mother of Science, Now I feel thy Power
Within me clear, not only to discern

Things in their Causes, but to trace the ways
Of highest Agents, deemed however wise.
Queen of this Universe, do not believe
Those rigid threats of Death; ye shall not Die:
How should ye? by the Fruit? it gives you Life
To Knowledge? By the Threatener, look on me,
Me who have touched and tasted, yet both live,
And life more perfect have attained than Fate
Meant me, by venturing higher than my Lot.
Shall that be shut to Man, which to the Beast
Is open? or will God incense his ire
For such a pretty Trespass, and not praise
Rather your dauntless virtue, whom the pain
Of Death denounced, whatever thing Death be,
Deterred not from achieving what might lead
To happier life, knowledge of Good and Evil;
Of good, how just? of evil, if what is evil
Be real, why not known, since easier shunned?
God therefore cannot hurt ye, and be just;
Not just, not God; not feared then, nor obeyed:
Your fear itself of Death removes the fear.
Why then was this forbid? Why but to awe,
Why but to keep ye low and ignorant,
His worshippers; he knows that in the day
Ye Eat thereof, your Eyes that seem so clear,
Yet are but dim, shall perfectly be then
Opened and cleared, and ye shall be as Gods,
Knowing both Good and Evil as they know.
That ye should be as Gods, since I as Man,
Internal Man, is but proportion meet,
I of brute human, ye of human Gods.
So ye shall die perhaps, by putting off
Human, to put on Gods, death to be wished,
Though threatened, which no worse than this can bring
And what are Gods that Man may not become
As they, participating God-like food?
The Gods are first, and that advantage use
On our belief, that all from them proceeds,
I question it, for this fair Earth I see,
Warmed by the Sun, producing every kind,
Them nothing: If they all things, who enclosed

Knowledge of Good and Evil in this Tree,
That whoso eats thereof, forthwith attains
Wisdom without their leave? and wherein lies
The offence, that Man should thus attain to know?
What can your knowledge hurt him, or this Tree
Impart against his will if all be his?
Or is it envy, and can envy dwell
In heavenly breasts? these, these and many more
Causes import your need of this fair Fruit.
Goddess humane, reach then, and freely taste.'
He ended, and his words replete with guile
Into her heart too easy entrance won.

[Eve sins]
9:780. So saying, her rash hand in evil hour
Forth reaching to the Fruit, she plucked, she ate:
Earth felt the wound, and Nature from her seat
Sighing through all her Works gave signs of woe,
That all was lost.

Blaise Pascal, *Pensées* (1670)

Blaise Pascal was born in 1623 at Clermont-Ferrand, in France. When he was only three his mother died and he and his two sisters were educated by their father. He was an infant prodigy, especially in the area of maths and science. He designed and produced the first calculator (computer), paved the way for the invention of the barometer and pioneered the theory of probability. He demonstrated the existence of the vacuum in nature, favouring an experimental, inductive approach over the deductive approach of most of his contemporaries – such as the philosopher René Descartes, who claimed on the basis of pure reason that it was impossible for a vacuum to exist.

In 1646 Pascal came across the Jansenists. Jansenism was a seventeenth-century 'Puritan' movement within the Roman Catholic Church which aroused deep controversy, especially in France. Cornelius Jansen was the Roman Catholic bishop of Ypres. He was concerned that the Roman Catholic Church was becoming morally lax and was drifting away from Augustine's teaching on grace. He himself studied Augustine's works intensely and wrote a massive exposition of his teaching, entitled *Augustinus*, whose publication he prudently delayed until after his death in 1640. This met with immediate opposition from the Jesuits, the party most opposed to Augustinianism. They induced the pope in 1653 to condemn five propositions, allegedly drawn from the *Augustinus*, but this did not end the controversy. The Jansenists responded by accepting that the condemned propositions were heretical, but denying that Jansen had taught them. During Pascal's lifetime there was a bitter struggle between the Jesuits and the Jansenists, with the latter fighting for their survival.

Through the Jansenists, the Pascal family were converted to a more serious religious commitment. Blaise continued with his scientific pursuits. In 1651 his father died, and one of his sisters became a nun at Port Royal, the centre of Jansenism. Blaise was opposed to this at the time, but in 1654 he underwent a second conversion, a two-hour long mystical experience late one night, the so-called 'night of fire'. He wrote about this in his *Memorial*, which he carried with him to his death (*Pensées* 913, below). After his conversion, Pascal's links with Port Royal were strengthened. The year 1655 was a time of crisis for Jansenism. Antoine Arnauld, the leader of the movement, was on trial before the Sorbonne for his views.

Pascal's fame today rests on two works. From 1656 to 1657 he wrote nineteen satirical *Provincial Letters*, against the Jesuits. The anonymous author presents himself as a puzzled bystander writing about events at Paris to a country friend. In particular, he ridiculed the Jesuit doctrine of 'probabilism', whereby they were able to allow low moral standards. The doctrine simply stated that where there was a difference of opinion among moral theologians, the confessor is obliged to follow that opinion which most favours the sinner. Thus if one reputable authority (e.g. a Jesuit) held something not to be sin, the confessor was forbidden to impose a stricter view on the penitent, even if all other writers were united in condemning it as sin. This doctrine was originally designed to protect the penitent from over-harsh confessors who might on their own authority refuse absolution. But the Jesuits were using it to reduce to a bare minimum the definition of sin – because any action defended by any one authority, however outrageously, could no longer be treated as a sin.

The *Provincial Letters* make entertaining reading, but refer to a controversy long dead. Pascal's better-known work is his projected *Apology for the Christian Religion*. He did not live to complete this but left behind extensive fragments, some of which he had arranged under various headings. These were first published in 1670, after his death, with the title *Pensées (Thoughts)*. There are almost a thousand fragments, which vary in length from a few words to several pages. Two themes predominate, which Pascal himself identifies near the beginning. The first is the 'wretchedness of man without God' and that 'nature is corrupt' – this he sought to demonstrate from nature itself. The second is the 'happiness of man with God' – Pascal sought to demonstrate from Scripture that 'there is a Redeemer'. On the second theme his thoughts were not especially original and are considerably dated in the light of more recent biblical studies. On the first theme, however, his sayings have a considerable psychological and spiritual depth and his penetrating diagnosis of the human condition has rightly earned this work, fragmentary and largely disorganized though it may be, the status of a classic. Although his work was to have been an *Apology*, it is not a merely rational defence of the Christian faith. While recognizing the legitimate role of reason, he argued that revelation goes beyond, though not against, reason. His apologetic method consists as much in pointing to the wretchedness of the human condition as to the reasonableness of the Christian remedy. In a culture obsessed with human worth and self-esteem Pascal's work is a much needed corrective from the past.

———————————————————

131: Nothing jolts us more rudely than this doctrine [of original sin], and yet, but for this mystery, the most incomprehensible of all, we remain incomprehensible to ourselves. The knot of our condition was twisted and turned in that abyss, so that it is harder to conceive of man without this mystery than for man to conceive of it himself.

170: *Submission*. One must know when it is right to doubt, to affirm, to submit. Anyone who does otherwise does not understand the force of reason. Some men run counter to these three principles, either affirming that everything can be proved, because they know nothing about proof, or doubting everything, because they do not know when to submit, or always submitting, because they do not know when judgment is called for.

173: If we submit everything to reason our religion will be left with nothing mysterious or supernatural. If we offend the principles of reason our religion will be absurd and ridiculous.

183: Two excesses: to exclude reason, to admit nothing but reason.

185: Faith certainly tells us what the senses do not, but not the contrary of what they see; it is above, not against them.

188: Reason's last step is the recognition that there are an infinite number of things which are beyond it. It is merely feeble if it does not go as far as to realize that.

192: Knowing God without knowing our own wretchedness makes for pride. Knowing our own wretchedness without knowing God makes for despair. Knowing Jesus Christ strikes the balance because he shows us both God and our own wretchedness.

423: The heart has its reasons of which reason knows nothing: we know this in countless ways.

449: [Christianity] teaches men then these two truths alike: that there is a God, of whom men are capable, and that there is a corruption in nature which makes them unworthy. It is of equal importance to men to know each of these points: and it is equally dangerous for man to know God without knowing his own wretchedness as to know his wretchedness without knowing the Redeemer who can cure him. Knowing only one of these points leads either to the arrogance of the philosophers, who have known God but not their own wretchedness, or to the despair of the atheists, who know their own wretchedness without knowing their Redeemer.

471: For my part, I confess that as soon as the Christian religion reveals the principle that men are by nature corrupt and have fallen away from God, this opens one's eyes so that the mark of this truth is everywhere apparent: for nature is such that it points at every turn to a God who has been lost, both within man and without, and to a corrupt nature.

562: There are only two kinds of men: the righteous who think they are sinners and the sinners who think they are righteous.

617: Anyone who does not hate the self-love within him and the instinct which leads him to make himself into a God must be really blind. Who can fail to see that there is nothing so contrary to justice and truth? For it is false that we deserve this position and unjust and impossible to attain it, because everyone demands the same thing. We are thus born into an obviously unjust situation from which we cannot escape but from which we must escape.

However, no [other] religion has observed that this is a sin, that it is innate in us, or that we are obliged to resist it, let alone thought of providing a cure.

632: Man's sensitivity to little things and insensitivity to the greatest things are marks of a strange disorder.

695: Original sin is folly in the eyes of men, but it is put forward as such. You should therefore not reproach me for the unreasonable nature of this doctrine, because I put it forward as being unreasonable. But this folly is wiser than all men's wisdom, it is wiser than men [1 Corinthians 1:25]. For without it, what are we to say man is? His whole state depends on this imperceptible point. How could he have become aware of it through his reason, seeing that it is something contrary to reason and that his reason, far from discovering it by its own methods, draws away when presented with it?

737: We are usually convinced more easily by reasons we have found ourselves than by those which have occurred to others.

741: The adding-machine [like the computer today] produces effects closer to thought than anything done by the animals, but it does nothing to justify the assertion that it has a will like the animals.

792: I maintain that, if everyone knew what others said about him, there would not be four friends in the world; this is evident from the quarrels caused by occasional indiscreet disclosures.

913: [*Memorial*: Pascal's record of his conversion, 23 November 1654]
Fire
'God of Abraham, God of Isaac, God of Jacob,' not of philosophers and scholars.
Certainty, certainty, heartfelt, joy, peace.
God of Jesus Christ.
. . .
Jesus Christ.
I have cut myself off from him, shunned him, denied him, crucified him.
Let me never be cut off from him!

He can only be kept by the ways taught in the Gospel.
Sweet and total renunciation.
Total submission to Jesus Christ and my director.
Everlasting joy in return for one day's effort on earth.
I will not forget thy word [Psalm 119:16]. Amen

975: Men often take their imagination for their heart, and often believe they are converted as soon as they start thinking of becoming converted.

Philipp Jakob Spener, *Holy Desires*
(1675)

Philipp Jakob Spener was born in Alsace in 1635. He received a godly upbringing and went on to become a pastor. He was senior pastor at Frankfurt from 1666 and while there became the 'patriarch' or chief founder of Pietism. In 1686 he left Frankfurt to become court chaplain at Dresden and moved on from there in 1691 to be a pastor at Berlin. He died in 1705.

By the mid-seventeenth century, all was not well with Lutheranism. All citizens were baptized as infants and were therefore believed to be regenerate or 'born again'. All baptized Lutherans were considered to be Christians. But while everyone might belong to the church and receive instruction in Lutheran doctrine, there was a shortage of practical Christian living. It was this deficiency which Pietism sought to rectify. Spener set out his goals in a manifesto for pietist reform, his *Pia Desideria* or *Holy Desires* or Heartfelt Desire for a God-pleasing Reform of the True Evangelical Church, Together with Several Simple Christian Proposals Looking Toward this End, published in 1675. Spener was influenced by Johann Arndt, whose *True Christianity* (1606–9) paved the way for Pietism. *Holy Desires* was initially published as the preface to a volume of Arndt's sermons.

Holy Desires falls into three main parts: an account of the corrupt conditions of the church in Spener's time; the possibility of better conditions in the church and six proposals to correct conditions in the church. These proposals are:

1. 'A more extensive use of the Word of God among us;'

2. 'The establishment and the diligent exercise of the spiritual priesthood;'

3. The need to teach people that 'it is by no means enough to have knowledge of the Christian faith, for Christianity consists rather of practice';

4. 'We must beware how we conduct ourselves in religious controversies with unbelievers and heretics;'

5. 'That the office of the ministry be occupied by men who, above all, are themselves true Christians and, then, have the divine wisdom to guide others on the way of the Lord;'

6. 'That sermons be so prepared by all that their purpose (faith and its fruits) may be achieved in the hearers to the greatest possible degree.'

The Pietists stressed the importance of a living personal faith in Jesus Christ. It is not enough just to be a baptized church member, just to assent to Lutheran doctrine. We need to be born again, to be converted. (Spener did not deny the Lutheran doctrine that infants are born again in baptism, but he held that this grace is normally lost.) True Christianity is not just doctrine to be believed, it is an experience of the Holy Spirit in conversion and new life.

This stress on a living, personal faith did not lead Spener to regard sound doctrine as unimportant, but it did put it in its place. Better a Calvinist (or even a Roman Catholic!) with a living faith in Jesus Christ, than a strictly orthodox Lutheran without such faith. Pietism was a protest against the preoccupation of that time with the minor details of Lutheran orthodoxy. The reform of doctrine had led to an obsession with the minutiae of orthodoxy while the great need was for a reform of life.

Spener stressed the importance of Bible study. It was not sufficient merely to use the Bible to prove Lutheran doctrine and to score points in debate against the enemies of Lutheranism. We need the Holy Spirit to speak to our hearts through the Scriptures and to apply them to us personally. The Bible needs to be read and preached in a devotional way, leading to a changed lifestyle.

Spener lamented the number of unregenerate pastors whose lives did not exemplify what they taught. He urged that theological training should not be preoccupied with teaching the intricacies of Lutheran orthodoxy. It should aim at changing the lives of the students and preparing them to preach practically from the Bible and to care for others pastorally.

Spener introduced an early form of home Bible study group to further these aims. These brought together clergy and laity. Spener believed strongly in Luther's doctrine of the priesthood of all believers and the need for all Christians to exercise a spiritual ministry. Spener's most important convert was A. H. Francke (1663–1727), the other great leader of the early pietist movement. Francke was active mainly at Halle, where a new university was founded on pietist lines.

The influence of Pietism has been immense. It has remained a force within the Lutheran churches, especially in certain areas, such as Württemberg in southern Germany, and Norway. Spener's godson, Count Zinzendorf (1700–60), played a leading role in the Moravian church, the influence of which spread throughout the world. The Wesleys were deeply influenced by the Moravians, and through them the whole evangelical movement. Evangelicalism is to the Anglo-Saxon world what Pietism is to Lutheranism. Pietists, Moravians and Evangelicals have all played a leading role in the missionary movement.

Today 'pietist' has become almost entirely a derogatory word. The popular image of the Pietist is of someone who is excessively preoccupied with their own personal salvation, who sees salvation in terms of withdrawal from the world and inner peace of mind. Their aim is to save individuals, but they have no concern for society at large; they are so concerned about the world to come that they have little time for the needs of this world. It is true that Pietism has sometimes degenerated into this caricature, but this was not true of the original Pietists. The pietist and evangelical traditions, when they have been healthy and vigorous, have balanced the individual and the corporate, the this-worldly and the other-worldly.

———————————————

Salutation. Let us remember that in the last judgment we shall not be asked how learned we were and whether we displayed our learning before the world; to what extent we enjoyed the favour of men and knew how to keep it; with what honours we were exalted and how great a reputation in the world we left behind us; or how many treasures of earthly goods we amassed for our children and thereby drew a curse upon ourselves. Instead, we shall be asked how faithfully and with how childlike a heart we sought to further the kingdom of God; with how pure and godly a teaching and how worthy an example we tried to edify our hearers amid the scorn of the world, denial of self, taking up the cross, and imitation of our Saviour; with what zeal we opposed not only error but also wickedness of life; or with what constancy and cheerfulness we endured the persecution or adversity thrust upon us by the manifestly godless world or by false brethren, and amid such suffering praised our God.

Part 1. When men's minds are stuffed with such a theology which, while it preserves the foundation of faith from the Scriptures, builds on it with so much wood, hay and stubble of human inquisitiveness that the gold can no longer be seen, it becomes exceedingly difficult to grasp and find pleasure in the real simplicity of Christ and his teaching. This is so because men's taste becomes accustomed to the more charming things of reason, and after a while the simplicity of Christ and his teaching appears to be tasteless. Such knowledge, which remains without love, 'puffs up' [1 Corinthians 8:1]. It leaves man in his love of self; indeed, it fosters and strengthens such love more and more. Subtleties unknown to the Scriptures usually have their origin, in the case of those who introduce them, in a desire to exhibit their sagacity and their superiority over others, to have a great reputation, and to derive benefit therefrom in the world. Moreover, these subtleties are themselves of such a nature that they stimulate, in those who deal with them, not a true fear of God but a thirst for honour and other impulses which are unbecoming in a true Christian.

* * *

There are not a few who think that all that Christianity requires of them (and that having done this, they have done quite enough in their service of God) is that they be baptized, hear the preaching of God's Word, confess and receive absolution, and go to the Lord's Supper, no matter how their hearts are disposed at the time, whether or not there are fruits which follow, provided they at least live in such a way that the civil authorities do not find them liable to punishment.

Part 2. Let no one think that we here intend and seek too much. . . . If one seeks perfection one must leave this world and enter the world to come. Only there will one encounter something perfect; one cannot hope for it before then. To those who raise this kind of objection I reply thus: First, we are not forbidden to seek perfection, but we are urged on toward it. And how desirable it would be if we were to achieve it! Second, I cheerfully concede that here in this life we shall not manage that, for the farther a godly Christian advances, the more he will see that he lacks, and so he will never be farther removed from the illusion of perfection than when he tries hardest to reach it.

It is like the observation that as a rule those who have made the most progress in their studies are far less likely to consider themselves learned than others who have just begun to look into books a half-year ago. With the passing of time the former come to a fuller understanding of what true erudition means than they could have had before. So in spiritual matters, too, there is more cause to be concerned about beginners who think themselves to be perfect than about those who have already taken some steps in that direction.

Henry Scougal,
The Life of God in the Soul of Man
(1677)

Henry Scougal was born in 1650 and died in 1678. His father was a minister who became bishop of Aberdeen. Henry went to study at King's College, Aberdeen at the age of fifteen, graduated in 1668 and became a tutor the following year. In 1672 he was ordained and left Aberdeen to serve in a parish but two years later was recalled to become professor of divinity at Aberdeen. His aim in his teaching was to ensure that his lectures encouraged holy living as well as correct believing. He held the post for only four years before his early death from consumption at the age of twenty-eight.

During his brief life Scougal wrote a number of minor works, as well as the one brief but significant work for which he is famous. In 1677 he published *The Life of God in the Soul of Man, or the Nature and Excellency of the Christian Religion*, which became a devotional classic, prized beyond his own Episcopalian tradition. It is in three parts:

1. 'Religion, the Natural and Divine Life, and the Exemplification of Divine Life in our Blessed Saviour.' The root of the divine life is faith and it has four chief branches: 'love towards God', 'charity towards men', 'purity' and 'humility'.

2. 'The Excellency of Religion and Divine Love.' Scougal expounds the excellency and the advantages of each of the four chief branches.

3. 'The Difficulties and Duties of the Christian Life.' Scougal enumerates 'God's provision for the despondent' and 'the course we ought to take' to attain spiritual growth. He also proposes particular subjects of meditation designed to produce the four chief branches.

The Life of God in the Soul of Man made its mark upon the leaders of the Evangelical Revival in the following century. Susanna Wesley recommended it to her sons and it strongly influenced John in his early years at Oxford, together with Thomas à Kempis's *The Imitation of Christ* (see pages 186–89). Charles Wesley lent a copy to George Whitefield, who states that it showed him the nature of true religion and made him realize his need of the new birth. It is simply written and supremely practical and well deserves its status as a classic.

1:1. The Nature of True Religion

I cannot speak of religion but I must regret that among so many pretenders to it so few understand what it means, some placing it in the understanding, in orthodox notions and opinions; and all the account they can give of their religion is that they are of this or the other persuasion, and have joined themselves to one of those many sects whereinto Christendom is most unhappily divided. Others place it in the outward man, in a constant course of external duties and a model of performances. If they live peaceably with their neighbours, keep a temperate diet, observe the returns of worship, frequenting the church or their closet, and sometimes extend their hands to the relief of the poor, they think they have sufficiently acquitted themselves. Others again put all the religion in the affections, in rapturous hearts and ecstatic devotion; and all they aim at is to pray with passion, and think of heaven with pleasure, and to be affected with those kind and melting expressions wherewith they court their Saviour, till they persuade themselves they are mightily in love with him, and from thence assume a great confidence of their salvation, which they esteem the chief of Christian graces.

Thus are these things which have any resemblance of piety, and at the best are but means for obtaining it, or particular exercises of it, frequently mistaken for the whole of religion. Nay, sometimes wickedness and vice pretends to that name. I speak not now of those gross impieties wherewith the heathen were wont to worship their gods. There are but too many Christians who would consecrate their vices and follow their corrupt affections, whose rugged humour and sullen pride must pass for Christian severity, whose fierce wrath and bitter rage against their enemies must be called holy zeal, whose petulancy towards their superiors or rebellion against their governors must have the name of Christian courage and resolution.

But certainly religion is quite another thing and they who are acquainted with it will entertain far different thoughts and disdain all those shadows and false imitations of it. They know by experience that true religion is a union of the soul with God, a real participation of the divine nature, the very image of God drawn upon the soul or, in the Apostle's phrase, it is 'Christ formed within us' [Galatians 4:19]. Briefly, I know not how the nature of religion can be more fully expressed than by calling it a *divine life*.

2:3. Purity

a. Its excellency

That which I named as a third branch of religion was purity; and you may remember I described it to consist in a contempt of sensual pleasures and resoluteness to undergo those troubles and pains we may meet with in the performance of our duty. Now the naming of this may suffice to recommend it as a most noble and excellent quality. There is no slavery so base as that whereby a man becomes a drudge to his own lusts, nor any victory so glorious as that which is obtained over them. Never can that person be capable of anything that is noble or worthy, who is sunk in the gross and feculent [fetid] pleasures of sense or bewitched with the light and airy gratifications of fancy. But the religious soul is of a more sublime and divine temper. It knows it was made for higher things and scorns to step aside one foot out of the ways of holiness for the obtaining of any of these.

3:1. God's Provision for the Despondent
f. The need to bestir ourselves

Away then with all perplexing fears and desponding thoughts! To undertake vigorously and to rely confidently on the divine assistance is more than half the conquest. 'Let us arise and be doing and the Lord will be with us' [1 Chronicles 22:16]. It is true, religion in the souls of men is the immediate work of God and all our natural endeavours can neither produce it alone nor merit those supernatural aids by which it must be wrought. The Holy Ghost must come upon us and the power of the Highest must overshadow us, before that holy thing can be begotten and Christ be formed in us. But yet we must not expect that this whole work should be done without any concurring endeavours of ours. We must not lie loitering in the ditch and wait till Omnipotence pull us from thence. No, no: we must bestir ourselves and put forth ourselves in our utmost capacities and then we may hope that 'our labour shall not be vain in the Lord' [1 Corinthians 15:58].

John Bunyan, *The Pilgrim's Progress*
(1678)

John Bunyan was born in 1628 at Elstow (near Bedford), the son of a poor brazier or tinker. He served with the Parliamentary army from 1644 to 1646 or 1647. In 1649 he married the daughter of godly parents and through her began to seek after God. But it was only after several years of deep inner turmoil (described in his spiritual autobiography *Grace Abounding to the Chief of Sinners*) that he eventually came to find peace with God. He was greatly helped by John Gifford, the Independent pastor of St John's Church in Bedford. In 1653 Bunyan became a member of this congregation and before long began to preach. He was outstanding as a preacher – John Owen, one of the most learned men of the time, on being asked by Charles II why he listened to an uneducated tinker, replied: 'Could I possess the tinker's abilities for preaching, please your majesty, I would gladly relinquish all my learning.'

In 1660 the monarchy was restored, with the return of Charles II, and this meant persecution for those who would not conform to the new Anglican settlement. Bunyan was imprisoned that year for preaching and remained in jail almost continuously until 1672, because he would not undertake to cease preaching. He was also briefly imprisoned in 1677. It was while in prison that he wrote his best-known works, *Grace Abounding* and *Pilgrim's Progress*. He died in 1688, as the persecution of the dissenters was coming to an end.

Pilgrim's Progress is Bunyan's great masterpiece. It was published in 1678 and sold for eighteen pence. It has since been translated into about 100 different languages and has been printed countless times. In 1684 Bunyan published a second, not so well known, volume or part. This is the account of how Christian's wife and children embark on the same journey.

Although largely uneducated, Bunyan was a naturally gifted writer and produced one of the masterpieces of English literature. He took the perennial theme of the Christian life as a journey and dramatized this in narrative form. (Channel 4 produced an excellent televised version entitled 'Dangerous Journey', words taken from Bunyan's subtitle.) Christian (the pilgrim) sets out on a journey from the City of Destruction to the Celestial City. The progress of the Christian life is illustrated by the places on the way: such as The Slough of Despond, Vanity Fair, Doubting Castle. There is also encouragement and warning to be derived from the characters that Christian meets on the way: such as Obstinate, Pliable, Talkative, and godly characters such as Faithful and Hopeful. Bunyan describes the trials and the temptations, the joys and the comforts of the Christian life in a way that has appealed to many far removed from his particular Calvinist, Baptist tradition.

In *Grace Abounding* Bunyan described his own experience in very personal terms. It is highly introspective and involves his struggles with questions that plagued some people at that time, such as 'Am I elect?' and 'Have I committed the sin against the Holy Spirit?' The pattern of his conversion would be of direct relevance to only a few. Pilgrim's experience in *Pilgrim's Progress* is more straightforward, but still gruelling and heroic. His family's journey in Part 2 is easier, with less struggle prior to conversion and with a guide to direct them on their path. If the first part describes the 'heroic' Christian and is based on Bunyan's own experience, the second part describes the 'ordinary' Christian and is based more upon Bunyan's pastoral experience.

Pilgrim's Progress has also inspired a number of other works. Of particular interest is a short story by the nineteenth-century American writer Nathaniel Hawthorne, called *The Celestial Railway*, which effectively relates Bunyan's tale to our modern age, with its more liberal values.

As I walked through the wilderness of this world, I lighted on a certain place where there was a den. And I laid me down in that place to sleep and as I slept I dreamed a dream. I dreamed, and behold I saw a man clothed with rags, standing in a certain place with his face from his own house, a book in his hand and a great burden upon his back. I looked and saw him open the book and read therein. And as he read, he wept and trembled, and not being able longer to contain he brake out with a lamentable cry, saying, 'What shall I do?'

* * *

Now I saw in my dream that the highway up which Christian was to go was fenced on either side with a wall and that wall was called Salvation. Up this way, therefore, did burdened Christian run, but not without great difficulty because of the load on his back. He ran thus till he came at a place somewhat ascending; and upon that place stood a cross and a little below, in the bottom, a sepulchre. So I saw in my dream that just as Christian came up with the cross, his burden loosed from off his shoulders and fell from off his back, and began to tumble and so continued to do till it came to the mouth of the sepulchre, where it fell in and I saw it no more.

Then was Christian glad and lightsome and said with a merry heart, 'He hath given me rest by his sorrow, and life by his death.' Then he stood still a while to look and wonder; for it was very surprising to him that the sight of the cross should thus ease him of his burden. He looked, therefore, and looked again even till the springs that were in his head sent the waters down his cheeks. Now as he stood looking and weeping, behold, three Shining Ones came to him and saluted

him with, 'Peace be to thee.' So the first said to him, 'Thy sins be forgiven thee,'
the second stripped him of his rags and clothed him with change of raiment, the
third also set a mark on his forehead and gave him a roll with a seal upon it,
which he bid him look on as he ran and that he should give it in at the celestial
gate. So they went their way. Then Christian gave three leaps for joy and went on
singing.

* * *

So I saw in my dream, that [Christian and his companion] went on together till
they came in sight of the gate [to the Celestial City]. Now I further saw that
betwixt them and the gate was a river, but there was no bridge to go over and the
river was very deep. At the sight, therefore, of this river the pilgrims were much
stunned; but the men that went with them said, 'You must go through or you
cannot come at the gate.' . . . The pilgrims then, especially Christian, began to
despond in their mind and looked this way and that, but no way could be found
by them by which they might escape the river. Then they asked the men if the
waters were all of a depth. They said, 'No;' yet they could not help them in that
case for, said they, 'you shall find it deeper or shallower as you believe in the King
of the place.'

Then they addressed themselves to the water, and entering Christian began
to sink and crying out to his good friend Hopeful, he said, 'I sink in deep waters;
the billows go over my head; all his waves go over me.' Then said the other, 'Be of
good cheer, my brother. I feel the bottom and it is good.' Then said Christian, 'Ah!
my friend, the sorrows of death have compassed me about; I shall not see the land
that flows with milk and honey.' And with that a great darkness and horror fell
upon Christian, so that he could not see before him. Also here he in a great
measure lost his senses, so that he could neither remember nor orderly talk of any
of those sweet refreshments that he had met with in the way of his pilgrimage.
But all the words that he spoke still tended to discover that he had horror of mind,
and heart-fears that he should die in that river and never obtain entrance in at the
gate. Here also, as they that stood by perceived, he was much in the troublesome
thoughts of the sins that he had committed, both since and before he began to be
a pilgrim. . . .

Hopeful therefore here had much ado to keep his brother's head above
water; yea, sometimes he would be quite gone down, and then, ere a while, he
would rise up again half dead. Hopeful did also endeavour to comfort him, saying,
'Brother, I see the gate, and men standing by to receive us;' but Christian would
answer, 'It is you, it is you they wait for; for you have been hopeful ever since I
knew you.' 'And so have you,' said he to Christian. 'Ah, brother,' said he, 'surely
if I was right he would now arise to help me; but for my sins he hath brought me

into the snare and hath left me.' Then said Hopeful, 'My brother, you have quite forgot the text where it is said of the wicked, "There are no bands in their death, but their strength is firm; they are not troubled as other men, neither are they plagued like other men" [Psalm 73:4–5]. These troubles and distresses that you go through in these waters are no sign that God hath forsaken you; but are sent to try you, whether you will call to mind that which heretofore you have received of his goodness and live upon him in your distresses.'

Then I saw in my dream that Christian was in a muse a while. To whom also Hopeful added these words, 'Be of good cheer, Jesus Christ maketh thee whole.' And with that Christian brake out with a loud voice, 'Oh, I see him again and he tells me, "When thou passest through the waters, I will be with thee; and through the rivers, they shall not overflow thee"' [Isaiah 43:2]. Then they both took courage and the enemy was after that as still as a stone, until they were gone over. Christian, therefore, presently found ground to stand upon and so it followed that the rest of the river was but shallow. Thus they got over. . . .

Now while I was gazing upon all these things, I turned my head to look back and saw Ignorance come up to the river side; but he soon got over, and that without half the difficulty which the other two men met with. For it happened that there was then in that place one Vain-Hope, a ferryman, that with his boat helped him over; so he, as the other I saw, did ascend the hill to come up to the gate; only he came alone, neither did any man meet him with the least encouragement. When he was come up to the gate, he looked up to the writing that was above and then began to knock, supposing that entrance should have been quickly administered to him; but he was asked by the men that looked over the top of the gate, 'Whence come you? and what would you have?' He answered, 'I have ate and drank in the presence of the King and he has taught in our streets.' Then they asked him for his certificate, that they might go in and show it to the King: so he fumbled in his bosom for one and found none. Then said they, 'Have you none?' but the man answered never a word. So they told the King, but he would not come down to see him, but commanded the two shining ones, that conducted Christian and Hopeful to the city, to go out and take Ignorance and bind him hand and foot and have him away. Then they took him up and carried him through the air to the door that I saw in the side of the hill and put him in there. Then I saw that there was a way to hell even from the gate of heaven, as well as from the City of Destruction. So I awoke and behold it was a dream.

Brother Lawrence, *The Practice of the Presence of God* (1691)

Nicholas Herman was born in 1611 in the French province of Lorraine. After some eighteen years of military service he became a lay brother in the Discalced Carmelite order at Paris, taking the name Brother Lawrence. He served as a humble cook for thirty years until forced by blindness to retire from this duty. He died in 1691.

Brother Lawrence learned to retain a sense of God's presence and communion with him in the midst of his busy duties in the kitchen. He wrote about this in a few letters to various people and in some spiritual notes and maxims. After his death these were gathered together by Abbé Joseph de Beaufort, the vicar general of the cardinal archbishop of Paris, and published in 1691. He also included summaries of some conversations that he had had with Lawrence in 1666 and 1667. In due course this collection received the appropriate title of *The Practice of the Presence of God*.

The Practice of the Presence of God immediately achieved popularity and rapidly came to be seen as a spiritual classic by Catholics and Protestants alike. Lawrence's great strength is his ability to express profound truths in very simple language. He speaks from his own experience about the way to attain an awareness of the presence of God even in the hustle and bustle of an active life.

Letter 5: To a Religious

I have not found my manner of life covered in books so, although I have no difficulty about it, yet for greater security I should be glad to know your thoughts about it. In a conversation some days ago with a person of piety, he told me that the spiritual life was a life of grace, which begins with servile fear, is increased by the hope of eternal life and is consummated by pure love; and that each of these states had its different stages, by which one arrives at last at that blessed consummation.

I have not followed all these stages. On the contrary, from I know not what instincts, I found they discouraged me. It was for this reason that, at my entrance into religion, I resolved to give myself up to God, as the best satisfaction I could make for my sins, and for the love of him to renounce all. For the first years during the time set apart for devotion I commonly meditated on death, judgment, hell, heaven and my sins. I continued thus some years applying my mind carefully for the rest of the day (even in the midst of my work) to the presence of God, whom I considered always as with me, often as in me.

At length I came insensibly to do the same thing during my set time of prayer, which caused in me great delight and consolation. This practice produced in me so high an esteem for God, that faith alone was capable to satisfy me in that point. That is how I began. And yet I must tell you that for the first ten years I suffered much: the fear that I was not as devoted to God as I wished to be, the constant thought of my past sins and the great unmerited favours of God to me, were the matter and source of my sufferings. During this time I repeatedly fell and rose again. It seemed to me that creatures, reason and God himself were against me and that only faith was for me. I was troubled sometimes with thoughts that it was presumptuous to believe that I had received at once such favours which others attained with difficulty; at other times that it was a wilful delusion, and that there was no salvation for me.

When I was resigned to end my days in these troubles (which did not at all diminish my trust in God, but served only to increase my faith) I found myself changed all at once. And my soul, which till that time was troubled, felt a profound inward peace, as if she were in her centre and place of rest. Ever since that time I walk before God simply, in faith, with humility and with love, trying hard to do nothing and think nothing that would displease him. I hope that when I have done what I can, he will do with me what he pleases.

I cannot express what passes in me at present. I have no pain or difficulty about my state because I have no will but that of God, which I endeavour to fulfil in all things. I am so resigned to it that I would not pick up a straw from the ground against his order or from any other motive than sheer love to him. I have quitted all forms of devotion and set prayers except those to which my state obliges me. And I make it my business only to remain in his holy presence by a simple attentiveness and a general fond regard to God. This I may call an actual presence of God – or, to speak better, a habitual, silent and secret conversation of the soul with God. It causes in me inward joys and raptures, which sometimes also appear outwardly. They are so great that I am forced to use means to moderate them and prevent them appearing to others.

In short, I am assured beyond all doubt that my soul has been with God above these thirty years. I pass over many things lest I bore you, but I think it proper to inform you how I consider myself before God, whom I behold as my King. I consider myself as the most wretched of men, full of sores and corruption, who has committed all sorts of crimes against his King. Touched with remorse, I confess to him all my wickedness, I ask his forgiveness, I abandon myself in his hands, that he may do what he pleases with me. This King, full of mercy and goodness, far from chastising me embraces me with love, makes me eat at his table, serves me with his own hands and gives me the key of his treasures. He converses and delights himself with me incessantly, in a thousand and a thousand ways, and treats me in all respects as his favourite. It is thus I consider myself from time to time in his holy presence.

My most usual method is this simple attentiveness and such a general passionate regard to God, to whom I find myself often attached with greater sweetness and delight than that of an infant at its mother's breast – so that, if I dare use the expression, I should choose to call this state the breasts of God because of the inexpressible sweetness which I taste and experience there. If sometimes my thoughts wander from it by necessity or infirmity, I am presently recalled by inward motions, so charming and delicious that I am ashamed to mention them. I desire your reverence to reflect rather upon my great wretchedness, of which you are fully informed, than upon the great favours which God does me, all unworthy and ungrateful as I am.

As for my set hours of prayer, they are only a continuation of the same exercise. Sometimes I consider myself there as a stone before a mason, from which he is to make a statue. Presenting myself thus before God, I desire him to make his perfect image in my soul and render me entirely like himself. At other times, when I apply myself to prayer, I feel all my spirit and all my soul lift itself up without any care or effort of mine; and so it continues as it were suspended and firmly fixed in God, as in its centre and place of rest.

I know that some charge this state with inactivity, delusion, and self-love. I confess that it is a holy inactivity and would be a happy self-love, if the soul in that state were capable of it, because while she is in this repose she cannot be disturbed by such acts as she was formerly accustomed to. Previously they helped her support, but now they would rather hinder than assist her. Yet I cannot bear that this state should be called delusion, because the soul which thus enjoys God desires in it nothing but him. If this be delusion in me it is for God to remedy it. Let him do what he pleases with me, I desire only him and to be wholly devoted to him.

You will, however, oblige me in sending me your opinion, for which I always have great respect, for I have a singular esteem for your reverence, and am yours in our Lord.

William Law, *A Serious Call to a Devout and Holy Life* (1728)

William Law was born in 1686 in the village of King's Cliffe in Northamptonshire. He studied at Emmanuel College, Cambridge where he became a fellow in 1711. The same year he was ordained to the ministry. In 1716, however, Law was deprived of his fellowship because he was unwilling to swear an oath of allegiance to King George I, believing that the Stuarts were the legitimate kings and that James II had been illegally deposed in the Glorious Revolution of 1688. This was the end of Law's public life.

For ten years (1727–37) Law took up a post as tutor to the Gibbon family, tutoring the father of the famous historian Edward Gibbon. Around 1740 he returned to the village of his birth, entering into 'semi-monastic retirement' in a small community with two women, one being the sister of his former pupil. There he remained until his death in 1761, living an ordered and austere life.

Law is famous above all for his *Serious Call*, written in 1728. It has been claimed that its influence is second only to Bunyan's *Pilgrim's Progress* (see pages 339–42) among English post-Reformation writings. Like Bunyan, Law illustrates his points by portraying specific people as examples. John and Charles Wesley were influenced by it in their early years. In the mid 1730s Law began to read the works of Jakob Boehme (1575–1624), a heterodox German Lutheran mystic. Boehme's influence is seen in his later writings, such as his *Spirit of Prayer* (1749, 1750) and *Spirit of Love* (1752, 1754). These writings did not meet with the approval of many of the admirers of his *Serious Call*, such as John Wesley.

The *Serious Call* is a sustained attack on nominal Christianity. He mocks the idea that religious practices suffice to make one a Christian. Being a Christian implies submitting to God in the whole of one's life, in the 'secular' as well as the 'religious' realm. His expectations are demanding and while he concedes that the genuine Christian will commit sin he is unwilling to accommodate anything less than a firm intention and resolve to do God's will.

Law is strong on the law, on the challenge of discipleship, on the call to sanctification. His book is after all, as the title states, a call to 'a devout and holy life', a call much needed by the church today. But Law is weak on the gospel, on the grace of God, on the gift of justification. He taught that we have a right to expect mercy only for sins arising from 'unavoidable weaknesses and infirmities', not for those which involve a lack of intention on our part. Again, a careless life is 'unworthy of the mercy of God' (chapter 3). It is vital to hold together the free gift of forgiveness and the demand of discipleship and Law is weak here. While so many today offer the former without the latter, Law is in danger of the opposite. Yet as a corrective to today's emphasis his work has a real value.

Law has also been criticized for seeing all activities as either virtue or vice, leaving no room for innocent relaxation or entertainment. As a modern interpreter puts it, 'the bow must always be taut, never relaxed'. This omission, by no means peculiar to Law, may be acceptable for those seeking to live in semi-monastic retirement, but is a serious weakness if one seeks to advise those living in the world. Similarly, for Law learning was suspect and culture was seen as dangerous.

Chapter 1: Concerning the nature and extent of Christian devotion

Devotion is neither private nor public prayer; but prayers, whether private or public, are particular parts or instances of devotion. Devotion signifies a life given or devoted to God. He therefore is the devout man, who lives no longer to his own will, or the way and spirit of the world, but to the sole will of God, who considers God in everything, who serves God in everything, who makes all the parts of his common life parts of piety by doing everything in the name of God and under such rules as are conformable to his glory. . . .

It is for want of knowing, or at least considering, this that we see such a mixture of ridicule in the lives of many people. You see them strict as to some times and places of devotion, but when the service of the church is over they are but like those that seldom or never come there. . . . This is the reason why they are the jest and scorn of careless and worldly people – not because they are really devoted to God but because they appear to have no other devotion but that of occasional prayers. . . .

Is it not therefore exceeding strange that people should place so much piety in the attendance upon public worship, concerning which there is not one precept of our Lord's to be found, and yet neglect these common duties of our ordinary life, which are commanded in every page of the Gospel? . . .

If self-denial be a condition of salvation, all that would be saved must make it a part of their ordinary life. If humility be a Christian duty, then the common life of a Christian is to be a constant course of humility in all its kinds. If poverty of spirit be necessary, it must be the spirit and temper of every day of our lives. If we are to relieve the naked, the sick and the prisoner, it must be the common charity of our lives as far as we can render ourselves able to perform it. If we are to love our enemies, we must make our common life a visible exercise and demonstration of that love. . . . If we are to follow Christ, it must be in our common way of spending every day.

Chapter 2: An inquiry into the reason why the generality of Christians fall so far short of the holiness and devotion of Christianity

It may now be reasonably inquired how it comes to pass that the lives even of the better sort of people are thus strangely contrary to the principles of Christianity. . . .

Now the reason of common swearing is this: it is because men have not so much as the intention to please God in all their actions. For let a man but have so much piety as to intend to please God in all the actions of his life, as the happiest and best thing in the world, and then he will never swear more. It will be as impossible for him to swear, whilst he feels this intention within himself, as it is impossible for a man that intends to please his prince to go up and abuse him to his face. . . .

Here, therefore, let us judge ourselves sincerely. Let us not vainly content ourselves with the common disorders of our lives, the vanity of our expenses, the folly of our diversions, the pride of our habits, the idleness of our lives and the wasting of our time, fancying that these are such imperfections as we fall into through the unavoidable weakness and frailty of our natures. But let us be assured that these disorders of our common life are owing to this, that we have not so much Christianity as to intend to please God in all the actions of our life, as the best and happiest thing in the world. So that we must not look upon ourselves in a state of common and pardonable imperfection, but in such a state as wants [i.e. lacks] the first and most fundamental principle of Christianity, viz. an intention to please God in all our actions.

Chapter 4: We can please God in no state or employment of life but by intending and devoting it all to his honour and glory

As a good Christian should consider every place as holy because God is there, so he should look upon every part of his life as a matter of holiness because it is to be offered unto God. . . .

Men of worldly business, therefore, must not look upon themselves as at liberty to live to themselves, to sacrifice to their own humours and tempers, because their employment is of a worldly nature. But they must consider that, as the world and all worldly professions as truly belong to God as persons and things that are devoted to the altar, so it is as much the duty of men in worldly business to live wholly unto God as it is the duty of those who are devoted to divine service. . . .

If, therefore, we desire to live unto God, it is necessary to bring our whole life under this law: to make his glory the sole rule and measure of our acting in every employment of life. For there is no other true devotion but this of living devoted to God in the common business of our lives. . . .

If a glutton was to say, in excuse of his gluttony, that he only eats such things as it is lawful to eat, he would make as good an excuse for himself as the greedy, covetous, ambitious tradesman that should say he only deals in lawful business. For as a Christian is not only required to be honest but to be of a Christian spirit, and make his life an exercise of humility, repentance and heavenly affection, so all tempers that are contrary to these are as contrary to Christianity as cheating is contrary to honesty.

Chapter 6: Containing the great obligations, and the great advantages of making a wise and religious use of our estates and fortunes

I have quoted this passage [Matthew 25:31–46] at length, because if one looks at the way of the world one would hardly think that Christians had ever read this part of Scripture. For what is there in the lives of Christians that looks as if their salvation depended upon these good works? And yet the necessity of them is here asserted in the highest manner and pressed upon us by a lively description of the glory and terrors of the day of judgment.

Some people, even of those who may be reckoned virtuous Christians, look upon this text only as a general recommendation of occasional works of charity – whereas it shows the necessity not only of occasional charities now and then, but the necessity of such an entire charitable life as is a continual exercise of all such works of charity, as we are able to perform.

You own that you have no title to salvation if you have neglected these good works, because such persons as have neglected them are, at the last day, to be placed on the left hand and banished with a 'Depart, ye cursed.' There is, therefore, no salvation but in the performance of these good works. Who is it, therefore, that may be said to have performed these good works? Is it he that has some time assisted a prisoner, or relieved the poor or sick? This would be as absurd as to say that he had performed the duties of devotion who had some time said his prayers.

Philip Doddridge, *The Rise and Progress of Religion* (1745)

Philip Doddridge was born in London in 1702, the twentieth child of his parents. The family had Puritan roots, his grandfather having like Richard Baxter been expelled from his ministry for refusing to conform to the 1662 Act of Uniformity. He was educated at the Dissenting Academy (a place for Nonconformists to study, the universities of Oxford and Cambridge being open to Anglicans only) at Kibworth, a few miles north west of Market Harborough. He then became a minister at Kibworth from 1723 to 1729. In that year he became principal of an academy at Market Harborough, which he then transferred the short distance south to Northampton on becoming minister there. For the remaining years of his life, from 1729 till his death from tuberculosis in 1751, he combined ministry of the Independent Church at Northampton with leadership of the academy. He devoted these years to training generations of Nonconformist ministers. One of his innovations was to lecture in English rather than Latin. He was competent in maths and physics as well as theology and taught and presented papers on these subjects. He was also noted as a philanthropist and pioneered overseas mission.

Doddridge, like Brother Lawrence as described in his *Practice of the Presence of God* (see pages 343–45), sought to enjoy communion with God:

> *When I awake in the morning, which is always before it is light, I address myself to him and converse with him, speak to him while I am lighting my candle and putting on my clothes, and have often more delight before I come out of my chamber, though it hardly be quarter of an hour after my awaking, than I have enjoyed for whole days, perhaps weeks of my life. He meets me in my study, in secret, in family devotions.*

Some of Doddridge's hymns are still sung – especially 'O happy day, that fixed my choice' and 'Hark the glad sound! The Saviour comes'. But he is best known today for his book *The Rise and Progress of Religion*, which was first published in 1745 and has been translated into many languages. The idea for the book came from the hymn-writer Isaac Watts, who had planned to write the book himself. When ill health prevented this Watts encouraged Doddridge to take on the project. It was a highly influential book leading to the conversion of many, including William Wilberforce.

The Rise and Progress is addressed to the nominal Christian, a term that in Doddridge's day would describe a substantial proportion of the populace of England.

Each of the thirty chapters concludes with a prayer, which helps to apply the teaching to the heart and will of the reader and not just to the mind. His aim (as described in his summary of the book below) was to lead those who were unconcerned about spiritual matters to an awareness of their sin and guilt before God, and thence to a grasp and acceptance of the good news of the gospel.

―――――――――――

Chapter 1: The Introduction to the Work, with Some General Account of its Design

7. In forming my general plan, I have been solicitous that this little treatise might, if possible, be useful to all its readers, and contain something suitable to each. I will therefore take the man and the Christian in a great variety of circumstances. I will first suppose myself addressing one of the vast number of thoughtless creatures who have hitherto been utterly unconcerned about religion, and will try what can be done, by all plainness and earnestness of address, to awaken him from this fatal lethargy, to a care (chapter 2), an affectionate and an immediate care about it (chapter 3). I will labour to fix a deep and awful conviction of guilt upon his conscience (chapter 4), and to strip him of his vain excuses and his flattering hopes (chapter 5). I will read to him, O! that I could fix on his heart that sentence, that dreadful sentence, which a righteous and an Almighty God hath denounced against him as a sinner (chapter 6), and endeavour to show him in how helpless a state he lies under this condemnation, as to any capacity he has of delivering himself (chapter 7). But I do not mean to leave any in so terrible a situation: I will joyfully proclaim the glad tidings of pardon and salvation by Christ Jesus our Lord, which is all the support and confidence of my own soul (chapter 8). And then I will give some general view of the way by which this salvation is to be obtained (chapter 9); urging the sinner to accept of it as affectionately as I can (chapter 10); though nothing can be sufficiently pathetic, where, as in this matter, the life of an immortal soul is in question.

8. Too probable it is that some will, after all this, remain insensible; and therefore that their sad case may not encumber the following articles, I shall here take a solemn leave of them (chapter 11); and then shall turn and address myself as compassionately as I can, to a most contrary character; I mean, to a soul overwhelmed with a sense of the greatness of its sins, and trembling under the burden, as if there were no more hope for him in God (chapter 12). And that nothing may be omitted which may give solid peace to the troubled spirit, I shall endeavour to guide its inquiries as to the evidences of sincere repentance and faith (chapter 13); which will be farther illustrated by a more particular view of

the several branches of the Christian temper, such as may serve at once to assist the reader in judging what he is, and to show him what he should labour to be (chapter 14). This will naturally lead to a view of the need we have of the influences of the blessed Spirit to assist us in the important and difficult work of the true Christian, and of the encouragement we have to hope for such divine assistance (chapter 15). In an humble dependence on which, I shall then enter on the consideration of several cases which often occur in the Christian life, in which particular addresses to the conscience may be requisite and useful.

9. As some peculiar difficulties and discouragements attend the first entrance on a religious course, it will here be our first care to animate the young convert against them (chapter 16). And that it may be done more effectually, I shall urge a solemn dedication of himself to God (chapter 17), to be confirmed by entering into a communion of the church, and an approach to the sacred table (chapter 18). That these engagements may be more happily fulfilled, we shall endeavour to draw a more particular plan of that devout, regular and accurate course, which ought daily to be attended to (chapter 19). And because the idea will probably rise so much higher than what is the general practice, even of good men, we shall endeavour to persuade the reader to make the attempt, hard as it may seem (chapter 20); and shall caution him against various temptations, which might otherwise draw him aside to negligence and sin (chapter 21).

10. Happy will it be for the reader, if these exhortations and cautions be attended to with becoming regard; but as it is, alas! too probable that, notwithstanding all, the infirmities of nature will sometimes prevail, we shall consider the case of deadness and languor in religion, which often steals upon us by sensible degrees (chapter 22); from whence there is too easy a passage to that terrible one of a return into known and deliberate sin (chapter 23). And as the one or the other of these tends in a proportionable degree to provoke the blessed God to hide his face, and his injured Spirit to withdraw, that melancholy condition will be taken into particular survey (chapter 24). I shall then take notice also of the case of great and heavy afflictions in life (chapter 25), a discipline which the best of men have reason to expect, especially when they backslide from God and yield to their spiritual enemies.

11. Instances of this kind will, I fear, be too frequent; yet, I trust, there will be many others, whose path, like the dawning light, will 'shine more and more unto the perfect day' (Proverbs 4:18). And therefore we shall endeavour, in the best manner we can, to assist the Christian in passing a true judgment on the growth of grace in his heart (chapter 26), as we had done before in judging of its sincerity. And as nothing conduces more to the advancement of grace than the lively

exercise of love to God, and a holy joy in him, we shall here remind the real Christian of those mercies which tend to excite that love and joy (chapter 27); and in the view of them to animate him to those vigorous efforts of usefulness in life, which so well become his character, and will have so happy an efficacy in brightening his crown (chapter 28). Supposing him to act accordingly, we shall then labour to illustrate and assist the delight with which he may look forward to the awful solemnities of death and judgment (chapter 29). And shall close the scene by accompanying him, as it were, to the nearest confines of that dark valley through which he is to pass to glory; giving him such directions as may seem most subservient to his honouring God and adorning religion by his dying behaviour (chapter 30). Nor am I without a pleasing hope, that, through the Divine blessing and grace, I may be, in some instances, so successful as to leave those triumphing in the views of judgment and eternity, and glorifying God by a truly Christian life and death, whom I found trembling in the apprehensions of future misery; or, perhaps, in a much more dangerous and miserable condition than that I mean, entirely forgetting the prospect, and sunk in the most stupid insensibility of those things, for an attendance to which the human mind was formed, and in comparison of which all the pursuits of this transitory life are emptier than wind and lighter than a feather.

Jonathan Edwards,
The Religious Affections (1746)

Jonathan Edwards was born in 1703 at East Windsor, Connecticut. In 1716 he went to Yale College as a student and later became a tutor there. While he was religious from his youth, he had in the early 1720s a conversion experience which brought home to him in a deeper way the sovereignty and the grace of God. In 1727 he became minister of the Congregational Church at Northampton in Massachusetts, in succession to his grandfather, Solomon Stoddard. During Edwards's time at Northampton there was revival in the parish – in 1734 or 1735 arising from his own preaching, and from 1740 arising out of the ministry of George Whitefield in New England. But Edwards's relationship with his congregation was not wholly satisfactory. He sought to tighten the requirements for membership, which had been relaxed by his grandfather, and as a result was dismissed by the congregation in 1750. The following year he went to Stockbridge as a missionary to the Native Americans and while there wrote a number of his greatest works. In reaching out to the Native Americans he was following the example of David Brainerd, whose *Life and Diary* he had edited in 1749 (see pages 359–62). In 1757 he was invited to be president of the College of New Jersey (now Princeton University) and reluctantly accepted. On his arrival in 1758 he was inoculated against smallpox, because of an epidemic, but died soon after from the side effects.

Edwards has been called the greatest American philosopher, largely on the basis of his *Freedom of the Will*, published in 1754. He was the father of New England Theology – a leading exponent of which was his son Jonathan Edwards Junior (1745–1801). In due course this gave birth to New Haven Theology, as seen in Charles Finney.

Jonathan Edwards was both a defender and a critic of the revivals of his time. In 1741, at Enfield, Connecticut, he preached a notorious sermon on 'Sinners in the Hands of an Angry God'. This sermon, in which he laid especial stress on God's wrath, was one of those which sparked off revival.

The God that holds you over the pit of hell, much as one holds a spider or some loathsome insect over the fire, abhors you and is dreadfully provoked. His wrath towards you burns like fire; he looks upon you as worthy of nothing else, but to be cast into the fire; he is of purer eyes than to bear to have you in his sight; you are ten thousand times more abominable in his eyes than the most hateful venomous

serpent is in ours. You have offended him infinitely more than ever a stubborn
rebel did his prince – and yet it is nothing but his hand that holds you from
falling into the fire every moment.

In 1737 he wrote *A Faithful Narrative* in which he describes the effects of the earlier revival. But as time went by he discovered that not all of the conversions during the revival were genuine – some of those who professed conversion soon lapsed into their old godless ways. This led Edwards to preach on the subject in 1742 and 1743 and to develop these sermons into a book, his *Treatise Concerning the Religious Affections*, published in 1746. Here he examined the nature of true religion, a question which he deems to be most important:

> *There is no question whatsoever that is of greater importance to mankind and*
> *what is more concerns every individual person to be well resolved in, than this:*
> *What are the distinguishing qualifications of those that are in favour with God,*
> *and entitled to his eternal rewards? Or, which comes to the same thing, What is*
> *the nature of true religion? And wherein do lie the distinguishing notes of that*
> *virtue and holiness that is acceptable in the sight of God? (Author's Preface)*

Against the rationalist opponents of the revivals, Edwards maintains that true religion lies not merely in the mind but chiefly in the 'affections' (the heart, inclination, will). But against uncritical supporters of the revivals, he points out that not all religious affections are an evidence of God's grace. They can be fervent, lead to an outward change of life, lead to confidence before God and to moving testimonies – yet without there being a true change of heart. In particular, Edwards devotes the twelve chapters of Part 2 to listing signs which can be present without there being a true work of God's grace:

1. 'That religious affections are very great or raised very high;'

2. 'That they have great effects on the body;'

3. 'That they cause those who have them to be fluent, fervent, and abundant, in talking of the things of religion;'

4. 'That persons did not excite them of their own contrivance and by their own strength;'

5. 'That they come with texts of Scripture, remarkably brought to the mind;'

6. 'That there is an appearance of love in them;'

7. 'Persons having religious affections of many kinds, accompanying one another;'

8. 'That comforts and joys seem to follow awakenings and convictions of conscience, in a certain order;'

9. 'That they dispose persons to spend much time in religion, and to be zealously engaged in the external duties of worship;'

10. 'That they much dispose persons with their mouths to praise and glorify God;'

11. 'That they make persons that have them exceeding confident that what they experience is divine, and that they are in a good estate;'

12. 'That the outward manifestations of them, and the relation persons give of them, are very affecting and pleasing to the godly.'

Edwards is warning people not to derive assurance of salvation from the presence of these signs and also warning against a superficial reading of the revival that assumed that all whose emotions were aroused were true Christians. He then devotes the twelve chapters of Part 3 to listing signs that are evidence of a true work of God:

1. 'Truly gracious affections arise from divine influences and operations on the heart;'

2. 'Their ground is the excellent nature of divine things, not self-interest;'

3. 'They are founded on the loveliness of the moral excellency of divine things;'

4. 'They arise from the mind's being enlightened to understand or apprehend divine things;'

5. 'They are attended with a conviction of the reality and certainty of divine things;'

6. 'They are attended with evangelical humiliation;'

7. 'They are attended with a change of nature;'

8. 'They are attended with the lamblike, dovelike spirit and temper of Jesus Christ;'

9. 'They are attended with a Christian tenderness of spirit;'

10. 'They have beautiful symmetry and proportion;'

11. 'The higher they are raised, the more is a longing of soul after spiritual attainments increased;'

12. 'They have their exercise and fruit in Christian practice.'

Edwards's book is a valuable corrective to those who have a superficial idea of what is involved in conversion and who are too ready to assume the genuineness of a conversion on an inadequate basis. It is wrong, however, to seek assurance of salvation by an introspective self-examination looking for the twelve signs. Such a procedure will lead either to loss of assurance or to a Pharisaic self-confidence. The signs are a valuable secondary test, but the foundation of assurance must remain Christ and the promises of the gospel.

Edwards's book has much to say to the issues raised by the modern charismatic movement. He wholeheartedly approves of a felt and experienced 'heart religion', but warns powerfully about the dangers of being misled by a superficial emotionalism.

———

1:2:2. The Author of the human nature has not only given affections to men, but has made them very much the spring of men's actions. As the affections do not only necessarily belong to the human nature, but are a very great part of it; so (inasmuch as by regeneration persons are renewed in the whole man, and sanctified throughout) holy affections do not only necessarily belong to true religion, but are a very great part of it. And as true religion is of a practical nature, and God hath so constituted the human nature, that the affections are very much the spring of men's actions, this also shows, that true religion must consist very much in the affections. . . .

As in worldly things worldly affections are very much the spring of men's motion and action; so in religious matters the spring of their actions is very much religious affections. He that has doctrinal knowledge and speculation only, without affection, never is engaged in the business of religion.

1:2:3. Nothing is more manifest in fact, than that the things of religion take hold of men's souls no further than they affect them. There are multitudes that often hear the word of God, and therein hear of those things that are infinitely great and important, and that most nearly concern them, and all that is heard seems to be wholly ineffectual upon them, and to make no alteration in their disposition or behaviour; and the reason is, they are not affected with what they hear. . . .

I am bold to assert that there never was any considerable change wrought in the mind or conversation of any person, by anything of a religious nature that ever he read, heard or saw, who had not his affections moved. Never was a natural man engaged earnestly to seek his salvation; never were any such brought to cry after wisdom, and lift up their voice for understanding, and to wrestle with God in prayer for mercy; and never was one humbled, and brought to the foot of God, from anything that ever he heard or imagined of his own unworthiness and deserving of God's displeasure; nor was ever one induced to fly for refuge unto Christ, while his heart remained unaffected. Nor was there ever a saint awakened out of a cold, lifeless flame, or recovered from a declining state in religion, and brought back from a lamentable departure from God, without having his heart affected. In a word, there never was anything considerable brought to pass in the heart or life of any man living, by the things of religion, that had not his heart deeply affected by those things.

1:3. Having thus considered the evidence of the proposition laid down, I proceed to some inferences.

1. We may hence learn how great their error is, who are for discarding all religious affections, as having nothing solid or substantial in them. . . .

2. If it be so, that true religion lies much in the affections, hence we may infer, that such means are to be desired, as have much of a tendency to move the affections. Such books, and such a way of preaching the word, and administration of ordinances, and such a way of worshipping God in prayer, and singing praises, is much to be desired, as has a tendency deeply to affect the hearts of those who attend these means. . . .

3. If true religion lies much in the affections, hence we may learn, what great cause we have to be ashamed and confounded before God, that we are no more affected with the great things of religion. It appears from what has been said, that this arises from our having so little true religion. . . .

So has God disposed things, in the affair of our redemption, and in his glorious dispensations, revealed to us in the gospel, as though everything were purposely contrived in such a manner, as to have the greatest possible tendency to reach our hearts in the most tender part, and move our affections most sensibly and strongly. How great cause have we therefore to be humbled to the dust, that we are no more affected!

David Brainerd, *Life and Diary* (1749)

David Brainerd is remembered above all as a pioneer missionary among Native Americans. He was born in 1718 at Haddam (Connecticut) and in 1739, at the age of twenty-one, experienced conversion. This prompted him to enrol that autumn at Yale College with a view to the Congregational ministry. In his third year Brainerd made a private comment about a tutor that he had 'no more grace than this chair' – motivated according to Jonathan Edwards by an 'intemperate, imprudent zeal'. This was reported to the rector, who demanded of Brainerd a public recantation. The latter refused to comply and so was expelled from Yale. He continued to study for the ministry, now privately with a Congregational minister. Having gained his licence to preach, Brainerd was persuaded to apply for a job with the Scottish Society for the Propagation of Christian Knowledge (SPCK). This led to him being offered and accepting a call to work as a missionary among Native Americans – a task that he undertook with some hesitation.

The rest of Brainerd's brief life was devoted to his missionary task. This began with some Mahican Indians at Kaunameek in upstate New York, in between Albany and Stockbridge (Massachusetts). He worked among them from April 1743 to April the following year, under the guidance of John Sergeant, another missionary to the Indians based at Stockbridge. During this time Sergeant taught him the received wisdom of Indian outreach, but Brainerd came to question some of this. In May 1744 Brainerd was posted to the Delaware Indians in eastern Pennsylvania, with whom he worked for a year. He saw little visible fruit among them and even less from more remote groups that he visited deeper in Pennsylvania. Wrestling with this led him to realize that missionaries should measure success not by the number of converts but by their fidelity to their calling. This insight was to encourage many involved in the nineteenth-century missionary movement – many of whom were to see little fruit, even in areas of the world (such as Africa) where future generations were to see phenomenal church growth. That growth was based on the foundations laid by pioneer missionaries who themselves saw few results.

In June 1745 Brainerd preached to another group of Delaware Indians in New Jersey. Here he met with a much more positive response, winning converts within a few weeks. He remained with the group for sixteen months, helping them to move to new lands at Cranberry, New Jersey. This work was cut short because Brainerd suffered increasingly from tuberculosis and moved east in the hope of recovery. He stayed in Jonathan Edwards's home at Northampton and was nursed by his daughter Jerusha, whom he would have married had he lived. Instead he died in October 1747 at the young age of twenty-nine, followed a few months later by Jerusha, who had contracted the disease from him. They are buried next to each other.

Brainerd kept a private journal. In 1746 he himself published selections from this, in two parts: *The Rise and Progress of a Remarkable Work of Grace among a Number of Indians in the Provinces of New Jersey and Pennsylvania and Divine Grace Displayed, or the Continuance of a Remarkable Work of Grace* . . . . When he realized that he was dying he gave strict instructions that his private journal should not be published, but Jonathan Edwards managed to persuade him to the contrary. After his death Edwards edited and published Brainerd's diary, journal and private correspondence as *An Account of the Life of the Late Reverend Mr. David Brainerd, Minister of the Gospel, Missionary to the Indians . . . Chiefly Taken from his Own Diary, and Other Private Writings Written for his Own Use* (1749). In the original edition Edwards did not include those passages which Brainerd had himself published in 1746 (which include the extract below) but these were added in many later editions. This became Edwards's most popular work and was highly influential on generations of missionaries, including William Carey. Edwards was not uncritical of Brainerd. He acknowledged his melancholy temperament that could lead him to dejection and also that he was 'excessive in his labours, not taking due care to proportion his fatigues to his strength' – i.e. a workaholic.

August 8 [1745]. In the afternoon I preached to the Indians. Their number was now about sixty-five persons, men, women and children. I discoursed from Luke 14:16–23 and was favoured with uncommon freedom in my discourse. There was much visible concern among them while I was discoursing publicly; but afterwards when I spoke to one and another more particularly, whom I perceived under much concern, the power of God seemed to descend upon the assembly 'like a mighty rushing wind' [Acts 2:2], and with an astonishing energy bore down all before it.

I stood amazed at the influence which seized the audience almost universally, and could compare it to nothing more aptly than the irresistible force of a mighty torrent or swelling deluge, that with its insupportable weight and pressure bears down and sweeps before it whatever is in its way. Almost all persons of all ages were bowed down with concern together and scarcely one was able to withstand the shock of this surprising operation. Old men and women, who had been drunken wretches for many years, and some little children, not more than six or seven years of age, appeared in distress about their souls, as well as persons of middle age. And it was apparent that these children, some of them at least, were not merely frighted with seeing the general concern but were made sensible of their danger – the badness of their hearts – and their misery without Christ, as some of them expressed it. The most stubborn hearts were now obliged to bow. A principal man among the Indians, who before was most secure and self-righteous, and thought his state good because he knew more than the generality of the Indians had formerly done, and who with a great degree of confidence the day before told me, 'He had been a Christian more than ten years,' was now brought under solemn concern for his soul and wept bitterly. Another man, considerable in years, who had been a murderer, a powwow (or conjurer) and a notorious drunkard, was likewise brought to cry for mercy, with many tears, and to complain much that he could be no more concerned when he saw his danger to be so great.

They were almost universally praying and crying for mercy in every part of the house, and many out of doors, and numbers could neither go nor stand. Their concern was so great, each one for himself, that none seemed to take any notice of those about them, but each prayed as freely for themselves and appeared to their own apprehension as much retired as if they had been every one by themselves in the thickest desert. I believe they thought nothing about any one but themselves and their own state and so were every one praying apart, although all together.

It seemed to me that there was now an exact fulfilment of that prophecy, Zechariah 12:9–12. There was now *a great mourning, like the mourning of Hadadrimmon*; and each seemed to 'mourn apart'. I thought this had a near resemblance to the day of God's power mentioned in Joshua 10:14. I never saw *any day like it* in all respects – it was a day wherein I am persuaded the Lord did much to destroy the kingdom of darkness among this people.

This concern in general was most rational and just. Those who had been awakened any considerable time complained more especially of the badness of their hearts; those newly awakened of the badness of their lives and actions past. And all were afraid of the anger of God and of everlasting misery as the desert of their sins. Some of the white people who came out of curiosity to 'hear what this babbler would say' [Acts 17:18] to the poor ignorant Indians were also much awakened and some appeared to be wounded with a view of their perishing state. Those who had lately obtained relief were filled with comfort at this season; they appeared calm and composed and seemed to rejoice in Christ Jesus. Some of them took their distressed friends by the hand, telling them of the goodness of Christ and the comfort that is to be enjoyed in him, and thence invited them to come and give up their hearts to him. I could observe some of them in the most honest and unaffected manner, without any design of being taken notice of, lifting up their eyes to heaven as if crying for mercy, while they saw the distress of the poor souls around them.

There was one remarkable instance of awakening this day that I cannot but take particular notice of here. A young Indian woman, who I believe never knew before she had a soul, nor ever thought of any such thing, hearing that there was something strange among the Indians, came to see what was the matter. In her way to the Indians she called at my lodgings, and when I told her I designed presently to preach to the Indians she laughed and seemed to mock, but went to them. I had not proceeded far in my public discourse before she felt *effectually* that she had a soul, and before I had concluded my discourse was so convinced of her sin and misery and so distressed about her soul's salvation that she seemed like one pierced through with a dart and cried out incessantly. She could neither go, nor stand, nor sit without being held up. After public service was over she lay flat on the ground, praying earnestly and would take no notice nor give any answer to any that spoke to her. I hearkened to hear what she said and perceived the burden of her prayer to be 'Have mercy on me and help me to give thee my heart.' Thus she continued praying incessantly for many hours together.

This was indeed a surprising day of God's power and seemed enough to convince an Atheist of the truth, importance and power of God's word.

George Whitefield, *Sermons* (pre-1770)

George Whitefield was born in Gloucester in 1714 to an innkeeper. Growing up in such an environment he acquired godless habits, such as swearing and lying. Although George's schooling was interrupted by the poor family finances, the generosity of a family friend enabled him to study at Pembroke College, Oxford. There Charles Wesley lent him a copy of Henry Scougal's *The Life of God in the Soul of Man* (see pages 336–38). He later commented that 'he never knew what true religion was' until he read Scougal. It was this that made him realize his need of the new birth.

Having himself seen the light, George resolved to devote his life to preaching it. This he did for thirty-three years, from 1737 to his death in 1770. In addition to preaching regularly around Great Britain, he also visited America seven times where he helped to spread the flames of revival. About eighty percent of all American colonists heard him preach. In 1739 he started an orphanage and school outside Savannah, Georgia, for which he raised funds throughout his life. Whitefield found that his gospel message did not meet with the favour of all of the Anglican clergy and many pulpits were closed to him. As a result be began to preach in the open air, a tactic later adopted by the Wesleys. His sermons were regularly heard by crowds numbering tens of thousands. He had a very powerful voice and the deist Benjamin Franklin, who became a close friend, estimated that he could easily be heard by over thirty thousand people.

Whitefield had great oratorical and acting skills and a recent book about him is entitled *The Divine Dramatist*. He also pioneered the use of newspaper adverts as advance publicity for his sermons, despite an initial reluctance, finding that it increased attendance. His opponents called him a 'Pedlar in Divinity', comparing his methods with those of travelling salesmen. It is estimated that he preached over eighteen thousand times and that he was heard by some ten million people.

Whitefield and the Wesleys had much in common but fell out over doctrine. Whitefield was a Calvinist, believing that we choose God because he has first chosen us, while the Wesleys were Arminians, believing that God gives his grace to all and that it is up to us whether or not to accept it. They agreed to go their separate ways, but retained their respect for each other. Whitefield asked for John Wesley to preach his funeral sermon. The Wesleys left behind them a highly organized movement that in due course split from the Church of England to become the Methodist Church. Whitefield remained in the Church of England but was very happy to preach in other churches. He did not organize his converts into groups and left no ecclesiastical group behind him. Yet his influence has been immense in that many later preachers, like Billy Graham, have looked to him for inspiration.

During his lifetime many of Whitefield's sermons were published, separately and in small collections. In due course a fuller collection emerged of up to seventy-five *Sermons on Important Subjects*. There were various editions in the nineteenth century. One of the most famous of his sermons is that on 'The Almost Christian', based upon the words of King Agrippa, 'Paul, almost thou persuadest me to be a Christian' (Acts 26:28).

Amongst those who gladly receive the word, and confess that we speak the words of truth and soberness, there are so few who arrive at any higher degree of piety than that of Agrippa, or are any farther persuaded than to be 'almost Christians', that I cannot but think it highly necessary to warn my dear hearers of the danger of such a state. . . .

I. And, *first*, I am to consider what is meant by an almost Christian

An almost Christian, if we consider him in respect to his duty to God, is one that halts between two opinions; that wavers between Christ and the world; that would reconcile God and Mammon, light and darkness, Christ and Belial. It is true, he has an inclination to religion, but then he is very cautious how he goes too far in it. His false heart is always crying out, 'Spare thyself, do thyself no harm.' He prays indeed that 'God's will may be done on earth, as it is in heaven' [Matthew 6:10]. But notwithstanding, he is very partial in his obedience and fondly hopes that God will not be extreme to mark every thing that he wilfully does amiss, though an inspired apostle has told him that 'he who offends in one point is guilty of all' [James 2:10]. But chiefly, he is one that depends much on outward ordinances, and on that account looks upon himself as righteous and despises others; though at the same time he is as great a stranger to the divine life as any other person whatsoever. In short, he is fond of the form, but never experiences the power of godliness in his heart. . . .

But to proceed in the character of an almost Christian: If we consider him in respect of himself, as we said he was strictly honest to his neighbour, so he is likewise strictly sober in himself – but then both his honesty and sobriety proceed from the same principle of a false self-love. It is true, he runs not into the same excess of riot with other men; but then it is not out of obedience to the laws of God, but either because his constitution will not away with intemperance, or rather because he is cautious of forfeiting his reputation, or unfitting himself for temporal business. But though he is so prudent as to avoid intemperance and excess, for the reasons before-mentioned, yet he always goes to the extremity of what is lawful. It is true, he is no drunkard; but then he has no Christian self-denial. He cannot think our Saviour to be so austere a Master as to deny us to indulge ourselves in some particulars, and so by this means he is destitute of a sense of true religion, as much as if he lived in debauchery or any other crime whatever. . . .

II. I proceed to the second general thing proposed – to consider the reasons why so many are no more than almost Christians

1. And the first reason I shall mention is because so many set out with false notions of religion; though they live in a Christian country, yet they know not what Christianity is. This perhaps may be esteemed a hard saying, but experience sadly evinces the truth of it; for some place religion in being of this or that communion; more in morality; most in a round of duties, and a model of performances; and few, very few acknowledge it to be what it really is, a thorough inward change of nature, a divine life, a vital participation of Jesus Christ, a union of the soul with God; which the apostle expresses by saying, 'He that is joined to the Lord is one spirit' [1 Corinthians 6:17]. . . .

2. A second reason that may be assigned why so many are no more than almost Christians is a servile fear of man: multitudes there are and have been who, though awakened to a sense of the divine life, and have tasted and felt the powers of the world to come, yet out of a base sinful fear of being counted singular, or condemned by men, have suffered all those good impressions to wear off. . . . No wonder that so many are no more than almost Christians, since so many 'love the praise of men more than the honour which cometh of God' [John 12:43].

3. A third reason why so many are no more than almost Christians is a reigning love of money. . . . And thus many, both young and old, nowadays come running to worship our blessed Lord in public, and kneel before him in private, and inquire at his gospel, what they must do to inherit eternal life – but when they find they must renounce the self-enjoyment of riches and forsake all in affection to follow him they cry, 'The Lord pardon us in this thing! We pray thee, have us excused' [2 Kings 5:18; Luke 14:18–19]. But is heaven so small a trifle in men's esteem as not to be worth a little gilded earth? Is eternal life so mean a purchase as not to deserve the temporary renunciation of a few transitory riches? Surely it is. But however inconsistent such a behaviour may be, this inordinate love of money is too evidently the common and fatal cause why so many are no more than almost Christians.

4. Nor is the love of pleasure a less uncommon or a less fatal cause why so many are no more than almost Christians. Thousands and ten thousands there are who despise riches, and would willingly be true disciples of Jesus Christ, if parting with their money would make them so; but when they are told that our blessed Lord has said, 'Whosoever will come after him must deny himself' [Mark 8:34]; . . . they go away sorrowful for they have too great a love for sensual pleasures. . . . Tell

them of the necessity of mortification and self-denial and it is as difficult for them to hear as if you were to bid them 'cut off a right hand, or pluck out a right eye' [Matthew 5:29–30]. They cannot think our blessed Lord requires so much at their hands, though an inspired apostle has commanded us to 'mortify our members which are upon earth' [Colossians 3:5]. . . . But some men would be wiser than this great apostle, and chalk out to us what they falsely imagine an easier way to happiness. They would flatter us, we may go to heaven without offering violence to our sensual appetites and enter into the strait gate without striving against our carnal inclinations. And this is another reason why so many are only almost, and not altogether Christians.

5. The fifth and last reason I shall assign why so many are only almost Christians is a fickleness and instability of temper. It has been, no doubt, a misfortune that many a minister and sincere Christian has met with, to weep and wail over numbers of promising converts who seemingly began in the Spirit, but after a while fell away and basely ended in the flesh; and this not for want of right notions in religion, nor out of a servile fear of man, nor from the love of money, or of sensual pleasure, but through an instability and fickleness of temper. They looked upon religion merely for novelty, as something which pleased them for a while; but after their curiosity was satisfied, they laid it aside again. . . .

III. Proceed we now to the general thing proposed, namely, to consider the folly of being no more than an almost Christian

1. And the *first* proof I shall give of the folly of such a proceeding is that it is ineffectual to salvation. It is true, such men are almost good; but almost to hit the mark is really to miss it. God requires us 'to love him with all our hearts, with all our souls, and with all our strength' [Luke 10:27]. He loves us too well to admit any rival because, so far as our hearts are empty of God, so far must they be unhappy. The devil, indeed, like the false mother that came before Solomon, would have our hearts divided as she would have had the child; but God, like the true mother, will have all or none. 'My Son, give me thy heart,' thy whole heart, is the general call to all – and if this be not done, we never can expect the divine mercy.

Charles Wesley, *Hymns* (1788)

Charles was the younger brother of John Wesley, born in 1707 as the eighteenth child in the family. Like John he studied at Christ Church, Oxford, where he was also one of the founders of the 'Holy Club'. He accompanied John in his abortive mission to Georgia. Again like John, on his return to England he was influenced by the Moravian Peter Böhler and also read Luther's commentary on Galatians. As a result, on Whit Sunday 1738, he had a conversion experience leading to a sense of peace with God. On this occasion he beat his brother to it – by three days!

Charles gave himself to preaching, in churches and in the open air. But it was not for his preaching that he was to become famous. He was an outstandingly gifted hymn-writer, probably the greatest English hymn-writer ever. Of the more than seven thousand hymns that he composed the majority have (deservedly) passed into oblivion, but the best are among the finest ever written in English. (Those who compare the worst of contemporary worship songs with the cream of the hymns of the past should remember that the latter are a tiny minority selected from a very mixed bunch.)

The Evangelicals had a faith to preach. They also had a faith to sing about. The basic tenets of the evangelical message can be summarized from Charles's hymns:

● The centrality of Jesus Christ;

● Atonement through the cross of Christ;

● The transforming experience of conversion;

● Assurance of salvation;

● Holiness of life;

● Sharing the good news.

These themes are all amply illustrated in the hymns printed below. They are taken from the 1782 edition of the Methodist hymn book, hymns and verses being numbered as they there appear. I have, however, included some other verses which did not appear in this particular edition, these verses being unnumbered. This serves as a reminder that with many hymns the verses that appear today in hymn books are a selection from a greater number.

Hymn number 1

1 O for a thousand tongues to sing
My dear Redeemer's praise,
The glories of my God and King,
The triumphs of his grace!

2 My gracious Master and my God,
Assist me to proclaim,
To spread through all the earth abroad
The honours of thy name.

3 Jesus! the name that charms our fears,
That bids our sorrows cease;
'Tis music in the sinner's ears,
'Tis life, and health, and peace.

4 He breaks the power of cancelled sin,
He sets the prisoner free;
His blood can make the foulest clean,
His blood availed for me.

He speaks, and, listening to his voice,
New life the dead receive,
The mournful, broken hearts rejoice,
The humble poor believe.

5 Hear him, ye deaf; his praise, ye dumb,
Your loosened tongues employ;
Ye blind, behold your Saviour come,
And leap, ye lame, for joy.

In Christ your Head, you then shall know,
Shall feel your sins forgiven;
Anticipate your heaven below,
And own that love is heaven.

Glory to God, and praise and love
Be ever, ever given,
By saints below and saints above,
The church in earth and heaven.

On this glad day the glorious Sun
Of Righteousness arose;
On my benighted soul he shone
And filled it with repose.

Sudden expired the legal strife,
'Twas then I ceased to grieve;
My second, real, living life
I then began to live.

Then with my heart I first believed,
Believed with faith divine,
Power with the Holy Ghost received
To call the Saviour mine.

I felt my Lord's atoning blood
Close to my soul applied;
Me, me he loved, the Son of God,
For me, for me he died!

I found and owned his promise true,
Ascertained of my part,
My pardon passed in heaven I knew
When written on my heart.

6 Look unto him, ye nations, own
Your God, ye fallen race;
Look, and be saved through faith alone,
Be justified by grace.

7 See all your sins on Jesus laid:
The Lamb of God was slain,
His soul was once an offering made
For every soul of man.

8 Awake from guilty nature's sleep,
And Christ shall give you light,
Cast all your sins into the deep,
And wash the Æthiop white.

Harlots and publicans and thieves
In holy triumph join!
Saved is the sinner that believes
From crimes as great as mine.

Murderers and all ye hellish crew
In holy triumph join!
Believe the Saviour died for you;
For me the Saviour died.

9 With me, your chief, ye then shall know,
Shall feel your sins forgiven;
Anticipate your heaven below,
And own that love is heaven.

Hymn number 36

1 Jesus! the Name high over all,
In hell or earth or sky;
Angels and men before it fall,
And devils fear and fly.

2 Jesus! the Name to sinners dear,
The Name to sinners given!
It scatters all their guilty fears,
It turns their hell to heaven.

3 Jesus! the prisoner's fetters breaks,
And bruises Satan's head;
Power into strengthless souls it speaks,
And life into the dead.

4 O that the world might taste and see
The riches of his grace!
The arms of love that compass me
Would all mankind embrace.

5 O that my Jesu's heavenly charms
Might every bosom move!
Fly, sinners, fly into those arms
Of everlasting love.

Thee I shall constantly proclaim,
Though earth and hell oppose;
Bold to confess thy glorious Name
Before a world of foes.

6 His only righteousness I show,
His saving truth proclaim;
'Tis all my business here below
To cry 'Behold the Lamb!'

7 Happy, if with my latest breath
I may but gasp his Name,
Preach him to all and cry in death,
'Behold, behold the Lamb!'

Hymn number 193

1 And can it be that I should gain
An interest in the Saviour's blood?
Died he for me, who caused his pain,
For me, who him to death pursued?
Amazing love! How can it be,
That thou, my God, shouldst die for me?

2 'Tis mystery all: the Immortal dies!
Who can explore his strange design?
In vain the firstborn seraph tries
To sound the depths of love divine.
'Tis mercy all! Let earth adore;
Let angel minds inquire no more.

3 He left his Father's throne above
So free, so infinite his grace;
Emptied himself of all but love,
And bled for Adam's helpless race:
'Tis mercy all, immense and free,
For O my God, it found out me!

4 Long my imprisoned spirit lay,
Fast bound in sin and nature's night;
Thine eye diffused a quickening ray;
I woke, the dungeon flamed with light!
My chains fell off, my heart was free,
I rose, went forth, and followed thee.

Still the small inward voice I hear,
That whispers all my sins forgiven;
Still the atoning blood is near,
That quenched the wrath of hostile heaven.
I feel the life his wounds impart;
I feel the Saviour in my heart.

5 No condemnation now I dread;
Jesus, and all in him, is mine;
Alive in him, my living Head,
And clothed in righteousness divine,
Bold I approach the eternal throne,
And claim the crown, through Christ my own.

Hymn number 318

1 O thou who camest from above,
The pure celestial fire to impart,
Kindle a flame of sacred love
On the mean altar of my heart.

2 There let it for thy glory burn
With inextinguishable blaze,
And trembling to its source return,
In humble love and fervent praise.

3 Jesus, confirm my heart's desire
To work and speak and think for thee;
Still let me guard the holy fire,
And still stir up thy gift in me.

4 Ready for all thy perfect will,
My acts of faith and love repeat,
Till death thy endless mercies seal,
And make my sacrifice complete.

Hymn number 334

1 O for a heart to praise my God,
A heart from sin set free!
A heart that always feels thy blood
So freely spilt for me.

2 A heart resigned, submissive, meek,
My great Redeemer's throne,
Where only Christ is heard to speak,
Where Jesus reigns alone.

3 O for a lowly, contrite, heart,
Believing, true and clean,
Which neither life nor death can part
From him that dwells within.

4 A heart in every thought renewed
And full of love divine,
Perfect and right and pure and good,
A copy, Lord, of thine.

5 Thy tender heart is still the same,
And melts at human woe:
Jesu, for thee distressed I am,
I want thy love to know.

6 My heart, thou know'st, can never rest
Till thou create my peace;
Till of my Eden repossessed,
From every sin, I cease.

7 Fruit of thy gracious lips, on me
Bestow that peace unknown,
The hidden manna, and the tree
Of life, and the white stone.

8 Thy nature, gracious Lord, impart;
Come quickly from above;
Write thy new name upon my heart,
Thy new, best name of Love.

Hymn number 374

1 Love divine, all loves excelling,
Joy of heaven to earth come down;
Fix in us thy humble dwelling;
All thy faithful mercies crown!
Jesus, thou art all compassion!
Pure unbounded love thou art;
Visit us with thy salvation!
Enter every trembling heart.

Breathe, O breathe thy loving Spirit,
Into every troubled breast!
Let us all in thee inherit;
Let us find that second rest.
Take away our bent to sinning;
Alpha and Omega be;
End of faith, as its Beginning,
Set our hearts at liberty.

2 Come, Almighty to deliver,
Let us all thy grace receive;
Suddenly return and never,
Never more thy temples leave.
Thee we would be always blessing,
Serve thee as thy hosts above,
Pray and praise thee without ceasing,
Glory in thy perfect love.

3 Finish, then, thy new creation;
Pure and spotless let us be.
Let us see thy great salvation
Perfectly restored in thee;
Changed from glory into glory,
Till in heaven we take our place,
Till we cast our crowns before thee,
Lost in wonder, love, and praise.

John Wesley, *Journal* (1791)

John Wesley was born in 1703, the fifteenth child of Susanna and Samuel, the rector of Epworth in Lincolnshire. When John was only five the rectory burnt to the ground one night. He was trapped upstairs and was rescued at the last minute from an upper window. This led his mother to view him as 'a brand plucked from the fire' (Zechariah 3:2), preserved for a special task. He studied at Christ Church, Oxford, and was ordained in 1725. He returned to Oxford to be a fellow of Lincoln College and while there helped to found the 'Holy Club', which was for those who were serious about the practice of their religion. At this time Wesley was influenced by William Law's *A Serious Call to a Devout and Holy Life* (see pages 346–49). He belonged to the High Church tradition in the Church of England, which sometimes failed to grasp the doctrine of justification by faith. In 1735 Wesley went as a missionary to Georgia, but failed dismally. His inadequacies were exposed the very day after his arrival, by a Moravian pastor, as described in the second extract, below. (The Moravians were Pietists, in the tradition of Spener.)

By the time of his return to England in 1738 Wesley was even more aware of his spiritual need. But deliverance was at hand. Wesley received further help from the Moravians, especially one Peter Böhler, and matters came to a head later that year. On 24 May he went to an evening meeting where he heard a reading from Luther's preface to the Epistle to the Romans. During the course of this John felt his heart 'strangely warmed' and received an assurance that his sins were forgiven.

Traditionally, this is seen as Wesley's conversion. It seems probable that he had already been a committed Christian for some years. The new element, derived from the Moravians, was the assurance of salvation, based on justification by faith. (Interestingly, John's father, who himself came from a Puritan, nonconformist family, had told him on his deathbed that the strongest proof of Christianity is the inward witness of the Holy Spirit.) To many in the Church of England it seemed presumptuous to claim any such assurance. But Wesley came to see it as 'the very foundation of Christianity' and 'the main doctrine of the Methodists'.

John Wesley was not the only one to undergo such a conversion. His younger brother Charles preceded him by three days, as did George Whitefield by several years. They began to preach the message of salvation by faith in Jesus Christ. But such teaching was not welcome in the pulpits of the Church of England. This was a time of considerable moral and religious decline in England. Unbelief was becoming fashionable and many of the clergy preached little more than a barren moralism. The preaching of the Wesleys and the other Evangelicals, or 'Methodists' as they came to be called because of their methodical approach to spirituality, came as a clarion call to return to the gospel, the good news of salvation in Jesus Christ. As pulpits closed to them, first Whitefield and then Wesley began, in 1739, to preach in the open air. Circumstances had pushed them into the most effective way of reaching the mass of the populace, many of whom were not touched by the churches.

Evangelical preachers went about preaching in the market places and wherever they could gather an audience. John Wesley himself travelled some 5,000 miles on horseback each year, at a time when the major roads resembled the country dirt tracks of today. (Not for nothing has he been called 'God's horseman'.) He would stop several times a day and preach to whoever would listen. 'I look upon all the world as my parish. Thus far I mean, that in whatever part of it I am, judge it meet, right and my bounden duty to declare, unto all that are willing to hear, the glad tidings of salvation.' Sometimes, especially in the early years, he would meet with a hostile reception, including stoning. But he persevered and was still preaching in the open air at the age of eighty-seven, shortly before his death in 1791. There are few areas in England where Wesley did not preach.

Wesley and the other evangelical preachers had to face opposition, from the clergy and from all levels of society. But at the same time, many responded. Through their preaching Britain experienced the Evangelical Revival and many were brought into a living personal knowledge of Jesus Christ. As a result of the revival, Evangelicalism became a major factor in Anglo-Saxon Protestantism – and for much of the time since then, the dominant factor. The Wesleys gathered their converts into societies, which existed alongside the local parish churches. But the hostility of the Church of England led to their separation from the established church to form the Methodist Church. Not that the Church of England itself was untouched. As a result of the revival, the Evangelicals became in due course the major group in the Church of England, a position that they retained until the latter part of the nineteenth century. The traditional free churches (the Presbyterians, Congregationalists and Baptists), which had declined in numbers and vitality, were also revived and grew rapidly.

The revival dramatically influenced the church in England. But its effects were not merely ecclesiastical. Through the revival the lower classes were touched by the gospel in a way that had not previously occurred. Indeed, all levels of society were affected and the moral tone of the nation changed significantly. It has been said that without the revival Britain would probably have faced a revolution like the French Revolution. In the nineteenth century the 'nonconformist conscience' was a powerful factor in politics. The roots of the trades union movement and the Labour Party go back into Evangelicalism. The social and political life of the nation was profoundly affected in many ways.

When he went to Oxford Wesley began to keep an exact account of how he spent every hour of every day. This he continued for fifteen years. When he sailed for Georgia he began instead to keep a journal recording the events and activities of each day, beginning on 14 October 1735. The last entry was on 24 October 1790, a few months before his death the following March. Throughout his life Wesley kept both a diary, written in a cipher which has since been cracked, and a journal, written in full. Sometimes the journal is found in a number of different written versions. During his lifetime Wesley himself published extracts from his journal in regular instalments, beginning soon after his return from Georgia. It has been said that 'Wesley's *Journal* is still his best biography.' It is a lively account of his life and ministry through which his own character shines. It is rightly regarded as a spiritual classic.

The passages below are from his published versions, with extra material from the handwritten originals added within square brackets.

14 October 1735. [About nine in the morning] Mr Benjamin Ingham, of Queen's College, Oxford; Mr. Charles Delamotte, son of a [sugar] merchant, in London, [aged twenty-one,] who had offered himself some days before, [and showed an earnest desire to bear us company;] my brother, Charles Wesley, and myself, took boat for Gravesend, in order to embark for Georgia. Our end in leaving our native country was not to avoid want, God having given us plenty of temporal blessings, nor to gain riches or honour [which we trust he will ever enable us to look on as no other than dung and dross;] but singly this – to save our souls, to live wholly to the glory of God.

8 February 1736. [I asked Mr. Spangenberg's advice with regard to myself] – to my own conduct. He told me he could say nothing till he had asked me two or three questions. 'Do you know yourself? Have you the witness within yourself? Does the Spirit of God bear witness with your Spirit, that you are a child of God?' I was surprised, and knew not what to answer. He observed it, and asked, 'Do you know Jesus Christ?' I paused and said, 'I know he is the Saviour of the world.' 'True,' replied he, 'but do you know he has saved you?' I answered, 'I hope he has died to save me.' He only added, 'Do you know yourself?' I said, 'I do.' But I fear they were vain words.

24 January 1738. We spoke with two ships, outward-bound, from whom we had the welcome news of our wanting but one hundred and sixty leagues of the Land's End. My mind was now full of thought, part of which I writ down as follows:

> I went to America, to convert the Indians; but oh, who shall convert me? who, what is he that will deliver me from this evil heart of unbelief? I have a fair summer religion. I can talk well; nay, and believe myself, while no danger is near. But let death look me in the face, and my spirit is troubled. Nor can I say, 'To die is gain' [Philippians 1:21]!

24 May 1738. In the evening I went very unwillingly to a society in Aldersgate Street, where one was reading Luther's preface to the Epistle to the Romans. About a quarter before nine, while he was describing the change which God works in the heart through faith in Christ, I felt my heart strangely warmed. I felt I did trust in Christ, Christ alone for salvation; and an assurance was given me that he had taken away *my* sins, even *mine*, and saved *me* from the law of sin and death.

24 October 1790. I explained, to a numerous congregation in Spitalfields church, 'the whole armour of God' [Ephesians 6:11]. St Paul's, Shadwell, was still more crowded in the afternoon while I enforced that important truth, 'One thing is needful' [Luke 10:42]; and I hope many, even then, resolved to choose the better part.

William Carey, *An Enquiry in the Obligations of Christians* (1792)

William Carey was born in 1761 in rural Northamptonshire. His father was a weaver but later became a schoolmaster. William himself was apprenticed to a shoemaker when he was about fourteen years old. One of his fellow apprentices introduced him to a nonconformist prayer meeting as a result of which he began in 1779 to attend a nearby Congregationalist chapel. He came to reject infant baptism and was rebaptized as a believer in 1783. In addition to his work as a shoemaker he began to preach in a Baptist church and also to study Hebrew, Greek and Latin. In 1785 he became a pastor, while also making shoes and teaching in a school. In 1789 he became pastor of a larger Baptist church in Leicester.

Carey read the accounts of James Cook's exploration of the South Seas and was moved to consider the duty of European Christians to preach the gospel in such regions. He was also influenced by reading David Brainerd's *Life and Diary* (see pages 359–62). But not all of his fellow Baptists agreed with Carey. At an association meeting he proposed that Christ's command to teach all nations was binding on all generations. One minister is reported to have responded: 'Young man, sit down, sit down! You are an enthusiast. When God pleases to convert the heathen, he'll do it without consulting you or me.' Carey realized that his case needed to be argued carefully.

In 1792 he published his classic work, *An Enquiry into the Obligations of Christians to Use Means for the Conversion of the Heathens*. It was published in Leicester and cost one shilling and six pence. This brief work sets out abiding principles for overseas mission, in five parts or sections. In the first section Carey argues that Christ's commission to preach the gospel to the whole world was not for the apostolic age only but is still binding upon the church. This is followed by a short review of the history of mission from Pentecost, mostly drawn from Acts with a brief account of later endeavours. Section three is a country by country survey of the world, continent by continent, giving for each country its dimensions, its population and its religion. Regarding the last, his main categories are 'Protestants', 'Papists', 'Greek Christians', 'Jews', 'Mahometans' and 'Pagans'. Hindus, Buddhists and Confucianists are included in the last category. This section is an early and crude version of what is done today by Patrick Johnstone's popular *Operation World*. The fourth section argues for the practicality of doing more for the conversion of the heathen. The final section concerns the duty of Christians and how the missionary task should be promoted.

A few days after the publication of his *Enquiry* Carey preached a famous sermon on Isaiah 54:2–3 at the annual meeting of the Northamptonshire Association of Baptist

Churches. Here he declared that God was about to extend the kingdom of Jesus throughout the whole world. He urged his hearers to expect great things and, in the light of that, to attempt great things. This later became the slogan 'Expect great things from God. Attempt great things for God.'

An insular British perspective has entitled Carey 'the father of modern missions'. In fact Continental Christians such as the Moravians had already been engaged in the task since the beginning of the eighteenth century. Carey's role was to facilitate the awakening of the British to this opportunity and task. He was the chief founder of the Baptist Missionary Society in 1792 and helped to stimulate the interest and concern that led to the huge missionary outreach from Britain in the nineteenth century and which in due course transformed Christianity into the first truly global religion.

Carey practised what he preached. In 1793 he set sail for India, where he remained until his death in 1834. Originally he went to Calcutta but he soon moved north to the Danish settlement of Serampore where there was greater freedom to evangelize. Carey realized that Indians, not Europeans, would make the most effective evangelists and so founded Serampore College to train Indian Christians. He also, with helpers, translated the Bible into six Indian languages and produced grammars and dictionaries for a number of languages.

―――――――――――――――――

Section 5. An Enquiry into the Duty of Christians in General, and What Means Ought to Be Used, in Order to Promote This Work

One of the first, and most important of those duties which are incumbent upon us, is *fervent and united prayer*. However the influence of the Holy Spirit may be set at nought, and run down by many, it will be found upon trial, that all means which we can use, without it, will be ineffectual. If a temple is raised for God in the heathen world, it will not be 'by might, nor by power', nor by the authority of the magistrate, or the eloquence of the orator; 'but by my Spirit, saith the Lord of Hosts' [Zechariah 4:6]. We must therefore be in real earnest in supplicating his blessing upon our labours. . . .

Many can do nothing but pray, and prayer is perhaps the only thing in which Christians of all denominations can cordially, and unreservedly unite; but in this we may all be one, and in this the strictest unanimity ought to prevail. Were the whole body thus animated by one soul, with what pleasure would Christians attend on all the duties of religion, and with what delight would their ministers attend on all the business of their calling.

We must not be contented however with praying, without *exerting ourselves in the use of means* for the obtaining of those things we pray for. Were 'the children of light', but 'as wise in their generation as the children of this world' [Luke 16:8], they would stretch every nerve to gain so glorious a prize, nor ever imagine that it was to be obtained in any other way. . . .

Suppose a company of serious Christians, ministers and private persons, were to form themselves into a society, and make a number of rules respecting the regulation of the plan, and the persons who are to be employed as missionaries, the means of defraying the expense, etc., etc. This society must consist of persons whose hearts are in the work, men of serious religion, and possessing a spirit of perseverance; there must be a determination not to admit any person who is not of this description, or to retain him longer than he answers to it.

From such a society a *committee* might be appointed, whose business it should be to procure all the information they could upon the subject, to receive contributions, to enquire into the characters, tempers, abilities and religious views of the missionaries, and also to provide them with necessaries for their undertakings. . . .

In respect to *contributions* for defraying the expenses, money will doubtless be wanting; and suppose the rich were to embark a portion of that wealth over which God has made them stewards, in this important undertaking, perhaps there are few ways that would turn to a better account at last. Nor ought it to be confined to the *rich*; if persons in more moderate circumstances were to devote a portion, suppose a *tenth*, of their annual increase to the Lord, it would not only correspond with the practice of the Israelites, who lived under the Mosaic Economy, but of the patriarchs Abraham, Isaac, and Jacob, before that dispensation commenced. Many of our most eminent forefathers amongst the *Puritans* followed that practice; and if that were but attended to now, there would not only be enough to support the ministry of the gospel at home, and to encourage *village preaching* in our respective neighbourhoods, but to defray the expenses of carrying the gospel into the heathen world.

If congregations were to open subscriptions of *one penny*, or more per week, according to their circumstances, and deposit it as a fund for the propagation of the gospel, much might be raised in this way. By such simple means they might soon have it in their power to introduce the preaching of the gospel into most of the villages in England; where, though men are placed whose business it should be to give light to those who sit in darkness, it is well known that they have it not. Where there was no person to open his house for the reception of the gospel, some other building might be procured for a small sum, and even then something considerable might be spared for the baptist, or other committees, for propagating the gospel amongst the heathen. . . .

We are exhorted 'to lay up treasure in heaven, where neither moth nor rust doth corrupt, nor thieves break through and steal' [Matthew 6:19]. It is also declared that 'whatsoever a man soweth, that shall he also reap' [Galatians 6:7]. These scriptures teach us that the enjoyments of the life to come, bear a near relation to that which now is; a relation similar to that of the harvest, and the seed. It is true all the reward is of mere grace, but it is nevertheless encouraging; what a *treasure*, what a *harvest* must await such characters as Paul, and [John] Elliot, and [David] Brainerd, and others, who have given themselves wholly to the work of the Lord. What a heaven will it be to see the many myriads of poor heathens, of Britons amongst the rest, who by their labours have been brought to the knowledge of God. Surely a 'crown of rejoicing' [1 Thessalonians 2:19] like this is worth aspiring to. Surely it is worth while to lay ourselves out with all our might, in promoting the cause, and kingdom of Christ.

William Wilberforce,
A Practical View (1797)

William Wilberforce was born at Hull in 1759, into a wealthy merchant family. When he was nine his father died and William was sent to stay with a wealthy uncle and aunt. Through their influence he was converted in 1771, to the displeasure of his mother. She took him away from his uncle and aunt and sent him instead to a boarding school, where he spent five years. This had the desired effect and he lost his interest in religion.

In 1776 Wilberforce, by now a wealthy man, went to study at St John's College, Cambridge. At this stage he was living a thoroughly worldly life and was very popular. He devoted more time to socializing than to study. After three years at Cambridge he moved to London where he became friends with William Pitt. Both decided to enter Parliament and Wilberforce was elected MP for Hull in 1780. Pitt failed to get elected that year but succeeded the next and at the end of 1783 became Britain's youngest ever prime minister at the age of twenty-four. Wilberforce remained a close friend, but was independent-minded as a politician.

In 1784 Wilberforce toured the Continent in the company of Isaac Milner, an evangelical clergyman later to become president of Queens' College, Cambridge. They read together Doddridge's *The Rise and Progress of Religion* (see pages 350–53) and the New Testament. Over the period of a year or more Wilberforce came to accept basic Christian doctrines and experienced conversion (the 'great change' as he called it) after a period of conviction of sin. He considered the ordained ministry but was dissuaded by Pitt and by the hymn-writer John Newton, on the grounds that he was needed in the political realm. After hesitation and prayer Wilberforce became convinced that God had set him two tasks: 'the suppression of the slave trade and the reformation of manners [morality]'. John Newton had himself been a slave trader and encouraged Wilberforce to oppose it. John Wesley's last letter, written on his deathbed, encouraged him in the task. It was to be a long struggle, with many setbacks, and it was not until 1807 that the bill abolishing the slave trade passed both houses of Parliament and gained royal assent. It was in 1833, just after Wilberforce's death, that his ultimate aim, a bill abolishing slavery, was passed into law.

Wilberforce's other task was furthered by his book: *A Practical View of the Prevailing Religious System of Professed Christians in the Higher and Middle Classes in this Country, Contrasted with Real Christianity* (1797). The publisher was none too confident and printed only five hundred copies, but it proved to be hugely popular and there was a fifth edition by the end of the year. It was a best-seller and played a key role in the spread of evangelical Christianity among the upper classes in Britain early in the nineteenth century. It has remained popular and in print – though it was not just the title that was rather long and most modern editions abridge it. Wilberforce commends 'serious religion' as a cement for civil society. By stressing the mutual obligations of rich and poor it would help to hold society together – the French Revolution showing what could happen when the Christian basis of society was lost.

Wilberforce achieved all that he did despite physical frailty. He was short (called a 'shrimp' by James Boswell) and suffered from poor eyesight, a bad back and weak digestion. He had three near brushes with death earlier in his life. It was his iron will and his commitment to his calling that enabled him to overcome these disabilities.

Chapter 5: The Excellence of Christianity in Certain Important Particulars

The virtues most strongly and repeatedly enjoined in Scripture and by our progress in which we may best measure our advancement in holiness, are the fear and love of God and of Christ; love, kindness and meekness towards our fellow-creatures; indifference to the possessions and events of this life, in comparison with our concern about eternal things; self-denial and humility. . . .

Take then the instances of loving kindness and meekness towards others and observe the solid foundation which is laid for them in self-denial, in moderation as to the good things of this life and in humility. The chief causes of enmity among men are pride and self-importance, the high opinion which men entertain of themselves and the consequent deference which they exact from others, the over-valuation of worldly possessions and of worldly honours and, in consequence, a too eager competition for them. The rough edges of one man rub against those of another, if the expression may be allowed, and the friction is often such as to injure the works and disturb the just arrangements and regular motions of the social machine. But by Christianity all these roughnesses are filed down, every wheel rolls round smoothly in the performance of its appointed function, and there is nothing to retard the several movements or break in on the general order.

The religious system indeed of the bulk of nominal Christians is satisfied with some tolerable appearances of virtue and accordingly, while it recommends love and beneficence, it tolerates pride and vanity in many cases; it even countenances and commends the excessive valuation of character and at least allows a man's whole soul to be absorbed in the pursuit of the object which he is following, be it what it may, of personal or professional success. But though these latter qualities may, for the most part, fairly enough consist with a soft exterior and courtly demeanour, they cannot so well accord with the genuine internal principle of love. Some cause of discontent, some ground of jealousy or of envy will arise; some suspicion will corrode; some disappointment will sour; some slight or calumny will irritate and provoke reprisals. In the higher walks of life, indeed, we learn to disguise our emotions, but such will be the real inward feelings of the soul, and they will frequently betray themselves when we are off our guard or when we are not likely to be disparaged by the discovery. . . .

But Christianity is not satisfied with producing merely the specious guise of virtue. She requires the substantial reality, which may stand the scrutinizing eye of that Being 'who searches the heart' [Jeremiah 17:10]. Meaning therefore that the Christian should live and breath in an atmosphere, as it were, of benevolence, she forbids whatever can tend to obstruct its diffusion or vitiate its purity. It is on this principle that emulation is forbidden, for besides that this passion almost insensibly degenerates into envy and that it derives its origin chiefly from pride and a desire of self-exaltation, how can we easily love our neighbour as ourselves, if we consider him at the same time our rival and are intent upon surpassing him in the pursuit of whatever is the subject of our competition?

Christianity, again, teaches us not to set our hearts on earthly possessions and earthly honours and thereby provides for our really loving or even cordially forgiving those who have been more successful than ourselves in the attainment of them, or who have even deignedly thwarted us in the pursuit. 'Let the rich,' says the apostle, 'rejoice in that he is brought low' [James 1:9–10]. How can he who means to attempt, in any degree, to obey this precept be irreconcilably hostile towards any one who may have been instrumental in his depression?

Christianity also teaches us not to prize human estimation at a very high rate and thereby provides for the practice of her injunction, to love from the heart those who justly or unjustly may have attacked our reputation and wounded our character. She commands not the show but the reality of meekness and gentleness and by thus taking away the aliment [food] of anger and the fomenters of discord, she provides for the maintenance of peace and the restoration of good temper among men, when it may have sustained a temporary interruption.

John Henry Newman,
Sermons Preached before the University of Oxford (1843)

John Henry Newman was born in 1801 into an evangelical family. When he was fifteen he was deeply influenced by various Calvinist writings and underwent an evangelical conversion: 'I fell under the influences of a definite Creed, and received into my intellect impressions of dogma which, through God's mercy, have never been effaced or obscured.' He studied at Oxford and in 1822 became a fellow of Oriel College. Here his evangelical convictions were undermined. First, he experienced a drift towards liberalism. Then he received a strong impulse in a different direction, from John Keble. Keble pointed him to the Early Church Fathers and this influenced his thinking in a more 'Catholic' direction.

In 1833 Keble preached his famous sermon on National Apostasy and this is traditionally seen as the launching of the Oxford Movement. Ironically, in the light of later developments, the occasion for the launch was the threat to the Church of England posed by the Catholic Emancipation Act of 1829 (giving Roman Catholics greater political freedom) and the plan to weaken the Church of England in (Roman Catholic) Ireland. The positive principles of the movement included the following beliefs: episcopacy as the divinely-appointed means of church government; the apostolic succession of bishops who stand in an unbroken line from the apostles, succeeding to their authority; the right of the church to govern herself without state interference; the importance of the sacraments; baptismal regeneration (new birth through baptism), the real presence of Christ's body and blood in the eucharist; the eucharist as a sacrifice offered to God. In many ways the Oxford Movement was a reaffirmation of traditional High Church views. But its founders introduced a radically new element by turning to the Early Church in *opposition* to the Protestant Reformation. Some of them were violently hostile to the Reformers.

The movement's views were expounded in a series of *Tracts for the Times* – begun in 1833 – with the result that its adherents were called 'Tractarians'. The anti-Protestant tone caused much offence. Newman at this stage, in common with others, saw the Church of England as the middle way between Protestantism and Roman Catholicism. He still retained the traditional belief that the pope was the Antichrist. The Early Church he saw as the golden age, to which they were returning in pursuit of a pure Catholic faith, not tainted by medieval Rome. The Catholic faith was to be discerned by the principle enunciated by Vincent of Lérins (early fifth century): 'we hold to that which has been believed everywhere, always and by everyone [within the Catholic Church]'. In 1841 Newman wrote *Tract Ninety*.

In this he argued that the *Thirty-nine Articles* (see pages 264–68) were compatible with the teaching of the (Roman Catholic) Council of Trent. While the articles were *ambitious* of a Protestant interpretation, they were *patient* of Catholic interpretation. This tract aroused a storm of protest, which led to the termination of the series. One leading figure observed that he would no longer trust Newman with his silver.

Newman was disappointed at this time by the actions of the bishops. They were making decisions which seemed to indicate that despite the claims of the Tractarians the Church of England was after all a Protestant church. Newman lost his faith in the Church of England and gradually withdrew from involvement in it, leaving Oxford for a monastic retreat at nearby Littlemore. Intuitively he had come to feel that it was Rome after all which was the true Catholic Church. But while his heart was won, his head knew that in many ways Rome differed from the Early Church. How could his head be reconciled to his heart? Gradually he came to see the answer in the concept of the *development of doctrine*. He set this out in his famous *Essay on the Development of Christian Doctrine*, written while an Anglican as a defence of his conversion to Rome. The *Essay* was published unaltered after his conversion in 1845, with a postscript submitting it to the judgment of the church.

Newman's ideas met with a frosty reception in the ultra-dogmatic nineteenth-century Roman Catholic Church. It was his fellow ex-Evangelical, Henry Manning, who became cardinal archbishop of Westminster (although Newman was eventually made a cardinal in 1879). Manning was of a different temper to Newman. 'The appeal to history is heresy and treason,' he maintained. But Newman's day was to come. If the First Vatican Council (1869–70), which defined papal infallibility, was Manning's council, the Second Vatican Council (1962–65), which acknowledged development in doctrine, may be called Newman's council. It has even been claimed, with tongue in cheek, that in the long run it was the Roman Catholic Church which was converted to Newman, not vice versa.

Newman wrote many famous works which are still in print. One of his more accessible works, of abiding value, is the series of fourteen (later fifteen) *Sermons Preached before the University of Oxford* between 1826 and 1843 (often referred to as his *University Sermons*). These have often been reprinted. There is a theme that runs through about half of the sermons, the relation between faith and reason. The final sermon, preached in 1843, was on the theme that was preoccupying him at that time, the development of doctrine.

Sermon 11 (later 12). Love the Safeguard of Faith Against Superstition

1. Faith, considered as an exercise of reason, has this characteristic – that it proceeds far more on antecedent grounds than on evidence; it trusts much to presumptions, and in doing this lies its special merit. Thus it is distinguished from knowledge in the ordinary sense of that word. We are commonly said to know a

thing when we have ascertained it by the natural methods given us for ascertaining it. Thus we know mathematical truths, when we are possessed of demonstrative evidence concerning them; we know things present and material by our senses. We know the events of life by moral evidence; we know things past or things invisible, by reasoning from certain present consequences of the facts, such as testimony borne to them. When, for instance, we have ascertained the fact of a miracle by good testimony, the testimony of men who neither deceive nor are deceived, we may be said to know the fact; for we are possessed of those special grounds, of that distinct warrant in its behalf, which the nature of the case assigns and allows. These special grounds are often called the evidence; and when we believe in consequence of them, we are said to believe upon reason.

5. To maintain that faith is a judgment about facts in matters of conduct, such, as to be formed, not so much from the impression legitimately made upon the mind by those facts, as from the reaching forward of the mind itself towards them – that it is a presumption, not a proving – may sound paradoxical, yet surely is borne out by the actual state of things as they come before us every day. Can it, indeed, be doubted that the great majority of those who have sincerely and deliberately given themselves to religion, who take it for their portion, and stake their happiness upon it, have done so, not on an examination of evidence, but from a spontaneous movement of their hearts towards it? They go out of themselves to meet him who is unseen, and they discern him in such symbols of him as they find ready provided for them. Whether they examine afterwards the evidence on which their faith may be justified or not, or how far soever they do so, still their faith does not originate in the evidence, nor is it strong in proportion to their knowledge of the evidence; but, though it may admit of being strengthened by such knowledge, yet it may be quite as strong without it as with it. They believe on grounds within themselves, not merely or mainly on the external testimony on which religion comes to them.

7. The same view of faith, as being a presumption, is also implied in our popular mode of regarding it. It is commonly and truly said, that faith is a test of a man's heart. Now, what does this really mean, but that it shows what he thinks likely? – and what he thinks likely, depends surely on nothing else than the general state of his mind, the state of his convictions, feelings, tastes and wishes. . . . That the evidence is something, and not every thing; that it tells a certain way, yet might be more; he will hold, in either case: but then follows the question, what is to come of the evidence, being what it is, and this he decides according to (what is called) the state of his heart.

11. As faith may be viewed as opposed to reason, in the popular sense of the latter word, it must not be overlooked that unbelief is opposed to reason also. Unbelief indeed, considers itself especially rational, or critical of evidence; but it criticizes the evidence of religion, only because it does not like it, and really goes upon presumptions and prejudices as much as faith does, only presumptions of an opposite nature. This I have already implied. It considers a religious system so improbable, that it will not listen to the evidence of it; or, if it listens, it employs itself in doing what a believer could do, if he chose, quite as well, what he is quite as well aware can be done; viz., in showing that the evidence might be more complete and unexceptionable than it is. On this account it is that unbelievers call themselves rational; not because they decide by evidence, but because, after they have made their decision, they merely occupy themselves in sifting it.

36. Such, then, under all circumstances, is real faith; a presumption, yet not a mere chance conjecture; a reaching forward, yet not of excitement or of passion; a moving forward in the twilight, yet not without clue or direction; a movement from something known to something unknown, kept in the narrow path of truth by the law of dutifulness which inhabits it, the light of heaven which animates and guides it, – and which, whether feeble and dim as in the heathen, or bright and vigorous as in the Christian, whether merely the awakening and struggling conscience, or the 'minding of the Spirit', whether as a timid hope, or in the fullness of love, is, under every dispensation, the one acceptable principle commending us to God for the merits of Christ. And it becomes superstition or credulity or enthusiasm or fanaticism, or bigotry, in proportion as it emancipates itself from this spirit of wisdom and understanding, of counsel and ghostly strength, of knowledge and true godliness, and holy fear. And thus I would answer the question how it may be secured from excess, without the necessity of employing what is popularly called reason for its protection – I mean processes of investigation, discrimination, discussion, argument, and inference. It is itself an intellectual act, and it takes its character from the moral state of the agent. It is perfected, not by mental cultivation, but by obedience. It does not change its nature or its function, when thus perfected. It remains what it is in itself, an initial principle of action; but it becomes changed in its quality, as being made spiritual. It is as before a presumption, but the presumption of a serious, sober, thoughtful, pure, affectionate, and devout mind. It acts, because it is faith; but the direction, firmness, consistency, and precision of its acts, it gains from love.

John Charles Ryle, *Holiness* (1877)

J.C. Ryle was born in 1816 into a godly Methodist family. His father was a Member of Parliament. After going to school at Eton he proceeded to Christ Church, Oxford. While there he underwent an experience of conversion, through hearing Ephesians 2:8 read in church – 'For by grace are ye saved through faith; and that not of yourselves: it is the gift of God.' This impressed upon Ryle his own sinfulness and the need to be born again.

The Methodist Ryle had planned a career in politics, like his father, but instead was ordained into the Anglican ministry in 1841. For the next thirty-nine years he served in a number of parishes, on all of which he made a significant impact. In 1880 he was appointed the first bishop of the new diocese of Liverpool. Within ten years he had transformed the diocese with a massive programme of church building, an increase in the number of clergy and the appointment of lay 'Scripture Readers'. This increase was matched by a near doubling of the number of people confirmed. Ryle retired early in 1900 owing to poor health and died a few months later.

Ryle was a great preacher. In one of his churches he had carved on the pulpit the words, 'Woe is unto me if I preach not the Gospel' (1 Corinthians 9:16). He also published a number of his sermons as tracts. He believed in presenting his message clearly and simply and one of his tracts was entitled *Simplicity in Preaching*. He also wrote over thirty books, many of which are still in print. Between 1856 and 1869 he wrote a multi-volume set of *Expository Thoughts* on each of the Gospels. His *Knots Untied: Being Plain Statements on Disputed Points in Religion from the Standpoint of an Evangelical Churchman* (1898) has remained popular. But perhaps his greatest work was his *Holiness: Its Nature, Hindrances, Difficulties, and Roots*, first published in 1877. Here he expounds the traditional Reformed doctrine of sanctification, in opposition to a number of contrary ideas that were prevalent, such as the idea that sanctification is by faith alone, without any human effort – 'don't wrestle, nestle'. In an age where any mention of the demands of discipleship is liable to be rejected as legalistic and guilt-inducing, Ryle's message is still highly relevant.

Chapter 1: Sin

He that wishes to attain right views about Christian holiness must begin by examining the vast and solemn subject of sin. He must dig down very low if he would build high. A mistake here is most mischievous. Wrong views about holiness are generally traceable to wrong views about human corruption. I make no apology for beginning this volume of papers about holiness by making some plain statements on sin.

The plain truth is that a right knowledge of sin lies at the root of all saving Christianity. Without it such doctrines as justification, conversion, sanctification are 'words and names' which convey no meaning to the mind. The first thing, therefore, that God does when he makes anyone a new creature in Christ is to send light into his heart and show him that he is a guilty sinner. . . . If a man does not realize the dangerous nature of his soul's disease, you cannot wonder if he is content with false or imperfect remedies. I believe that one of the chief wants [lacks] of the church in the nineteenth century has been, and is, clearer fuller teaching about sin. . . .

'A sin' consists in doing, saying, thinking or imagining anything that is not in perfect conformity with the mind and law of God. 'Sin' in short, as the Scripture says, is 'the transgression of the law' [1 John 3:4]. The slightest outward or inward departure from absolute mathematical parallelism with God's revealed will and character constitutes a sin, and at once makes us guilty in God's sight. . . .

The sinfulness of man does not begin from without, but from within. It is not the result of bad training in early years. It is not picked up from bad companions and bad examples, as some weak Christians are too fond of saying. No! It is a family disease which we all inherit from our first parents, Adam and Eve, and with which we are born. . . . The fairest babe that has entered life this year and become the sunbeam of a family, is not, as its mother perhaps fondly calls it, a little 'angel' or a little 'innocent' but a little sinner. Alas! As it lies smiling and crowing in its cradle, that little creature carries in its heart the seeds of every kind of wickedness! Only watch it carefully, as it grows in stature and its mind develops, and you will soon detect in it an incessant tendency to that which is bad, and a backwardness to that which is good. You will see in it the buds and germs of deceit, evil temper, selfishness, self-will, obstinacy, greediness, envy, jealousy, passion – which if indulged and let alone will shoot up with painful rapidity. Who taught the child these things? Where did he learn them? . . .

The greatest proof of the extent and power of sin is the pertinacity with which it cleaves to man even after he is converted and has become the subject of the Holy Ghost's operations. To use the language of the Ninth Article [of the *Thirty-Nine Articles* – see pages 264–68], 'this infection of nature doth remain, yea even in them that are regenerate.' So deeply planted are the roots of human corruption, that even after we are born again, renewed, 'washed, sanctified, justified' [1 Corinthians 6:11] and made living members of Christ, these roots remain alive in the bottom of our hearts and, like the leprosy in the walls of the house, we never get rid of them until the earthly house of this tabernacle is dissolved. Sin, no doubt, in the believer's heart has no longer *dominion*. It is checked, controlled, mortified and crucified by the expulsive power of the new principle of grace. The life of a believer is a life of victory and not of failure. But the very struggles which go on within his bosom, the fight that he finds it needful to fight daily, the watchful jealousy which he is obliged to exercise over his inner man, the contest between the flesh and the spirit, the inward 'groanings' which no one knows but he who has experienced them – all, all testify to the same great truth, all show the enormous power and vitality of sin. Mighty indeed must that foe be who even when crucified is still alive! Happy is that believer who understands it and while he rejoices in Christ Jesus has no confidence in the flesh; and while he says, 'Thanks be unto God who gives us the victory' [1 Corinthians 15:57] never forgets to watch and pray lest he fall into temptation! . . .

No proof of the fullness of sin, after all, is so overwhelming and unanswerable as the cross and passion of our Lord Jesus Christ, and the whole doctrine of his substitution and atonement. Terribly black must that guilt be for which nothing but the blood of the Son of God could make satisfaction. Heavy must that weight of human sin be which made Jesus groan and sweat drops of blood in agony at Gethsemane and cry at Golgotha, 'My God, my God, why hast thou forsaken me?' [Matthew 27:46]. . . .

One point only remains to be considered on the subject of sin, which I dare not pass over. That point is its *deceitfulness*. It is a point of most serious importance and I venture to think it does not receive the attention which it deserves. You may see this deceitfulness in the wonderful proneness of men to regard sin as less sinful and dangerous than it is in the sight of God; and in their readiness to extenuate it, make excuses for it and minimize its guilt. . . . I fear we do not sufficiently realize the extreme subtlety of our soul's disease. We are too apt to forget that temptation to sin will rarely present itself to us in its true colours saying, 'I am your deadly enemy and I want to ruin you for ever in hell.' Oh no! Sin comes to us like Judas, with a kiss; and like Joab, with outstretched hand and flattering words. The forbidden fruit seemed good and desirable to Eve; yet it cast her out of Eden. The walking idly on his palace roof seemed harmless enough to David; yet it ended in adultery and murder. Sin rarely seems sin at first beginnings. Let us then watch and pray, lest we fall into temptation. We may give wickedness smooth names, but we cannot alter its nature and character in the sight of God. Let us remember St Paul's words: 'Exhort one another daily, lest any be hardened through the deceitfulness of sin' [Hebrews 3:13]. It is a wise prayer in our Litany: 'From the *deceits* of the world, the flesh and the devil, good Lord deliver us.' . . .

For my part I am persuaded the more light we have, the more we see our own sinfulness; the nearer we get to heaven, the more we are clothed with humility. In every age of the church you will find it true, if you will study biographies, that the most eminent saints. . . have always been the humblest men.

On the other hand I ask my readers to observe *how deeply thankful we ought to be for the glorious Gospel of the grace of God*. There is a remedy revealed for man's need as wide and broad and deep as man's disease. We need not be afraid to look at sin and study its nature, origin, power, extent and vileness, if we only look at the same time at the Almighty medicine provided for us in the salvation that is in Jesus Christ. Though sin has abounded, grace has much more abounded. . . .

A Scriptural view of sin will prove an admirable *antidote to the low views of personal holiness* which are so painfully prevalent in these last days of the church. . . . I am afraid that Christ-like charity, kindness, good-temper, unselfishness, meekness, gentleness, good-nature, self-denial, zeal to do good and separation from the world are far less appreciated than they ought to be and than they used to be in the days of our fathers. . . . It may be that the vast increase in wealth in the last twenty-five years has insensibly introduced a plague of worldliness and self-indulgence and love of ease into social life. What were once called luxuries are now comforts and necessaries, and self-denial and 'enduring hardness' are consequently little known. . . .

We must then try to realize that it is *terribly possible* to live a careless, easy-going, half-worldly life and yet at the same time to maintain evangelical principles and call ourselves evangelical people! Once let us see that sin is far viler and far nearer to us and sticks more closely to us than we supposed and we shall be led, I trust and believe, to get nearer to Christ.

Henry Drummond,
The Greatest Thing in the World (1883)

Henry Drummond was born in Stirling, Scotland, in 1851. At the age of fifteen he went to Edinburgh University, where he eventually studied theology. He was uncertain about his vocation to the pastoral ministry, but found his true calling in a slightly different direction. He helped with the 1873–75 mission to Britain by Dwight Moody and Ira Sankey, speaking at student meetings and individually counselling those who were seeking. Moody was so impressed with Drummond's gifts that he invited him to join his team in America. Drummond declined, but helped again with Moody's next mission to Britain in 1882–84. He did, however, pay a number of visits to the United States where he made a deep impact on university campuses, including Harvard, Yale and Princeton. Drummond also went on speaking tours to continental Europe, Africa and the Far East. His preaching ministry was directed especially to students, calling the uncommitted to conversion and encouraging the converted to a life of service, especially in overseas mission. He died in 1897 at the early age of forty-five from a painful bone disease.

Drummond was ordained and spent some time in ministry in Edinburgh and Glasgow. He also devoted himself to scientific studies, teaching science at the Free Church College in Glasgow, where he became a professor. He was particularly interested in the relation between theology and Darwin's theory of evolution, expounded in the latter's *The Origin of Species by Means of Natural Selection* (1859) and *The Descent of Man and Selection in Relation to Sex* (1871). Drummond sought a synthesis between Darwinian evolution and evangelical faith, which he expounded in his *Natural Law and the Spiritual World* (1883). This approach he developed in some lectures given at Boston and published as *The Ascent of Man* (1894). By no means all were happy with Drummond's theistic-evolution approach, though he played a significant pioneering role in the attempt to relate science and theology. He retained his essential evangelical beliefs, but tampered too much with traditional orthodoxy for many people's liking.

Although Drummond's *Natural Law and the Spiritual World* was a best-seller, it is not that for which he is famous today. In 1884 he spoke at Moody's invitation on 1 Corinthians 13, Paul's great hymn on love, to a group of Christian workers. Moody was so impressed by the talk that he prevailed upon Drummond to preach it again in America. Eventually he prepared it for publication as *The Greatest Thing in the World* (1887). This also became a best-seller, translated into many other languages, and has never gone out of print.

The Greatest Thing in the World is a short piece, well under 10,000 words in length. It is divided into four sections. After a brief preliminary section extolling love as the *summum bonum*, there is a section on 'The Contrast' between love and other things (verses 1–3). The longest section is 'The Analysis' which identifies the nine ingredients of the 'spectrum of love', just as a prism breaks light into the colours of the rainbow (verses 4–7). Finally, 'The Defence' points to love as the thing that lasts (verses 8–13). Drummond concludes by challenging his readers to join him in reading the chapter once a week for the next three months. 'A man did that once and it changed his whole life. Will you do it? It is for the greatest thing in the world.'

The Analysis

After contrasting love with these things Paul, in three verses, very short, gives us an amazing analysis of what this supreme thing is. I ask you to look at it. It is a compound thing, he tells us. It is like light. As you have seen a man of science take a beam of light and pass it through a crystal prism, as you have seen it come out on the other side of the prism broken up into its component colours, red, and blue, and yellow, and violet, and orange, and all the colours of the rainbow, so Paul passes this thing, love, through the magnificent prism of his inspired intellect and it comes out on the other side broken up into its elements. And in these few words we have what one might call the Spectrum of Love, the analysis of love. Will you observe what its elements are? Will you notice that they have common names; that they are virtues which we hear about every day; that they are things which can be practised by every man in every place in life; and how, by a multitude of small things and ordinary virtues, the supreme thing, the *summum bonum*, is made up?

The Spectrum of Love has nine ingredients: . . .

Patience, kindness, generosity, humility, courtesy, unselfishness, good temper, guilelessness, sincerity – these make up the supreme gift, the stature of the perfect man. . . .

Generosity. 'Love envieth not' [verse 4]. This is love in competition with others. Whenever you attempt a good work you will find other men doing the same kind of work, and probably doing it better. Envy them not. Envy is a feeling of ill-will to those who are in the same line as ourselves, a spirit of covetousness and detraction. How little Christian work even is a protection against unchristian feeling. That most despicable of all the unworthy moods which cloud a Christian's soul assuredly waits for us on the threshold of every work, unless we are fortified with this grace of magnanimity. Only one thing truly need the Christian envy, the large, rich, generous soul which 'envieth not'.

And then, after having learned all that, you have to learn this further thing, *humility* – to put a seal upon your lips and forget what you have done. After you have been kind, after love has stolen forth into the world and done its beautiful work, go back into the shade again and say nothing about it. Love hides even from itself. Love waives even self-satisfaction. 'Love vaunteth not itself, is not puffed up' [verse 4].

The fifth ingredient is a somewhat strange one to find in this *summum bonum: courtesy*. This is love in society, love in relation to etiquette. 'Love doth not behave itself unseemly' [verse 5]. Politeness has been defined as love in trifles. Courtesy is said to be love in little things. And the one secret of politeness is to love. Love *cannot* behave itself unseemly. You can put the most untutored person into the highest society, and if they have a reservoir of love in their heart, they will not behave themselves unseemly. They simply cannot do it. . . .

So much for the analysis of love. Now the business of our lives is to have these things fitted into our characters. That is the supreme work to which we need to address ourselves in this world, to learn love. Is life not full of opportunities for learning love? Every man and woman every day has a thousand of them. The world is not a playground; it is a schoolroom. Life is not a holiday, but an education. And the one eternal lesson for us all is *how better we can love*. What makes a man a good cricketer? Practice. What makes a man a good artist, a good sculptor, a good musician? Practice. What makes a man a good linguist, a good stenographer? Practice. What makes a man a good man? Practice. Nothing else. There is nothing capricious about religion. We do not get the soul in different ways, under different laws, from those in which we get the body and the mind. If a man does not exercise his arm he develops no biceps muscle; and if a man does not exercise his soul, he acquires no muscle in his soul, no strength of character, no vigour of moral fibre, nor beauty of spiritual growth. Love is not a thing of enthusiastic emotion. It is a rich, strong, manly, vigorous expression of the whole round Christian character – the Christlike nature in its fullest development. And the constituents of this great character are only to be built up by ceaseless practice.

[Conclusion]

In the Book of Matthew [25:31–46], where the Judgment Day is depicted for us in the imagery of One seated upon a throne and dividing the sheep from the goats, the test of a man then is not, 'How have I believed?' but 'How have I loved?' The test of religion, the final test of religion, is not religiousness, but love. I say the final test of religion at that great Day is not religiousness, but love; not what I have done, not what I have believed, not what I have achieved, but how I have discharged the common charities of life. Sins of commission in that awful indictment are not even referred to.

By what we have not done, by sins of omission, we are judged. It could not be otherwise. For the withholding of love is the negation of the spirit of Christ, the proof that we never knew him, that for us he lived in vain. It means that he suggested nothing in all our thoughts, that he inspired nothing in all our lives, that we were not once near enough to him to be seized with the spell of His compassion for the world.

Charles Haddon Spurgeon, *Sermons*

(1855–92)

Charles Haddon Spurgeon was born near Colchester in 1834, the eldest son of an Independent minister. His formal education was mediocre, but he supplemented it with his own reading of Foxe's *Book of Martyrs* (see pages 259–63) and Puritan writers. He is reported to have read Bunyan's *Pilgrim's Progress* (see pages 339–42) over a hundred times. This upbringing gave him a good knowledge of the Christian faith and a conviction of its truth, but did not bring him peace with God. He was deeply conscious of his sin and sensed God's wrath against him. Then at the age of fifteen, in January 1850, he was diverted by a snowstorm to a Primitive Methodist chapel where a mediocre lay preacher was preaching on Isaiah 45:22: 'Look unto me and be ye saved, all the ends of the earth.' As Spurgeon recounts in his *Autobiography*, 'He had not much to say, thank God, for that compelled him to keep on repeating his text, and there was nothing needed, by me at any rate, except his text.' Through this sermon he was led to a saving encounter with Christ. A few months later he was baptized in a river a few miles away.

Spurgeon soon became a well-known preacher. He preached his first sermon, unexpectedly and without preparation, at the age of sixteen. Before long he became the pastor of the Baptist Church at Waterbeach, near Cambridge. His fame spread and attendance increased tenfold. At the age of nineteen he was called to be minister of the important New Park Street Chapel in London. Here his preaching was equally successful. The chapel almost immediately needed to be extended and while this was underway Spurgeon preached at Exeter Hall. This hall, seating over 4,000, was not big enough for Spurgeon and in 1856 he began to preach instead at the Surrey Music Hall, which seated 10,000. In 1861 he preached in the Crystal Palace without amplification to nearly 24,000 people, the largest recorded indoor crowd. That year the Metropolitan Tabernacle was opened, seating 6,000, and this became his base for the next thirty-one years until his death in 1892.

Spurgeon's preaching was immensely popular and special trains were put on to bring people to hear him. But he was a controversial figure, not lacking in detractors. One commented that the difference between St Paul's Cathedral and the Metropolitan Tabernacle was that in the former the pulpit was in the nave while in the latter the knave was in the pulpit! A local newspaper objected that his preaching was 'redolent of bad taste, vulgar and theatrical'. Spurgeon was unrepentant. He had no intention of being vulgar, but he was concerned to preach the gospel simply and forcefully to ordinary people, and in this he was hugely successful. He is reckoned to have preached to some ten million people – the same number as George Whitefield, but as a local church minister rather than an itinerant evangelist. Almost eleven thousand people were baptized under his London ministry. He is a strong contender for the title of the greatest preacher in the history of the church.

Spurgeon's preaching had great power. On one occasion he was testing the acoustics in the Agricultural Hall and cried out, 'Behold the Lamb of God which taketh away the sin of the world' [John 1:29]. A worker up in the rafters heard this and was converted! On another occasion a woman was converted through reading a single page of a sermon that had been used to wrap some butter. Yet Spurgeon did not start to prepare his Sunday evening sermons until that afternoon and his notes were normally contained on one side of a piece of paper, sometimes the back of an envelope. The bulk of his preparation came in the form of his reading. Throughout his ministry he regularly read six books a week – and managed to remember much of what he read. At his death he owned some twelve thousand volumes.

Spurgeon began to publish his sermons in 1855. Eventually 3,544 sermons were published in the sixty-three volumes of *The New Park Street Pulpit* and *The Metropolitan Tabernacle Pulpit* – comprising over twenty million words, the equivalent of the twenty-seven volumes of the ninth edition of the *Encylopedia Britannica*. Over a million copies of this series have been sold. There is more material by Spurgeon in print than by any other Christian author of the past or present.

A Sermon Delivered on Sabbath Morning, October 16th, 1859, at the Music Hall, Royal Surrey Gardens

'And the Spirit and the bride say, Come. And let him that heareth say, Come. And let him that is athirst come. And whosoever will, let him take the water of life freely' [Revelation 22:17].

The cry of the Christian religion is the simple word, 'Come.' The Jewish law said, 'Go, and take heed unto thy steps as to the path in which thou shalt walk. Go, and break the commandments, and thou shalt perish; Go, and keep them, and thou shalt live.' The law was a dispensation of the whip, which drove men before it; the gospel is just of the opposite kind. It is the Shepherd's dispensation. He goeth before his sheep, and he bids them follow him, saying unto them, 'Come.' The law repels; the gospel attracts. The law shows the distance between God and man; the gospel bridges that distance. . . .

Let us go at once to our text – 'Whosoever will, let him take the water of life freely.' Now, there are four things very plain from our text, namely, that first, *there is a 'water of life'*; that secondly, *the invitation is very wide – 'Whosoever will'*; that thirdly, *the path is clear*, for it says, *'Whosoever will, let him come'*; and then again, that, fourthly, *the only rule that is prescribed is – 'let him take it freely'*. That is the only price demanded, and the only condition, which indeed is not a condition, but a death-blow to all conditions. 'Let him come and take the water of life freely.'

I. First, then, remember I am about to preach a very simple sermon this morning, dealing with simple souls. I am longing to see sinners brought to Christ, my heart yearns after the multitude of men who see no beauty in him that they should desire him. God has saved many in this place; may he be pleased this morning to bring some wanderer to the Father's house, through the merit of the Son's cross by the Spirit's influence. Well, then, *there is a 'water of life'*. Man is utterly ruined and undone. He is lost in a wild waste wilderness. The skin bottle of his righteousness is all dried up, and there is not so much as a drop of water in it. The heavens refuse him rain, and the earth can yield him no moisture. Must he perish? He looks aloft, beneath, around, and he discovers no means of escape. Must he die? Must thirst devour him? Must he fall upon the desert and leave his bones to bleach under the hot sun? No; for the text declares there is a fountain of life. . . . This sacred fountain, established according to God's good will and pleasure in the covenant, opened by Christ when he died upon the cross, floweth this day to give life and health, and joy and peace to poor sinners dead in sin, and ruined by the fall. There is a 'water of life'. . . .

II. In the second place we observe from the text that the invitation is very wide – *'Whosoever will, let him take the water of life freely.'* How wide is this invitation! There are some ministers who are afraid to invite sinners. Then why are they ministers, for they are afraid to perform the most important part of the sacred office? There was a time I must confess when I somewhat faltered when about to give a free invitation. My doctrinal sentiments did at the time somewhat hamper me. I boldly avow that I am unchanged as to the doctrines I have preached; I preach Calvinism as high, as stern, and as sound as ever; but I do feel, and always did feel an anxiety to invite sinners to Christ. And I do feel also, that not only is such a course consistent with the soundest doctrines, but that the other course is after all the unsound one, and has no title whatever to plead Scripture on its behalf. . . . I glory in the avowal that I preach Christ even to *insensible sinners* – that I would say even to the dry bones of the valley, as Ezekiel did, 'Ye dry bones live!' [37:4–6] doing it as an act of faith; not faith in the power of those that hear to obey the command, but faith in the power of God who gives the command to give strength also to those addressed, that they may be constrained to obey it. But now listen to my text; for here, at least, there is no limitation. But sensible or insensible, all that the text saith is, 'Whosoever *will*, let him come and take the water of life freely.' . . .

III. And now I am about to show you, in the third place, how clear the path is. *'Whosoever will, let him come and take the water of life freely.'* That word 'let' is a very curious word, because it signifies two opposite things. 'Let' is an old-fashioned word which sometimes signifies 'hinder'. 'He that letteth shall be taken away' [2 Thessalonians 2:7] – that is, 'He that hindereth.' But here, in our text, it means the removing of all hindrance. *'Let* him come': Methinks I hear Jehovah speaking this. Here is the fountain of love and mercy. But you are too unworthy, you are too vile. Hear Jehovah! He cries, '*Let him come*, he is willing. Stand back! Doubts and fears, away with you, let him come; make a straight road; let him come if he be but willing.' Then the devil himself comes forward and striding across the way, he says to the poor trembling soul, 'I will spill thy blood; thou shalt never have mercy. I defy thee; thou shalt never believe in Christ, and never be saved.' But Christ says, '*Let him come*'; and Satan, strong though he be, quails beneath Jehovah's voice, and Jesus drives him away, and the path stands clear this morning, nor can sin, nor death, nor hell, block up the way, when Jehovah Jesus says, '*Let* him come.' . . .

IV. And now this brings me to the last head, the condition which is the death of all conditions – *Let us take it freely.* Methinks I see one here who is saying 'I would be saved and I will do what I can to be worthy of it.' The fountain is free, and he comes with his halfpenny in his hand, and that a bad one, and he says, 'Here, sir, give me a cup of this living water to drink; I am well worthy of it for see the price is in my hand.' Why, man, if thou could'st bring the wealth of Potosi, or all the diamonds of Galconda, and all the pearls of Ormuz, you could not buy this most costly thing. Put up your money, you could not have it for gold or silver. The man brings his merit, but heaven is not to be sold to meritmongers. Or perhaps you say 'I will go to church regularly, I will give to the poor, I will attend my meeting-house, I will take a sitting, I will be baptized, I will do this and the other, and then no doubt I shall have the water of life.' Back, miserable herd, bring not your rags and rubbish to God, he wants them not. Stand back, you insult the Almighty when you tender anything as payment. Back with ye; he invites not such as you to come. He says come freely. He wants nothing to recommend you. . . . .

And as my Master is true and faithful, he cannot cast away one soul that cometh, for 'him that cometh unto me I will in no wise cast out' [John 6:37]. O Spirit, now draw reluctant hearts, and now give timid souls courage to believe for Jesus' sake. Amen.

Thérèse of Lisieux, *Story of a Soul*
(1897)

Marie Françoise Thérèse Martin was born in 1873 at Alençon in Normandy (France). She herself divided her early years into three phases. The first was a happy period until her mother died in 1877. This trauma plunged her into a 'winter of trial', a period of sadness and religious scruples that lasted for eight years. Last was the period between her conversion in 1886 and her entry into a convent in 1888.

In 1881 the family moved from Alençon to Lisieux, where Thérèse attended the Benedictine Abbey school. In 1883 she endured for three months a mysterious illness involving convulsions and hallucinations, before experiencing an instantaneous cure while praying before a statue of the Virgin Mary. Thérèse had been religious from her earliest years but on Christmas Day 1886 she experienced an instant change which she called her 'conversion'. This occurred on her return home from midnight Mass and led her to desire to suffer for God and to resolve to enter the Discalced Carmelite convent at Lisieux, where two of her sisters were already nuns. The nuns wanted to accept Thérèse but the ecclesiastical superior of the convent felt that she should wait until she was twenty-one. Thérèse and her father appealed to the bishop and, while awaiting the outcome, went on pilgrimage to Rome. In April 1888, at the age of fifteen, she was allowed to enter the convent.

Life in the convent was not easy, due especially to the behaviour of the prioress. Thérèse avoided becoming involved in internal politics, devoting herself to a life of prayer and fidelity to the rule of the order. In 1893 she was appointed acting mistress of novices and in this role she set forth her 'Little Way' of drawing near to God. There was nothing new about this but it was a fresh restatement of basic Christian ideas.

In 1896 she developed symptoms of tuberculosis, from which she died eighteen months later. Thérèse had written various pieces, in the form of letters written to her two older sisters and to a superior in the convent. The first, forming nearly two thirds of the whole and written in 1895–96, covers her life to 1894 when another of her sisters entered the convent. The second, written in four days in September 1896 is quite brief. The third, written in the last few weeks of her life, covers her time in the convent. This touches on the practicalities of life in a religious community, including the petty tensions, and Thérèse's reactions to them. As her end drew near she asked her sister to collect and edit these writings. A year after her death a version of this 'autobiography', edited to improve the style and take account of the sensibilities of her fellow nuns, was published privately and sent to other Carmelite convents. Such was the response that it was soon reprinted and within fifteen years over a million copies were printed. In the 1950s her original text was published, based on her handwritten manuscript. It is variously known by the English titles *Autobiography* and *Story of a Soul*.

Thérèse is commended for the way in which, as Pope Pius XI put it, she achieved sanctity 'without going beyond the common order of things'. Given her simple and uncomplicated approach it is ironical that she has also made a significant theological contribution. In the sixteenth century the Council of Trent produced a *Decree on Justification* which set out Roman Catholic teaching in opposition to the Reformation. Perhaps the most controversial statement in this is that justified Christians can 'be considered to have fully satisfied God's law, according to this state of life, by the deeds they have wrought in him and to have truly merited to gain eternal life'. This was opposed by some of those at the Council. The highly important *Catechism of the Catholic Church* (1994) summarizes the teaching of Trent on justification, but also adds a quotation from Thérèse's *Story of a Soul* which effectively neutralizes the objectionable statement:

> *After earth's exile, I hope to go and enjoy you in the fatherland, but I do not want to lay up merits for heaven. I want to work for your* love alone. . . . *In the evening of this life, I shall appear before you with empty hands, for I do not ask you, Lord, to count my works. All our justice is blemished in your eyes. I wish, then, to be clothed in your own* justice *and to receive from your* love *the eternal possession of* yourself. *(§2011)*

───────────────

Book 3, Chapter 34. Little Sacrifices of the Cloister

Meditating on these words of Jesus [John 15:13], Mother, I began to see how imperfect my own love was; it was so obvious that I didn't love my sisters as God loved them. I realize, now, that perfect love means putting up with other people's shortcomings, feeling no surprise at their weaknesses, finding encouragement even in the slightest evidence of good qualities in them. . . .

Always, when I act as charity bids, I have this feeling that it is Jesus who is acting in me; the closer my union with him, the greater my love for all the sisters without distinction. What do I do when I want this love to grow stronger in me? How do I react, when the devil tries to fix my mind's eye on the defects of some sister who hasn't much attraction for me? I remind myself, in a great hurry, of all that sister's good qualities, all her good intentions. True enough, she's made a slip this time; but who's going to tell us how often she's fought temptation and conquered it, only she was too humble to let us notice it?

There's one sister in the community who has the knack of rubbing me up the wrong way at every turn; her tricks of manner, her tricks of speech, her character, just strike me as unlovable. But, then, she's a holy religious [nun]; God must love her dearly; so I wasn't going to let this natural antipathy get the better of me. I reminded myself that charity isn't a matter of fine sentiments; it means doing things. So I determined to treat this sister as if she were the person I loved best in the world. Every time I met her, I used to pray for her. . . . But I didn't confine myself to saying a lot of prayers for her, this sister who made life such a tug-of-war for me; I tried to do her every good turn I possibly could. When I felt tempted to take her down with an unkind retort, I would put on my best smile instead, and try to change the subject; doesn't the *Imitation [of Christ]* [see pages 186–89] tell us that it's better to let other people have their way in an argument, than to go on wrangling over it? . . .

   She was quite unconscious of what I really felt about her, and never realized why I behaved as I did; to this day, she is persuaded that her personality somehow attracts me.

References & Acknowledgments

For the online editions of texts the web address given is normally that of the home page of the organization displaying the text, rather than the address of the text itself. This is because the former is much less likely to change than the latter. Thus for the huge collection held by the Christian Classics Ethereal Library (www.ccel.org) one should click on the link to the author or title listing of the works. The address www.ccel.org/fathers2 takes one to the Ante-Nicene Fathers series and to the two Nicene and Post-Nicene Fathers series. Likewise, with www.creeds.net, one follows the links to Ancient, Lutheran and other creeds.

Abbreviations

[Details of publishers and locations refer to those who currently market these series.]

ANF   *Ante-Nicene Fathers* (Grand Rapids: Eerdmans, many reprints).
Also available on CD-ROM and online.

NPNF   *Nicene and Post-Nicene Fathers* (Grand Rapids: Eerdmans, many reprints).
Also available on CD-ROM and online.

NPNF(2)   *Nicene and Post-Nicene Fathers*, Second Series. (Grand Rapids: Eerdmans, many reprints).
Also available on CD-ROM and online.

ACW   *Ancient Christian Writers* (New York and Mahwah, New Jersey: Paulist Press;
London: SPCK).

FoC   *The Fathers of the Church* (Washington, D.C.: Catholic University of America Press).

LCC   *The Library of Christian Classics* (London: SCM; Philadelphia: Westminster Press).

CWS   *The Classics of Western Spirituality* (New York and Mahwah, New Jersey: Paulist Press;
London: SPCK).

1. Ignatius of Antioch, *Letters*

ANF 1 and J.B. Lightfoot, *The Apostolic Fathers* (London: Macmillan, 1891) [changed];
www.ccel.org/fathers2
Modern editions: M. Staniforth and A. Louth (trs), *Early Christian Writings: The Apostolic Fathers*
(Harmondsworth: Penguin Classics, 1987, revised edition); ACW 1; FoC 1.

2. Justin Martyr, *First Apology*

ANF 1 [changed]; www.ccel.org/fathers2
Modern editions: ACW 56; FoC 6.

3. *The Martyrdom of Polycarp*

ANF 1 and J.B. Lightfoot, *The Apostolic Fathers* (London: Macmillan, 1891) [changed];
www.ccel.org/fathers2
Modern editions: M. Staniforth and A. Louth (trs), *Early Christian Writings: The Apostolic Fathers*
(Harmondsworth: Penguin Classics, 1987, revised edition); ACW 6; FoC 1.

4. *The Epistle to Diognetus*

ANF 1 and J.B. Lightfoot, *The Apostolic Fathers* (London: Macmillan, 1891) [changed];
www.ccel.org/fathers2
Modern editions: M. Staniforth and A. Louth (trs), *Early Christian Writings: The Apostolic Fathers*
(Harmondsworth: Penguin Classics, 1987, revised edition); ACW 6; FoC 1.

5. Irenaeus, *Against Heresies*

ANF 1 [changed]; www.ccel.org/fathers2
Modern edition: ACW 55 [more volumes to follow].

6. Tertullian, *Apology*
ANF 3 [changed]; www.ccel.org/fathers2
Modern edition: FoC 10.

7. *The Passion of Perpetua and Felicitas*
ANF 3 [changed]; www.ccel.org/fathers2
Modern edition: W.H. Shewring, *The Passion of SS. Perpetua and Felicity* (London: Sheed & Ward, 1931 and 1976 reprint).

8. Cyprian, *Letter to Donatus*
ANF 3 [changed]; www.ccel.org/fathers2
Modern edition: FoC 36.

9. Origen, *Against Celsus*
ANF 4 [changed]; www.ccel.org/fathers2
Modern edition: Origen, *Contra Celsum* (Cambridge: Cambridge University Press, 1953 and later reprints).

10. Eusebius of Caesarea, *The History of the Church*
NPNF(2) 1 [changed]; www.ccel.org/fathers2
Modern editions: Eusebius, *The History of the Church* (Harmondsworth: Penguin Classics, 1965); FoC 19.

11. Athanasius, *The Incarnation of the Word*
NPNF(2) 4 [changed]; www.ccel.org/fathers2
Modern edition: Athanasius, *Contra Gentes* and *De Incarnatione* (Oxford: Oxford University Press, 1971).

12. Athanasius, *The Life of Antony*
NPNF(2) 4 [changed]; www.ccel.org/fathers2
Modern edition: Athanasius, *The Life of Antony and the Letter to Marcellinus* [CWS] (New York: Paulist Press, 1980).

13. *Sayings of the Desert Fathers [and Mothers]*
B. Ward (tr.), *The Sayings of the Desert Fathers* (London and Oxford: Mowbray, 1981, revised edition).

14. Cyril of Jerusalem, *Catechetical Lectures*
NPNF(2) 7 [changed]; www.ccel.org/fathers2
Modern editions: W. Telfer (ed.), *Cyril of Jerusalem and Nemesius of Emesa* [LCC 4] (London: SCM, 1955) [12 lectures only]; FoC 61 and 64.

15. Basil of Caesarea, *The Long Rules*
Saint Basil, *Ascetical Works* (Washington, D.C.: Catholic University of America Press, 1950, reprinted 1962 and 1990) = FoC 9.

16. Gregory of Nazianzus, *Theological Orations*
NPNF(2) 7 [changed]; www.ccel.org/fathers2 [24 of the 45 *Orations*]
Modern editions: E.R. Hardy and C.C. Richardson (eds), *Christology of the Later Fathers* [LCC 3] (London: SCM, 1954) [*Theological Orations* only; NPNF translation with minor changes]; F.W. Norris, *Faith Gives Fullness to Reasoning: The Five Theological Orations of Gregory Nazianzen* (Leiden: E.J. Brill, 1990) [*Theological Orations* only; introduction, commentary and translation].

17. Pseudo-Macarius, *Fifty Spiritual Homilies*
Pseudo-Macarius, *The Fifty Spiritual Homilies and the Great Letter* [CWS] (New York: Paulist Press, 1992).

18. John Chrysostom, *The Priesthood*
NPNF 9 [changed]; www.ccel.org/fathers2
Modern edition: Chrysostom, *The Priesthood* (New York: Macmillan, 1955).

19. Ambrose, *The Duties of Ministers*
NPNF(2) 10 [changed]; www.ccel.org/fathers2

20. Gregory of Nyssa, *The Life of Moses*
Gregory of Nyssa, *The Life of Moses* [CWS] (New York: Paulist Press, 1978).

21. Augustine, *Confessions*
Saint Augustine, *Confessions*, translated by R.S. Pine-Coffin (Harmondsworth: Penguin Classics, 1961).
Copyright © R.S. Pine-Coffin, 1961. Reproduced by permission of Penguin Books Ltd.
NPNF 1 version at www.ccel.org/fathers2; www.ccel.org [1955 translation]
Other modern editions: FoC 21; Saint Augustine, *Confessions* (Oxford: Oxford University Press, 1991).

22. Augustine, *The Spirit and the Letter*
NPNF 5 [changed]; www.ccel.org/fathers2
Modern edition: Augustine, *Later Works* [LCC 8] (London: SCM, 1955).

23. Augustine, *The City of God*
NPNF 2 [changed]; www.ccel.org/fathers2
Modern edition: Augustine, *The City of God* (London: Penguin Classics, 1984).

24. John Cassian, *Conferences*
NPNF(2) 11 [changed]; www.ccel.org/fathers2
Modern editions: O. Chadwick (tr.), *Western Asceticism* [LCC 12] (London: SCM, 1958) [selected
Conferences]; John Cassian, *Conferences* [CWS] (New York: Paulist Press, 1985) [selected Conferences];
ACW 57 [complete].

25. Cyril of Alexandria, *Third Letter to Nestorius*
Own translation. NPNF(2) 14:201–18 at www.ccel.org/fathers2
Modern editions: Cyril of Alexandria, *Select Letters* (Oxford: Oxford University Press, 1983); FoC 76.

26. Leo, *Tome*
Own translation. NPNF(2) 12:38–43 and 14:254–58 at www.ccel.org/fathers2
Modern edition: FoC 34.

27. *The Definition of Chalcedon*
Own translation. NPNF(2) 14:262–65 at www.ccel.org/fathers2
Modern edition: R.A. Norris (ed.), *The Christological Controversy* (Philadelphia: Fortress Press, 1980), 155–59.

28. The Athanasian Creed
www.creeds.net [older translation]
Modern edition: J.N.D. Kelly, *The Athanasian Creed* (London: Adam & Charles Black, 1964), 17–20.

29. Boethius, *The Consolation of Philosophy*
Boethius, The Consolation of Philosophy (Harmondsworth: Penguin Classics, 1969); www.ccel.org [1902]

30. Council of Orange, *Canons*
J.H. Leith, *Creeds of the Churches* (Atlanta: John Knox Press, 1982, 3rd edition). Older translation at
www.creeds.net

31. *The Rule of Benedict*
O.H. Blair (ed.), *The Rule of Benedict* (Fort Augustus: Abbey Press, 1886) [changed]. 1949 translation at
www.ccel.org
Modern edition: O. Chadwick (tr.), *Western Asceticism* [LCC 12] (London: SCM, 1958).

32. Gregory the Great, *Pastoral Rule*
NPNF(2) 12 [changed]; www.ccel.org/fathers2
Modern edition: ACW 11.

33. Maximus the Confessor, *Four Hundred Chapters on Love*
Excerpts from Maximus Confessor, *Selected Writings*, translation and notes by George C. Berthold, from The Classics of Western Spirituality, Copyright © 1985 by George Berthold, Paulist Press, Inc., New York/Mahwah, N.J. Used with permission of Paulist Press, www.paulistpress.com

34. Bede, *A History of the English Church and People*
Bede, *A History of the English Church and People*, translated by Leo Sherley-Price, revised by R.E. Latham (Harmondsworth: Penguin Classics, 1955, revised edition, 1968). Copyright © Leo Sherley-Price, 1955, 1968. Reproduced by permission of Penguin Books Ltd.
Older translation at www.ccel.org

35. John of Damascus, *The Orthodox Faith*
NPNF(2) 9 [changed]; www.ccel.org/fathers2
Modern edition: FoC 37.

36. Symeon the New Theologian, *Catechetical Discourses*
Symeon the New Theologian, *The Discourses* [CWS] (New York: Paulist Press, 1980).

37. Anselm, *Cur Deus Homo*
Anselm of Canterbury, *The Major Works* (Oxford: Oxford University Press, 1998). Older translation at www.ccel.org

38. Bernard of Clairvaux, *The Steps of Humility and Pride*
Bernard of Clairvaux: The Steps of Humility and Pride, translated by M. Ambrose Conway osco. Copyright Cistercian Publications, Kalamazoo, Michigan 49008.

39. Bernard of Clairvaux, *Loving God*
Bernard of Clairvaux: On Loving God, translated by Robert Walton osb. Copyright Cistercian Publications, Kalamazoo, Michigan 49008. Older translation at www.ccel.org

40. Peter Lombard, *Sentences*
Unpublished translation by F.L. Battles, revised. Other version at www.franciscan-archive.org/lombardus [incomplete]
Modern edition: E.R. Fairweather (ed.), *A Scholastic Miscellany: Anselm to Ockham* [LCC 10] (London: SCM, 1956) [brief selections].

41. Richard of St Victor, *The Twelve Patriarchs*
Richard of St Victor, *The Twelve Patriarchs, The Mystical Ark, Book Three of the Trinity* [CWS] (London: SPCK, 1979).

42. Thomas of Celano, *First Life of Francis of Assisi*
Thomas of Celano, *The First Life of Saint Francis of Assisi* (London: Triangle, 2000). Older translation at www.fordham.edu/halsall [extracts]

43. Bonaventure, *The Soul's Journey into God*
Bonaventure, *The Soul's Journey into God, The Tree of Life, The Life of St Francis* [CWS] (New York: Paulist Press, 1978). Older translation at www.ccel.org

44. Thomas Aquinas, *The Sum of Theology*
Thomas Aquinas, *The 'Summa Theologica' of St Thomas Aquinas*, 22 vols (London: Burns Oates & Washbourne, 1920–25, revised edition) [changed]; www.ccel.org
Modern edition: Thomas Aquinas, *Summa Theologiae*, 60 vols (London: Eyre & Spottiswoode, first volume printed 1964).

45. Johann Tauler, *Sermons*
Johannes Tauler, *Sermons* [CWS] (New York: Paulist Press, 1985).

46. *The German Theology*

B. Hoffmann (ed.), *The Theologia Germanica of Martin Luther* [CWS] (London: SPCK, 1980). Other version at www.ccel.org [translation of Würzburg version by Susanna Winkworth]

47. Catherine of Siena, *The Dialogue*

Catherine of Siena, *The Dialogue* [CWS] (New York: Paulist Press, 1980). Modernized 1896 translation at www.ccel.org

48. Thomas à Kempis, *The Imitation of Christ*

Thomas à Kempis, *The Imitation of Christ*, translated by Leo Sherley-Price (Harmondsworth: Penguin Classics, 1952). Copyright © 1952 by Leo Sherley-Price. Reproduced by permission of Penguin Books Ltd. Modern translation at www.ccel.org

49. Desiderius Erasmus, *The Praise of Folly*

Erasmus, *Praise of Folly and Letter to Maarten van Dorp, 1515* (London: Penguin Classics, 1971, revised 1993). Older translation at www.ccel.org

50. Martin Luther, *The Freedom of a Christian*

H.J. Grimm (ed.), *Luther's Works*, vol. 31 (Philadelphia: Muhlenberg Press, 1957). Older translation at www.fordham.edu/halsall

51. William Tyndale, *The New Testament*

Taken from facsimile of the original.
Modern editions: William Tyndale, *The New Testament 1526*, W.R. Cooper (ed.) (London: British Library, 2000) [original spelling]. Also D. Daniell (intr.), *Tyndale's New Testament* (New Haven and London: Yale University Press, 1989) [1534 edition with modern spelling].

52. *The Schleitheim Confession*

From *The Schleitheim Confession*, translated and edited by John Howard Yoder, Herald Press, Scottdale, Pennsylvania, USA. All rights reserved. Used with permission of Herald Press.
Another translation is at www.anabaptists.org/history. Earlier printed in J.H. Yoder (ed.), *The Legacy of Michael Sattler* (Scottdale, Pennsylvania: Herald Press, 1974); www.creeds.net

53. Martin Luther, *The Small Catechism*

Translation by R.E. Smith (22 May 1994; Version 1.1, 22 December 1994) found online at www.ccel.org
Modern edition: R. Kolb and T.J. Wengert (eds), *The Book of Concord* (Minneapolis, Minnesota: Fortress Press, 2000).

54. *The Augsburg Confession*

F. Bente and W.H.T. Dau (eds), *Concordia Triglotta* (St Louis, Missouri: Concordia, 1921) [changed]; www.creeds.net
Modern edition: R. Kolb and T.J. Wengert (eds.), *The Book of Concord* (Minneapolis, Minnesota: Fortress Press, 2000).

55. Ulrich Zwingli, *Exposition of the Faith*

G.W. Bromiley (ed.), *Zwingli and Bullinger* [LCC 24] (London: SCM, 1953).

56. John Calvin, *Institutes of the Christian Religion*

John Calvin, *Institutes of the Christian Religion*, H. Beveridge (tr.) (Edinburgh: Calvin Translation Society, 1845, often reprinted) [changed]; www.ccel.org
Modern edition: J. Calvin, *Institutes of the Christian Religion* [LCC 20–21] (London: SCM, 1960).

57. John Calvin, *Short Treatise on the Lord's Supper*

John Calvin, *Tracts and Treatises*, vol. 2 (Edinburgh: Calvin Translation Society, 1849), reprinted in H. Beveridge and J. Bonnet (eds), *Selected Works of John Calvin*, vol. 2 (Grand Rapids: Baker, 1983) [changed].
Modern edition: J.K.S. Reid (ed.), *Calvin: Theological Treatises* [LCC 22] (London: SCM, 1954) [above translation with minor changes].

58. Ignatius Loyola, *Spiritual Exercises*

Excerpts from Ignatius of Loyola, *The Spiritual Exercises and Selected Works*, edited by George E. Ganss, S.J., from The Classics of Western Spirituality, Copyright © 1991 by George E. Ganss, S.J., Paulist Press, Inc., New York/Mahwah, N.J. Used with permission of Paulist Press, www.paulistpress.com
Older translation at www.ccel.org

59. Heinrich Bullinger, *Decades*

Heinrich Bullinger, *The Decades*, 4 vols (Cambridge: Cambridge University Press, 1849–52) [changed].

60. Martin Bucer, *The Kingdom of Christ*

W. Pauck (ed.), *Melanchthon and Bucer* [LCC 19] (London: SCM, 1969) [lacks section on divorce earlier translated by Milton].

61. Thomas Cranmer, *The Book of Common Prayer*

The Boke of Common Prayer (London: Edward Whytchurch, 1552); www.ccel.org
Modern edition: E.C.S. Gibson (intr.), *The First and Second Prayer Books of Edward VI* (London: J.M. Dent, 1910; London: Prayer Book Society, 1999).

62. Menno Simons, *The Cross of the Saints*

Menno Simons, *The Complete Writings* (Scottdale, Pennsylvania: Herald Press, 1956 and reprints).

63. Philip Melanchthon, *Loci Communes*

C.L. Manschreck (ed.), *Melanchthon on Christian Doctrine* (Oxford: Oxford University Press, 1965; reprinted Grand Rapids: Baker, 1982) [from 1555 German edition].
Other modern edition: W. Pauck (ed.), *Melanchthon and Bucer* [LCC 19] (London: SCM, 1969) [1521 edition].

64. John Knox, *The Scots Confession*

A.C. Cochrane (ed.), *Reformed Confessions of the 16th Century* (London: SCM, 1966); www.creeds.net

65. *The Heidelberg Catechism*

A.C. Cochrane (ed.), *Reformed Confessions of the 16th Century* (London: SCM, 1966); www.creeds.net

66. John Foxe, *Book of Martyrs*

John Foxe, *The Acts and Monuments*, 8 vols, J. Pratt (ed.) (London: Religious Tract Society, 1877) is the last full edition of the work. There are numerous shorter modern editions which heavily abridge and paraphrase Foxe, some even extending the account three centuries beyond Foxe's death; www.ccel.org

67. *The Thirty-nine Articles*

Book of Common Prayer; www.creeds.net

68. *The Formula of Concord*

F. Bente and W.H.T. Dau (eds), *Concordia Triglotta* (St Louis, Missouri: Concordia, 1921) [changed]; www.bookofconcord.org
Modern edition: R. Kolb and T.J. Wengert (eds), *The Book of Concord* (Minneapolis, Minnesota: Fortress Press, 2000).

69. Teresa of Avila, *The Interior Castle*

Teresa of Avila, *The Interior Castle* [CWS] (London: SPCK, 1979), reprinted in Teresa of Avila, *The Collected Works*, vol. 2 (Washington, D.C.: Institute of Carmelite Studies, 1980); www.catholicfirst.com/catholicclassics.cfm

70. John of the Cross, *The Dark Night of the Soul*

From *The Collected Works of St John of the Cross*, translated by Kieran Kavanaugh and Otilio Rodriguez. Copyright © 1964, 1979, 1991 by Washington Province of Discalced Carmelites, ICS Publications, 2131 Lincoln Road, N.E., Washington, D.C. 20002-1199, U.S.A. www.icspublications.org
Older translation at www.ccel.org

71. Richard Hooker, *A Learned Discourse of Justification*
Richard Hooker, *Works*, vol. 3 (Oxford: Oxford University Press, 1888); www.ccel.org
Modern edition: P. Secor (ed.), *The Sermons of Richard Hooker* (London: SPCK, 2001) [in modern English].

72. William Perkins, *The Cases of Conscience*
William Perkins, *The Whole Treatise of the Cases of Conscience* (Cambridge: John Legat, 1606–1608).
Modern edition: T.F. Merrill (ed.), *William Perkins 1558–1602: English Puritanist* (Nieuwkoop: De Graaf, 1966) [slightly abridged].

73. Francis de Sales, *Introduction to a Devout Life*
1876 translation at www.ccel.org
There are many modern editions.

74. Richard Sibbes, *The Bruised Reed and the Smoking Flax*
A.B. Grosart (ed.), *Works of Richard Sibbes*, vol. 1 (Edinburgh: Banner of Truth, 1973 and reprints); Richard Sibbes, *The Bruised Reed* (Edinburgh: Banner of Truth, 1998).

75. George Herbert, *The Country Parson*
George Herbert, *The Country Parson, The Temple* [CWS] (London: SPCK, 1981); www.ccel.org

76. *The Westminster Confession of Faith*
J.H. Leith, *Creeds of the Churches* (Atlanta: John Knox Press, 1982, 3rd edition), and many other sources; www.creeds.net

77. Richard Baxter, *The Saints' Everlasting Rest*
W. Orme (ed.), *The Practical Works of the Rev. Richard Baxter*, vols 22–23 (London: James Duncan, 1830); www.ccel.org [abridged version]
Modern edition: Richard Baxter, *The Saint's Everlasting Rest* (Fearn, Ross-shire: Christian Focus, 2000).

78. Jeremy Taylor, *The Rule and Exercises of Holy Dying*
Jeremy Taylor, *The Rule and Exercises of Holy Dying* (London: RR, 1651); www.ccel.org
Modern edition: Jeremy Taylor, *Holy Living and Holy Dying*, vol. 2 (Oxford: Oxford University Press, 1989).

79. John Owen, *Temptation*
W.H. Goold (ed.), *The Works of John Owen*, vol. 6 (Edinburgh: Banner of Truth, 1967 and reprints); www.ccel.org

80. Samuel Rutherford, *Letters*
Letters of Samuel Rutherford (Edinburgh: Banner of Truth, 1984). A selection also at www.ccel.org and www.puritansermons.com/ruth/ruthindx.htm

81. John Milton, *Paradise Lost*
From www.ccel.org
Modern editions: John Milton, *Paradise Lost* (London: Penguin Classics, 1989) and many others.

82. Blaise Pascal, *Pensées*
Blaise Pascal, *Pensées*, translated by A.J. Krailsheimer (Harmondsworth: Penguin Classics, 1966).
Copyright © A.J. Krailsheimer, 1966. Reproduced by permission of Penguin Books Ltd.
Older translation at www.ccel.org

83. Philipp Jakob Spener, *Holy Desires*
Philipp Jakob Spener, *Pia Desideria* (Philadelphia: Fortress, 1964).

84. Henry Scougal, *The Life of God in the Soul of Man*
Henry Scougal, *The Life of God in the Soul of Man* (London: C. Smith and W. Jacob, 1677); www.ccel.org
Modern editions: Henry Scougal, *The Life of God in the Soul of Man* (Fearn, Ross-shire: Christian Focus, 1996) and many others, which mostly alter the text in some way.

85. John Bunyan, *The Pilgrim's Progress*
From www.ccel.org
Modern editions: John Bunyan, *The Pilgrim's Progress* (Oxford: Oxford World's Classics, Oxford University Press, 1998) and many others.

86. Brother Lawrence, *The Practice of the Presence of God*
From www.ccel.org [changed]
Modern editions: Brother Lawrence, *The Practice of the Presence of God* (London: Hodder and Stoughton, 1981) and many others.

87. William Law, *A Serious Call to a Devout and Holy Life*
From www.ccel.org
Modern edition: William Law, *A Serious Call to a Devout and Holy Life; The Spirit of Love* [CWS] (London: SPCK, 1978).

88. Philip Doddridge, *The Rise and Progress of Religion*
Philip Doddridge, *The Rise and Progress of Religion* (London, 1745); www.ccel.org
Modern edition: There is a recent abridged edition (Grace Publications, 1993), but the complete work is available only online.

89. Jonathan Edwards, *The Religious Affections*
Jonathan Edwards, *Select Works of Jonathan Edwards, Volume III: Treatise Concerning the Religious Affections* (Edinburgh: Banner of Truth, 1961 and reprints); www.ccel.org

90. David Brainerd, *Life and Diary*
J. Edwards, *Life and Journal of the Rev. David Brainerd* (Edinburgh: H.S. Baynes, 1826); www.ccel.org
Modern editions: J. Edwards, *The Life of David Brainerd* (*The Works of Jonathan Edwards*, vol. 7) (New Haven and London: Yale University Press, 1985); J. Edwards, *The Life and Diary of David Brainerd* (Sovereign Grace Publications, 2000). There are also many modern abridgements.

91. George Whitefield, *Sermons*
George Whitefield, *Sermons on Important Subjects* (London: William Tegg, 1854); www.ccel.org [59 sermons]

92. Charles Wesley, *Hymns*
J. Wesley (ed.), *A Collection of Hymns, for the Use of the People Called Methodists* (London: J. Paramore, 1782); www.ccel.org
Modern editions: innumerable hymn books.

93. John Wesley, *Journal*
N. Curnock (ed.), *The Journal of the Rev. John Wesley A.M.*, 8 vols (London: Robert Culley, 1909–16).
Modern edition: A.C. Outler et al. (eds.), *The Works of John Wesley* (Nashville: Abingdon Press; Oxford: Oxford University Press, first volume printed 1975), vols 18–24 for complete *Journal*.
There have also been numerous abridged editions. Also at www.ccel.org [from 1951 Moody Press edition]

94. William Carey, *An Enquiry in the Obligations of Christians*
William Carey, *An Enquiry into the Obligations of Christians to Use Means for the Conversion of the Heathens* (Leicester: Ann Ireland, 1792). Facsimile of original (London: Baptist Missionary Society, 1942); www.thebaptistpage.com
Modern edition: William Carey, *An Enquiry into the Obligations of Christians to Use Means for the Conversion of the Heathens* (Dallas, Texas: Criswell Publications, 1988).

95. William Wilberforce, *A Practical View*
William Wilberforce, *A Practical View of the Prevailing Religious System of Professed Christians in the Higher and Middle Classes in this Country, Contrasted with Real Christianity* (London: T. Cadell and W. Davies, 1797).
Modern edition: William Wilberforce, *Real Christianity* (London: Hodder and Stoughton, 1989) [modernized and abridged].

96. John Henry Newman, *Sermons Preached before the University of Oxford*
John Henry Newman, *Sermons, Chiefly on the Theory of Religious Belief, Preached Before the University of Oxford* (London: Rivington and Oxford: Parker, 1843); www.newmanreader.org
Modern edition: John Henry Newman, *Fifteen Sermons Preached Before the University of Oxford between A.D. 1826 and 1843* (Notre Dame, Indiana: University of Notre Dame Press, 1998).

97. John Charles Ryle, *Holiness*
John Charles Ryle, *Holiness, and other Kindred Subjects* (London: William Hunt, 1877, 2nd edition); www.iserv.net/~mrbill (ch. 1–5)
Modern editions: John Charles Ryle, *Holiness* (Evangelical Press, 1979 and Charles Nolan Publishing, 2001).

98. Henry Drummond, *The Greatest Thing in the World*
From www.ccel.org
There are many modern editions.

99. Charles Haddon Spurgeon, *Sermons*
Modern edition: Charles Haddon Spurgeon, *The New Park Street Pulpit* and *The Metropolitan Tabernacle Pulpit* (Pasadena, Texas: Pilgrim Publications, 1969–80); www.ccel.org

100. Thérèse of Lisieux, *Story of a Soul*
Thérèse of Lisieux, *Autobiography of a Saint* (London: Harvill, 1958).
Other modern edition: J. Clarke (ed.), *Story of a Soul: The Autobiography of Saint Thérèse of Lisieux* (Washington, D.C.: Institute of Carmelite Studies, 1996).